THE TRANSFORMATION OF
RURAL
CHINA

—— ASIA AND THE PACIFIC ——

Series Editor: Mark Selden, Binghamton University

Exploring one of the most dynamic and contested regions of the world, this series includes contributions on political, economic, cultural, and social changes in modern and contemporary Asia and the Pacific.

Asia
and
the
Pacific

THE TRANSFORMATION OF
RURAL
CHINA

JONATHAN UNGER

AN EAST GATE BOOK

M.E.Sharpe
Armonk, New York
London, England

An East Gate Book

Library of Congress Cataloging-in-Publication Data

Unger, Jonathan.
  The transformation of rural China / by Jonathan Unger.
    p. cm.—(Asia and the Pacific)
  "East gate book."
  Includes bibliographical references and index.
  ISBN 0-7656-0551-1 (alk. paper); ISBN 0-7656-0552-X (pbk.: alk. paper)
    1. China—Rural conditions. 2. China—History—1949- 3. Villages—China. 4.
  Communism and argiculture—China. I. title. II. Asia and the Pacific (Armonk, N.Y.)

  HN733.5.U54 2002
  307.72′0951—dc21   2002017527

Printed in the United States of America

BM (c)   10   9   8   7   6   5   4   3   2   1
BM (p)   10   9   8   7   6   5   4   3   2

For my wife and best colleague,

Anita Chan,

and for our daughter Carla

Contents

Acknowledgements

A debt of gratitude is owed to Mark Selden and Anita Chan for reading and critiquing all of the manuscript. The book has gained very considerably from their insightful comments and suggestions. A debt is owed, too, to Bennis Wai Yip So, who provided comments on Chapter 7; Carl Riskin and Scott Rozelle, who commented on earlier versions of Chapter 9; and Lam Tao-chiu, who critiqued Chapter 10.

A number of scholars have conducted research with me in the Chinese countryside, and they contributed to my knowledge of the sites we examined together. In particular, Jean Hung has collaborated with me in conducting interviews in a wide range of villages in Yunnan Province in 1988; Eva Hung, Lam Tao-Chiu and Anita Chan worked together with me in Xiqiao Township in Guangdong during 1997; and Zhu Xiaoyang and I conducted interviewing together in the countryside of Qinghai Province in 2000. Richard Madsen and Anita Chan have graciously provided their interview transcripts concerning Chen Village, a community about which we earlier co-authored a book.

Several scholars have also kindly shared their research findings with me. Gong Xiaoxia provided extensive notes on documentation regarding the Cultural Revolution in the countryside. Dai Jianzhong, X.L. Ding, Gao Mobo, Hua Linshan, Isabelle Thireau, Andrew Walder, Yan Yunxiang and Zhu Xiaoyang provided helpful information about the Cultural Revolution from their personal stores of knowledge. And Chris Buckley, Janek Rowinski and X.L. Ding provided valuable pointers to, or copies of, recent Chinese-language newspaper and magazine reports on rural China.

Portions of some of the chapters have appeared, in earlier versions, in articles that I have published, and I am grateful to several publishers for permission to make use of this material. For this, credit is due to *The Journal of Peasant Studies* (for some of the material that appears in Ch. 1); Cambridge University Press (Ch. 2); *The China Quarterly* (Ch. 3); M.E. Sharpe (Chs. 4 and 10); *Pacific Affairs* (Ch. 5); and *The China Journal* (Ch. 8).

Susanna Sharpe copy-edited the chapters, Angela Grant prepared the book's Index and Heli Brecht almost single-handedly took charge of the book's production. Their contributions are gratefully acknowledged.

THE TRANSFORMATION OF
RURAL
CHINA

Introduction

The Chinese countryside has experienced not one but two extraordinary transformations. In the 1950s it was plunged into revolutionary change, in which all of the former political institutions were overturned and the land tenure system was destroyed and replaced by collectives. Every village in China was dramatically affected by the two decades of at times radical Party programs that lasted until after Mao's death in 1976. As is well known, in an extraordinary turnabout a second transformation ensued under Deng, in which most of the programs of the Maoist period were reversed and villagers returned to family farming.

This book focuses on the most salient features and themes of each period, for it will be seen that the latter period grew out of the first in many important ways. To understand what is transpiring in China today, one must understand the shape of that previous period. In fact, as the final chapters of this book will show, the contours of the rural political system changed less in the post-Mao era than many observers have supposed.

The first four chapters probe the earlier period of collective agriculture—highlighting the institutions through which the Party dominated the countryside, the mind-set of the peasantry during the heyday of Maoism, and the tensions that developed over the years as a consequence of radical Maoist policies. The opening chapter explores the complex interactions between the Party-state's political machinery and China's farmers, while two of the following chapters (Chapters Two and Four) focus on two of the most extraordinary, and most misunderstood, aspects of the Maoist effort: the "class line" and the utopian systems of remuneration that were introduced into villages. These two policy areas represented the very crux of Maoism, and they provide excellent illustrations of the hold that Party ideology gained over villagers' beliefs—ultimately with unexpected consequences. To examine the tensions of the Maoist period, a further chapter (Three) focuses on the Cultural Revolution upheavals of 1966–68, when a wide variety of group antagonisms and conflicts were laid bare across rural China.

The latter seven chapters of the book explore the post-Mao period, examining the situation in both poor and prosperous parts of the countryside. These chapters trace how, along with the institutional frameworks and practices inherited from the past, decollectivization resolved some of the dilemmas of the collective period, offered new opportunities to farmers, and created new dilemmas and tensions. One chapter examines how the land and collective assets were divided among farming families to create a new system that in most respects resembles independent farms. Other chapters examine the growing gaps in incomes and opportunities among villagers, the plight of rural migrant laborers, the rise of private industrial entrepreneurs in the most prosperous parts of the countryside, the persistence of poverty in the hinterlands, the nature of the rural economic and political elites today, the protests that peasants have mounted against the abuses of the system by local officials, and the movement to introduce grassroots elections.

The special, powerful (albeit changing) character of the rural political system provides the thread that binds this book together. For in China, more than in almost any other country, the state–peasant relationship over the course of the past half–century has loomed large in the shaping of livelihoods and lives and local events. No matter what the immediate topic of any section of any chapter, the influence of the state is visible.

A second thread that figures centrally in the book, running through almost every chapter, involves the question of equality. The Communist revolution promised a leveling of economic disparities among village households, and we will examine the efforts that were made to achieve this during the first three decades of the People's Republic. A second aspect of equality involves social stratification, and here too efforts were made to overturn and destroy the class structures of pre-revolution times—erecting in their stead an unusual new perverted form of "revolutionary" class hierarchy. It will be seen in these pages how—and why—both the economic leveling and the new forms of social stratification were eventually abandoned, and we will observe the re-emergence of prosperous and poor within the same village and the renewed formation of class structures. We will see, too, the trade-offs over the course of time between equality, repression, corruption, development, class and caste.

Most of the information, analysis, and "feel" for rural China in this book are drawn from extensive interviewing over a long period of time. I first started interviewing rural Chinese people in the mid-1970s, and at that time often discussed with interviewees not only the current conditions in their village but also what had gone on in the village as far back as the early 1960s. Consequently, the book is able to examine, with specific examples, how Mao-era policies operated in the countryside starting from the time, after the Great Leap Forward's collapse in 1959–60, when a stable system of rural collectives was first put into place.

My interview research has continued intermittently up to the present day. Since the mid-1970s, in a series of research projects conducted from Hong Kong (before it was possible for a non-Chinese to do such research inside China) and then within China starting in the 1980s, I have had an opportunity to conduct in-depth interviews with people from well over a hundred Chinese villages.

I was not alone in conducting interviews in Hong Kong. Much of the research on China during the period when Mao was in command took place in Hong Kong, and a couple of generations of researchers developed methods to meet the question of interviewee reliability. Anita Chan, Richard Madsen and I were able to draw upon this experience when we undertook interviewing with more than two dozen people from one village for our book *Chen Village*,[1] and I employed similar

---

[1]   Anita Chan, Richard Madsen and Jonathan Unger, *Chen Village: The Recent History of a Peasant Community in Mao's China* (Berkeley: University of California Press, 1984). A considerably updated and expanded edition was published in 1992 under the title *Chen Village Under Mao and Deng*.

techniques in the early 1980s in interviews with several dozen other respondents who had recently come to Hong Kong from the Chinese countryside.[2]

When I began interviewing inside Chinese villages in the latter half of the 1980s, I was able to confirm the veracity of the information I had obtained in Hong Kong. During repeated research trips over the past dozen-plus years into the countryside of six coastal and inland provinces, I was able to visit many dozens of rural households in poor and prosperous districts alike, and was also able to interview a large number of local officials, from hamlet cadres up through county heads.[3] The most recent such research trip was in November–December 2000, into villages in six poor counties in Qinghai Province in western China. Just as during my previous research in Hong Kong, everywhere that I have visited in rural China I have asked rounds of questions relating to the local economy, family livelihoods, and the local political administration.

Some of what I discovered was written up and published as journal articles and book chapters, but many of my findings remained in interview transcripts and memoranda to myself. I was looking forward ultimately to publishing a book like this. It is a mixture of previously published and never-before-published material, interwoven to create what I hope is a coherent, integrated account of the transformation and re-transformation of the Chinese countryside. A few of the chapters are in a form quite similar to work that I have previously published: for instance, Chapters 2–4, which explore aspects of the Maoist period, were first written after the close of that period, when it had become possible to attain a perspective on the whole era. Some other chapters are partially based upon previous writings but have been substantially updated, rethought and reshaped to take account of further research trips that I undertook, the ongoing changes in China, and new debates and findings in the China studies field. Other chapters have been written expressly for this book. They cover topics I had never previously written about but which I consider important to include.

---

[2]   The interviewing methods that were developed, and discussions on the reliability of such research, are addressed in Martin K. Whyte and William L. Parish: "Appendix 1: Methodological Notes," *Urban Life in Contemporary China* (Chicago: University of Chicago Press, 1984), p. 384; and a similar discussion appears in William L. Parish and Martin K. Whyte, *Village and Family in Contemporary China* (Chicago: University of Chicago Press, 1978), p. 345. The methodologies of Hong Kong interviewing are also discussed in Andrew Walder, "The Hong Kong Interviews: An Essay on Methods," in *Communist Neo-Traditionalism: Work and Authority in Chinese Industry* (Berkeley: University of California Press, 1986), pp. 255-69; and Jonathan Unger "The Hong Kong Connection: The Advantages of China Research from the Room Next Door," *China Information*, Vol. 2, No. 2 (Spring, 1987), pp. 27-36.

[3]   The methodologies of fieldwork inside rural China are discussed in Anne Thurston and Burton Pasternak (eds.), *The Social Sciences and Fieldwork in China: Views from the Field* (Boulder: Westview Press, 1986); and Elisabeth Croll, "Short-term Field Investigation in China: A Personal View," *China Information*, Vol. 2, No. 1 (Summer 1987), pp. 17-26.

Given the vast size of China's rural population—some 900 million villagers—the transformation of the countryside, first in revolution and then through a dramatic reform, is, I believe, one of the more significant stories of our time. A number of books and articles have engaged one or another period or have pursued the story in one locale. Here an effort will be made to come to grips with the most salient aspects of this drama across regions and across the whole span of time, from the era of Maoist radicalism up to the present day.

I

The Countryside Under Mao

Chapter One

STATE POWER AND THE VILLAGES

The collectivization of the Chinese countryside under Mao was one of the largest efforts in world history to reorganize people's lives and livelihoods. Almost a sixth of humankind was swept up in the successive waves of revolutionary change in the 1950s that culminated in a collective system of agriculture. Collectivization not only entailed an entirely new system of property ownership. It also gave rise to new types of work relations, and as will be seen in later chapters, this dramatically reshaped social relationships in many thousands of villages. In addition, and equally important, collectivization implanted a new strict form of political hierarchy and political teachings that—as will be seen— penetrated every corner of China and brought rural households firmly under the sway of the state.

My own vicarious knowledge of this period derives from extended interviews starting in the mid-1970s with farmers and village officials, in which they discussed an already established system of collective agriculture that had been put in place in the early 1960s. Most of the interviewees were not old enough to remember well the tumultuous events of the late 1940s and the 1950s when, in a dizzying succession of events, the farmers of China experienced first a land reform and then an escalating series of progressively higher forms of collectivization, leading into the utopian and ultimately tragic Great Leap Forward of 1958-60. The specific type of system of collectives that will be the focus of our attention was created out of the ashes of that tragedy, but to understand how China reached that pass, let us very briefly sketch the agrarian revolution of the 1950s.

The First Attempt

In the late 1940s in parts of northern China and in the early 1950s in the rest of the country, the Communist Party had carried out a land reform. As a first step, teams of Party activists entered villages to lead "class struggle" against local landlords and rich peasants. Following an orchestrated campaign of village-wide meetings to pour out grievances and "settle accounts" against them, their land was redistributed to the landless and land-deficient households.[1] Through this

---

[1]   A beautifully written and highly recommended description of the tumultuous 1947 land reform in one village in north China is William Hinton's *Fanshen: A Documentary of*

land-reform campaign, the power of the local elite was effectively broken in each village, and its place taken by a new leadership of poorer peasants loyal to the Party.

To make the new, relatively egalitarian peasant smallholdings economically viable, seasonal mutual-aid groups were soon established under the Party's guidance; and these gradually were shaped over the following years into agricultural producer cooperatives, each containing about two dozen families. By 1955, China contained some 17 million. In these, farmers received a portion of the harvest yields in exchange for having allowed their land and draft animals to be used by the cooperative and another harvest portion based on their contribution of labor. Within the space of another year, Party organizations everywhere in China in 1956 were competing to convert these cooperatives into collectives, enlarged to contain some 40 to 200 households. Even villages that had not yet formed cooperatives were being ushered directly into collectives. In these, farmers had to permanently give up their land and draft animals, sometimes willingly and sometimes grudgingly. In exchange, each household received a share of the collective's agricultural yields based entirely upon its contributions of labor. During the winter and other agricultural slack seasons, the collectives were to organize this labor to build new irrigation channels, terrace hillsides, and in other ways augment the local infrastructure.[2]

Although the new collectives ran into serious teething problems, and many effectively were retrenched or collapsed during the first year of operation, Mao and other Party radicals in 1958 pushed forward a far more ambitious program: the Great Leap Forward. By April 1958 the first "commune" was proclaimed. With local officials anxiously clambering to get on board, it was announced by November that practically every one of China's villagers belonged to one.[3] These gathered together in one massive unit a rural market town and all of the villages that surrounded it. In some extraordinary cases a single giant commune swallowed up several market towns and scores of villages. At the height of the Great Leap Forward, the cadres in the market-town command posts of the new communes directed the labor of many thousands of villagers. Stories were circulated in China's mass media about miraculous achievements in far-flung

---

Revolution in a Chinese Village (1966), republished in 1997 by the University of California Press.

[2]   See, e.g., Franz Schurmann, *Ideology and Organization in Communist China* (Berkeley: University of California Press, 1966), pp. 440-64; and Vivienne Shue, *Peasant China in Transition: The Dynamics of Development Toward Socialism, 1949-1956* (Berkeley: University of California Press, 1980).

[3]   On the origins of the Great Leap Forward, see Frederick C. Teiwes and Warren Sun, *China's Road to Disaster: Mao, Central Politicians, and Provincial Leaders in the Unfolding of the Great Leap Forward, 1955-1959* (Armonk: M.E. Sharpe, 1999); and David Bachman, *Bureaucracy, Economy, and Leadership in China: The Institutional Origins of the Great Leap Forward* (Cambridge: Cambridge University Press, 1991).

parts of the country. In a competition to achieve similar miracles, the large squads of farmers were instructed to plant seeds so tightly packed together that the seedlings crowded each other out; they were ordered off to work at hastily planned dam sites during the agricultural busy seasons; they were told to eat free meals in public mess halls and to melt their own metal cooking utensils in primitive backyard steel furnaces that produced useless junk. Huge quantities of grain were shipped off to the cities and onward for export as rural officials competed to exaggerate the size of local harvest yields. The consequence of all this was a collapse in rural production during 1959 and 1960 and a plunge into starvation in many parts of the countryside.[4]

After the excesses of the collectivization drives and the Great Leap Forward, rural China needed to be re-organized once again. In the early 1960s a more feasible system of rural governance was established that endured for some two decades, from 1960 to the early 1980s. A generation of rural people came of age entirely within the contours of this structure. This first chapter covers this long period of institutionalized socialism. It explores how a "workable" system of layered responsibilities and controls was created in the 1960s that involved local hierarchies of production teams, production brigades and communes. It will also be seen how this new administrative structure enabled the Party leadership in Beijing to penetrate the villages and rural households with new programs and new values. And the chapter will show, finally, how this system was wracked by tensions between peasant interests on the one side and those of the Party-state on the other, in ways that ultimately spelled the demise of the collectives. Unless otherwise noted, the information and analyses about this period of two decades are based upon my own interview research—but I have also sought to confirm the validity of the chapter's generalizations by keeping in mind the descriptions contained in a dozen and a half books that have been published about specific Chinese villages.[5]

---

[4]   On this see, e.g., Dali L. Yang, *Calamity and Reform in China* (Stanford: Stanford University Press, 1996).

[5]   The village studies and biographies of villagers that contain material on the 1960s and 1970s include Stephen Endicott, *Red Earth: Revolution in a Sichuan Village* (Toronto: NC Press, 1989); Edward Friedman, Paul G. Pickowicz and Mark Selden, *Revolution, Resistance and Reform in Village China* (New Haven: Yale University Press, forthcoming); He Liyi, *Mr. China's Son: A Villager's Life* (Boulder: Westview Press, 1993); William Hinton, *Shenfan: The Continuing Revolution in a Chinese Village* (New York: Random House, 1983); Mobo Gao, *Gao Village: Rural Life in China Since the Revolution* (London: Hurst & Co.; Honolulu: University of Hawaii Press, 1999); Philip Huang, *The Peasant Family and Rural Development in the Yangzi Delta* (Stanford: Stanford University Press, 1990); Huang Shumin, *The Spiral Road: Change in a Chinese Village Through the Eyes of a Communist Party Leader* (Boulder: Westview Press, 1989), pp. 89-98; Jun Jing, *The Temple of Memories: History, Power, and Morality in a Chinese Village* (Stanford: Stanford University Press, 1996); Ellen R. Judd, *Gender and Power in Rural North China* (Stanford: Stanford

Production Teams: The Basis for Agriculture

When the collectives were reorganized and consolidated in the early 1960s, agricultural production within each village was placed in the hands of "production teams" (*shengchan dui*). This was a term carried over from the Great Leap Forward, but it was given new content. Each production team, comprising a hamlet or village neighborhood and containing some 10 to 50 households, owned a block of agricultural land, and its member households worked the land together as a group and shared in the proceeds. In the wake of the Great Leap Forward's failure, the idea was to create a collective unit small enough for members to perceive the relationship between their own contribution of labor, their team's productivity, and their family's benefits from this.

To encourage the farmers to accept their team head's leadership, the head was normally either elected by team members or informally chosen by consensus, though in a minority of cases the team heads were actually selected from above by the Party organization. In some other cases, even if elected, the production team head was chosen by one large kinship group or clique to the detriment of other such groups, and cases were reported of nepotism, favoritism, and abuses of power. But despite such occurrences, on the whole the teams were relatively democratic in the way leaders were chosen—which had no parallel in any other parts of the Chinese political system.[6]

The new system contained a number of attractive features. By providing farmers with a share in a larger stretch of land than any family could farm on its own, the system gave each of the households protection against personal ruin in the event of a flooded plot of land or unexpected illness. It also provided for a relatively equitable distribution of incomes among households. And it organized and paid for a range of public services. In many villages, by the late 1960s or 1970s almost-free health care and elementary schooling were being provided

---

University Press, 1994); Sulamith Heins Potter and Jack M. Potter, *China's Peasants: The Anthropology of a Revolution* (Cambridge: Cambridge University Press, 1990); Gregory A. Ruf, *Cadres and Kin: Power, Authority, and Corporatism in a West China Village, 1937-1991* (Stanford: Stanford University Press, 1998); Peter J. Seybolt, *Throwing the Emperor from His Horse: Portrait of a Village Leader in China, 1923-1995* (Boulder: Westview Press, 1996); Helen F. Siu, *Agents and Victims in South China* (New Haven: Yale University Press, 1989); Yunxiang Yan, *The Flow of Gifts: Reciprocity and Social Networks in a Chinese Village* (Berkeley: University of California Press, 1996); and Zhang Letian, *Gaobie lixiang: Renmin gongshe zhidu yanjiu* (Departing from Ideals: Research into the System of the People's Commune) (Shanghai: Dongfang Chubanshe, 1998). Also taken into account was a village study in whose authorship I played a part: Anita Chan, Richard Madsen and Jonathan Unger, *Chen Village Under Mao and Deng* (Berkeley: University of California Press, 1992); the same village is also described in Richard Madsen, *Morality and Power in a Chinese Village* (Berkeley: University of California Press, 1984).

6   On this topic see, for example, John Burns, *Political Participation in Rural China* (Berkeley: University of California Press, 1988).

through production-team revenues—reaching much of rural China for the first time in history. Production teams also paid for the sustenance of orphans, widows and the childless elderly. In much of rural China, mortality rates declined dramatically, and the length of villagers' lives began to approach those of developed nations.

The countryside was able to achieve these gains in part because the state under Mao was strong and penetrated communities effectively. The state's drive to transform villages had a downside, however, in the political and economic spheres. Although Mao and other Party leaders were willing to tolerate a system of ownership and production by relatively small production teams, and were willing for the farmers to select their own production-team heads, at the same time the national leaders were unwilling to give the team memberships enough leeway in figuring out what crops to grow or enough say on how their own teams and villages were run. The system ultimately was top-down. The belief at the helm of the Party was that China's villagers, left to their own devices, would not continue to move China forward into ever higher forms of socialist society. The villages needed to be controlled and prodded for their own good. And there was a second important factor. The national leadership was convinced that to develop the national economy, agricultural surpluses needed to be squeezed from the countryside. Without strong institutional mechanisms in place, the villagers would not so willingly sacrifice their own material interests for the greater good of China by providing the state with cheap agricultural provisions to help build up Chinese industry.

Controlling Agricultural Production

The consequence was that in the new system of governance that was put in place after the collapse of the Great Leap Forward, the production teams sat at the very bottom of an administrative hierarchy, and they were dominated by a top-down chain of Party rule that reached from Beijing into each and every village. When I first began conducting interviews with Chinese from rural areas in the 1970s, during the collective era, my interviewees were in accord on this point. They saw the power of China's central authorities as overwhelming and irresistible; villages had options to shape their own policies only in those spheres that the central authorities did not decide to dominate.

The national Party leadership became increasingly assertive as the years passed and the Party's memories of the Great Leap Forward and its disastrous consequences faded. Within less than a decade, even the question of what to produce in what fields was not always left to the good sense and experience of the team heads and farmers. In the mid-1970s an interviewee from subtropical Guangdong Province provided a striking anecdote:

> Very often the orders from above completely have ignored our local conditions. In 1971, for example, there was an order to grow winter wheat. [The top leadership in Beijing had gotten the notion that every province should grow supplies of wheat, including provinces where wheat was not traditionally eaten.] Our production team leader complained bitterly. He said that in 1958

[the Great Leap Forward] we had similarly been forced to plant a winter crop of wheat and it had been a total failure. He added that we wouldn't have enough fertilizer for all of our crops, and so the spring crop of rice would be badly affected. But it was to no avail. Our team had to pay out of its own funds to buy wheat seeds, and in the end there wasn't any wheat to harvest, just as the farmers had predicted.

Sometimes the commands from above could be in the guise of "requests" or "suggestions," but that phrasing did not necessarily provide the peasantry and their agricultural production teams with any greater leeway. An interviewee from another Guangdong village recollects a "request" of 1969:

> From way above our village the Party leadership asked us farmers to dedicate rice to the commune and nation as a gift. We had had a good harvest that year, and we naturally wanted to keep the extra grain. But our agricultural production team was required to have someone stand up as a representative of the peasants and say "Let's dedicate this rice to the revolution and the world." We farmers felt, "Here we have a good harvest, but of what good is that to us?" But no-one dared to say this openly. So the rice was donated, and we got no money for it. Later they reversed this policy, but they didn't give back the rice.

These exactions occurred in the midst of mini-campaigns launched from on high. Onerous though they were, a greater burden to the peasant economy was the annual fixed demand for cheap sales of foodstuffs to the state. These took the place of agricultural taxes (the latter remained at a low level throughout the collective era). Instead, the government relied upon purchases of agricultural produce at below the cost of production. It was intent upon extracting steadily growing quantities of this agricultural produce from the villages in order to develop the urban economy more rapidly. It was a classic case of forced industrialization based upon a primitive accumulation of capital.

To ensure this predictable supply of basic foodstuffs to the cities at depressed prices, the state dictated to the production teams which of their fields needed to be devoted to grain and other specified crops and precisely how large a quota of grain each team needed to sell to the state at a low price. They were required to ignore comparative advantage and market prices and to concentrate on the production of this low-priced grain.[7]

---

[7] Reviewing the effects of this policy, the economist Nicholas Lardy has concluded that state policies were "inimical to peasant interests," and he cited "a long-term tendency for the state systematically to constrain peasant income-earning opportunities and to inhibit the efficient use of resources in agriculture." "State Intervention and Peasant Opportunities," in William L. Parish (ed.), *Chinese Rural Development: The Great Transformation* (Armonk: M.E. Sharpe, 1985), p. 34.

To be sure, the peasantry sometimes *did* react self-protectively. But a distinction must be made here. Laying out dozens of interview transcripts side by side suggests that grain concealments and unreported plots of land were much more common in the hamlets of poor districts than in the better-off settlements of the deltas and plains. Since the latter villages normally were able to produce enough grain to retain a grain cushion even after their quota deliveries, the upper administrative levels scrupulously monitored their crop yields. By contrast, the unwritten bureaucratic rule of thumb when squeezing foodstuffs from the poorest districts was that, notwithstanding the officially imposed grain levies, enough needed to be left in the hands of the peasantry to ensure their survival. Thus in dealing with such villages, the officialdom tended to look the other way even when the production teams there engaged in fairly clumsy machinations to hide a portion of their harvests. They kept the locations of some of their mountain fields secret, reported good grain as having been spoiled, handed in heavy soaked grain in the place of dry grain, and cooked their account books. An interviewee from a poor hilly district confided in the 1970s,

> Our team secretly distributed a hundred kilos of rice to each of us before the team handed in anything to the government. The team heads gave us a lot of detailed instructions to cover up the discrepancies. If we were ever questioned by higher-level cadres coming down, we were to say each person in the team received only 15 kilos per month on the average. The big charts up at the team office showing the grain rations of each person and family were for show, to con outsiders. The team kept two separate account books, one real, one false.[8]

It is clear from interviews that such poor teams could get away with committing transgressions of a sort that members of more prosperous communities did not dare contemplate.

The concerns of the teams in richer communities instead revolved around efforts to resist the urgings from higher-level officials to donate, or sell cheaply, their *above*-quota grain to the state. This resistance also included attempts, after fulfilling their quotas, to secretly move field markers in order to shift bits of land away from grain production and into crops like vegetables or peanuts, which fetched better prices. The farmers considered such diversions of land as simply making good business sense for their team collective, whereas the state denounced such practices as "capitalist roading." The local Party officials had to

---

[8]   This "hidden economy" was not, of course, included in the Chinese government's data on national agricultural production. To this extent, economists perhaps have tended to underestimate total grain production and *per capita* levels of rural consumption under Mao.

keep a watchful eye to control production teams in these sporadic games of hide-and-seek.[9]

In short, production-team leaders in both poor and prosperous villages sought, if they could get away with it, to sidestep some of the demands coming down from above. The production-team leaders, after all, remained peasants. They shared the farmers' interests and were directly concerned with their neighbors' livelihoods. They themselves worked almost full time in the fields, and like other peasants they received their wages in "work points" that depended on the value of the team's annual income. The real reward for their pains lay only in petty perquisites and the esteem of neighbors. When production did poorly or the state's exactions rose, peasant disgruntlement mounted and the team heads were likely to consider throwing in the towel and quitting. But whatever their desires to protect the team's interests, they were in a very weak position to openly or directly resist the impositions of the bureaucracy. Their base was only a hamlet or a small village neighborhood; they quite often were illiterate and lacked the knowledge and confidence to speak up effectively at meetings in defense of their teams' interests when faced by articulate, overbearing political superiors; and if they did take a stand they could always be dismissed from on high. When the peasantry and team heads resisted national policies, it could only be covertly and marginally through cheating (especially, as seen, in the poorest districts) or through unorganized passivity, as in the response to the Three Loyalties Campaign of 1968-69, when peasants throughout China showed their discontent with new state-enforced impositions by markedly slowing down in their work.[10]

Private vs. Collective

At the same time, the team heads were often at odds with their own members over a different aspect of the new agrarian system: private plots. The rights of peasants to engage in private sideline production had been guaranteed by the state (with temporary local exceptions during radical campaigns) since 1962.[11] China's leaders had learned through the disastrous experiences of the Great Leap Forward, in which private plots were abolished, that the private agricultural sector,

---

[9]   Other examples of team stratagems in what Jean Oi calls "the war over the harvest" are contained in Chapter 6 of her excellent book *State and Peasant in Contemporary China* (Berkeley: University of California Press, 1989).

[10]   The peasantry's reaction to this campaign is discussed in Chan, Madsen and Unger, *Chen Village Under Mao and Deng*, Ch. 6.

[11]   "Regulations on the Work of the Rural People's Communes (Revised Draft), September 1962," *Documents of the Chinese Communist Party Central Committee, September 1956–April 1969*, Vol. I (Hong Kong: Union Research Institute, 1971), pp. 719-22.

particularly the private plot, was a "necessary adjunct to the socialist economy."[12] The regulations of 1962 let the teams set aside 5 to 7 percent of their arable land for these private plots. Because most Chinese villages have little land per capita, the plots were relatively tiny.[13] A family held only temporary use rights to them; and the size of its plot got readjusted from time to time as additional children were born and older children married out. The peasants were also permitted to raise animals such as pigs, chickens and ducks privately,[14] to plant limited numbers of fruit trees in courtyards and on hilltop wasteland, and to fish or produce cottage handicrafts after hours.

These private activities were essential to the peasants' livelihoods in two ways. Whereas the collective fields provided almost all of China's grain, the private sector provided the bulk of the farmers' vegetables and meat. This was reflected in the saying, "For the bottom of the ricebowl rely on the collective. For the top of the bowl rely on ourselves." The private endeavors were also the peasants' most important source of cash income. At the end of each collective harvest each household's cumulative workpoints were computed and the family was paid in both kind and cash. Payment in kind came first, and the team was supposed to guarantee to each family the staple foodgrains that it needed even if it had insufficient workpoints and had to go into debt to the team. Such families received no cash from the collective and depended entirely upon their private sidelines for cash. In poor villages, many families found themselves in this circumstance. But even the best-off households in prosperous villages did not have much ready money to meet the costs of a family funeral or a son's wedding. On such occasions, peasants sold what they jokingly referred to as their "piggy banks"—one or more of their hogs. For all peasants, prosperous or impoverished alike, a second rural saying applied: "For eating rice rely on the collective. For money rely on your private sidelines."

Partly because of the government's own pricing mechanisms, under which much of the collective grain was sold cheaply to the state under the quotas while vegetables and pork procured far better prices, farmers could earn considerably more per hour from their private endeavors than from collective labor. All told, from among all the villages for which I have such information through interviewing, approximately one-quarter to one-third of the peasants' gross

---

[12] *People's Daily* (Beijing), quoted in Kenneth Walker, *Planning in Chinese Agriculture: Socialization and the Private Sector, 1956-1962* (London: Frank Cass & Co., 1965), p. 93.

[13] I have calculated the size of the private plots in Chen Village in Guangdong Province, which, because it adjoined a mountain range and could cultivate slopes, had more land than other villages in the area. There, the private plots ranged from a minimum of one-thirtieth of an acre for a single person or married couple to a maximum of one-tenth of an acre for families with six or more members.

[14] To enable farmers to grow pig fodder, the government allowed an extra small allotment of private plot for each sow that a family owned.

annual income (including both in kind and cash) derived from the private sector.[15] In two of the poorest villages for which I have interview data, where the earnings from the collective fields were very low, up to half of the family income derived from such private activities.

This was a source of conflict between team leaders and farmers: for the peasants' natural desire to focus on this valuable private production inevitably impinged upon the productivity of the collective sector. A former team head remarked to me, "We knew that any person's energies are limited and that if farmers are so energetic on their own land then they're slighting the team's land." Team leaders were constantly on the lookout to stop team members sneaking off early from work, constantly preventing peasants from clearing too much barren land to expand their private production, constantly haranguing members to actually rest during rest breaks rather than scramble off to their private endeavors.

From above, the Party-state periodically reacted to keep the private endeavors quite limited in extent and under tight control. One means, used especially during the 1970s, was to deny the farmers a free market at which to sell their private produce. This steered the sales of private produce toward the state's own purchasing depots, which offered lower prices than a free market would have. In what became for some villages a game of cat and mouse, private marketing could be largely curtailed but never altogether suppressed. For one thing, a fair number of urban people relied on private purchases to supplement the shriveled vegetables and skin-and-bones poultry available in state stores, and on their days off from work rode buses out into the countryside to privately purchase foodstuffs.

During radical periods, the officialdom not only clamped down on this, but also sometimes launched campaigns to directly tighten the reins on private plots. These campaigns were usually backed vociferously by ideologues among the Party leaders, who warned shrilly that private undertakings encouraged a selfish "small producer mentality" among the peasantry. The last major campaign of this type, the Line Education Campaign (*Luxian jiaoyu yundong*) of 1974-75, was pushed by the group around Mao later dubbed the Gang of Four, and was so

---

[15]   Other researchers have come up with somewhat similar findings. In the suburbs of Guangzhou city, according to John Burns, one-third to one-half of a farm family's total *cash* income in the 1970s came from private endeavors. (John Burns, "The Radicals and the Campaign to Limit Bourgeois Rights in the Countryside," *Contemporary China*, Vol. 1, No. 4 (January 1977), p. 27). Deborah Davis-Friedman, who did extensive interviewing in the 1970s about rural Guangdong Province, calculated that generally 20 to 40 percent of a rural family's total income derived from private sources. (Deborah Davis-Friedman, "Strategies for Aging: Interdependence Between Generations in the Transition to Socialism," *Contemporary China*, Vol. 1, No. 6 (March 1977), p. 36). In the model communes visited by S. J. Burki in the 1960s about 20 percent of total family income came from this. S. J. Burki, *A Study of Chinese Communes, 1965* (Cambridge: Harvard University East Asian Research Center, 1969), pp. 40-1.

draconian that it needed to be removed from local cadre hands. Even the production team heads and village heads, after all, relied upon private endeavors to supplement their family's earnings. Squads of officials sent from above momentarily needed to take over many of China's villages to push the campaign through: in Guangdong Province alone, 120,000 officials were dispatched into villages.[16] They forced through reductions in the size of private plots, implemented very strict limits on the numbers of ducks and chickens farmers could raise, and imposed harsh fines equivalent to several days' wages on any team member who took leave during the day to attend to private matters.

The Production Brigade and Party Control

The production teams were all part of a "production brigade." Each large village (or in the absence of sizable villages, each cluster of small neighboring hamlets) had been designated a "brigade." The brigade government (that is, the village government) ran the local primary school and perhaps a rudimentary health clinic, sometimes established and operated small village factories and repair shops, controlled and coordinated the irrigation system that fed into the teams' fields—and oversaw political campaigns. This was because the brigade was the lowest level at which a Party branch operated. It provided the principal avenue through which the Party leadership in Beijing could penetrate and politically dominate village life—for the branch Party secretary was empowered to supervise the workings of the village government and the production teams. Although each village had a brigade head and deputy brigade heads and other official posts, they were subordinate to the Party branch and its Party secretary. To make sure the brigade Party secretary was attuned to the wishes of the Party, he (few Party secretaries were women) was always selected by the Party levels above.

The leadership of the brigade—the Party secretary and the brigade officials alike—often had reason to feel trapped uncomfortably between the grassroots production teams and upper-level interests. They had all risen from the local peasantry, felt loyal to their village, and very much wanted to help shape a more prosperous community and higher peasant morale. At the same time, they held postings that they were eager to preserve and found themselves under very strong pressures from above.

Put in a nutshell, politics within Chinese villages often revolved around an intrinsic conflict between the production teams—economic entities that were somewhat democratic—versus the brigade level, a political entity, essentially autocratic and under pressure to uphold and enforce Party policy. That, in simple terms, was the framework, and to a surprising extent village politics did operate along these lines. Even though brigade leaders often were intent, first and foremost, upon protecting their own interests, not those of the Party and state, the

---

[16]   *Far Eastern Economic Review*, October 25, 1974, p. 15.

balance of pressures that they faced normally put them at the service of the Party state.

Generally speaking, where a brigade was coterminous with a single village, its leaders were in a far better position to bring daily pressure to bear on the teams below them, as compared to localities where the brigade was composed of a string of separate hamlets. In the latter circumstances, the brigade level seemed an artificial administrative device imposed from outside, and the brigade leadership had no natural constituency. In contrast, in a compact single-village brigade, the brigade heads could project themselves as the leaders of the community, and could appeal to the peasants' loyalty to their own village.[17] Politically, a village-wide leadership has always represented its village to the world outside; socially, the village and not the neighborhood (production team) is the sphere the peasant had always inhabited; economically, especially in south China, the vital water-supply system had to be coordinated at village level, not by the teams alone. In a single-village brigade, the brigade leaders—that is, the village leaders—were always nearby and daily interacted with the men who led the production teams. In such a situation, even a team's longer-term economic course was sometimes influenced as much by the brigade leadership as by the team heads. Elsewhere, say a production team that constituted its own semi-isolated mountain hamlet, the team by necessity not only controlled its own day-to-day affairs, but also needed to take over some of the functions that were ordinarily held by a brigade. A comparison of interviews that I conducted about several dozens of rural communities suggests that Party campaigns could be more vigorously implemented in single-village brigades than in those composed of several hamlets.

Brigade leaderships tended to be proactive, and when opportunities arose they were apt to take the initiative. They had been given leeway by the state to establish village enterprises, and especially in the 1970s they took advantage of this to seek out niches where profits could be made through small labor-intensive industry. Brickworks, sawmills, agricultural processing plants and very simple manufacturing plants soon dotted parts of the countryside. As these were "collectives," they were allowed to keep the profits. But as a brigade did not have its own ready sources of capital, starting a village enterprise often entailed negotiations with the production teams. In return for capital, each team would be promised a given number of industrial jobs for its own team members and, in some villages, modest dividends. Perhaps more important, it was understood that if the brigade government could generate its own income, it would not have to turn to the teams each year to fund all of the village's services.

---

17   This is precisely the type of appeal that the brigade heads were able to put forward successfully in Chen Village, a community that was not only a single brigade/village but also a single lineage. (Chan, Madsen and Unger, *Chen Village Under Mao and Deng*, passim.)

Success in industrializing tilted the balance of power between teams and brigade further in the brigade's direction. A brigade administration that ran profitable enterprises now controlled a sizeable budget that it could use at its own discretion; and it had gained a constituency of workers that it directly employed. Not only did such a brigade not have to bargain and compromise with the village's teams to finance its own operations; it also found itself in a less dependent position *vis-à-vis* the authorities above the village. In short, village officials discovered that enterprises were an effective tool for augmenting their own political security and status. As a group, the officials in such villages not only became increasingly entrepreneurial; they also gained experience in the rough and tumble of market competition. The rapid rural industrialization of the 1980s and 1990s, which for most of the Deng era was spurred by collective industry, has its origins in this prior period.

The Commune: A Bridge to the State

Above the brigade and its Party branch sat the commune government.[18] The commune no longer held the type of direct and totalistic control over all rural activity that briefly had been put into its hands during the Great Leap Forward. The largest of the Great Leap Forward communes had been reduced in size, and a commune now consisted of a small rural market town and the dozen or so surrounding agricultural villages.[19] The commune administration sometimes owned and operated several small rural factories and perhaps a few orchards, ran the local secondary school and sometimes established a rudimentary hospital. Most essentially, though, the commune served the role of a political watchdog: the seat of a local Party machine that kept a close watch on the villages within its jurisdiction and relayed the state's policies and commands to the village Party secretaries. The commune and its Party secretary were needed as a "bridge" between the rural communities and the central state. This was because the rural counties, which comprised the next higher level in the chain of political command, normally contained upward of a hundred villages, too large a number to be supervised directly by the government organs in the county capital.

The higher in the rural administration that an official sat, the more closely he or she found it personally worthwhile to abide by the Party-state's demands. For one thing, the officials at the commune and county levels, unlike the village-level

---

[18] Ezra Vogel has written an excellent detailed discussion of the commune-level administration, along with detailed discussions of the brigade and production team administrations, in A. Doak Barnett, with Ezra Vogel, *Cadres, Bureaucracy, and Political Power in Communist China* (New York: Columbia University Press, 1967), pp. 313-424.

[19] For an interesting and influential discussion of the economic and administrative necessity for the commune to conform to the contours of the local rural marketing district, see G. William Skinner, "Marketing and Social Structure in Rural China, Part III," *Journal of Asian Studies*, Vol. 24, No. 3 (May 1965), pp. 386-99.

brigade leadership, were out of sight and out of range of the peasants' frustrations. Nor did they feel particularly attached to the rural district where they were stationed. In fact, the commune leaders normally were rotated from one commune to another rather than serve in their own native commune district, just as the county's leaders were rotated in from elsewhere.[20] (This was very much in keeping with the long-standing practices of the Chinese emperors, who had sent officials to rule counties and regions of which they were not natives so as to circumvent the dangers of localist loyalties and connections.) Unlike lower-level cadres, they were paid by and received their promotions from the state; and if we can intuit from the policies that these county and commune officials sometimes pushed, it would seem that their jobs were not jeopardized by crop failures out in the villages or stagnating peasant living standards, just so long as the grain-quota exactions and Beijing's commands got met. William Hinton's *Shenfan*, a book about a village in the 1960s and 1970s, draws a graphic picture of a rigid self-serving political bureaucracy that was inclined "to issue blind directives, to order unreasonable projects, and recommend impractical schemes . . . unable to co-exist with any kind of pluralism, any grass-roots initiative, any lower-level dissent."[21]

During the 1970s, the rural bureaucrats were still smarting from the terrible buffeting that all levels of the officialdom had endured during the Cultural Revolution upheaval of 1966-68. In its wake, Chinese politics remained tense and unpredictable. The safest course was to avoid taking any initiatives themselves, and instead to dogmatically apply whatever policies came down from above. National policy preferences did not always even have to be spelled out in firm directives; informal comments by national leaders or repeated reports in the national press praising some new rural endeavor often were enough to spark its enforced implementation, as provincial, prefectural and county officials scrambled to jump aboard.[22] They were vying nervously to avoid seeming laggard compared to officials in the regions next door. It was in this fashion that the irrational planting of winter wheat, discussed above, was imposed on Guangdong farmers and that the gifts of free "loyalty grain" were enforced.

What is striking in looking at interview transcripts is the similarity of such bureaucratic responses over vast distances. Even when the Party Central Committee in Beijing did not issue specific national directives, far-flung villages

---

[20]   This rule of avoidance was more strictly adhered to before the Cultural Revolution of 1966-68 than afterward. In the 1970s the rule of thumb was that someone could initially rise to a top leadership position within his or her own commune in the wake of the Cultural Revolution turmoil, but subsequently would be rotated sideways. This became true, too, of rural county leaderships. This system of rotation is still practiced today, especially at the county level, with much the same consequences.

[21]   William Hinton, *Shenfan: The Continuing Revolution in a Chinese Village*, pp. 757, 755.

[22]   On this, also see David Zweig, *Agrarian Radicalism in China, 1968-1978* (Cambridge, Mass.: Harvard University Press, 1989).

were forced to shift in the same direction at the same time as if, to use the Chinese term for this phenomenon, there had been a "single stroke of the knife." Nationwide, the same coercive pressures were at work everywhere.

When the Maoist state chose to intervene in local affairs, in short, it could do so with dramatic effect. But sometimes the situation was more ambiguous. Where the Party-state did *not* press an issue, village and production-team leaders had some room to maneuver, and they sometimes sought to protect themselves and their localities. Brigade leaders carefully appraised whether unwanted policies originated at levels high in the Party, in which case they fulsomely mouthed support and made sure their own brigade toed the line, as compared to programs that were concocted at the commune level. If the latter, they could surreptitiously stall in implementing the program until the wave of commune initiatives had passed. Or they could even risk a public show of resistance on behalf of their village, knowing that the commune administration, when acting on its own, was the weakest level in the Party-state's chain of command. Interviewees report that a commune generally held few economic assets of its own, had no natural constituencies that its leadership could turn to for support, and had to depend upon the borrowed power of the state to get its way.

Before the Communist revolution and collectivization, villagers had oriented themselves toward their local market town, which normally became transformed into the commune's headquarters. They had congregated there to buy and sell, to exchange news and socialize.[23] But after the Mao-era collectives were established, produce was sold directly to the state, and only one or two people in each production team needed to be assigned to venture into the market town to deliver it. Peasants no longer took an active interest either in the town or in the other villages of their marketing district, now dubbed a commune. Among other things, throughout much of the 1970s the peasants' free markets in the market town had been suppressed and thereby lateral trade between villages had been cut off, making the villages dependent instead upon the state both as the purchaser of their products and as the provider of consumer and investment goods. And the religious festivals that formerly had brought them into town on special occasions had been branded as "feudal" and eliminated, giving farmers even less reason to venture into town.

As the relevance to them of the market town and the local marketing district (commune) declined, the attention of the peasantry and of village cadres became focused, more strongly than ever before, upon their own neighborhoods and villages. The peasantry, after all, no longer were independent smallholders but were bound together economically in the production teams. They now shared a common harvest and a common fate with their immediate neighbors. And they felt this bind to the team and village and this common fate especially strongly

---

[23]   G. William Skinner, "Marketing and Social Structure in Rural China, Part I," *Journal of Asian Studies*, Vol. 24, No. 1 (1964).

during these decades because they could no longer depart. A rigid system of residential permits (*hukou*) had been established in 1960 that prevented people from moving to another district or working away from home without government permission—and this was rigorously enforced. For better or worse, people knew that they were now bound to their community.

At the very same time, as has been observed, the village became tied directly and strongly into national movements and national demands. Its economy became shaped by the needs of the state, and its local politics shaped by the ebbs and flows of national campaigns. In sum, then, as the "intermediate" world beyond the village—the local marketing district/commune—shrank in importance to villagers, both the village community and the larger national world outside became increasingly significant to the peasants and village cadres. But one unfortunate consequence was that as the economic and social significance of the marketing district weakened, the village now faced the state on its own, naked as it were, as it was largely isolated from neighboring villages.[24]

Politically oriented administrative organs have a general tendency to seek to enlarge their own sphere of influence, and commune administrations were no exception. Given the weakness of their position, the communes' Party leaders frequently sought to strengthen their own leverage over the localities by way of the political campaigns that punctuated rural life throughout the period of Mao's rule. During campaigns, all issues became politicized, and the commune Party committee, as the organ directly above the brigade Party branches, could enforce the lower levels' compliance by claiming to be the official local guardian and interpreter of Mao's Thought. Placed in that politically sacrosanct context, in a campaign atmosphere of "struggle meetings" and purges, resistance to commune programs became fraught with political dangers. "Since it's to the commune level's advantage when campaigns come along," an interviewee of the mid-1970s observed, "the communes like to push lots of small intra-Party campaigns as a means of keeping politics alive. Between the peaks of campaigns and between major campaigns, the commune level's powers to get compliance otherwise wanes."

The commune officials were not the only ones to utilize political campaigns as a means to grasp greater power over the levels below them. So, too, did all levels in the system. The "continuing revolution" that the Left in China promoted in the 1960s and 1970s, the Maoist emphasis upon "Politics in Command," and the recurring bouts of campaign fever that Mao and his followers initiated all served to strengthen upper-level controls over the lower levels and a cowed

---

[24]   On this point, my findings differ entirely from the main premise of Vivienne Shue's *The Reach of the State* (Stanford: Stanford University Press, 1988). Shue posited that a "cellular" commune provided an effective buffer between the village community and the Communist state, deflecting and frequently thwarting the state's initiatives. All of the information that I have obtained from interviews and documentation strongly suggest the opposite.

populace. Even brigade leaders welcomed campaigns that allowed them to pull the agricultural production teams below them into line and to build brigade-level powers at the expense of the teams. The uncertainty and fears generated by campaigns, and the political demands then for total ideological obeisance, cut through and obviated any self-protective resistance by lower levels.

While the uncertainty and fears generated by the recurrent bouts of campaigns strengthened upper-level controls over the populace, some of these campaigns were also turned by Mao against the local officialdom itself, to keep officials in line. A massive initiative of this type, the Four Cleanups campaign, shook the countryside during the first half of the 1960s, orchestrated by so-called "workteams" of higher-level officials who took over villages for the duration of the campaign and organized villagers to criticize errant village officials.[25] This campaign was followed shortly by the Cultural Revolution upsurge of 1966-68, during which villagers were given a freer rein to attack local power-holders. In both campaigns, local officials who had abused their positions and engaged in corruption were pulled up short, as ordinary people responded to the calls from China's top leaders to lay accusations. Such campaigns served, intermittently, as the main buttress against corruption in a system that had few other safeguards. But for the most part, the political campaigns tightened controls on the rural populace rather than loosened them, demanding even greater conformity from the populace than in ordinary times. By targeting both ordinary people and officials, rule by campaigns in China served a role not dissimilar to the centralizing function filled by the secret police in Stalin's Russia.

Radical Decentralization vs. Administrative Hierarchy: Party vs. Government Control

Ironically, as seen earlier, the extraordinary county and commune-level efforts to conform to upper-level whims occurred at a time when, in the wake of the radical Cultural Revolution turmoil of 1966-68, China ostensibly had decentralized the economy's administration. To understand this seemingly contradictory result, we must briefly examine the two different models of socialist administration that China adhered to. The first of these was imported from Stalin's Russia in the 1950s, and in it each of the central government ministries held strong decision-making powers for its own area of administration (say, the Ministry of Agriculture would establish the priorities for that sector of the economy and the Ministry of Education for the educational sector) and directives flowed downward and outward to the localities through each of the hierarchical ministry's chains of command. This type of supervision by a complex multilayered ministerial organ

---

[25]   This is described in Madsen, *Morality and Power in a Chinese Village*, Ch. 3; also in Chan, Madsen and Unger, *Chen Village Under Mao and Deng*, Chs. 1-3. On the elite politics that underpinned this campaign, see Richard Baum, *Prelude to Revolution: Mao, the Party and the Peasant Question, 1962-66* (New York: Columbia University Press, 1975).

assumes routine administration and bureaucratically planned economic development.

The alternative model was one in which the Party committee of each region or district would hold direct responsibility over the multifaceted activities within its boundaries, including, say, agriculture and education; and in turn, each lower Party committee would be responsible for all the decisions affecting its own smaller geographic area.[26]

Mao distrusted the ministries and their bureaucracies. He felt, apparently, that they tended to regard orderly administration as a *goal*, which in effect would place them in opposition to the continued transformations of the economy and society that Mao so grandly and dogmatically envisioned. Mao and his closest followers instead preferred the regional Party model. Relinquishing a comprehensive range of responsibilities to a region meant that a Party committee rather than professional ministry functionaries—the "reds" rather than the "experts"—would establish the priorities and set the tone, would promulgate the local policy decisions and control and allocate the financing. Party committees were far better positioned than ministerial bureaucracies to initiate mass mobilization and to manage the upsurge of political campaigns. The followers of Mao could point proudly to this model as facilitating "Politics in Command," as the Maoist saying went, while disparaging the other framework as mechanically placing routinized "Economics in Command."

This is not to say that periods when the local-region-based system of Party committees were more firmly in control, such as the Great Leap Forward and the first half of the 1970s, were in any way periods of democratic "mass line" or of local mass participation in decision-making. Quite to the contrary, the phrase "Politics in Command" denoted, among other things, that top-down ideological and political controls were to be tightened, almost as if to offset the degree of autonomy that the local regions were gaining in the economic sphere. The official demand during such times was for "monolithic leadership" (*yiyuanhua lingdao*), a term that connoted a more dictatorial political grip over both government bureaus and lower Party committees by Mao and the Party Central Committee in Beijing. In fact, one of the charges that the proponents of regional Party committee control leveled against the system of ministerial chains of command was that in the latter framework officials were too inclined to ignore the top Party commanders' "monolithic leadership" in pursuit of the ministries' own interests and policies.

---

[26] The important distinctions between these two models of administration are discussed in detail in Jonathan Unger, "The Struggle to Dictate China's Administration: The Conflict of Branches vs. Areas vs. Reform," *The Australian Journal of Chinese Affairs*, No. 18 (July 1987), pp. 15-45. Also see Franz Schurmann, *Ideology and Organization in Communist China*, (Berkeley: University of California Press, 1966), pp. 174-8.

This distinction between administrative models applies well to the period of Great Leap Forward radicalism. Even though economic/administrative decentralization into the hands of provincial and local Party committees was introduced, a book by Alfred Chan about the Great Leap Forward shows how the Party leaderships of provinces and districts as geographically diverse as Guangdong Province in the south and Liaoning Province in the north anxiously sought to keep in the good graces of their political superiors by rigidly pursuing all of the Leap-inspired programs in the very same way. They did so regardless of whether these policies made sense in the local context; indeed, no discernible efforts were made whatsoever to protect regional institutional interests.[27] Hamlets and villages across China had to march quick-step to a single drumbeat. At no other time, in fact, was that phrase "a single stroke of the knife" truer or more devastatingly applied. As we have observed in earlier pages, the same sort of political anxiety, conformity and irrational rural policy directives again prevailed more than a decade later in the early 1970s, when in the wake of the Cultural Revolution turmoil Mao once again hobbled some of the ministries and decentralized China into the hands of Party committees.

During the Great Leap Forward and similar radical periods of decentralization, political discipline tightened to such an extent that military terminology became fashionable; rural communities in the Leap metaphorically were seen as units of a large revolutionary army. It was then that the term "brigade" first came to designate a village, that village neighborhoods and hamlets became "teams" (the Chinese term for an army squad), and that peasants marched into the fields in massed formations following a red banner.

Over the following two decades, the repeated demands that the villages conform rigidly to the dictates of the national leadership, the terrible political pressures upon all sectors of the bureaucracy and all sectors of the populace, the militant conformity demanded during the upsurges of campaigns, and the universal adulation of a supreme leader all bore a totalitarian stamp. So, too, the Maoist-era designations of "enemies of the state" who needed to be controlled and in some cases extirpated remind us of certain other totalitarian regimes.

We ought not, however, infer from the use of this term that the state's writ extended to *all* spheres of local life. Even totalitarian polities leave notable gaps in the controls they impose. Particularly between campaigns, villagers found ways to pursue private pleasures. And village officials and even ordinary peasants repeatedly sought ways to turn national programs to their own local and personal ends, all the while spouting revolutionary slogans. Indeed, an often Byzantine informal local politics flourished, based not only on that inherent conflict between the brigade and team levels, but also based upon conflicts between different lineage groups or between neighborhoods, or conflicts stemming from family

---

[27]   Alfred Chan, *Mao's Crusade: Politics and Policy Implementation in China's Great Leap Forward* (Oxford: Oxford University Press, 2001).

grudges of generations past, or conflicts rooted in the conflicting ambitions of different local leaders. When national political "struggle campaigns" erupted, village heads and peasants alike were apt to try to turn these toward their own purposes, targeting and persecuting personal enemies and unpopular local scapegoats. All of this was true, too, of Stalin's Russia. The crucial points that should be borne in mind, though, are that when the Maoist or the Stalinist state chose to intervene in local affairs, it could do so with dramatic effect, and that its intervention at times touched so many spheres of activity. It is in this sense that the term "totalitarian" rang true for both states. If anything, one of the essential distinctions between the Soviet Union and China was that in China the reach of the Party-state in the countryside was considerably more penetrating and comprehensive, not least because, quite unlike the warfare waged by the urban Stalinist regime against the Russian peasant from the late 1920s onward, the Chinese Party had succeeded in gaining large numbers of adherents within the villages. The result was that the Chinese Party's authority over the villages, as shall be seen below, was grounded in a complex mixture of tacit fears and genuine acceptance, rather than stark Stalinist coercion.

True Believers

Dating back to the time of the Chinese civil war in the 1930s and 1940s and the land reform of the early 1950s, the Party had enjoyed a reservoir of popularity and trust in the countryside. For many years thereafter, it was able to rely upon strong constituencies in the villages that were responsive to the revolution's appeals to political militancy and economic egalitarianism. The same interviewees who in the 1970s described to me the coercive side to village–state relations under Mao's rule often spoke in the next breath of this element of support, as in the following discussion about the early 1970s, conducted in Hong Kong with an interviewee from a village in Guangdong Province's hill country:

> There's no way to oppose state policy. But you know, it's funny, the peasants who were impoverished before the revolution feel that even if they see no good points in a program, in the end things will work out well. They *believe* in the Party and have real feelings of gratitude toward it.

Beginning in the early 1960s, the Party had felt a need to take strong organizational measures to perpetuate these feelings. Memories of the Party's popular civil-war and land-reform policies were fading, and amidst the terrible economic depression that followed the collapse of the Great Leap Forward the loyalties of China's former have-nots could no longer be taken for granted. Meetings to "remember past bitterness and think of present sweetness" (*yiku sitian*) were organized to encourage the peasants to keep firmly in mind their debt of gratitude to the Party and Mao. Alongside this, in village after village, networks of "mass organizations" (*qunzhong zuzhi*) were re-activated—Poor and Lower-middle Peasant Associations, the Women's Association, Communist Youth League branches, and so forth—and all of these chorused simplified and emotionally charged versions of the Party teachings, often in the shape of sacrosanct quotations from Chairman Mao.

Interviewees confirmed that a great many farmers fell under the thrall of these teachings. We shall observe this in several of the chapters that follow, especially Chapters Two and Four, which deal with "class struggle" and with utopian efforts to install egalitarian systems of rural pay.

Mao and the Party machinery under him took advantage of this acceptance in the eyes of much of the peasantry to attempt to transform the villagers' outlook. During the more ambitious of the Party-led campaigns, they were pushed to abandon their customs and religious practices. To promote this, the Party-state forcefully penetrated not just the rural community but even the privacy of homes. An interviewee from an inland village remembers, for example:

> In 1964 there was a "destroy superstition" campaign. The farmers in my village didn't dare to say what they thought of it, but all of them destroyed their household gods, old and young people alike. They were asked to destroy them with their own hands. People were scared to, but they did it. The cadres took the lead. The political teachings and the meetings on this pressed down level by level. People had to do it; otherwise they'd badger you, they'd keep you in meetings every night until you acted on it.

Yet whatever the means, the Party *did* succeed in profoundly reshaping belief systems in a great many of China's villages—and coercion, though ever-present, was not even the most important element in the Party's success. A large number of the peasants who destroyed their household gods pasted up posters of Mao where the altar had stood, filling the void with a new form of worship. And this was not simply a ritual substitution to satisfy Party cadres. A new worldview had struck roots.

To be sure, alongside the new beliefs, an old faith in geomancy (*fengshui*), fate and supernatural phenomena often persisted. It would have been surprising had this not been so; changes in belief system are not like a simple change of clothes. Indeed, even when a peasant did entirely discard some particular previous item of faith, the older belief sometimes could remain in the peasant's repertoire of *potential* beliefs—held in abeyance, as it were—and later, when faith in the Mao cult flagged, could again come to the fore. Today, some of the traditional religious practices once again flourish in the rural districts, and even some of the peasantry who in their own minds had altogether put aside such beliefs have today taken them up again in middle or old age.

Historians record similar periods of dramatic changes in belief followed by partial or complete reassertions of traditional belief patterns. To cite just one example from European history, Bohemia at the start of the Thirty Years War was caught up in fervent Protestant revolt, but subsequently, in the exhaustion of Bohemia's defeat, Catholicism was readopted in most households as if alternative beliefs had never erupted.[28] Just as observers of the Czech Republic today would

---

[28]   C.V. Wedgwood, *The Thirty Years War* (London: Jonathan Cape, 1944).

be wrong to assume that Prague had always been staunchly Catholic, so too observers of rural China today ought not presume that alterations to beliefs during the Maoist interregnum had been merely skin deep and that a primordial peasant worldview had prevailed largely untouched throughout. The worldviews of some of the peasantry had been reshaped in very marked ways—and yet today have reshifted again.

Upending the Maoist Effort

The crux of the matter was that the peasantry's faith could not endlessly be tested, year after exhausting year and decade upon decade, in the crucible of irrational Party policies, heavy grain exactions and stagnating rural living standards. As we shall examine in later chapters, by the 1970s peasant patience, even among recent true believers, was beginning to run thin; and disillusionment and stalled production eventually led to the abandonment of agrarian socialism after Mao's death. Nonetheless, the litany of failed Party programs and demands should not lead us to believe that almost everything that occurred during those decades went against the interests of the farmers. As was noted earlier, there was much that had been good in the collective system: in the provision of economic security, basic health care, education, and welfare for the needy. Significantly, it is also clear from interviews during the 1970s with émigrés from the countryside that in the sphere of agricultural production, the production teams, if left to their own devices, could have operated reasonably efficiently and productively. As production cooperatives, they provided a much-needed mechanism to organize the farmers' labor during slack seasons so as to improve the irrigation infrastructure. They also provided a means to marshal funds for investment in agriculture, on a scale often beyond what individual households can now muster. In these respects, the peasantry could see the benefits of collective agriculture; interviews during the 1970s revealed clearly that there had been acceptance and a large degree of support for the team-based effort. Had the state been differently organized, had it allowed the agricultural production teams a much wider degree of independence in their economic operations, it is conceivable that the system of teams would have persisted successfully over the long term.

But for most of the two decades in which Chinese agriculture operated through production teams, China's Party-state could not keep its hands off. One good example—the topic of Chapter Four—is the radical Dazhai wage program that ultimately proved unfeasible. In the end, as will be seen in these pages, it was incessant political interference from above that destroyed the viability of collective production and the peasants' willingness to participate in cooperative labor: political despotism ultimately destroyed rural socialism.

Chapter Two

THE RURAL "CLASS" SYSTEM IN THE MAO ERA

Among all of the concepts that were promoted by Mao and the Party, the strong play given to "class" is perhaps the least understood and the most often misinterpreted outside of China. These "class" teachings provide us with a particularly clear window into how far the worldview propagated by the Party penetrated the thinking of farmers, and enables us to witness the profound effects such teachings had upon the fabric of village society.

In a nutshell, for the first three decades after the establishment of the People's Republic, class labels strongly influenced the lives of each and every Chinese. A class label did not refer to a person's current income, social position, or relationship to the ownership of the means of production. It did not, in short, denote class membership in the existing socio-economic structure, whether understood in Marxist or Weberian terms. Rather, a class label had been affixed to each household in the early 1950s after the revolution's victory, categorizing the family's economic and/or political position under the *ancien regime*. During the next thirty years these capsule designations weighed heavily in determining social and political statuses.[1]

The New Class Pyramid: A Case Study

In order to observe the nuances of how this system operated and how it influenced the mentalities and shaped the lives of rural people, one good approach is to study the effects of this "class" system in one locale. My discussion will therefore draw upon the example of the village that I know best, a rural community in south China's Guangdong Province called Chen Village.[2]

---

[1]   An excellent overall study of the effects of these teachings about class is Richard Kraus, *Class Conflict in Chinese Socialism* (New York: Columbia University Press, 1981). A study of how class teachings affected urban students is Jonathan Unger, *Education Under Mao: Class and Competition in Canton Schools, 1960-1980* (New York: Columbia University Press, 1982).

[2]   During a period of a decade and a half starting in 1975, two dozen emigrants from this village were interviewed in Hong Kong by Anita Chan, Richard Madsen and myself for the book *Chen Village Under Mao and Deng*. The book depicted the recent history of the village, and there was no specific study in it of the "class" system. Most of the quotes and descriptions of the following pages are based on these interviewees' reconstructions of the period from the mid-1960s through the mid-1970s, the decade in which "class" distinctions were most clearly and forcefully felt in Chinese villages.

Chen Village contained approximately 250 families during the 1960s and 1970s, about average in size for its district. It contained a single lineage, as do many of the villages in south China. It was not particularly well off, but neither was it noticeably poor by the standards of Guangdong. It had never been promoted by the government as a political or economic showcase for other villages to emulate, but neither was it ever considered politically backward. Interviewees from the village felt that its internal "class" stratification was typical of the villages in the surrounding district. Based on my reading of the Chinese media and personal interviews with farmers from a couple of dozen other villages, there is no reason to assume that their impression was in any sense misleading for rural China of the 1960s and 1970s as a whole.

During land reform in 1950, shortly after the success of the Communist revolution, a workteam of cadres sent by the Party had carried out careful investigations to determine how much property each Chen family had owned on the eve of the revolution. The apex of the village's socio-economic pyramid had been occupied by a small number of landlords and rich peasants. Below them was a considerably larger number of middle peasants, who owned enough land to be basically self-sufficient, and upper-middle peasants, whose incomes before land reform had derived largely from their own labor, but who had also hired a laborer or rented out modest amounts of land beyond what family members themselves could till. But the bulk of the village population had consisted of tenants who owned only small plots (or no land at all) and landless laborers.[3] All of those at the bottom of the pyramid subsequently were grouped together under a "poor peasant" label (see Figure 1).

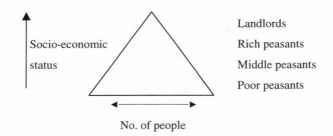

No. of people

Figure 1:   Pre-land reform

---

[3]   For more complete discussions of the class distinctions and labels deriving from land reform, see William Hinton, *Fanshen* (New York: Random House, 1966), pp. 623-26, 400-10 (for north China in 1948); and C.K. Yang, *A Chinese Village in Early Communist Transition* (Cambridge, Mass.: MIT Press, 1959), p. 141 (for Guangdong in 1950).

During land reform this traditional pyramid was shattered. Economic exploitation was eliminated from Chen Village and the rest of the Chinese countryside. But in the process new socio-political distinctions were created. The pre-revolutionary class designations were stored in dossiers, and eventually a new system of caste-like rigidity was devised on the basis of these files.

At the very top stood families whose heads had served in the revolutionary wars as Party officials or military officers (and who therefore now held the "class" designation of a "revolutionary cadre" household) or whose heads had died in the revolution (dubbed "revolutionary martyrs"). They were considered the "reddest" (that is, the most pure and stalwart supporters of the revolution's goals) and were therefore given the highest status in this "class" system. Rural districts in north China sometimes contained a few such families, inasmuch as the Party's battles against the Japanese in World War II and then against the Kuomintang regime in the civil war were waged in the north. But Guangdong Province lies in the south of China, and there were no such households in Chen Village.

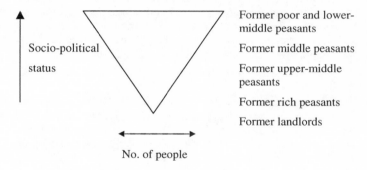

Figure 2:   Post-revolution

Within the village, the former poor peasants were placed officially at the top of a new inverted pyramid (see Figure 2), on the grounds that they could be counted upon to support revolutionary change. But the government wanted to broaden its popular appeal beyond this category and eventually granted almost the same privileged status to the former lower-middle peasants (who made up approximately a quarter of Chen Village's population). Before Liberation, the main source of the lower-middle peasants' earnings had been their own small landholdings, but they had had to supplement their income by renting additional land or by hiring themselves out as part-time laborers. They, too, had benefited from land reform.

Together, over the next three decades, they and the former poor peasants were to comprise the village's "good-origin" *(chengfen hao)* families. Indeed, in the mid-1960s the Party reaffirmed and strengthened the lower-middle peasantry's good-class credentials by establishing a Poor-and-Lower-Middle Peasants Association in Chen Village. Though a poor-peasant label continued to be recognized locally as superior, good-class Chen Villagers thereafter became accustomed to referring to themselves as being "poor-and-lower-middle peasants" *(pinxiazhongnong)*. This term was used as if it denoted a single word and a single "class" category. In most respects it did.

Between 80 and 85 percent of the families in Chen Village belonged to this privileged stratum of former poor-and-lower-middle peasants. Another 10-12 percent belonged to the middling stratum of former middle and upper-middle peasants.

During and after the land reform, there had been fears in Beijing that the old village elites might informally retain influence over local affairs. This fear had prompted repeated official efforts through the mid-1950s to discredit and isolate the overthrown classes. Landlords were targeted for physical attack and the expropriation of most of their land and property during the land reform, and the rich peasants were stripped of their property and residual influence during the subsequent organization of cooperatives and collectives. But for reasons explored below, the temporary measures that were employed to discredit the former village elites became transformed into permanent fixtures of village society. By the mid-1960s, all of the "bad-class" households in Chen Village (4-5 percent of the village population) had been consigned to an outcaste status.[4]

The Village Outcasts

A household was bad class when it was headed by a "four-bad categories element" *(si lei fenzi)*, defined as a landlord, rich peasant, counter-revolutionary, or "rotten element" *(huai fenzi)*. Among these, the true pariahs in Chen Village were the village's two former landlords: "They were treated like lepers. If you so much as said hello to them your class stand was considered questionable. They had no friends. They didn't dare to talk to each other, either." The former rich peasantry, though facing stiff discrimination, never suffered this same degree of isolation and unremitting contempt.

The remaining two types of "four-bad elements" (the counter-revolutionaries and rotten elements) were not categories based upon economic class origins. The counter-revolutionaries included people who had committed serious acts to destroy the Party, as well as officials of the former Kuomintang regime and the

---

4   William L. Parish and Martin K. Whyte, in a survey of sixty-three Guangdong villages, calculated that 73 percent of the peasantry had been classified as poor and lower-middle peasants, 13 percent as middle peasants, another 3 percent as upper-middle peasants, 4 percent as rich peasants and 2 percent as landlords; see *Village and Family in Contemporary China* (Chicago: University of Chicago Press, 1978), p. 99. By these figures, Chen Village had a slightly higher proportion of poor and lower-middle peasants and, perhaps, a slightly lower proportion of bad-class households than the average village.

leaders of rural militias that fought the Party during the civil war. There were no such men from Chen Village. The rotten elements were people who had committed serious criminal or social offenses or had cooperated too closely with the former regime. For example, they included people who, even if poor peasants before land reform, had been designated village bullies (e'ba) in the employ of the Kuomintang or landlords. More significantly, these latter two categories also subsequently covered people who committed serious felonies or political errors after the Party came to power. A good-origin peasant thus had to bear in mind that the punishment for a major transgression could be a permanent four-bad-element "hat." The prime example from Chen Village was a former bandit-turned-guerrilla who had been rewarded after Liberation with a petty post in urban government. Caught in an act of theft, he had attacked and injured his supervisor. The offender was officially branded a "rotten element" and sent back to Chen Village to face long-term "class" discrimination.

As a symbol of polluted status, during the 1960s and 1970s the dozen or so elderly "four-bad elements" (the designation included their wives and widows) had to sweep dung from the village square before mass meetings were to be held there. To symbolize further that most of them were irredeemably among the damned, they were not permitted to attend any political sessions or participate in Mao Study groups. If a production team was caught concealing the size of its harvest in order to reduce the government's grain quotas, the four-bad members of the team could expect to be pinned with part of the blame. Though in reality they would have been too frightened to participate in these efforts, they were deemed by the authorities to be a corrupting influence on better-class team members. In most of the various political campaigns of the 1960s and 1970s, bad-class villagers became the targets of struggle sessions, during which they were subjected to abuse, to remind the audience of past exploitation and the persistence of "bad-class" hostility toward the new order. During the Cleansing of Class Ranks campaign of 1968-69 (by far the fiercest campaign in Chen Village since land reform), fifteen out of the twenty campaign victims who spent time in the village jail were either "four-bad elements" or their close relatives.[5] A number were beaten in the highly emotional climate of the struggle sessions.

The poor and lower-middle peasants' suspicions of the "bad elements" were, if anything, fueled by this maltreatment. Many of the good-class peasants

---

[5]   Not all of Chen Village's four-bad elements came under attack during campaigns. For example, two rich-peasant brothers from Chen Village were among the men most knowledgeable about agriculture, and they regularly had made this knowledge available to their team's leaders. Moreover, they were industrious workers and went out of their way never to give offense to any of their better-class neighbors. As a result, they were the only members of the four-bad categories whose legal "hats" had been removed by the village and commune cadres (though they continued to be counted as bad-class). In comparison, their mother and the wife of one of them were quarrelsome. Their hats remained in place, and they were among those "struggled" against and jailed in the Cleansing of Class Ranks campaign.

reasoned that if they themselves had been so miserably treated they would want to seek vengeance. This rationale allowed some villagers to indulge in a hysteria that conveniently reconfirmed and underscored the bad elements' status as class enemies:

> After a period in which they'd been struggled against, we became very careful when walking in the lanes at night. Who knows? If they couldn't get over the humiliation might they not club you down in the dark? It was a custom in the village at such times to put some fish in the wells, to test whether there's any poison in the drinking water.

The young people from bad-class homes were not themselves "elements." The government had never given them political hats placing them under the "dictatorship" and supervision of the masses. They held the various rights of citizenship; they could vote in team elections and attend Mao Study sessions. The official rhetoric consistently held that these young people, like those from all other class categories, were politically "educable" and could be "united with." Alongside this rhetoric, however, the government implicitly endorsed the argument that worldviews were hereditary: that the thinking of bad-class children had been dangerously contaminated by their parents. "Actually," a former Chen Village cadre commented in the mid-1970s, "you should be more on guard against the landlord's son. The old landlord himself is already just a useless old stick." Official discrimination was invited against all bad-class descendants by noting their father's class origin label prominently in their personal dossiers. Parallel to traditional patrilineal Chinese practices, class origin labels were hereditary only in the patriline, and the sons of the bad-class sons (but not the children of bad-class daughters) bore the stigma in turn. Even had they been allowed to leave Chen Village, the dossiers and labels of the bad-class grandchildren would follow them through life.[6]

Many of the bad-class descendants grew up burdened by confused feelings of inferiority. A rich-peasant grandson from Chen Village, interviewed in his late twenties in the 1970s, recalled that even when he was just a small child,

> I didn't quarrel much. People called me "landlord son" [sic]. I felt inferior, hopeless, as if things were beyond my control. It was so unfair. Take me; I was born after the peace [n.b. he did not, as most Chinese would, use the word "Liberation" here]. Even if my parents had done something wrong, exploited other people, why should I be discriminated against? I felt inferior, never dared to do anything. Even before I got involved in any quarrel, I'd already say to myself: "eh, the only thing I can do is to live with my head down." . . . Usually at school the teachers treated me like any other kid. But if I did something

---

6   The son of the old guerrilla who had been labeled a rotten element was luckier than the descendants of landlords and rich peasants, since he could legally claim a "poor peasant" origin—even though an officially tainted one.

wrong and got a scolding, they'd bring out my class background: "You mean you side with your parents rather than the poor and lower-middle peasants?!"

Most bad-class young people quietly kept to their own kind. A good-class peasant from another village observed in a 1976 interview:

> Ordinarily, the young children of the four-bad elements get together in the evenings. Those of good-class background separately get together. They make up different social sets. The poor-peasant kids don't hate the others, but they're worried to visit with them.

Why did this system of rigid discrimination persist in Chen Village into the 1960s and 1970s? Certainly, the Party's reasoning of the early 1950s no longer held. By the mid-1950s, Party leaders had already concluded, I think correctly, that the former rural elites were nearly powerless. They no longer controlled any private or lineage properties and had been excluded from the networks of political power that the Party was erecting on the basis of the new cooperatives and collectives. Accordingly, in 1956 the Party leadership's assumption was that the period of class struggle was drawing to a close.[7] Class origins—the younger generation's especially—no longer were to be rigidly taken into account.

This being the case, was the re-introduction of harsh class policies in the 1960s merely in response to the desires and demands of the peasantry? Certainly, in the case of Chen Village in the 1950s, and even into the 1960s, some of the good-class peasants did feel a strong personal hostility toward some of the four-bad elements. As a former Chen Villager remarks: "Those old folks really felt it. They'd experienced it. They knew what landlords were like before." But the perpetuation of class discrimination beyond the fifties had to be rooted in more than just these personal antagonisms. Had revenge been the main spur, discrimination should have faded with the passage of time as memories grew dimmer and new generations emerged. Yet quite the reverse occurred. The stress upon "class feelings" and the rituals of class hatred were stronger in the 1960s and 1970s than in the 1950s.

Why? The discrimination against the tiny minority of bad-class people was partly a consequence of renewed state sponsorship. But the Chen Village peasants did cooperate fully. Could it be, then, that discrimination against an outcaste group was in accord with the cultural traditions and attitudes of people in this region?

---

[7] For example, "The Political Report of the Party Central Committee" (September 1956) states: "Except in a few localities, the feudal landlords have . . . been eliminated as a class. The rich peasants are also being eliminated as a class. Landlords and rich peasants who used to exploit the peasants are being reformed; they are making a fresh start in life and becoming people who live by their own work." See *Eighth National Congress of the Communist Party of China* (Beijing: Foreign Languages Press, 1956), Vol. 1, p. 15.

Cultural Roots?

Certainly historical antecedents can be found; the practices of any society are necessarily colored by its traditions. Confucian thought did stress that social stability depended upon a hierarchic ordering in human relations. Early Chinese religious thought contained notions of collective retribution through the patrilineage; descendants were often thought to be paying through ill fortune for the transgressions of their parents or grandparents. The premise existed, too, of collective legal guilt. In imperial law, punishments for the most serious crimes sometimes extended to relatives of the perpetrator, even collaterals much removed. These historically grounded notions of social order and of collective religious and legal guilt were still evident in rural thought during the 1960s. An interviewee who had been a leading member of Chen Village's public security committee turned implicitly to all of these arguments when she justified to me the treatment meted out to the four-bad elements' relatives during the village's Cleansing of Class Ranks campaign of 1968.

In considering these historical legacies, however, the essential point to note is that late-imperial China did not have any strong traditions of caste or estate-like structures.[8] True, at the very bottom of the social system certain pariah groups were permanently banned from taking the examinations to become officials, and people in this category (such as boat people and entertainers) were often deemed to be unfit even to associate with ordinary Chinese. But these socially degraded groups constituted only a small fraction of 1 percent of China's total population. They were social isolates, not present in a farming village; and, as much to the point, their pariah statuses were upheld by imperial dicta rather than by popular sentiment. Thus, with the Yongzheng emperor's emancipatory edicts of 1723-35, all but the culturally and occupationally distinct "boat people" of south China melted easily into the general populace.[9] Indeed, during recent centuries, against the realities of grinding poverty and limited life chances, it had been a belief of the *laobaixing,* the "ordinary people," that upward mobility was an intrinsic right, available to those with luck and wits.[10] It was a social myth that helped to legitimize and protect the status quo.

---

[8]   On this, see Philip Kuhn, "Chinese Views of Social Classification," in James Watson (ed.), *Class and Social Stratification in Post-Revolution China* (Cambridge: Cambridge University Press, 1984), pp. 16-28.

[9]   See, for example, Ho Ping-ti, *The Ladder of Success in Imperial China* (New York: Columbia University Press, 1962), pp. 18-19, 55-56; Mark Elvin, *The Pattern of the Chinese Past* (Stanford: Stanford University Press, 1973), p. 248; Ch'u T'ung-tsu, "Chinese Class Structure and Its Ideology," in John K. Fairbank (ed.), *Chinese Thought and Institutions* (Chicago: University of Chicago Press, 1957), pp. 249, 387; Eugene Anderson, "The Boat People of South China," *Anthropos,* Vol. 65, Nos. 1-2 (January 1970), p. 253.

[10]   Mark Elvin. *The Pattern of the Chinese Past,* p. 258, shares that perception: "Chinese rural society in the nineteenth and the early twentieth century was . . . one of the most fluid in the

Isolated exceptions existed, such as the hereditary slaves (relatively few in number) maintained as symbols of prestige by wealthy members of powerful lineages.[11] But Chen Village, like most peasant communities, did not share in that practice; it was far too poor. In Chen Village all men were Chens; and, notwithstanding the richer households' economic exploitation of their poor agnates, religious and social beliefs held that all Chens were equal before the common ancestors. The weight of traditional attitudes precluded notions of sharp hereditary distinctions within the village.

In short, the intellectual and emotional support for a new system of hereditary strata did not stem from cultural antecedents in Chen Village. Instead, for a complex set of reasons, the Chen peasants were responding favorably to a new system of beliefs and behavioral norms fostered by the Party.

Underpinnings of Discrimination: Party Tactics and the Self-image of the Good Classes

The Party's initiatives of 1956 to dampen the significance of class origins were short-lived. For one thing, by the early 1960s the top Party leaders apparently feared that the feelings among the former poor and lower-middle peasants of a debt of gratitude (*bao'en*) toward the Party were rapidly subsiding. In the early sixties, Mao and Party officials felt it was essential to remind the peasantry of this debt of gratitude. Mao's directive of late 1962—"Never forget class struggle"— was propagated at a time when the nation was just recovering from the terrible economic depression and famine caused by the Great Leap Forward. The peasants were not to judge the government in terms of the present difficulties; through "class education" they were to bear in mind how much they owed to the Party.

They were to keep constantly in mind that the great divide in China was not between themselves and their leadership but between the masses and "class enemies" who wanted to destroy the new society. Throughout China, the message was drilled home through textbooks at school, through films, on radio and in village political-education meetings that the national revolutionary cause was perpetually threatened by enemy forces that lurked half-hidden everywhere in China. On the surface, these hidden enemies might seem like harmless neighbors: as Mao had written, they might even "assume the guise of a beautiful young maiden."[12] But Mao had pressed the point that one must never let down one's

---

world, lacking any of the status and caste restraints which typified late pre-modern Japan or India."

[11]   James L. Watson, "Chattel Slavery in Chinese Peasant Society: A Comparative Analysis," *Ethnology,* Vol. 5, No. 4 (October 1976) and his "Transactions in People: The Chinese Market in Slaves, Servants and Heirs," in J.L. Watson (ed.), *Asian and African Systems of Slavery* (Oxford: Basil Blackwell; and Berkeley: University of California Press, 1980).

[12]   Mao Zedong, "Carry the Revolution Through to the End," in *Selected Words of Mao Tse-tung*, Vol. IV (Beijing: Foreign Languages Press, 1961), p. 304. In that same essay, Mao famously

guard against them and indeed needed to be pitiless in suppressing them. The "bad class" people in each village were officially targeted as tangible living examples of these half-hidden enemies. During the Four Cleanups campaign in Chen Village (1965-66), the Party pushed this message with greater emotional force than ever before.[13] It portrayed a Manichean world of righteous classes—the agricultural and industrial proletariat led by the Party—pitched in combat against the dark forces represented by the suspect classes.

A new workteam of Party cadres had come into Chen Village to carry out the Four Cleanups. To reinforce the legitimacy and significance of class distinctions, the cadres laboriously reinvestigated the "class" designations of each household. It was declared that some people might have lied during the 1950s land reform about their circumstances or that there may have been some oversight by fellow villagers or the land reform workteam. Repeatedly in meetings, the peasants were now urged in 1965 to recall who had owned precisely how much property before land reform. "But there purposely were very few changes in class labels," one of the Four Cleanups workteam's helpers recalls:

> It only involved the different gradations of middle peasants. For example, a landlord can *never* become a rich peasant, can *never* change, even if the land reform had been wrong. A case of a middle peasant could be corrected because it was less "political" in its implications than that of a bad-class family. . . .
> But [even here] the workteam's assumption was that unless the evidence strongly contradicted the household's "class" appellation, the land reform's appraisal would continue to be considered correct. The workteam wanted few alterations, because the Party wanted to pursue class struggle.

Class struggle required that the lines differentiating each category of household be reaffirmed, unchanged and sacrosanct.

As a result of the Four Cleanups, cadres in Chen Village became even harsher in their dealings with the four-bad households. Party officials had learned in the campaign that if they did not always exhibit an ostentatiously firm class stand, they might leave themselves open to attack. As one villager put it, "Of course they'd prefer to be more on the left than the right. Who'd dare to do anything that might later open them to accusations of having had relationships with bad elements?" Being harsh took on the coloring of political merit.

---

declared that "The Chinese people will never take pity on these snake-like scoundrels" (ibid). One of the most popular children's books of the 1960s, an allegory shaped from the Monkey King saga, carried precisely this message, even to the point of having the hero ruthlessly kill a snake demon who was artfully disguised as an innocent maiden. On this story and its violent "class struggle" message, see Unger, *Education Under Mao*, p. 88.

[13]   An excellent description and analysis of "class" and the use made of it in the Four Cleanups is Philip C.C. Huang, "Rural Class Struggle in the Chinese Revolution," *Modern China*, Vol. 21, No. 1 (January 1995), esp. pp. 128-30.

Villagers who wanted to get ahead politically followed the village cadres' lead. The more activist and righteous a person wanted to seem, the more loudly he or she would harangue the four-bad elements at struggle meetings. It became a contest among ambitious young activists.

In Chen Village and many other communities across China, the antagonism expressed at such sessions reflected sentiments that the great bulk of the villagers had come to share. But there were also communities where the peasants thought no-one warranted a "class enemy" label, and the class struggle sessions there simply became artificial performances acted out to satisfy higher authorities. As one obvious type of example, there were some poor villages where all of the residents before the revolution had been tenant farmers of absentee landlords or where all of the villagers had independently scratched out a living from a soil too poor to sustain any landlordism. But even in such villages, "class enemies" had to be designated for the benefit of enacting the political rituals. One example was the mountain hamlet of an interviewee, who explained:

> The only person who was really respected by everyone in the hamlet was a man in his fifties who'd been branded a historical counter-revolutionary, because in the old days he'd negotiated with bandits in the hamlet's behalf and somehow later became connected with them. There was no other four-bad element in our hamlet, so during campaigns he'd be dragged down to the commune headquarters for struggle meetings. I remember him being marched away one day, accompanied by representatives from the hamlet to struggle against him and with the hamlet militia to keep him under armed guard. But on the way back they offered him apologies and cigarettes, and when he came back later that day everyone slapped him on the back in a friendly way and he was warmly treated to dinners.

In Chen Village, in sharp contrast, cadres and young political activists were not ritualistically acting out a patently phony political rite that they and their neighbors privately scorned. Quite the contrary. Voluntarily at such sessions, ordinary peasants in Chen Village, even those who were not politically ambitious, sometimes joined in haranguing and humiliating the four-bad types. They *believed* in the strict class distinctions and in the legitimacy of class antagonisms. In a community such as Chen Village, in short, class struggle entailed more than what we have described thus far. The Party had provided the good-class peasantry with a complex set of emotional justifications and material reasons for discriminating against the bad-class households. Two concepts drawn from Max Weber's writings—specifying two quite different ways in which groups can claim superiority—help to explain the appeal of the Party's messages.

In the Four Cleanups campaign, the cadre workteam had been teaching the poor and lower-middle peasant households that they constituted what Weber has called a "negatively privileged" status group.[14] These are under-groups, like the early Christians and Jewish communities throughout history, whose dignity is sustained by the belief that as a group they have a providential mission and a special place before God. The workteam organized public "remember the bitterness" reminiscences and "remember the bitterness" meals consisting of wild vegetables and roots. In these ways the peasantry ritually relived the worst deprivations of pre-Liberation times. They were told that their former sufferings (or those of their parents or grandparents) had granted them a superior moral value, with sacred responsibilities. They were the "revolutionary masses"—the former wretched of the earth who had been entrusted with a mission to usher in a better future for China and the world. As such, they stood in a special, intimate relationship with Chairman Mao, "China's Savior."

These messages were propagated at Mao Study sessions, and provided the good-class peasants with new feelings of importance and self-pride. But there was a catch. To justify their newfound status, their behavior would have to conform to the Party's ideological image of them. As one young man from Chen Village commented: "When Mao Study was pushed in the 1960s the good-class kids in our village felt a responsibility to be progressive. You know, all those slogans and ideas praising the reliability of the poor and lower-middle peasants."

In this system of beliefs, the pariah classes served an important function as negative emulation models. They represented the mirror image of the good classes' proletarian virtues. The more that the good-class peasantry painted the bad-class households in black colors,[15] the more their own purported "redness" stood out in contrast.

In addition to the beliefs that they were a Chosen People, Party teachings simultaneously encouraged the good-class peasants to adopt the mythology of what Weber calls a "positively privileged status group." These are groups such as an aristocracy, whose claims to superiority lie in "this world," usually on the basis of a glorious inherited past and an innate superiority of genealogy. The poor and lower-middle peasants had become, within the village, an over-group in "this world"; in the words of one peasant, "they feel they're the masters of society." As a credential of their superiority some even proudly traced the purity of their poor and lower-middle peasant ancestry back four generations to establish a "blood-line" (xuetong) of "naturally red" (zilai hong) pedigree.

Weber points out that such beliefs in inherited superiority usually are employed to justify the monopolization of scarce goods and resources.[16] This was

---

[14]   H.H. Gerth and C. Wright Mills (eds.), *From Max Weber: Essays in Sociology* (Oxford: Oxford University Press, 1946), pp. 190, 276.

[15]   Tantamount to a racist slur, interviewees sometimes referred to these households as "black."

[16]   Gerth and Mills (eds.), *From Max Weber*, p. 190; W.G. Runciman (ed.), *Max Weber: Selections in Translation* (Cambridge: Cambridge University Press, 1978), p. 60; Max Weber, *Economy and Society* (Berkeley: University of California Press, 1978), p. 306.

certainly the case in Chen Village. Be it in schooling, medical care or job opportunities (e.g., an army career), the good-origin villagers could claim priority over their workmates of questionable origin.[17] Remarked an emigrant from the village in 1975: "Even if you go to Canton from the village to see a doctor, you don't have to stand so long in line; you show them your Poor-and-Lower-Middle Peasant Association card."

Examples of Good-Class Advantages

The "class line" (*jieji luxian*)—a Chinese term meaning to use class background as the basis for policies in order to favor the people of good class status—was pushed most strongly in rural China in the years between the end of the Cultural Revolution in 1968 and Mao's death in 1976.[18] But during these years, the application of the class line varied noticeably from one village to the next. The reason was that the class line was brought to bear precisely where local shortages in goods and services were most pronounced. Interviews with former school teachers from six Guangdong villages indicate, for instance, that villages which could not provide enough primary-school places enacted a strong class-line admissions policy, allowing in only children of good class background. This

---

[17]   There was an important exception here: in Chen Village the class line did *not* extend to wages. The landlord sons earned nearly as much as good-class men of equivalent labor power. In many other villages, however, there was economic discrimination against the bad-class peasantry. A letter to the editor from a Guangdong peasant—*Renmin ribao* (People's Daily), December 11, 1978—complained: "I am a young man born into a landlord family. Both of my parents died when I was very young and I was brought up by my brother who is a teacher. When the payments for labor were worked out, we people from an exploiting class background received only 70 percent of what other commune members were getting. What is the reason for this? The cadre . . . said: 'Although the upper levels have instructed that you're to get the same treatment as others, it must be in a manner suitable to local conditions. . . . You must receive less, because most of you are good at labor and have savings. If you're paid like the rest of the commune members, this will have a bad effect'."

[18]   For its own reasons, the Chinese government declared in 1977 that the Cultural Revolution had lasted until Mao's death, and many foreign and Chinese authors have adopted the Chinese government's new periodization of the term. Doing so obfuscates what occurred in China, as Anita Chan shows in her article "Dispelling Misconceptions about the Red Guard Movement: The Necessity to Re-Examine Cultural Revolution Factionalism and Periodization," *The Journal of Contemporary China*, Vol. 1, No. 1 (Fall, 1992), esp. pp. 73-5. If one is writing about leadership turmoil and violent mass purges among the Party elite during the Cultural Revolution, these were formally brought to an end at the Ninth Party Congress of 1969, when the new line-up of victors among the leadership was officially anointed. This date is best taken as the official end of the Cultural Revolution at the top, and a number of the best specialists on elite Chinese politics do so. If one is writing about the Cultural Revolution at the grassroots in the provinces, as I am, the Cultural Revolution was forcibly brought to a close in the latter part of 1968. In line with this, throughout the 1970s my interviewees from throughout China consistently referred to the Cultural Revolution as having ended in 1968.

policy gradually weakened as primary schooling expanded, but in these same villages a strong class line in admissions was again applied as the competition to get into local secondary schools increased.

In the same fashion, in some villages class-line decisions began to affect even the selection of teachers. In the 1950s, at a time when there was no real contest for secondary-school places, many former landlord and rich-peasant families pushed their sons through the educational system as the only means of providing for their futures. Where their services were needed, they became primary-school teachers without any local protest. But as education expanded in the 1960s and early 1970s, large numbers of good-class young people began to qualify to teach primary school. For the first time, teachers of unsavory class origins were suspected of spreading bad ideas among their poor and lower-middle peasant pupils. A good class background soon became the indispensable qualification for new teachers. In fact, the incumbent bad-class teachers in some villages were dismissed *en masse* to make room for good-class candidates. But in areas where teacher shortages still existed, a very different perception of the bad-class teachers sometimes prevailed. An interviewee from Canton who had been sent to settle in the countryside was recruited to be a teacher even though his father was a former capitalist:

> Nobody cared about that, because they had a shortage of teachers in the village junior high school. Even after I tried to run off to Hong Kong and got caught, the village leaders still wanted me to go back to teach in the school. They told me, "Don't worry about that little incident. The poor and lower-middle peasants still trust you."

In short, the class line could be turned on or off, depending on the local needs of the good-class peasantry.

They gained benefits from the class system in other respects as well. The privileged status of good-class men gave them an advantage in acquiring brides. This could be even more important to them than access to schools or jobs.

Peasant bachelors often needed this advantage. There is evidence of a demographic imbalance (with more young men than young women of marriageable age) in certain parts of rural China, including Chen Village, well into the 1970s. (This imbalance may be due to a persistence into the 1950s of the traditional strategy of female infanticide or neglect when food supplies were limited.)[19] In these circumstances, young men were willing, if need be, to accept a bride of worse class heritage than themselves. Since the official policy decreed that class labels are passed only through the patriline, these good-class bachelors knew that their children would inherit good credentials irrespective of their mother's origin.

---

[19]   See W.R. Geddes, *Peasant Life in Communist China* (Society for Applied Anthropology, Monograph No. 6, 1963).

Notwithstanding this, a woman's class status still made some difference to a prospective groom. This was especially true for those who had political aspirations. An interviewee in the 1970s observed of one Chen Villager: "He's a Party member and a cadre. If he married a wife with an unreliable class background, he would have a hard time taking responsibility for any important work. He wouldn't be considered trustworthy, because a wife can change a person."

In light of such beliefs, women who married into a better class status did not usually rise very far above their origin. If a poor or lower-middle-class peasant family could not find a satisfactory bride for their son within the circle of good-class households, they normally approached a middle-peasant family, while middle peasants who could not find marriage partners within their own category would look for brides among the bad classes. The groom's family would be wary, however, of a marriage that linked them to a bad-class family from their own or a nearby community. On their side, a bad-class woman's family knew that if she married near home, the stigma of her origin might continue to haunt her. Thus, whereas good-class and middle-peasant brides usually married into households nearby, the bad-class brides from Chen Village tended to marry into families from other counties.

Though the shortfall of rural women was only a few percentage points, it was enough to substantially dim the marriage prospects of the bad-class men. Such men came, after all, from the least marriageable 5 percent of the rural population. Bad-class parents therefore faced the prospect that none of their sons would be able to marry. Ironically, this was the converse of pre-Liberation times, when it was the poor peasants who did not always have the financial wherewithal to see their sons married.[20]

To keep the family line alive, bad-class households began resorting to a special strategy. "Just about the only way a landlord son can get married," noted a Chen Villager, "is through a swap with another household. . . . Both families sacrifice their daughters to keep the incense burning [i.e., to sustain the male line]." Normally such exchanges were arranged with other bad-class families. But this was not always the case. One of Chen Village's landlord families traded brides with an impoverished poor-peasant family whose only son was dimwitted and ugly.[21]

---

[20]   Edwin E. Moise, "Downward Social Mobility in Pre-Revolutionary China," *Modern China,* Vol. 3, No. 1 (January 1977), pp. 3-30.

[21]   Other interesting examples of how bad-class peasants found marriage partners can be found in Janet Salaff, "The Emerging Conjugal Relationship in the People's Republic of China," *Journal of Marriage and the Family,* No. 35 (1973), pp. 712-13.

Caught in the Middle: The Middle Peasantry and Sent-Down Urban Youths

The bad-class peasants in Chinese villages comprised only a small proportion of the population. Thus the poor and lower-middle peasants benefited most from their advantages over the upper-middle and middle peasants, who were considerably more numerous than the bad-class elements. The poor and lower-middle peasants usually stood ahead of them in line for the most coveted jobs, such as teaching. The middle peasants also lost out in the competition for the most desirable brides; in Chen Village they generally had to pay higher bride prices, to offset their lower status. Middle peasants could become brigade cadres and even village leaders. But to rise politically, a middle peasant had to be especially capable and exceptionally activist. Success was only likely when there were no good-class competitors of comparable ability. As one villager observed: "Our production team accountant was a politically active upper-middle peasant. Nobody else wanted the job; and this fellow seemed honest; and with so many poor and lower-middle peasants in our team we didn't worry that he would cause trouble—would turn the sky upside down."

The middle peasantry did not really object to the discrimination against the four-bad elements. In fact, many of them shared the common prejudices against the outcaste households. But the middle peasants wanted the class line drawn in a manner that placed them securely in the camp of the "masses." They wanted to be treated on terms similar to the good classes. They were wary of periods when the government pushed the rhetoric of class struggle. They knew that when emotions were stirred up against the suspect classes, suspicions about "reliability" could be leveled against themselves as well.

Many of the 18 million youths who came from the cities to settle in China's countryside in the 1960s and 1970s encountered difficulties similar to those that affected the middle peasantry. Like middle peasants, they did not bear the brunt of overt prejudice, but they were frustrated by the wall of class labels.

A contingent of fifty youths from Canton, mostly of middle-status class origins, arrived in Chen Village in 1964. Initially, as outsiders without any fixed niche in the hierarchy of village class statuses, they were simply referred to by the ambiguous label "students," which did not carry a class connotation. In this way the young people could be used to fill such high-status positions as Mao Study counselors or cashiers, for which the peasantry themselves did not have the necessary skills. But there were too few opportunities in a small village for all of these former students to be upwardly mobile, and as a consequence the young outsiders became intensely competitive among themselves. Seeing this, in 1965 the Four Cleanups workteam in Chen Village followed the Party's policies on class and granted the most desirable posts to a few of the urban youths who had good class origins. The peasants, following suit, began to view the urban-born youths in terms of their family statuses.

The bad-class families in Chen Village were of course too scared to protest against their own maltreatment; and the middle peasants always had to keep in mind that they were stuck in the village and might bear the consequences for the rest of their lives if they protested against class-line favoritism. But Chen Village's middle-class youths of urban origin did not face such constraints.

Young, unattached, unencumbered by village ties, and achievement-oriented, they were exasperated when they discovered that their expectations were being thwarted. By upbringing, they found it difficult to accept a second-class status. Whenever protests have erupted in China against the official distribution of privilege, it is usually people in just such circumstances (quite often middle class) who have been involved (e.g., the Hundred Flowers movement of 1957). During the Cultural Revolution, these urban, middle-class teenagers became the Rebel Red Guards in Chen Village (just as middle-class high school students comprised the core of the Rebel Red Guards in China's cities).[22] In the village, the young Rebels first attacked the Four Cleanups workteam and then the village cadres and an official Red Guard group composed exclusively of good-class youths. Their claim was that their ardent "devotion to Chairman Mao" proved that they were the true defenders of the revolution, in contrast to the good-class, but "suppressive," local power-holders. In the end, they achieved little through these accusations.

After the Cultural Revolution of 1966-68, peasant youths from Chen Village graduated from the local junior high school in rapidly growing numbers. To make room for them the sent-down youths of middle-class origin were eased out of whatever posts they still held. They became the victims of the same demographic process that was costing many bad-class teachers their jobs. Since Mao Zedong himself appeared to support a strict class line, these middle-class youths in Chen Village finally despaired of ever being appreciated or successful in China. The fault appeared to them to lie with the national polity rather than just local "power-holders." They had protested from within the political system during the Cultural Revolution, in the name of Mao, but gradually they became disaffected with the system itself. By 1974 the majority of Chen Village's urban-born Mao Study counselors and Communist Youth League members had swum to Hong Kong.

The 1970s: The Erosion of Beliefs in Class

Even though the nationwide favoritism shown to the good-class families had resulted in the disaffection of portions of the middle classes, the "Maoist" wing of the Party was willing to pay that price. Among other things, the Maoist wing presumably hoped to gain stronger support from the good-class peasantry. But in Chen Village and probably most other villages, that support did not materialize for long. By the mid-1970s, in fact, the Chen peasants' faith in Mao Thought and the Party was dissolving.

This decline in enthusiasm was due in part to the erratic nature of policy changes dictated by central authorities. Repeatedly the peasants heard programs

---

[22]   Anita Chan, Stanley Rosen and Jonathan Unger, "Students and Class Warfare: The Social Roots of the Red Guard Conflict in Guangzhou (Canton)," *The China Quarterly,* No. 83 (Autumn 1980), pp. 397-446.

and leaders fulsomely praised one day only to be condemned the next. Perhaps even more perturbing was the damage being done to Chen Village's economy by inflexible higher-level demands, similar to what we observed in the previous chapter about rural China as a whole. The village was pressed in Loyalty campaigns to contribute extra grain to the state at subnormal prices; to "self-reliantly" grow crops such as wheat and cotton that were woefully unsuited to the climate; to forego vegetable farming and to fill in profitable fish ponds in order to plant yet more grain. The Chen peasants watched in frustration as policies inimical to their interests were forced upon them from one year to the next.

In such circumstances, they were no longer so willing to accept the roles assigned to them by the Party's class teachings. When the Party bureaucracy demanded that they provide extra Loyalty grain or cut back on private plots, these "requests" invariably alluded to the innate political nobility of the poor and lower-middle peasants and their mission to achieve a higher level of socialism. The peasants did not want that type of nobility; many were becoming increasingly uneasy with the way class teachings were being utilized to justify actions that went against their interests.

The younger generation in Chen Village was also growing weary of the Party's rhetoric concerning the duty of poor and lower-middle peasants to be grateful for their deliverance from feudal tyranny. They had not themselves experienced the sufferings of the pre-Liberation era. Their concern was whether the Party was accomplishing anything for them in the present, not the past.

The patience of villagers, young and old alike, was strained yet further when, in the interminable evening political meetings, ambitious young activists rose to proclaim the depth of their "class hatred." In the local view, such declarations had become hypocritical: "All this talk about class struggle just seemed formalistic," an emigrant observed in 1978. "If the Party didn't keep rekindling the fire, the peasants wouldn't do it. . . . Everyone brought things to do at the meetings, and the women sewed and knitted. They've become numbed."

One of the central premises for perpetuating class discrimination had been that attitudes are inherited. By the mid-1970s, however, many young people were having private doubts on this score, too. How tainted, after all, could the sons, grandsons, and even great-grandsons of the four-bad elements really be? As some of these good-class peasants became skeptical of Party teachings they began to ignore some of the social barriers that had been imposed against the bad classes. A rich-peasant son commented in 1978: "In general the younger poor and lower-middle peasants nowadays don't think we should be treated like this, that we should be stepped on like this. Some of them began to talk with us."

This new attitude toward class discrimination may well have been reinforced by the fact that the benefits to be gained from the class line were no longer substantial. The poor and lower-middle peasants, after all, comprised 80-85 percent of the village population. At best, the class line had provided them with only a modest edge, and by the late 1970s, even that edge had diminished. To the young people's irritation, the best jobs increasingly were going to the relatives of village leaders; in practice, the "back door" of cadre privilege had begun displacing the class line. And by the mid-1970s the demographic imbalance between the sexes was receding. Only the weakest, poorest, and least capable of the young men had to worry seriously that they might not be able to find a suitable spouse. With or without the class line, in short, the life of the average good-class peasant would remain basically the same.

It should not, however, be assumed that the system of class discrimination no longer had any supporters in Chen Village. Some members of the older generation still clung to the feelings of the previous decades. But generally the beliefs were eroding. By the mid-1970s increasing numbers of the villagers were willing to see the system of class labels overturned.

Post-Mao: The Destruction of Class Barriers

Following Mao's death in 1976 his political successors moved to abandon the Party's policies of class discrimination. They evidently were aware that the old system no longer constituted an effective means of appealing to the majority of peasants. But more than this, the new leadership believed China needed a new era of social stability and economic progress, grounded in a new set of political premises. They wanted to end the sense of conflict that "class struggle" purposely had induced and the growing political disaffection among those who had lost out.

In particular, Party officials wanted to defuse the resentments of China's middle-class constituencies. Their concern here obviously included the middle peasants and the sent-down youths. But above all, the national Party leadership needed to win back the support of the urban intelligentsia and the middle-class technocrats who had been alienated by the intense class policies of the 1960s and 1970s. The success of the Four Modernizations campaign depended upon regaining their confidence.

Thus, for reasons partly tied to a new rural political strategy but partly also to the new drive to modernize China, Beijing made a series of sweeping announcements in late 1978 and 1979. To symbolize an end to class struggle throughout the nation, it was declared that most of China's four-bad elements, including the great majority of the old landlords, had "remolded" themselves over the past three decades. Though their class-origin labels would remain in dossiers, the Party Central Committee directed that their "hats"—the official stigmata—be permanently removed.[23] The former landlords and rich peasants who still wore legal hats now numbered only 50,000. Only months earlier, at the end of 1978, there had been more than 4 million such people in the Chinese countryside.[24]

Already weakened, the beliefs in the immutability of class labels collapsed in Chen Village in the wake of these pronouncements. Some of the older peasants

---

[23] *Renmin ribao* (People's Daily), January 30, 1979, in *Foreign Broadcast Information Service Daily Report: China,* February 1, 1979, pp. E17-20.

[24] See "Class Status in the Countryside: Changes Over Three Decades," *Beijing Review,* No. 3 (January 21, 1980), p. 14; and Party Central Committee Document, No. 4, 1979, in *Issues and Studies,* September 1979, p. 111.

were displeased initially, but their opposition soon subsided. Much as if rigid discrimination had never existed, the bad-class households eased back into the village's social and political life. For example, within two years one of the production teams elected a former rich peasant to serve as its team head, while a second team elected the son of the ex-guerrilla "rotten element" to serve as head. Remarkably, interviews in early 1982 revealed that class origins were no longer taken much into account even in marriage decisions. Bad-class youths could now obtain brides on almost equal terms with the young men of good-class backgrounds. In short, in a period of less than three years, a structure of discrimination based on class labels had simply disappeared, with scarcely a trace remaining.

The same Party leaders who ended class discrimination in 1979 had, in earlier decades, been firm adherents of the rural class policies. The reasons for the earlier line are apparent given the historical circumstances. The Party had been unable to live up to its economic promises of the collectivization "high tide" and Great Leap Forward; throughout the 1960s and 1970s most of the countryside remained impoverished. In lieu of prosperity, the Party could provide the majority of good-class peasants with marginal advantages (both material and nonmaterial) offered by the class line. These also gave the peasants the satisfaction of an honored status; the belief that they were bearers of a noble mission; and the feeling that they were innately superior to the scapegoats in bad-class households.

When these beliefs, along with their faith in the Party, began crumbling in the 1970s, a new means for appealing to the peasantry became necessary. By the late 1970s, national leaders wagered that peasant loyalties could be retained by introducing new material gratifications that would supplant the earlier symbolic rewards. It was clearly felt that a program of economic liberalization (with expanded free markets, larger private plots, and better prices for agricultural produce) would bring noticeable improvements in the peasantry's standard of living. Material improvements would render obsolete some of the political functions that the class system had served. As an emigrant from Chen Village commented to me in 1982: "It's not class origin which counts any more; what counts now is making money."

Chapter Three

THE CULTURAL REVOLUTION IN THE VILLAGES[*]

To comprehend the values held by villagers in the heyday of the Maoist era, as well as the multifaceted tensions that divided village society, no period is more fruitful to examine than the Cultural Revolution, between 1966 and 1968. In that period, as national and provincial turmoil paralyzed the Party machinery that stood above the villages, conflicts that had previously been suppressed under the Party's rule flared up in a large number of villages. In some cases, groups of villagers tried to oust the village leadership, and in others villagers fought among themselves. In yet others, as will be seen, any violence that occurred was entirely orchestrated from above by local county, commune, and village authorities, sometimes even in circumstances where there was no challenge to them from below.

By the outbreak of the Cultural Revolution, only a decade had passed since collectivization, and memories of pre-Communist times remained fresh in the minds of many of China's villagers. It is not surprising, then, that rural violence in the Cultural Revolution sometimes reflected animosities that were traditional, as exemplified by feuding between historically antagonistic lineages or villages. But it will also be seen that an equally important cause of conflict lay in the animosities that had been deliberately manufactured by the Party and government in the years since Liberation: a Frankenstein of Party teachings—including "class struggle"—that the Cultural Revolution activated and let loose in some rural areas and not others. One of the purposes of this chapter will be to delineate how the types of hostilities that were grounded in tradition and those engendered by the state intersected and played off each other in ways that extended and exacerbated conflicts in the countryside.

Among my interviewees, thirty-one in particular discussed with me what had occurred in their communities during the two and a half years of the Cultural Revolution (mid-1966 to late 1968).[1] Eighteen of them came from villages in

---

[*]   Special gratitude is owed to Gong Xiaoxia who, when I was researching this chapter, graciously provided me with summaries of a prodigious amount of Chinese documentation on the Cultural Revolution, and to Anita Chan, who shared interview transcripts with me. Thanks are also owed to Dai Jianzhong, X.L. Ding, Gao Mobo, Hua Linshan, Mark Selden, Isabelle Thireau, Andrew Walder, Yan Yunxiang and Zhu Xiaoyang for helpful information and comments.

[1]   All of my 31 interviewees on the Cultural Revolution are Han Chinese from entirely Han regions of the countryside, and so this chapter does not examine what occurred in the rural

Guangdong Province, and the remaining thirteen came from nine different provinces extending from Guangxi in the far south to Hebei in the north, and as far inland as Yunnan.[2] These interview materials will provide the main basis for my findings, but the chapter also draws on village studies by Western scholars,[3] an excellent article by Richard Baum drawing upon broadcasts and documentation from the Cultural Revolution,[4] and my own search of the available Chinese-language publications of the past three decades.[5]

---

districts occupied by China's ethnic-minority populations. The available evidence from such districts in the south of China strongly suggests that during the Cultural Revolution period of 1966-68 Han officials interpreted such people's nonconformity to the Han way of life as deviations from Chairman Mao's teachings, and efforts were often made in these rural regions by officials and mobs alike to impose Han mores by destroying the ethnic-minority people's religious sites and enforcing Han social practices. The worst reported repression of any ethnic minority during the Cultural Revolution occurred in the north, in Inner Mongolia, where Mongols were accused of conspiring to betray China in favor of Mongolia. Hundreds of thousands of Mongols were arrested in a witch hunt, many of them from the countryside, and tens of thousands reportedly were killed while in detention. On this see, for example, William R. Jankowiak, "The Last Hurrah? Political Protest in Inner Mongolia," *The Australian Journal of Chinese Affairs*, No. 19-20 (January–July 1988), pp. 273-88; also W. Woody, *The Cultural Revolution in Inner Mongolia* (Stockholm: Center for Pacific Asia Studies at Stockholm University Occasional Paper 20, 1993), 41 pp.; also Zheng Yi, *Hongse jinian bei* (The Red Memorial Plinth), (Taipei: Huashi Wenhua Gongsi, 1993), pp. 285-92.

[2]   These nine provinces are Anhui (two interviewees), Fujian, Guangxi (three), Hebei, Hunan, Jiangsu (two), Jiangxi, Shandong, and Yunnan.

[3]   These village studies are listed in Chapter 1, footnote 5. They are: Endicott, pp. 114-120; Friedman, Pickowicz, and Selden; Gao, pp. 144-59; Hinton, pp. 493-664; Philip Huang, pp. 130-31 (additional information on the same village's Cultural Revolution experience is contained in Huang's "Rural Class Struggle in the Chinese Revolution," *Modern China*, Vol. 21, No. 1 [January 1995]); Huang Shu-min, pp. 89-98; Potter and Potter, pp. 83-90; Ruf, Ch. 7; Seybolt, pp. 65-72; Siu, pp. 204-8; Chan, Madsen, and Unger, Chs. 2-5; and Madsen, Ch. 6.

[4]   Richard Baum, "The Cultural Revolution in the Countryside: Anatomy of a Limited Rebellion," in Thomas W. Robinson (ed.), *The Cultural Revolution in China* (Berkeley: University of California Press, 1971), pp. 367-476. By carefully piecing together where and when various types of incidents were reported to have occurred in the countryside, Baum was able to draw up an interesting chronological account of how the Cultural Revolution developed in the countryside, an account that examined the movement's ultimate spatial distribution. His documentary evidence suggested that the bulk of the commune towns and rural villages that experienced upheavals lay relatively close to cities, railway lines, major roads or ports and that, generally, the closer they were, the earlier they experienced Cultural Revolution turmoil.

[5]   My search revealed that in the three decades since Richard Baum gathered his material, relatively few new Chinese writings have been published about what occurred in the villages, in contrast to the outpouring of new materials during the past decade and a half on many other aspects of the Cultural Revolution. A vast national project during the 1980s and 1990s

Villages Unaffected by Turmoil

Slightly more than one-third of the villages of interviewees—eleven, to be exact—rode out the Cultural Revolution without any serious eruptions from below.[6] When compared to the near-ubiquity of turmoil in China's cities during the Cultural Revolution,[7] the very fact that a sizable proportion of rural communities were entirely unaffected by upheaval merits attention.

Some of these villages were effectively sealed off from the Cultural Revolution by their remoteness from the urban and county town–centered turmoil. An extreme illustration of this was provided by an interviewee from an Anhui county town who had romantically ventured far from town into a mountain district. He and his friends had hoped to arouse farmers' interest in the Cultural Revolution, only to discover a Hobbesian world of desperately poor and illiterate peasants who cared only about securing sufficient food to last the winter. They were scattered in tiny hamlets and were so little affected by the sweep of political events of the previous decade and a half that they still knew only the old Republican-era calendar. "Most of the stuff concerning the People's Republic stopped at the commune town. Mail and communications from above only irregularly reached even that far," he recalls.

---

has produced thick gazetteers for almost every county in China, and these sometimes include accounts of the Cultural Revolution, but they chronicle the combat in county towns and almost invariably stop short of the villages. A relatively small number of them contain scattered sentences on what occurred within particular villages—and in this chapter I cite the most relevant of these. The individual Chinese authors who, from personal interest, have turned their attention to the Cultural Revolution rarely examine what occurred in villages. Practically all of them have focused instead on the urban scene in which they themselves had participated. Two notable exceptions are Zhang Letian (see Ch. 1, fn. 5 [*vide* Ch. 6 of Zhang's book]) and the novelist Zheng Yi, who has done considerable research on rural massacres in Guangxi Province. See Zheng Yi, *Hongse jinian bei*, 686 pages. A greatly abridged version of the book has been published in English as *Scarlet Memorial: Tales of Cannibalism in Modern China* (Boulder: Westview Press, 1996), 199 pp. When Zheng Yi is cited in this chapter, the page numbers refer to the Chinese-langauge version.

[6]   When I write that one-third of the villages did not experience Cultural Revolution turmoil from below, I am referring only to efforts to topple village-level leaders or conflicts between different groups in these communities, as in inter-lineage struggles. I am not including persecutions mounted from above by officials, nor orchestrated movements to struggle against and physically abuse bad-class people. This occurred almost everywhere, and was not confined to the Cultural Revolution of 1966-68: as noted in Chapter Two, such persecutions were commonplace throughout most of the period of Mao's rule.

[7]   At one period or another between 1966 and 1968, almost every urban school, work unit and government office erupted in dissension and factionalism, very often spiraling into violence, in city after city throughout China. The pattern everywhere was rather similar. In every city, so-called Rebel and Conservative factions emerged from the melee and fought each other in the streets. On this, see for example, Hong Yung Lee, *The Politics of the Cultural Revolution* (Berkeley: University of California Press, 1978).

Such remote districts stood at one edge of a broad spectrum. As we have observed, most of rural China had been penetrated to a considerable extent by Party control and Party teachings and by periodic political campaigns. But even so, there was a decided reluctance among many Chinese farmers to do anything that might stir up disturbances within their communities. An interviewee from northern Guangdong observed, "There was just a bit of conflict in our village, because we peasants are pragmatic and know that we have to eat;" and another from Guangdong commented, "No matter whether the peasants wanted to rebel or not, they had to work."

As much to the point, most farmers had no desire to "rebel." According to interviewees, during the decade before the Cultural Revolution many of the villagers had reluctantly put up with having to participate in political campaigns that often inspired fear. Their habitual inclination in such circumstances was to make themselves inconspicuous by conforming to whatever actions others took, rather than take the initiative. Even if a farmer harbored a strong personal grievance, he or she knew that to defy village authority in this new Cultural Revolution campaign was likely to invite vengeance later from above. An interviewee from the countryside of Guangxi Province remembers that "A lot of the farmers in my village felt that the rebels were foolish. They'd remark: 'Such people are foolhardy to attack officials, since officials always have a net of mutual protection. Even if you feel you've got a chance to successfully struggle against the brigade Party secretary, how can you hope to struggle against the county leaders? If only one official doesn't fall, you'll be in trouble'." Many of those who, despite this, did rise up in the Cultural Revolution against their village leadership would ultimately discover the truth of that observation, to their great regret.

Another reason why the urban Red Guard youths who descended on villages found it difficult to stir up dissension was that many peasants felt tolerant about the local officials' shortcomings. One of these outside agitators, who subsequently left China and has written a book about his Cultural Revolution experiences in Guangxi, relates that after he had unsuccessfully made an impassioned speech to rouse peasants to attack their village's cadres for corruption, a farmer came up to him to explain that "of course the cadres take some advantages; otherwise who'd accept such posts." The peasants of this village were altogether unimpressed by these urban Red Guards' espousal of Cultural Revolution doctrine. When the arriving Red Guards denounced Liu Shaoqi and, implicitly, local cadres as "reactionaries" for giving priority to agricultural production rather than ideology and also for having earlier allowed enlarged private plots and free markets to exist, the villagers recoiled in the realization that the new campaign went against their own interests.[8]

---

[8]   See Hua Linshan, *Les années rouges* (Paris: Editions du Seuil, 1987), pp. 200-202.

The Opening Act: The Catalysts of Turmoil

The question, thus, is why, in light of all of the above constraining factors, upheavals from below nevertheless did occur in many villages. The evidence points to four specific types of political catalysts that helped push some villages past the threshold at which broad-based intra-village conflict would erupt:

(i) *Agitation by local students.* Relatively few village children continued their education into a secondary school at the commune headquarters town, but the numbers tended to be somewhat higher in China's more prosperous rural districts. When Mao gave orders in the spring of 1966 that schooling should be halted so that students could participate in the Cultural Revolution, the students at some of the commune-town schools, eager to exhibit their "political activism," excitedly followed the lead of the urban schools. This often constituted the initial event of the Cultural Revolution in such communes. In the summer and autumn of 1966, many of these secondary-school students returned to their villages to play out the "destroy the four olds" mini-campaign that they had heard was spilling out of urban schools. They stormed into peasants' homes and destroyed items that smacked to them of tradition. They especially ransacked the houses of people who before the revolution had been landlords or rich peasants.[9] In some cases it was these young people, and they alone, who initially responded positively to the Red Guards who came out from the cities seeking acolytes and allies.[10] Their activities sometimes provided the catalyst for later intra-village disturbances.

(ii) *Spill-over of turmoil from the county and commune towns.* The documentary evidence that has become available in China by way of the new county gazetteers of the 1980s and 1990s reveals that not only in the countryside close to the cities but also in the hinterlands, from the northern hinterlands of Shaanxi Province to the southern border province of Guangxi, a great many county capitals and commune towns experienced factional turmoil.[11] My

---

[9]   As just one example, an interviewee from Guangdong recalls that in mid-1966, "A whole group of secondary-school students marched into our village and held a rally next to the ancestral hall. They proclaimed they were going to 'destroy the Four Olds', and some of them smashed and burned the ancestral tablets in the hall, and then climbed onto the hall's roof and wrecked all the figurines that were up there. Because it was a new political campaign, the peasants who were watching were hesitant to stop them." On the following days, this group of local students chopped off the braids of young women as "feudal" and went through peasant houses ripping down pictures of kitchen gods and dragons and destroying other "superstitious" artifacts. More ominously, they proceeded to smash up the homes of former rich peasants and landlords, searching for Kuomintang flags or books, and when they could not find any they boisterously beat up a few of the old people.

[10]   In addition to my interviews, examples of urban Red Guards entering the countryside and, in some cases, trying to link up with such rural student Red Guards are contained in Richard Baum's article, "The Cultural Revolution in the Countryside," pp. 278-83.

[11]   This new material presents a picture of the Cultural Revolution as having been much more widespread in the countryside than previously presumed by foreign scholars. My interviews

interviews show, though, that in some rural districts these disruptive activities occurred almost exclusively in the county capitals and commune headquarters towns,[12] and did not directly affect most of the surrounding villages. But interviewees relate that in some other districts, the factional disputes in the towns spilled outward into the countryside as contending town-based factions sought allies, and that this sometimes encouraged contests for power within villages.

(iii) *Protests by sent-down urban youths.* Similar to Chen Village, a minority of China's villages during the mid-1960s contained rusticated urban young people.[13] Some of these youths had settled in the countryside because they had been unemployed in the cities; others had gone out of youthful idealism. Both types had soon discovered that they had been permanently assigned to a life of grueling labor, and in a village where they would always be considered "outsiders." As an interviewee observed: "The peasants didn't consider us their own people, but as people of a different surname who were not wanted there." When the Cultural Revolution erupted, the majority of these young people grasped the opportunity to protest against their treatment, but they did so indirectly. To air their personal grievances would have left them vulnerable to charges of "selfishness." Instead, they often resorted to the highly charged political rhetoric of the new Cultural Revolution to lay accusations against the local political leadership. Most of the disgruntled young people eventually tired of this and returned to their urban homes for the duration of the Cultural

---

are in accord with the new documentary material, revealing that even at a considerable distance from the cities, in some of the small towns that housed commune headquarters disgruntled junior commune-level cadres rose up against their superiors. In one of the commune towns in my interview sample, even the commune clerks organized their own Rebel group. In such communes, dissident groups of village youths that were too weak in their own community to cause any commotion could instead walk into the commune town to join in on one side or the other in the factional agitation.

[12]   The residents of the county capitals and rural towns had quite a different type of residence permit (*hukou*) than the peasants, and this provided them with a distinctly different set of circumstances in life: many of them worked in urban-like work units that paid regular salaries, not in agricultural production teams that shared out harvest yields. Economically, socially, and politically, their lives more closely resembled those of urban residents rather than peasants. The conflicts that embroiled many of the rural county capitals and towns during the Cultural Revolution seem to have closely followed the same chronology of events as the cities, and often the same type of factionalism arose there. (This observation is based in part on a separate set of interviews that I conducted with several former residents of county towns and in part on the descriptions of the Cultural Revolution in such towns that have been published in a large number of Chinese county gazetteers over the past decade.)

[13]   All told, between 1956 and 1966 inclusive, some 1.2 million urban young people were sent to live in the countryside. After the Cultural Revolution fighting, between late 1968 and 1976, an additional 14 million were dispatched. Jonathan Unger, *Education Under Mao: Class and Competition in Canton Schools, 1960-1980* (New York: Columbia University Press, 1992), p. 262, note 36.

Revolution turmoil, forming their own Red Guard groups in the cities to inveigh against "Liu Shaoqi's rustication policy."[14] But in the months before their departure from the villages, they stirred up a cauldron of charges and counter-charges, and sometimes succeeded in enlisting support among some of the village's excited secondary-school students and among those sectors of the local population who had their own reasons for feeling disgruntled. The dissension that they ignited sometimes outlasted their departure.[15]

(iv) *Legacy of the Four Cleanups campaign.* A final type of catalyst for village turmoil lay in the Four Cleanups campaign that had been under way in the countryside immediately preceding the Cultural Revolution. The campaign had not yet reached some of China's villages by the time the Cultural Revolution erupted in mid-1966, but where the Four Cleanups had been carried out it involved not just Mao Study programs and class struggle sessions against bad-class people, but also, principally, had involved an attack against village cadres for corruption and back-sliding. It was then, not during the Cultural Revolution, that villagers first witnessed the public humiliation of village officials, and learned the officially sanctioned political rhetoric that could, when opportunities arose, be utilized against them again.

For their part, those village officials who had just been ousted in the Four Cleanups nursed fresh grievances against those in the village who had turned against them, and grievances, too, against those who had been put into power in their stead. As the Four Cleanups campaign collapsed into the Cultural Revolution in the spring and summer of 1966, some of these ousted village power-holders perceived opportunities to recoup their positions. Those who had succeeded them in the seats of village power were equally determined to retain their new posts. And as the provincial and county levels of Party and government authority teetered and fell in the autumn and winter of 1966-67, the institutions of the state no longer were in any position to serve as the final arbiters in determining who held sway in these villages.[16]

In some other villages, the Four Cleanups workteams had overseen vitriolic attacks against village officials only to restore them to office in a later phase of

---

[14]   In addition to my interviews, the frustrating circumstances of sent-down youth during these months is described in Thomas P. Bernstein, *Up to the Mountains and Down to the Villages: The Transfer of Youth from Urban to Rural China* (New Haven: Yale University Press, 1977), pp. 264-68. On their leaving villages during the Cultural Revolution to return to the cities see Stanley Rosen, *The Role of Sent-down Youth in the Chinese Cultural Revolution* (Berkeley: Institute of East Asian Studies, University of California, 1981).

[15]   An example of this scenario is described in detail in Chan, Madsen and Unger, *Chen Village Under Mao and Deng*, Ch. 4. Similar scenes were played out in at least three other villages of interviewees.

[16]   A good example of this is described in Huang, *The Spiral Road*, pp. 91-3; also see Chan, Madsen and Unger, *Chen Village*, Ch. 4; also brief discussions in Baum, "The Cultural Revolution in the Countryside," pp. 376-77, 396-97.

the Cleanups campaign. Those villagers whom the workteams had only recently aroused to lay charges against the officials were thus left vulnerable to retaliation. In two of the villages of interviewees, pre-emptive attacks relatively early in the Cultural Revolution were launched against the newly restored officials by groups of people who were fearful for their own futures if they could not re-oust them.

In short, four different types of catalysts of rural unrest opened up opportunities for grievances and rivalries to pour out—and these tended largely to be grievances of a particular order. That is, what first found expression in the rural Cultural Revolution were tensions that were specifically tied to the workings of politically related institutions: whether within the new government school system, or within local Party and government bureaucracies, or emanating from the government's ideologically inspired program to dispatch urban young people to the countryside, or the tense, unsettled legacy of the Four Cleanups political campaign. The majority of the villages in my set of interviews where upheavals occurred had initially experienced one or the other of these four types of catalyst. The interviews suggest, too, that discontent was likely to remain dormant and suppressed where such catalysts were not present.[17]

Traditional Struggles for Dominance

To say that rural conflict was normally sparked off by tensions engendered by the political system should not imply that these tensions necessarily dominated the ensuing strife. Once the floodgates had been opened, different reasons for conflict that were more meaningful to many peasants frequently burst through. Interviews revealed that the tussles between contestants for village power and the infighting between the recent victims and beneficiaries of the Four Cleanups often overlaid deeper group antagonisms and cleavages that reached back many decades. Again and again, historically rooted conflicts between families, long-standing conflicts between lineage groups, and conflicts between hostile villages got played out in the ongoing Cultural Revolution violence. The nature and range of these long-festering conflicts can be illustrated by reference to several of the villages of interviewees.

A large brigade in Jiangxi Province consisted of three adjoining lineage villages, and the brigade Party Secretary was a Gao from Gao Village. This was

---

[17]   In only two of the villages discussed by interviewees did attacks to oust a local leader simply well up spontaneously in a disorganized fashion among the peasants. In the more dramatic of these two cases, the leader of a certain Jia Village in Anhui Province had had several fellow villagers beaten to death during the early 1960s, but since his lineage group, the Jias, dominated the village, he had not previously been called to account for his brutality. In the midst of the Cultural Revolution, a group of neighbors attempted to exact vengeance by drowning him in a large cesspool, but his kinsmen intervened to rescue him. In both of the cases from my interview files, such eruptions against hated officials lasted only days and faded away in disorganized confusion.

resented by the biggest of the three lineages, the Xus of Xu Village: "So Gao had remained in power only because the commune authorities protected him. The beginning of the Cultural Revolution, which removed protection from above, was the end of his career."[18]

Another brigade, in the southern part of Anhui Province, consisted of a single village containing a substantial number of surname groups, but all of the brigade officials came from three numerically dominant surnames. During the Cultural Revolution, the brigade largely split along these surname lines, but not entirely so. Some of the antagonisms stemming from the Four Cleanups campaign crosscut against the surname cleavages, and as a consequence, in the confusion of the alliances and counter-alliances that got shaped in the village, "some of the cadres betrayed lineage lines."

In yet another locale, located in hill country in Guangdong, a hamlet of twelve households comprised a production team. The hamlet was composed entirely of Hakka who had settled there only three generations earlier, and thus there were no lineages *per se*. But the hamlet had divided loosely into two sets of family groups that had vied to control the team leadership positions (and through that, the hamlet's resources) from the period of collectivization in the 1950s onward. The Cultural Revolution provided the setting for yet another round in this ongoing hamlet infighting, which would be played out again a couple more times during the political campaigns of the early 1970s.

A final example of lineage conflict occurred in a village in southern Jiangsu Province that consists of a large lineage, the Dings, and several smaller lineages. Here, the numerically largest branch of the Dings had allied itself in the period before the Cultural Revolution with the smaller Liu lineage to dominate the leadership posts in the brigade. In the Cultural Revolution another branch of the Ding lineage that had been excluded from posts joined forces with several small lineages to seek its share of power. The conflict escalated to the point where rifles were stockpiled by each side, but in the end violence was averted: in part, said the respondent, because the Dings on each side recognized the ties of common lineage. Generally, the evidence from the villages suggests that while lineage

---

[18] In this brigade, early in the Cultural Revolution, a Xu whom Party Secretary Gao had recently helped remove during the Four Cleanups on charges of corruption from a post as production-team accountant in Xu Village joined forces with a Gao man furious that his wife had openly become Secretary Gao's mistress. Together, the two men laid an unsubstantiated charge against the Party secretary, accusing him of having been a murderously active member of an anti-Communist militia before Liberation. Secretary Gao was quickly swept aside and his place was taken by his Xu accuser, who emerged as head of the new governing Revolutionary Committee of the brigade. (This information is drawn in part from personal communications with Mobo Gao, of Gao Village, and in part from his book *Gao Village*.)

differences contributed to conflict, membership in the same lineage—as in a single-lineage village—ameliorated conflict and the potential for violence.[19]

In all, ten of the villages in my set of interviews experienced conflicts between rival kinship and lineage groups—a third of all the villages of interviewees. This puts the rural Cultural Revolution in a new and quite different light than had been evident from the contemporaneous documentation from China.[20]

All of the villages of interviewees that experienced lineage conflict are located in the southern half of China: that is, they lie south of or within the Yangtze River basin. However, this phenomenon of inter-lineage warfare was not confined to the south: similar accounts show up in post-Mao writings about the Cultural Revolution experiences of northern Chinese villages. For instance, a former member of a village in Hebei Province reminisces that "there were two lineages in our village, Wang and Li. . . . From the very beginning, the two lineages fought each other without stopping. . . . Village head was a key position. Whoever took it would be able to control the other side. The Wang lineage had more people and always occupied that position, both under the Japanese and the Communist Party. . . . If you want to find out the roots of the Cultural Revolution, this is the longest and deepest one."[21]

Similarly, in Long Bow, the village in Shanxi Province that William Hinton has studied, two different lineages, the Lus and the Shens, predominated in the northern and southern halves of the village. The Lu lineage, in the north, "since Liberation at least, and possibly for a long time prior to that, had played an increasingly dominant role in village government. . . . To the ruling Lus, an uprising [during the Cultural Revolution] based on the Fourth Production Team in the south and the Sidelines Team led by Little Shen meant that southerners, instigated by Shens, were on the rampage and meant to take over."[22]

---

[19]   This distinction emerges in interviews with respondents from single-lineage villages, and a similar sense pervades written sources. The Party secretary of a village in Henan Province, as just one example, confided to his biographer, Peter J. Seybolt: "I was not severely criticized [during the Cultural Revolution] because most of us are in the same Wang family [lineage] here." Seybolt, *Throwing the Emperor from His Horse*, p. 68.

[20]   In his hundred-page article "The Cultural Revolution in the Countryside," Baum cites only two examples, both from provincial Chinese radio broadcasts, of local instances of "clan struggle" (p. 410). The emphasis in the Chinese newspapers and broadcasts of the time almost wholly centered on the surface political phenomena of factional struggles.

[21]   "The Cultural Revolution Has Been Under Way for Two Thousand Years," from Feng Jici's book of oral histories, *Yi baige ren de shinian*, translated in the collection "China's Great Terror: New Documentation on the Cultural Revolution," edited by Andrew G. Walder and Gong Xiaoxia, *Chinese Sociology and Anthropology*, Vol. 26, No. 1 (Fall 1993), pp. 13-14.

[22]   Hinton, *Shenfan: The Continuing Revolution in a Chinese Village*, p. 527. In this and the following example, also taken from a book-length village study, the authors delineate in a few sentences the fact that inter-lineage antagonisms were at work in the village's Cultural

Even when such lineage rivalries were at work, it was necessary that they be carried out within a Party-shaped political environment. One significant aspect of this was that only people who came from a sufficiently good class background could become involved in any Cultural Revolution activity, not everyone from the lineage group or village. People from households that contained former landlords or rich peasants, for instance, had to refrain from any role whatsoever lest the whole group be politically tarred. In a study of another north China village, in Hebei Province, this need shaped the very nature of the struggle between different lineages and sectors of the village: "Most active in the Cultural Revolution battles were the east end and west end of the village. The center, home of the old Southern Li [lineage] elite, was tranquil. Indeed, only poor peasants from the center were allowed into rebel organizations."[23]

Given the need to justify attacks and counter-attacks during the Cultural Revolution by way of "ideology," the traditionally based rivalries and antagonisms often were clothed in socialist rhetoric and got acted out in a newly "revolutionary" mode of stylized conflict. A quite extraordinary example of this, recounted by an interviewee, involved two neighboring villages in Guangdong Province that had long quarreled, sometimes violently, over water rights. Starting in the 1950s, the local Communist government administration had entirely suppressed armed conflict between the two villages. But when the Cultural Revolution erupted and young Red Guards in the cities had begun "destroying the four olds" in 1966, a group of young people from one of the villages, wearing Red Guard arm bands, had marched over to the other village and set fire to a temple there that was reputed to improve the *fengshui* of the village and the good fortune of its people. Their ostensible purpose was to put an end to reactionary feudal superstition (though notably, they themselves actually shared in these beliefs). A group of young Red Guards was quickly organized in the other village, and under the same slogan of combating feudal superstition they retaliated in kind by destroying an ancient tree near the other village that was believed to enhance the fertility of the brides who married into that village.[24]

Normally, however, inter-village conflicts were of a more serious and indeed sometimes murderous nature. The clashes reported in some of the interviews appear to have been neither more nor less than *xiedou*, the armed vendettas that traditionally had repeatedly pitted lineages or villages or even whole alliances of

---

Revolution infighting, but then "bury" this insight in a mass of chronological detail about the Cultural Revolution turmoil, to the extent that this underlying factor gets erased in readers' memories.

[23]   Friedman, Pickowicz and Selden, *Revolution, Resistance and Reform in Village China* (forthcoming), Ch. 3.

[24]   Such inter-lineage attacks on, or disputes over, structures that produced lucky or baleful *fengshui* were not uncommon in the countryside. One county recorded 961 inter-lineage disputes between 1961 and 1990 involving *fengshui*. *Fazhi ribao* (Law Daily), August 7, 1985, p. 1.

villages one against the other. In one incident, a Mai lineage village in Guangdong dispatched thirty men for some weeks to till the fields of a related Mai lineage in another commune, in order to free their distant relatives to mount a full-time battle against the hated Chens of Duanfen. In the 1940s, the Mais had similarly dispatched men to till the same set of fields while their distant Mai relatives of an earlier generation had battled the same hated Chens.[25]

Though often originally sparked by material issues such as irrigation rights or contested land ownership, through the generations such feuds usually had taken on a life of their own. Lucien Bianco, who has studied this phenomenon of traditional *xiedou*, notes that each time a new round of armed conflict between rival lineages or rival villages had been ignited, questions of honor plus "the dead call for vengeance, and feelings of insecurity" took over, and the turn to arms was "then seen as aggressive by the other party, who in turn use the smallest mistake as a pretext for reaction and punishment. To forgive an offence is interpreted as a sign of weakness, an invitation to encroach even more on the village or clan which is 'incapable' of defending its honor and its interests. It could even be said to threaten the survival of the group."[26]

---

[25]   This information comes from personal communications with Isabelle Thireau and Hua Linshan, who have co-authored a history of the first half of the 20th century of this Mai lineage village. A description of that 1940s *xiedou* is contained in their *Enquête sociologique sur la Chine 1911-1949* (Paris: Presses Universitaires de France, 1996), Ch. 8. Hua initially lived in the village during the 1970s as a sent-down youth, and he and Thireau have more recently conducted interviews on the years immediately preceding his stay there. They have related to me that during the Cultural Revolution, in addition to assisting those relatives in another commune, the Mais also made an unsuccessful attempt to wrest power from the leadership of their own brigade. Before Liberation, the Mai hamlet had been more prosperous than other nearby hamlets due to having relatives overseas, and they had paid the price during the period of collectivization in the 1950s when a poor lineage without Overseas Chinese connections gained control of the brigade leadership. During months of conflict in late 1966 and early 1967, a breakaway militia/Red Guard group that largely consisted of people from the Mai hamlet captured and beat the brigade Party secretary at a struggle meeting. But by the spring of 1968, when the Cleansing of Class Ranks campaign was announced, the former brigade cadres had recovered their power. About thirty Mai villagers were placed under political supervision and received formal "bad" labels, including that of counter-revolutionaries.

[26]   Lucien Bianco, "Rural Areas: Vendettas Are Back," *China Perspectives*, Vol. 1, No. 1 (September 1995), p. 27. On this theme of vengeance, also see Richard Madsen's analysis of the Cultural Revolution violence that had erupted in Long Bow Village, the village that was the subject of William Hinton's book *Shenfan*. Madsen observes how the factional loyalties in Long Bow were "rooted to a commitment to the past ... As the balance of power between the rival factions teetered back and forth, each faction accumulated injuries that demanded vengeful redress, deepening the spiral of violence." Richard Madsen, "The Politics of Revenge in Rural China During the Cultural Revolution," in Jonathan N. Lipman and Stevan Harrell (eds.), *Violence in China* (Albany: State University of New York Press, 1990), p. 187.

In the Cultural Revolution, the notions of uncompromising violent honor that fed a *xiedou* had opportunities to come to the fore. Indeed, the Mao quotations that were being brandished everywhere during the Cultural Revolution encouraged a similarly exaggerated, uncompromising righteousness and intolerance and a recourse to violence to destroy resistance. The extreme politics of the Cultural Revolution period meant, quite realistically, that losing out in a struggle was likely to entail severe persecution and perhaps even death. Such fears contributed to mounting cycles of violence and counter-violence—in cities as well as in the countryside, among worker and student groups as well as among farmers, and among self-interested contenders for rural political power as well as among the participants of *xiedou* vendettas. An interviewee observed, regarding the Cultural Revolution in her own village in Guangdong, that "seeking revenge afterwards is very common in China, and that's why people beat their victims down so hard: because they're afraid that if they can rise again they might take revenge. So you feel you need to totally demolish them."

The desperate need to win a decisive victory also explains why purely local conflicts within villages and between neighboring villages frequently became intertwined with factional alliances stretching upward and outward into the county capital and ultimately across whole provinces, until two vast factions battled for supremacy in the wider region. Local defeat or victory would depend upon that larger scene. If your opponent attached itself to one of the contesting alliances, your own local forces would need an equal degree of support from above to survive. Local antagonists sometimes became involved in pitched combat far removed from the village, desperate that their higher-order allies should prevail.[27]

Sometimes, too, even when there was no grassroots factionalism and when villages remained under the unchallenged control of village and commune Party leaders, contingents from the countryside became involved in this type of military engagement well outside the boundaries of their own district. They did so at the behest of the local officials for reasons—as will be explained in a later section—that were tied to notions of class struggle. To understand the mentality of these peasant corps, it is illuminating to examine first the tragic lengths reached by class discrimination in the countryside during the Cultural Revolution.

Local "Class" Violence Organized from Above

The Four Cleanups campaign, as noted, had caught a lot of village officials in its net on charges of corruption. But alongside such charges were accusations that some village officials had fraternized with or acted leniently toward bad-class fellow lineage members and neighbors. Village officials learned through the Four

---

[27]   A good description of this for a village in Fujian Province is contained in Huang Shu-min, *The Spiral Road*, pp. 93-94. There, members of the two village factions fought on opposite sides in the pitched battles of higher-level factions in and around the city of Xiamen.

Cleanups campaign that if they did not always exhibit an ostentatiously firm class stand, they might leave themselves open to such accusations—and that, conversely, vicious behavior toward four-bad households could help deflect any future attacks against themselves.

Knowing this, as the Cultural Revolution began to seep outward from the cities, many commune and village officials began to organize farmers to mete out severe persecution against the bad-class households. The local leaders apparently saw it as a means of self-protection to preside over such persecutions. They could see that one of the charges being leveled against urban Party leaders during the Cultural Revolution was that they had been insufficiently militant on behalf of Chairman Mao's line, and thus the local rural Party officials now appeared especially anxious to demonstrate their militancy in pursuit of bad-class enemies. Drumming up such "class struggle" was an important means for them to retain the initiative during the dangerous confusion of the Cultural Revolution.

Yet persecutions of "four-bad elements" did not occur in every village and hamlet, and where this did occur the farmers were not always enthusiastic about participating. China is vast, and as noted in the previous chapter, not every village had been penetrated equally by the Party teachings that encouraged "class hatred." In the brigade of one interviewee from Guangdong, when the commune leadership ordered struggle meetings against bad-class people during the Cultural Revolution, "as usual the four-bad elements were dragged out of their production teams and taken to the brigade center to be struggled against and beaten. It wasn't arranged to be done within the teams because everyone within a team had relations with each other and so they couldn't be trusted to carry this out."

The pressure to engage in "class struggle" could be intense, however, in a situation where higher-level rural officials were desperately intent upon protecting themselves by exhibiting "class militancy." As there was a conviction among many people in China that the "bad class" stain was biologically heritable, some rural officials demanded attacks on anyone who could be considered a close blood relation of one, with devastating results. For example, prior to the 1950s land reform the village of an interviewee in Guangdong Province had been a so-called "landlord village" that had dominated surrounding tenant villages. During the land reform period, most of the landlords had been massacred, and their young sons had been adopted and raised by good-class peasant families from the village as their own. They had, like other good-class youngsters, participated in the persecution of bad-class people during struggle meetings, and they were astonished when during the Cultural Revolution commune-level officials ordered that they themselves be persecuted as bad-class pariahs. In this particular village, the anger and resistance that this order aroused among their adoptive parents and grandparents provided the most memorable events of the Cultural Revolution.

But play-acting or resistance to "class struggle" appears to have occurred in only a small minority of villages. In most villages, those who bore bad-class labels were not adopted children, but rather families that had long been isolated as despised pariahs. There are numerous descriptions from interviews and Chinese documentation in which bad-class villagers, in one commune and village after another, were singled out for appalling treatment during the Cultural

Revolution, regardless of their lineage background or personal behavior. An interviewee from a single-lineage village in Shandong Province, the son of a "four-bad element," relates what occurred to his father—treatment that seems mild compared to what occurred in many other villages:

> My memory of the Cultural Revolution is that whenever there was something going on, such as a new Red Guard organization being set up or a group of outside Red Guards coming in to mobilize the villagers, we'd be horrified, because all of the factions would do the same thing to show their firm class stand—conduct struggle against four-bad elements. That meant my father would be brought to struggle meetings again and again. My father said that whenever a drum was heard in the village, he'd start to feel his legs shake. He would wear as much clothing as possible in preparation for being beaten. The next day, when we kids in the family went out, we were likely to be bullied by the other children.

In some districts, the psychology of hatred and of dehumanization of bad-class households led beyond struggle meetings and beatings to mass killings, as local officials and farmers channeled their frustrations, fears and aggressions into a collective hysteria. In the autumn of 1966, in one county near Beijing, all of the male kin of an interviewee's university classmate were wiped out during a mass pogrom against all local bad-class males, from the elderly through small children, and local officials and farmers proudly paraded into Beijing carrying banners proclaiming that theirs was the first rural district in China to be "purified."[28] Zheng Yi provides extensive, graphic examples of mass slaughters of bad-class families in rural Guangxi Province in one village after another.[29] Further north, Dao County in Hunan Province became particularly well known for such killings

---

[28]   This interview was conducted by Anita Chan. This may or may not have been the same incident that was discussed in 1968 by Xie Fuzhi (the head of China's public security forces, who was placed in charge of Beijing's municipal government during the latter part of the Cultural Revolution fighting). Xie noted that in a district of Daxing County "two men seized power and called a meeting of more than ten brigade Party secretaries and ordered the total slaughter of landlords, rich peasants, counter-revolutionaries, bad elements, and Rightists. In ten brigades, they and their children, including babies, were killed in one day." See *Selections from the Chinese Mainland Press*, No. 4225 (July 24, 1968), pp. 12-13. Also see Gao Gao and Yan Jiaqi, *Zhongguo Wenge shinianshi* (History of the Ten Years of the Chinese Cultural Revolution), Vol. 1 (Hong Kong: Dagongbao She, 1986), pp. 74-75.

[29]   Zheng Yi, *Hongse jinian bei* (The Red Memorial Plinth). One of the focuses of this book, remarkably, is the mass cannibalism that accompanied slaughters in parts of the Guangxi countryside. For a fascinating anthropological analysis of this gruesome occurrence, see Donald C. Sutton, "Consuming Counter-revolution: The Ritual and Culture of Cannibalism in Wuxuan, Guangxi, China, May to July 1968," *Comparative Studies in Society and History*, Vol. 37, No. 1 (July 1995), pp. 136-72.

on a massive scale.[30] An interesting paper by Gong Xiaoxia that looks across the whole of rural China has found that the massacres of bad-class people occurred largely in areas where the local authorities had been under heavy attack by a Rebel faction in the county but had managed to hold onto power.[31]

It is notable that even in parts of the countryside where systematic murder did *not* occur, there appears to have been a belief among farmers that they were licensed by the Party's ideological teachings to take the lives of "four-bad elements" with impunity. An interviewee from Guangdong Province recalled that although no-one in his own village was killed, during the struggle meetings called during the Cultural Revolution and during the succeeding Cleansing of Class Ranks campaign of 1968-69, "villagers with poor and lower-middle peasant labels had the right to beat to death people whose status was worse than rich peasant."

In some districts, as previously noted, anxious village officials egged on the brutal beatings of four-bad elements during the Cultural Revolution; but at times the inspiration and instructions came from far higher up. During the latter half of 1968, when the national leadership under Mao was at long last seeking to bring the Cultural Revolution fighting to a halt, the directives handed down from Beijing for the so-called Cleansing of Class Ranks campaign singled out bad-class people as targets alongside the local losers of Cultural Revolution conflict.[32] At the end of "struggle campaigns" and periods of upheaval it was a normal Party practice to "point the spear downward" toward vulnerable targets at the grassroots—to crack heads so as to restore order and obedience to Party hierarchy—and bad-class people made convenient targets. It was a tactic known as "killing the chickens to scare the monkeys," and it occurred in most of the villages of interviewees during these months. As one interviewee observed, "In the Cleansing of Class Ranks, no-one had any peace. Those controlling the

---

[30]   On this, see for example, "Dao Xian da zhusha" (The Great Slaughter in Dao County), *Kaifang zazhi* (Open Magazine) (Hong Kong), July 2001, pp. 63-80.

[31]   Gong Xiaoxia, "Perpetual Victims: Persecution of the 'Bad Classes' During the Cultural Revolution," *China Information*, Vol. 11, Nos. 2-3 (Autumn 1996), pp. 35-53.

[32]   A detailed description of how the Cleansing of Class Ranks campaign was carried out in one village is contained in Chan, Madsen and Unger, *Chen Village Under Mao and Deng*, Chs 5 and 6. The numbers of people persecuted during this campaign can be gauged by reference to Guangdong Province as a whole. In 1974, the recently restored provincial Party secretary, Zhao Ziyang, established a group to collect figures on the scale of repression in Guangdong during the Cleansing of Class Ranks period of 1968-69. The research group's findings were that in Guangdong Province alone, close to 40,000 people were killed during the Ranks campaign and about a million had been struggled against and put under "surveillance" or thrown into local jerry-built jails. See Anita Chan, Stanley Rosen and Jonathan Unger (eds.), *On Socialist Democracy and the Chinese Legal System* (Armonk: M.E. Sharpe, 1985), pp. 7, 41.

campaign 'got' (*gao*) the chickens in order to warn the 95 percent who were monkeys. While they got the 5 percent they scared everybody 100 percent."

In light of the repeated brutal persecution of bad-class people during Mao's rule, there was obviously nothing more dangerous to a *non*–bad class person than to be depicted and denounced in bad-class terms. It therefore is not surprising that even before the period of Cleansing of Class Ranks terror, in the emotional heat of local struggles between opposing camps in the Cultural Revolution the persecution of captured or defeated enemies often employed the same type of dehumanizing rhetoric as was wielded against bad-class people. After all, if "bad-class" labels such as "counter-revolutionary" or Rightist had been created in previous campaigns, why couldn't those whom one considered transgressors in the Cultural Revolution similarly be mentally designated as a new batch of bad-class elements? Zheng Yi's accounts of the murders of overthrown local officials and factional enemies in rural Guangxi show again and again that they were slaughtered at the very same time as and alongside "the four bad kinds of elements" in a single orgy of killing, treating them as one and the same, as if to cement this linkage in the minds of both onlookers and perpetrators.[33] Zheng Yi recounts, though, that sometimes participants could not bring themselves to fully equate the two types of victims as similarly beyond the pale of humanity and similarly easy to murder. Thus in one of the incidents in his book a few "four-bad elements" were first forced to kill a captured group of fallen cadres and factional enemies, lest the crowd of onlookers have the blood of non–bad class people on their own hands; and then the crowd beat the hapless "four-bad elements" to death.[34]

Again it should be noted that while such organized, sanctioned mass murders occurred only in a minority of districts, they represented the extreme pole of a belief in "class hatred" that was common to most of rural China. Not surprisingly, thus, in the midst of the Cultural Revolution fighting the antagonists were apt to fling charges not simply about each other but also regarding the impurity of each others' ancestors. So, too, factional members who were defeated could find the hereditary class labels of their households officially altered,[35] thereby permanently

---

[33]   A substantial number of such incidents are described in Section One (pp. 2-116) of Zheng Yi's book. One particularly chilling example is on p. 25.

[34]   See Zheng Yi, *Hongse jinian bei*, p. 14.

[35]   This occurred in at least two interviewees' villages (during most of my other interviews, it did not occur to me to ask). My presumption is that this same mechanism was at work in two counties in Shaanxi Province, as recorded in county gazetteers. In Qianyang County, during the Cleansing of Class Ranks campaign of 1968-69 that put to an end the Cultural Revolution fighting, 152 households were newly labeled as landlord and 130 as rich peasant, while in Shanyang County over a thousand households were re-labeled as landlords or rich peasants. *Qianyang Xianzhi* (Qianyang County Gazetteer), Xi'an: Shaanxi Renmin Jiaoyu Chubanshe, 1991, pp. 277-86; and *Shanyang Xianzhi* (Shanyang County Gazetteer), Xi'an:

demonizing their entire families. Fears of this became yet another of the elements that kept rural participants desperately fighting during the Cultural Revolution, no matter how good their class background. As one of the interviewees observed, "In a campaign like this, anyone might become a target. Even five generations back, if any one of your ancestors had done anything wrong it could be used against you. And of course in five generations someone must have made mistakes . . . or been rich."

Warfare Against Urban Centers

The state of mind that lent itself to the killing of bad-class people also ultimately contributed to the slaughter of urban people by rural militias during the final stages of the Cultural Revolution fighting. This, too, was the culmination of a pattern of events tied not to any historically grounded modes of thinking, but instead directly to the political logic of the Cultural Revolution in the countryside, and the proclivities and fears of the rural officialdom.

Both in rural communes where the *status quo* had won out against local opposition and in those where it had never been challenged, the authorities were apt to support the so-called Conservative-faction mass organizations of the county towns and prefectural capitals. The Conservative faction's membership tended to derive from among those people in the county towns who had been politically favored prior to the Cultural Revolution. The faction therefore tended to uphold the pre–Cultural Revolution county and prefectural leaders. This stance appealed to commune and village Party leaders. Their loyalty to their pre–Cultural Revolution superiors often appears to have remained informally intact. In many cases, such feelings of loyalty especially linked the communes' militia commanders[36] to the county militia headquarters, and in turn the county's Party and government leadership. The plight of the county-town authorities might not, in itself, have been enough to see the rural leaders and commune militia

---

Shaanxi Renmin Chubanshe, pp. 215-19. These documented examples were brought to my attention by Gong Xiaoxia.

[36] In a large number of counties, the power of the county and commune-level militia commanders had been greatly strengthened during the two years of Cultural Revolution turmoil. As provincial Party organs collapsed in early 1967, Party leaders at the county level sometimes strategically withdrew from their posts and let the militia commanders, who were protected by their military connections to the regional army command, pretend to assume authority while the county and commune Party leaders continued to control events from behind the scenes. In other cases, where the militia commanders were politically ambitious, they used the opportunity to make a play for real power at the county capital or commune. (This information derives from several interviewees. The assumption of authority by the militia heads can also be observed in the county gazetteers and Zheng Yi's volume: again and again in these sources, the leaders in the county Revolutionary Committees and at commune level who were in a position to instruct villages to carry out massacres in 1968 are identified as militia commanders.)

commanders become militarily involved. But in addition to their sympathy, they appear to have been fearful that a victory by the county-seat or urban-based Rebel factional alliance would jeopardize their own continued hold on power in the countryside. When the rural authorities received urgent calls to come to the aid of embattled county and prefectural leaders or to the rescue of flagging county-town or prefectural-city Conservative factions, the militia corps of farmers were ordered out of the villages and dispatched to do their duty.[37]

These armed attacks by the village militias against the urban Rebel organizations were often launched first at the county capital and then, when the rebellious forces there were crushed, progressively proceeded outward and upward toward the provincial capital. Liu Guokai, an author from Guangzhou who has written one of the best analyses of the Cultural Revolution thus far published, captures this set of shifts:

> After the start of violence, Rebels of the small county towns, unable to stand the [rural militias'] repeated onslaughts, ran off to the medium-sized cities in the prefectures. When the situation there became unbearable, they retreated to the provincial capitals, thus reinforcing the numerical superiority of Rebels in the big cities. The Conservatives then resorted to a Maoist quote made some thirty years earlier, that "the countryside should encircle the cities and seize power by armed force." . . . At a time when worker and student Conservatives were unable to gain the upper hand in violence, the peasants were sent to the front lines in tens of thousands by the district, county, and commune people's armed forces.[38]

In some places, county towns and cities became almost entirely Rebel, having driven out most of the Conservative forces or having absorbed some of them into Rebel ranks once the peasant militia onslaught commenced. In such cases the warfare quite clearly took on the complexion of urbanites versus peasant armies, and the animus that many peasants appear to have felt toward the comparatively privileged urban populace had an opportunity to rise to the surface. In turn, the urban people, whatever their factionalism, often felt a common solidarity of lifestyle and sentiment when menaced by the rural armies. A striking

---

[37] The militiamen often received remuneration for doing so. As a Jiangsu provincial radio broadcast of August 8, 1967, complained, "In some regions they practice counter-revolutionary economism and give supplementary workpoints, money and grain to commune members to take part in fighting . . . all to incite the peasants to enter the cities to fight the revolutionary mass organizations in factories, mines, administrative bureaux, and schools." Quoted in *China News Analysis*, No. 679 (September 29, 1967), p. 2. In two of the villages in my interview sample, ordinary villagers were paid in workpoints even for attending, in massed groups, vast struggle meetings that the commune authorities organized at the commune market town.

[38] Liu Guokai, "A Brief Analysis of the Cultural Revolution," *Chinese Sociology and Anthropology*, Vol. 11, No. 2 (Winter 1986-87), pp. 96-97.

illustration of this was provided by an interviewee from an Anhui county capital. News was received there that in an adjoining county the county Party chief, besieged by high-school Red Guards, had barricaded himself in that county's Party headquarters and had called upon thousands of rural militiamen, armed with rudimentary military equipment, hunting rifles, and swords, to free him by besieging the county town. When this news reached the interviewee's county, both of the factions in his county capital temporarily laid aside their conflict and joined forces, dispatching a convoy of more than two hundred trucks crammed with armed young people to break the siege. Their empathy for fellow town residents took precedence over their own factional warfare.

The peasant militiamen who rallied to attack county and provincial capitals sometimes appear to have perceived the besieged urban populace as "Others," beyond the pale of compassion. This was certainly the impression of an interviewee from Guangxi Province. It was as if they were transferring into a new context the manichean Maoist teachings about good versus evil and about the virtues of pitilessness that had justified the brutal mistreatment of bad-class people. In Nanning, the provincial capital of Guangxi, in the even larger city of Chengdu in Sichuan Province, and in a number of other cities across China, slaughters of urban Rebels by victorious rural militiamen ensued. Bodies of victims from the Guangxi massacres floated down-river all the way to Hong Kong.

The Tale of One County

I have thus far treated the different types of turmoil and violence in the countryside separately. But what occurred in many locales was more complex than that, intermingling different types of violence over the course of the Cultural Revolution. A good example of this is provided by an account of the conflict that erupted in a Guangdong county, related by a former Rebel senior high school student who rose briefly during the Cultural Revolution into the county's governing Revolutionary Committee.[39] His experience ties together in one setting several of the themes raised in this chapter, both of a traditional and a politically inspired nature. And it is, importantly, the story of someone whose activities moved between the world of the village and the wider conflicts of the county town and beyond, which was rare among interviewees. His tale links for us the Cultural Revolution of the villages with the broader mosaic of the Cultural Revolution.

The interviewee was attending school at the county capital thirty miles from home when the Cultural Revolution erupted. He quickly returned in excitement to

---

[39]   The following description is based on two interviews conducted in Hong Kong in 1978, supplemented by an article that the interviewee wrote about his village, including material on the Cultural Revolution, for a magazine that was published in Hong Kong during the late 1970s by a group of former Red Guards (*Huang He* [Yellow River], No. 5, March 1978).

his commune in the belief that the new campaign had granted him the liberty to show off his political activism. Naive and not quite knowing what if anything might warrant righteous criticism, he pasted up big character-posters in the commune town charging that the commune butchers were selling the best cuts of pork to relatives and officials. He also put up posters announcing that the four-bad elements sometimes carried shotguns to hunt birds, and wrote that if any were sighted doing so they would be killed:

> The peasants were impressed and felt, wow, those Red Guards can kill people if they like. There was actually only me, but the cadres trooped around after me as I tacked up my posters, and the peasants talked as if there must be many other Red Guards like me.

Within days, the commune authorities reacted to the obscure challenge that he posed by targeting for attack three teachers of non–good class origins at the commune's own high school: if there was to be "class struggle" the authorities would lead it. Nonetheless, some of the students there broke away from their control and joined the interviewee, in emulation of urban events, by enthusiastically posting up attacks against the commune Party secretary: "We accused him of *any*thing—of having hidden problems in his personal history, of poor results in agricultural production, of anything." They tried to persuade younger officials to join them in leveling these charges, but were unsuccessful; "they feared to participate." Within the interviewee's own brigade, fewer than a dozen young men became intermittently active as a largely ineffectual Rebel group: "They felt the brigade cadres were unfair, as individuals, in their leadership styles." But they were able to stir up just a "bit" of conflict that was easily suppressed.

What ended up troubling the brigade officials were not these ineffectual young people but rather that several of the hamlets in the brigade grasped the opportunity to take up arms against each other in disputes over local resources, reviving *xiedou*s of the past. In particular, the interviewee's own team and the team next door, which were separate hamlets, had had a dispute over a large stand of timber and bamboo as far back as villagers could remember. Prior to the revolution, periodic brawls between the two hamlets had taken a toll in casualties; his own father had been stabbed in one. When the Great Leap Forward collapsed and the Party organization's local power temporarily waned, fighting had re-erupted between the two hamlets, and now erupted again in the Cultural Revolution. Both sides resisted the weak efforts of the brigade to keep them from taking up arms: "Normally the county Public Security Office would have come to adjudicate and enforce an agreement. But with the county organs weakened by the Cultural Revolution chaos, our brigade government had no such backing."

The interviewee and a handful of young followers were obliged to retreat eventually from the commune town and concentrated their energies on the county capital. During the January Storm of 1967, when city governments were being overturned throughout China, the combined Rebel forces in the county capital were able to grab power there from a confused, dispirited county leadership. Disgruntled workers from the county-town factories had been enticed to join the rebels, but the bulk of the county, including most of its rural areas, remained in the hands of the Conservative faction, led by officials, that had emerged in opposition to the Rebels. Among the twelve communes in the county, only one was allied to the Rebels; and within the remaining eleven communes, only three brigades/villages were in the Rebel camp. These Rebel locales were all ones in which local Party Secretaries had been toppled. Everywhere else, the incumbent officialdom had survived, and they moved against the Rebel upstarts in the county capital.

When counties were ordered to patch together Revolutionary Committees in 1967 as the counties' new leadership organs, these rural officials in the interviewee's county controlled the majority of its membership. The county's Rebel faction desperately tried to resist lending it any authority and began organizing a preemptive armed coup against it. But the rural officials struck first with the rural militias, declaring the Rebels to be "counter-revolutionary" and, in one fell swoop, captured and arrested all of the Rebel leadership.

In mid-1968, when directives from on high began calling for the Cleansing of Class Ranks campaign to be implemented throughout China, delayed vengeance was exacted in this county against the defeated Rebels. The deputy head of the county Revolutionary Committee issued a set of instructions encouraging the commune militia heads to carry out executions, and in at least three communes that earlier in the Cultural Revolution had witnessed agitation from below, massacres ensued, with hundreds of Rebels killed.[40]

However, unlike some other provinces such as neighboring Guangxi, in Guangdong Province such locally initiated slaughters were not acceptable to the newly installed provincial power-holders. In December of 1968 an army unit entered the county to take control, and it arrested the deputy head of the county Revolutionary Committee, three commune militia commanders and, in the interviewee's own commune, three of the village militia heads. A fair number of officials throughout the county, at commune level and above, who had been active among the Conservative forces were ousted by the army corps, and local veterans of the PLA replaced them in leadership positions.

---

[40]   This was not an isolated case. As just one example, on the other side of China a parallel occurrence is recorded in the gazetteer published by Ziyang county in Shaanxi Province (Xian: Sanqin Chubanshe, pp. 521-26): During the nationwide wave of "power seizures" in early 1967, two antagonistic factions had emerged in the county capital—"Eryipai," to which the preponderance of teachers and secondary-school students belonged, and "Erliupai," based more heavily on cadres, peasants and workers. In 1968 the factional fighting in the county escalated, and in April military and police ammunition was seized by the two factions. Members of the weaker Eryipai soon thereafter fled the county and joined their allies in neighboring counties. Amid rear-guard armed fighting, many of the adherents of Eryipai who remained behind were rounded up, along with their families and members of the "bad classes." Over 400 were tortured and then murdered, including 211 labeled as "bad-class." By the end of 1968 a PLA unit entered the county to end the bloodshed. (I am indebted to Gong Xiaoxia for bringing this material to my attention.).

To bring the Cultural Revolution disturbances to a close and to force people of all sides obediently back into line, the PLA unit turned in early 1969 to the "class struggle" tools of the Cleansing of Class Ranks campaign, carrying out the campaign a second time, this time in a carefully controlled manner. Bad-class people numbered among those "struggled against" in mass meetings that were held in all the villages.

Summing Up

Similar to this interviewee's experience, a substantial number of informants and published village studies have recounted more than one type of conflict simultaneously being played out within a single village and commune town. In this respect, the Cultural Revolution in the countryside could, in some locales, be quite complex. Significantly, too, rural grassroots conflict was more widespread in China than previously reported. The villages of two-thirds of my interviewees witnessed upheavals from below in the shape of conflicts over village leadership and/or lineage-group rivalries. If we add to this the violence of "class struggle" against bad-class villagers and other forms of persecution that were mounted from above, the proportion of villages that were directly involved in Cultural Revolution conflict was quite high.

Whatever the diversity in local scenarios, the Cultural Revolution violence in the villages largely shared in a common set of underlying attitudes and prejudices. In village after village, this could be seen in the lineage-group loyalties and culturally based rural norms of vendetta and vengeance and in the politically sanctioned intolerance and "class hatred."

To an extent not previously recognized, concealed beneath the veneer of the high-blown Maoist political rhetoric that opponents hurled at each other, the lineage-group conflicts occupied a central place in the Cultural Revolution in the villages—occurring in fully half of all the villages of interviewees that witnessed conflict from below. Even so, it is notable that with the exception of this lineage feuding, all of the other ingredients of Cultural Revolution conflict owed heavily to Party teachings and to animosities that had been manufactured under Party rule. This can be seen not only in the genesis, perpetuation and intensification of orchestrated "class struggle" meetings, but also in the tense aftermath of the Four Cleanups Campaign, in the rural secondary-school students' "activist" behavior in the early stages of the Cultural Revolution, and in the manichean beliefs in good versus evil forces and dangerous "hidden counter-revolutionaries."

Notably, as has been seen, the intra-village conflicts tended to remain bottled up and repressed in those villages that did not first experience a catalyst from within the political arena. It has been seen, too, that the ensuing hostilities, even when between rival lineage and kin groups, often were strategically garbed in Maoist political rhetoric. As a consequence, they sometimes escalated well beyond the root causes of the initial conflict. In part, it was because the participants, once entangled in political conflict, were fearful of the penalties that the political system would impose if they ended up on the losing side. Once opened, thus, a Pandora's box of spiraling violence sometimes emerged. If the conflict in a village during this period had involved only a traditional-style *xiedou*, or only a contest for local power between rival leaders, it is unlikely that it would have gone any further than the violence that, in centuries past, had irregularly punctuated the rural scene in China. But in many villages across China, the Maoist rhetoric and the fears of losing out politically were like oil atop kindling. When a conflagration was sparked off in the Cultural Revolution, the traditional antagonisms, local rivalries, and Maoist ideological teachings could flare up in combination to create a tragedy of considerable dimension.

Chapter Four

IDEOLOGY AND THE RURAL WORK COMMUNITY: THE UTOPIAN DREAM AND ITS DEMISE

Maoist ideology was most clearly expressed in two extraordinary efforts to reshape the workings of rural communities. The first of these, as we have observed, was the new "class" system, and the second was a quintessentially "Maoist" system of remuneration that was supposed to promote selflessness. In some villages this new system was introduced prior to the eruption of the Cultural Revolution, and in many others it was first implemented at the end of the 1960s or in the early 1970s, in the years after the Cultural Revolution turmoil had ceased. To come to grips with the idealistic side of the Maoist ethos, it becomes illuminating to focus on this unusual program, its origins and the impact it had on community life.

In general, the countries that adopted Marxist agendas, from Russia to Cuba, found it difficult to devise rural payment systems that were at once economically viable and ideologically palatable. In wrestling with this problem, China more than any other socialist country, experimented after the collapse of the Great Leap Forward with a whole variety of remuneration schemes.[1] It will be seen here why each of these different wage systems was tried in turn. Attention will focus particularly upon what was called the Dazhai system—an explicit effort to reshape behavior in China's villages toward ends that Mao and his followers deemed morally superior. In the short term, the Dazhai system succeeded admirably in some villages. But by forcing villagers publicly to judge one another's attitudes and work performances, the program was eventually undermined in the 1970s by growing tensions among the peasantry.

To examine the shifts in attitudes among the peasants, I will again draw upon the experiences of Chen Village, the community with which I am best acquainted.

---

[1] In addition to the research presented in this chapter, several interesting analyses by economists of how these incentives systems operated have been published. These include James Kaisung Kung, "Egalitarianism, Subsistence Provision, and Work Incentives in China's Agricultural Collectives," *World Development*, Vol. 22, No. 2 (1994), pp. 175-87, and three studies by Louis Putterman: *Peasants, Collectives and Choice* (Greenwich: JAI Press, 1986); "The Incentive Problem and the Demise of Team Farming in China," *Journal of Development Economics*, Vol. 26, No. 1 (1987), pp. 103-27; and "Ration Subsidies and Incentives in the Pre-reform Chinese Commune," *Economica*, Vol. 55, No. 218 (May 1988), pp. 235-47.

Of the 2,000-plus pages of typed interview transcripts that Anita Chan, Richard Madsen and I obtained from more than two dozen Chen Village respondents during the 1970s and 1980s, almost 200 single-spaced pages dealt with the village's experiences with different remuneration systems.[2]

Cumulatively, the transcripts bring out clearly how each of these systems influenced work incentives, how each affected the ways in which the peasants interacted with each other, and how each system, by altering the perceptions of the villagers, influenced how they would react to the next system to be tried. The transcripts illustrate what became a history of increasingly sophisticated mechanisms that elicited increasingly complex responses from the labor force—a history that culminated, by the mid-1970s, in a disillusioned rejection of the idealistically Maoist Dazhai system. It is a story that clarifies why, after Mao's death, China has chosen to decollectivize agriculture.

This chronicle of Chen Village's experiences with socialist wage schemes begins with the failure of the Great Leap Forward. Because of the Leap, the village had had to re-erect a socialist economic structure beginning from square one.

Starting Over: The Trauma of the Great Leap Forward

The Great Leap had been economically catastrophic for Chen Village. In 1958-59, at the height of that confused utopian campaign, direct material incentives in Chen Village had gone by the board. Harvests had been siphoned off into an enormous pot the size of the entire local marketing district (commune) of nine villages. The peasantry had been allowed, free of charge, to eat as much as they wanted in public mess halls, as an advance on future harvests. Peasants sarcastically recall it as the Eat-it-all-up Period: for when disorganized production led to bad harvests in 1959, the public granaries had already been emptied. The Chen Village peasants responded in their own best interests. Had they still obeyed the cadres and gone out to labor in the fields, their yields would have been diverted into that oversized communal pot from which other villages could draw. The Chen Villagers would have expended precious calories without any assurances of adequate returns. A hungry peasant's wisest strategy was to stay at home conserving energy, leaving the village fields untended. The Chen Villagers remained unwilling to put in any effort even when the state subsequently reduced the collective pot to the size of the village. A pot that fed close to a thousand neighbors still provided insufficient incentives to resume work.

To rescue rural socialism from the nightmare into which it had fallen, the government in 1961 was obliged to rebuild the agrarian economy from the ground

---

[2]   Information that I separately gathered from emigrants from four other Guangdong villages suggests significant differences as well as similarities in different villages' reactions to wage systems. An excellent discussion of such variations, using a survey questionnaire covering sixty-three Guangdong villages, is in William Parish and Martin K. Whyte, *Village and Family in Contemporary China* (Chicago: University of Chicago Press, 1978), pp. 62-71.

up. A two-pronged program was enacted. As the first prong, each of Chen Village's five neighborhoods was organized into a production team, and each was granted ownership and control over a fifth of the village's land. This relatively small number of fifty households would be remunerated through the harvest yields from its own fields. To assure that the peasants would see a vested interest in working hard to improve their own livelihood, each of the five neighborhoods was further divided half a year later to form even smaller teams, each containing some twenty to twenty-five families.

Household Contracts

A new remuneration system in 1961 comprised the second prong of the state's efforts to end the economic depression. Taking account of the Great Leap Forward's debacle and the peasantry's withdrawal from collective labor, the new incentives program had best be one that did not require much cooperation among households nor much supervision from cadres. Under Liu Shaoqi's direction, the government accordingly gave its blessings to a system called *baochan dao hu*. It literally meant "contracting production to the household." In Chen Village, lots were to be drawn each year and a portion of lowland rice paddy and a portion of hill land parceled out to each family. At the start of the season, the family would be provided with fertilizer and seed and given sole responsibility for planting and weeding its allotted fields. Each plot of land had a quota attached to it. A certain field carried a quota, say, of 300 pounds of rice, and at harvest time the family would have to hand in that amount of grain in exchange for workpoints, say 300 workpoints. The team would sell most of the harvested grain to the state and would disburse the proceeds, both in money and in kind, to each family in accordance with the numbers of workpoints it had amassed.

Initially, a family was allowed under the household contract system to keep for itself any grain it had harvested above its quota. But after about a year this rule changed. The government wanted to regain greater control over grain supplies. So the grain was to be harvested collectively, and all of it was to go to the team. But to keep the families working hard to produce more, the household and team were to share the proceeds from the team's grain sales in the following way. Quotas were again set for each field, with workpoint penalties imposed now for under-quota harvests and a progressive workpoint bonus paid for all surpluses. An extra 150 pounds over the quota would, say, earn a family 200 extra workpoints.[3]

---

[3]   Teams selected their own method of contracting production. Other localities in the same region employed slightly different schemes. On this, see *Southern Daily* (Canton), June 21, 1962, p. 1, translated in *Union Research Service* (Hong Kong: Union Research Institute), Vol. 29, p. 323. Also see the Party documents from Bao'an County, Guangdong, in *Union Research Service*, Vol. 27, pp. 115, 124, 137-38, 142, and 151. Even earlier, in the mid-1950s, village cadres in many parts of China surreptitiously had resorted to contracting fields to the households in order to relieve the difficulties of coordinating and supervising

For the time being, the household contract system was popular. The Chen Villagers once more were working productively and eating regularly, and they were thankful. But some families did far better than others. Peasants who were adept at agricultural planning and who had a number of capable teenagers available to labor profited the most. They not only were able to earn those progressive bonuses; some of them even bid for extra plots of team land on which to raise vegetables and bid, too, for the special bonuses attached to tending the team's livestock. The household contracts did not particularly serve the interests, however, of families with children who were too young to work, or where the husband was weak or sickly or poor at agricultural planning. Inasmuch as losses as well as gains were exaggerated due to the system of progressive penalties and rewards, these families were struggling desperately simply to avoid falling short of their quotas. As the depression receded, a constituency in the village was building against the contract system.

This constituency had the support of the state. The authorities had encouraged the contracting to families only as a temporary, marginally socialist expedient. In 1963, once the crisis caused by the Great Leap Forward had eased, very strong "suggestions" began flowing down from Beijing to move back toward a more collective system.

Though it was the poorer households in Chen Village who welcomed the government's demands, even the better-off families went along without any reported grousing. All of the peasants, the labor-strong families included, lived precariously close to the border of economic survival. No matter how strong and capable a particular husband and wife might be, the possibility of an infestation of their own small plots or a broken leg or unexpected illness posed ever-present threats. According to interviewees, these Chen Villagers, like peasants elsewhere, wanted more than just a chance to maximize their incomes; they wanted also to minimize risks.[4] A major attraction of socialism in the 1950s, interviewees report, had been its promise of greater financial security. A system of collective agriculture provided a peasant with the cushion of sharing in broader economic resources than his or her family could manage on its own.

Task Rates

Under the new remuneration scheme, team members would cultivate the team's fields together and share in the revenues generated. Called *baogong* (contracted

---

collective cultivation. F.W. Crook, "Chinese Communist Agricultural Incentive Systems and the Labor Productive Contracts to the Households, 1956-65," *Asian Survey,* Vol. 13, No. 5 (May 1973).

[4]   This type of calculation has tended to be true of peasants the world over: "Living close to the subsistence margin and subject to the vagaries of weather and the claims of outsiders, . . . the peasant cultivator seeks to avoid the failure that will ruin him rather than attempting a big, but risky, killing." James C. Scott, *The Moral Economy of the Peasant* (New Haven: Yale University Press, 1976), p. 4.

work), the new arrangement employed task rates and piece rates to determine how big a slice from the collective pie each peasant earned.[5] It was necessarily a complex program, because of the complexity of crop rotation in China. Unlike work on a factory production line, a peasant often had to complete a fair number of different farm tasks in the course of a day, and entirely different sets of tasks in different seasons.

Some of these tasks were much more highly rewarded than others. In particular, those associated with men were markedly better paid than those associated with women. Men and women normally worked separately. In the dry season, for instance, when dredging the nearby river the men in Chen Village were the ones who dug out the mud from the river bottom while the women hauled it up the river bank and packed it into the dikes. The men were paid for each bucket they filled and the women for each one they toted. It was the women's work that required the greater skill and effort, since the dikes were tricky to ascend under the swaying loads of dredged mud. But over the course of an hour, the men's digging paid almost twice as much as the women's carrying. The village women did not complain, however; they concurred that their own lower status justified lower pay.

Most of the hundreds of chores required the constant supervision of workpoint recorders, who had to jot down precisely how much each laborer accomplished. But in a few of the agricultural seasons ways were found to dispense with the services of these workpoint recorders.[6] For instance, peasants at harvest time worked in tight-knit squads of a dozen or so members, much as they had done even in traditional times. Without having to break their work rhythm, half of the squad members cut the crop; others would rush the sheaves to a small thresher at the side of the field; two men worked the hand threshing machine; and the two strongest men hustled the loads of grain into the village. Since the pace of the squad members' work was so closely interlinked, workpoints were awarded to the squad as a whole based on the tonnage harvested. In this "group task work" the members would hold a post-harvest session to appraise each other's labor

---

[5]   Two studies of this type of remuneration system are: Andrew J. Nathan, "China's Work-Point System: A Study in Agricultural 'Splittism'," *Current Scene*, Vol. 2, No. 31 (April 15, 1964), and Frederick William Crook, "An Analysis of Work Payment Systems Used in Chinese Mainland Agriculture, 1956-1970," PhD. dissertation, Tufts University, 1970.

[6]   During the post-harvest season, the village might engage in road construction, and here each person was given a fixed length of road to dig for a fixed number of workpoints. As the reward for hard work, those who finished fastest were able to leave early to work on their private plots. Or, if there were no public project to finish and little need to push team members to labor efficiently, the strongest workers simply would be designated as grade A and would receive 10 workpoints per day, grade B workers would receive a flat 9 workpoints each day, grade C workers 8 points, and men who were grade D 7 points, irrespective of how much they accomplished. With no monetary incentives to work hard, people would take it easy, resting from the strains of the peak season.

contributions and to determine among themselves how to divide up the totality of squad workpoints.

But most of the year the peasants worked for individual task-rate payments. On the whole, they were satisfied with this. But particular problems arose that invited complaints. For one thing, individual task rates necessitated reams of accounts; yet most villagers were illiterate and basically innumerate, and there were too few trustworthy personnel in each team capable of doing the daily accounting. Worse, team members would constantly bicker with the workpoint recorders about how many workpoints they deserved, and some would also squabble and jockey each morning to get assigned to tasks that either provided the most workpoints for a day's work or were easy in terms of the workpoints allotted.

More significantly, the task-rate system primarily paid people for quantity, at the expense of quality. During the planting season, for instance, task rates rewarded women (transplanting was women's work) in terms of the numbers of rows of rice seedlings each could transplant in the flooded paddy field. Hurrying to earn more, the women did not always bother to push the seedlings' roots in firmly. Some plants eventually would disengage and float to the surface. The very way the payments were computed encouraged a woman to keep her eyes fixed just on the size of her own slice of the collective pie, not on the productivity and income of the team as a whole. It ultimately led to sub-optimal crop yields. Indeed, the task-rate system was less satisfactory in this respect than the household contract system, which had rewarded a peasant family only if it produced higher yields.

Learning from Dazhai

In early 1965 a cadre workteam entered Chen Village to push through the Four Cleanups campaign. This government workteam, which stayed for almost two years in the village, was made up of rural officials and a couple of university students. It had come into the village not only to root out corruption among the local cadres but also to revamp the methods of agricultural production and to regenerate the peasantry's faith in the Party and its ideology.[7] As part of these latter efforts, the Four Cleanups workteam introduced to Chen Village in early 1966 the blueprints for a brand-new system of remuneration—the Dazhai system.

Dazhai was a village in the hills of north China that Mao and the Party were promoting as the model for rural China.[8] Among its signal achievements, according to the workteam, was Dazhai's development of a new mutual-appraisal

---

[7]   For a detailed description, see Chan, Madsen and Unger, *Chen Village,* Chs. 2 and 3.

[8]   The Dazhai model, and the ways its achievements were exaggerated, are described in Jonathan Unger, "'Learn from Tachai': China's Agricultural Model," *Current Scene,* Vol. 9, No. 9 (September 1971). Also see Sun Qitai and Xiong Zhiyong, *Dazhai hongqi de shengqi yu zhuiluo* (The Rise and Fall of the Red Flag of Dazhai) (Henan Renmin Chubanshe, 1990).

wage program. Its underlying idea was to structure remuneration in ways that induced people to concentrate their attention upon the gains that would accrue from a larger team pie. Such a proposal was potentially feasible because the teams were, after all, profit-sharing cooperatives. If the team pie expanded, each family's portion would grow; it would gain if its neighbors worked harder. The Dazhai system played to this point. Under Dazhai, the peasants would sit in judgment of each other at periodic team meetings to determine what each peasant's work was worth. Rather than providing direct monetary spurs, the Dazhai system would employ social pressures.

This system of mutual appraisals was supposed to provide built-in quality controls on labor. During the transplanting season, for example, team members would see it in their own interests to commend and reward most highly an effective balance between speed and careful planting. There promised to be other advantages, too. If wages were to be apportioned at periodic appraisal meetings, a team could do without workpoint recorders and complex bookkeeping. It could eliminate the daily wrangling to get better work assignments.

But the Dazhai system was not just supposed to be economically and administratively advantageous. The workteam officials spoke of it as ideologically superior, and they denounced task rates as inimical to socialist ideals. The task-rate program, they said, had encouraged a selfish competitive concern to aggrandize one's own interests at the collective's expense. The system had daily corrupted the "proletarian" consciousness of the peasants. The Dazhai system would now give them the chance to prove and enhance their moral worth by pursuing the interests of the team as a whole.

The Dazhai method of mutual appraisals was merely one part of a larger package that the workteam was introducing into the village. Daily study sessions were inaugurated in which the workteam cadres and a group of urban-educated youths who had settled in the village taught Mao's quotes and incessantly impressed upon the peasantry the sanctity and relevance of the quotes. A perfervid atmosphere somewhat resembling a religious revivalist movement was whipped up—and put to the services of the new wage system. The rhetoric of the Mao study sessions and of a new village broadcasting system repeatedly intoned: fight personal selfishness, devote yourself to the collective. Villagers were supposed to concern themselves with the collective good even beyond the point where their own interests and the team's interests coincided. The politically moral man or woman was supposed to remain behind to finish up work in the dark even if no-one were around to notice it. At the approach of a thunderstorm, a moral person was supposed to collect the team's property first and only then look after his or her own animals and grain.

Paradoxically, even though a team member was not supposed to be thinking of personal gain, rewards for such selfless attitudes were built directly into the Dazhai wage system. In the mutual appraisals, not just a member's strength and accomplishments were to be evaluated, but also his or her orientation toward the collective and willingness to spur others on and to serve as a quick pace-setter. In short, the workpoint ratings were supposed to be treated as the community's judgment on each person's moral attainments.

These judgments on wages were intended also to have an ethical import in a separate respect. Under the task-rate system the strongest man in a team had been earning almost twice as much as the weakest man. An explicit goal of the Dazhai system was to narrow that gap. There was, again, a certain readiness within the village to pursue this. Many of the peasants, according to interviewees, agreed that the egalitarian leveling of the land reform and of the collectivization period of the 1950s had been justified.[9] The Dazhai system was presented as a further development of that tradition. It was supposed to reduce inequalities in earnings precisely because attitudes and not just strength would count. The weak man who tried his best would be given credit for it in his pay. The Four Cleanups workteam thus particularly could turn for active support to all those villagers who would directly benefit from the Dazhai program: the peasants who were weaker or, more precisely, who came from labor-weak households.

On the other side, whatever their agreement as to the greater morality of the Dazhai system, villagers who foresaw that their household's interests might be damaged generally were hesitant to embark on the new program. As one of the interviewees recalls, "Many of them thought that the task-rate system really wasn't so good; but since they themselves were good workers they wanted to keep it." Moreover, the new system entailed an untested risk; some of the team heads quietly voiced a concern that it would prove unmanageable and damage yields. They apparently felt that a community such as Chen Village, which was not far above the subsistence level of production, had precious little room for experiments. Had the choice been left in the hands of the teams, it seems doubtful that they would have ventured into the Dazhai system.

But in the midst of the Mao study campaign, no one was willing publicly to raise any self-interested arguments or conservative doubts about a program that so patently seemed progressive. There was a particular reluctance to object while the Four Cleanups workteam was in charge of village affairs. Only recently the workteam had investigated and browbeaten most of the peasant cadres for alleged acts of petty corruption. None now wanted to risk incensing the workteam by casting doubts upon its new mission. All ten production teams ended up endorsing the Dazhai experiment without serious public debate.

Operating Dazhai-Style: The First Years

The cadre workteam proceeded cautiously, knowing that the Dazhai method would not be easy to run effectively. One of the village's ten agricultural production teams—a team that had a very capable leadership and seemed the least divisive internally—was asked to pioneer the program with the workteam's aid. In the time-tested manner of campaigns, this production team served as the

---

9   Even a Chen Village landlord's son, whose family had lost everything due to the new order, remarked to me after he arrived in Hong Kong in the 1970s that "the good side of socialism is that earnings are more equal so that even the lame and the weak survive."

exemplar for the other nine teams. One of the members of that team recalls, "The team heads and team committees and Mao study counselors from all the production teams came to observe how our team did it. So did all of the village's Party and Communist Youth League members. That way, when they saw how our team could handle it, they wouldn't feel that it couldn't be done."

The onlookers went away largely convinced. It seems from interviews that most of the villagers wanted to believe in the new system's efficacy. Since their teams were already committed to the Dazhai program, they hoped it would confirm the promises made in the Mao study sessions. Some of them wanted the opportunity to prove their moral superiority; and all wanted to achieve improved living standards. If this new method could spur better work and higher production, they were willing to give it their best try. The Dazhai system, by its very nature, relied upon such a willingness. As one of the interviewees remarks, "In the beginning, *because* folks had trust in the Dazhai system, things went well in our village."

The success of early workpoint appraisal sessions depended not just on this spirit but also on careful planning. Before each of the appraisal sessions, the team head would gather together several strong, politically activist men to rehearse a smooth start to the session. It would be arranged for a few of them to volunteer from the audience to appraise themselves first, both to break the ice and to impart a proper atmosphere to the meeting. This was important because each person's appraisal was to start with a self-evaluation, something many peasants felt awkward to attempt in public.

At the main session, one of the prearranged volunteers would rise and deliver a short self-deprecating speech, to the effect that he had been making an attempt to follow the teachings of Chairman Mao, but to tell the truth, on such and such occasions he had not worked hard enough. He thought he deserved only 8.5 workpoints a day. He would try much harder in the future to work selflessly in the masses' interest.

Such a self-appraisal inevitably involved play-acting. There were a great many formal sessions in China in which people used an official rhetoric to say exactly what they were expected to say. They were now learning in Chen Village how to do so with self-evaluations. But in this initial phase of Chen Village's experience with the Dazhai system, say interviewees, the rhetoric was also taken seriously by many of the speakers. They did not want to seem hypocritical to themselves and others. Many of them did want to live up to Chairman Mao's teachings and do better work. When necessary, they did work overtime on their own. Moreover, such team members generally were determined that others should equally live up to their promises. A former Mao study counselor remarks, "People didn't dare make hypocritical promises at the meetings, because they'd get criticized if they didn't indeed do better. In the countryside this was easy to see."

After a person had presented his or her self-appraisal, other teammates would be asked to add their evaluations. But in those first months "they felt uncomfortable," recalls one of the villagers. "They'd never before judged other people right to their faces in this way. And besides, they felt that if they dared to speak out bluntly, when their own turn came people might raise lots of opinions about them." Those willing to speak up were usually the people who were beyond criticism—a few of the best male workers. For someone like that self-effacing activist who had requested 8.5 workpoints, they would offer praise and a suggestion that he receive a full 10 points a day—the top of the wage-point scale. One teammate after another would be called upon to concur.

At these early meetings, recollects an interviewee, not a single member of his team dared to request the full 10 workpoints. Almost all had requested less than they deserved and were subsequently upgraded by teammates. But all those who regularly had come late to work, or had lagged behind in their labor, or had missed team meetings came under criticism and saw the disapproval reflected in their workpoint rating.[10]

Every day, moreover, the team leaders and the strongest and most committed of the team members were organized to labor at a faster-than-usual clip that forced others to step up their own pace. Recalls the former Mao study counselor:

> These activists would be working very hard and would be mad others weren't trying so hard. [When the labor squad had its lunchtime Mao study session] they'd take the lead in speaking up about these things. They wouldn't mention any names. If you wanted to make a self-confession you decided on your own. But if they'd bring up a problem and you didn't correct yourself, then later you might get mentioned by name. "How come you aren't doing it right? We studied about this in the afternoon and you're still doing a bad job! Do you want your team to have enough to eat or not?" Ha, if you had these activists on the scene, you weren't going to have any laziness.

In these circumstances, the Chen Village teams did achieve an upward surge in production. The cadre workteam had introduced a Green Revolution rice strain. To grow properly, it required better water control and heavy amounts of fertilizers. New irrigation ditches needed to be dug; the paddy fields needed to be leveled; large quantities of extra compost needed to be collected. Under the Dazhai system, both the quantity and quality of the peasants' work rose more than

---

[10]   The scenario of these initial meetings was not successfully followed in the other four villages in my interview sample. The principal reason may have been that a Four Cleanups workteam had not played a hand in establishing the Dazhai method in these villages, nor organized a Mao study program to give the method the needed ideological underpinnings. In one of these other villages, "even in the very first evaluation meeting the people didn't really take political performance into consideration. When some did, others said, 'Are activist attitudes edible?' People would say, 'Counting task rates I'll work my ass off, but counting time, under this Dazhai stuff, I'll take the opportunity to have a rest'. . . . So both systems—task rates and time rates—were used simultaneously in my village without taking attitudes into consideration at all." Martin K. Whyte has also gathered descriptions from a number of interviewees from villages that similarly had set up the Dazhai program without the aid of a workteam and which, from the start, never got the system to operate properly. See Whyte's "The Tachai Brigade and Incentives for the Peasant," *Current Scene*, Vol. 7, No. 16 (August 15, 1969).

enough to meet the new labor demands. The Chen Villagers enjoyed the payoffs: by 1967, rice yields had nearly doubled. These successes boosted peasant morale and helped sustain intact the social pressures necessary for the Dazhai method's smooth operation.

A House Divided Against Itself

The Dazhai program was a double-edged sword, however, whose methods would, over time, cut both ways. On the one side, the system succeeded partly because the teams were communities whose members worried about each other's opinions. On the other side, the Dazhai program's eventual undoing was precisely this: it enouraged the peasants to be too sensitive about their standing among their neighbors. What created particular problems was the Dazhai system's concentration upon attitudes. Any judgments of a teammate's attitudes necessarily were subjective, in ways that observable and quantifiable criteria like strength or speed were not. This was one respect in which the Dazhai system was much more difficult to manage than the earlier group method of harvest-squad appraisals. Appraisals then had been confined to how much each member had produced; and since a man or woman could not help being weak or elderly, a low income under the earlier system had not impinged directly upon a person's sense of integrity. But now, under Dazhai, much more than just payments for work done had become involved in workpoint appraisals. The judgment on overall performance and attitudes was perceived as a measure of what the community thought of a member as a complete person. A lower appraisal implied a lower status. Indeed, the imprecise standard of attitudes inadvertently became a means to downgrade the ratings of people who were cantankerous and generally disliked. To retain their standing even more than to retain their earnings, such people learned to shed their reserve and to begin arguing vociferously for the workpoint rating they felt they deserved.

To reduce the acrimony, little more than a year after the introduction of the Dazhai system the team heads quietly abandoned attitudes as a criterion for the ratings. They never officially announced it; to follow the right political line, the fiction that good attitudes were being rewarded had to be preserved. The team heads simply steered appraisals toward the actual work accomplished.

Yet the mold had been set. Villagers had become accustomed to viewing the ratings as a measure of their comparative status, and most remained competitively alert to what they and their neighbors received. Many were intent to receive as good or better a rating than teammates they felt were of the same level, and at the same time they tried to prevent those who had been appraised lower than themselves from climbing up.

Within a couple of years, only the most politically devout team members any longer made a self-deprecating little speech or requested undervalued ratings. One interviewee who idealistically insisted on doing so discovered, to her considerable dismay, that two women with whom she was at odds quickly took the opportunity to congratulate her on her honesty, and that bemused teammates declined to speak up to rescue her from her own too-modest rating. At the next session she requested exactly what she considered she was worth.

A contrary manner of self-appraisal became increasingly common. Some participants began inflating their own appraisal in the hope that no one else would risk a quarrel by objecting. Rarely, though, did such a stratagem work: some teammate or other would insist upon keeping their own workpoint values higher than yours. Arguments gradually became rife. A wage system that specifically was intended to reinforce cooperation among teammates was becoming the cause of growing contention. The appraisal sessions increasingly were pitching personal interests and egos against the team members' common interests.

The weakest members of a team—the ill, the elderly and the handicapped—did not tend to be among the most quarrelsome at these sessions. They were embarrassed that they were a burden on the team and avoided making any scenes. Nor was it the strongest and most capable men who normally argued for better points. Their status was unchallengeable; they felt no need to quibble over a tenth of a workpoint, which comprised, after all, only 1 percent of their earnings—just a few cents per week. A tenth of a workpoint—the likely issue in disputes—only mattered to those concerned with fine distinctions in status. Almost always, interviewees agreed, these disputants were about average in their abilities. They felt they were making a real contribution to the team but some of them obviously felt insecure about their status and were jealous to safeguard it.

Interviewees agree, too, that teenagers tended to be a focus of the rating disputes. A teenager's physique and strength could show marked development from one agricultural season to the next, and their ratings therefore required constant re-evaluation. They normally were too embarrassed to speak up in their own behalf; but to their mortification, their mothers often felt no reluctance to pick up the gauntlet for them.

Indeed, almost every interviewee claimed that, to a very noticeable degree, women were more argumentative in these appraisal meetings than their husbands. Two reasons were discernible. First, as explained by a young woman from the village, men had far better opportunities to achieve a genuine status of their own. A majority of the men at one time or another would hold a post at the team or village level, but even the most capable and ambitious women were boxed in as women. The *symbol* of status represented by the workpoint system accordingly became more important to them. Second, being blocked from personal achievements, women more than men saw their social standing in the village as intertwined with that of their family and kin. Hence, they tended more than men to intervene in disputes to support the claims of relatives, thereby prolonging and widening the quarrels.

These difficulties were compounded in 1969 when the commune administration succeeded in forcing re-amalgamations of the very same teams that in 1962 had been divided in half. The new, larger teams would be able to control irrigation better and mechanize more efficiently. But with a doubling of each team's membership, the appraisal meetings became even more unwieldy. There were now twice as many teammates of one's own age and own capability with whom to compete, and more kin in the same team whom one could turn to for support. The government's national push in the late 1960s and early 1970s to combine teams inadvertently was undermining the government's simultaneous efforts to preserve the Dazhai system.

As the appraisal sessions in Chen Village grew more acrimonious, the best and most prestigious workers no longer were so willing to offer their disinterested appraisals. They did not want to risk getting unnecessarily caught up in a feud. The team heads themselves had to step in more regularly as the final arbiters of ratings. They began to dread the sessions.[11] Team members who received less than they had asked for carried their resentments out into the paddy fields; and the daily work of the cadres was made all the more difficult. The Dazhai method increasingly was generating what the Chinese call "mass/leadership contradictions."

Most team heads took the easy way out—scheduling fewer appraisal meetings. In 1966, when the system was first introduced, the meetings had been held every two weeks. According to government suggestions, once the system was successfully established fewer meetings would be needed; but Chen Village's cadres pushed for fewer sessions than the government could ever have expected. By 1971, the appraisal meetings were being convened only once every half year (at the very least, grain and cash had to be distributed after each of the two harvests).

But this avoidance of sessions only heightened the tensions when the peasants met. A half year's face was now at stake. Moreover, even the minuscule difference of a tenth of a workpoint per day now counted for something in monetary terms. Peasants who earlier had stayed out of the arguments found it worthwhile to expend that extra half hour at a meeting angling for a better rating. The sessions were becoming impossible to keep under control. Whereas the initial appraisal meetings of 1966 and 1967 had taken a couple of hours to settle, by 1970 the meetings frequently were lasting till dawn—and sometimes had to be resumed the next evening and occasionally even a third and fourth night. Each time the teams were left physically exhausted and internally divided.

By 1971 the team heads had concluded that the solution lay in simply giving each team member exactly the same rating as in the previous meeting. It seemed far better to have a brief meeting without appraisals than to endure the interminable arguments and subsequent backbiting. But by unofficially

---

[11]   An interviewee from another village recalls a somewhat different scenario. In that village the peasants feared getting on the wrong side of the team cadres and their families; and the team officers eventually controlled the sessions for their own benefits: "At the early sessions, the most difficult to appraise was the team head's wife. She was lazy but had the nerve to get up and say she ought to be considered top grade. For a whole hour, there was silence; no one stood up to support her, no one to oppose her. And the team head himself wouldn't step up and say anything once she'd made such claims. Eventually she got awarded a high rating. . . . My main complaints with Dazhai were that the cadres were better able to take advantage of it than they could with task rates, and that with Dazhai there was the feeling that if someone didn't work hard yet finagled high workpoints, then I won't work hard either."

converting the Dazhai system into a simple system of fixed salaries, the team heads were now granting people workpoints regardless of their work performance.[12]

The Dazhai program had entered the final phase in its decline. Up to now, whatever the terrible quarreling at appraisal sessions, the Dazhai method had operated reasonably well out in the fields. Teammates had continued to pressure each other into hard work. Some had been motivated by the prospects of higher yields and improved living standards all round. Others, less public spirited, had been angling to prove themselves better than their rivals. Still others had been spurred by their fear of scrutiny and criticism. But the Dazhai system itself had now been altered. Having evolved into fixed wages, even the incentives to compete for a higher status rating had been removed. Just as troubling, as far as the best workers were concerned, there no longer was even a fair spread in workpoints between the best and worst laborers.

Through the years, a group dynamic had been at work in the appraisal sessions. Whenever quarrels had arisen between workers of equivalent abilities, the teams had found that these could be resolved most conveniently by lifting the workpoint rating of the lower disputant to the same level as the higher, rather than infuriating the higher by lowering his or her points a notch. These inflationary compromises resulted eventually in a very narrow workpoint spread between the best and the worst, but any across-the-board attempt to re-widen the wage gap would have encountered the hostility of the many households that had benefited. The teams could not afford any additional divisiveness, and so cadres ignored the problem. In 1969, when a new cadre workteam stayed briefly in Chen Village, it expressed concern that the workpoint gap no longer provided equitable economic incentives, and the team heads concurred. But when the workteam left, not one of the teams tampered with the narrow spread.

Just how narrow the spread was can be seen in the following figures. At the initial 1966 appraisal meetings, the men's apportionments in one particular team had ranged from a low of 7.3 points to a high of 10, and the women's from a low of 5 points to a high of 7.5. By the early 1970s, the best still received 10, but the average man was getting 9.5 and the weakest 9.[13] The best male worker was now earning only a slim 5 percent more than the team's average and only 10 percent

---

[12] At a different village in my sample, the team leaders went a step further. They not only instituted a flat time wage; they entirely abandoned workpoint differentials and thereby removed the divisive associations between workpoints and status. "The highest—and the lowest—for a man was 10 points. All the women earned 9 points." Question: Why were there no differences at all in the wages of the men? "Because that would create conflicts."

[13] The elderly, semi-retired men who did odd chores for the team received 8.5 points, while the old women who had not yet retired were given 6.

more than his least capable and energetic neighbor. The spread among the women had become even narrower, from a high of 7.5 points to a low of 7.1.[14]

When production annually had been expanding, the strongest peasants had not particularly minded that their less productive neighbors were obtaining a disproportionate share through this gradual narrowing of workpoint differences. Since their own families were living better than ever before, they felt they could afford a measure of altruism: "They didn't want to hurt other people, so they felt 'Well, it doesn't really matter'." But by about 1970, the village's economy started souring.

Over the years the Green Revolution grain had been growing less resistant to blight, and the state was not providing substitute seed varieties of any quality. But a more potent factor in the village's economic troubles was, simply and purely, the heavy hand of China's bureaucracy. The national, provincial and county bureaucrats, having recently been pummeled in the turmoil of the Cultural Revolution, seemed concerned primarily with their own political skins. As noted in Chapter One, in the uncertain political winds of the early 1970s they were pushing any policy that seemed safely leftist. They pressed the village to "self-reliantly" grow crops such as wheat and cotton that were woefully unsuited to the climate; to forgo profitable team vegetable plots and to fill up money-making fish ponds in order to plant yet more grain; and then, as national slogans and policies periodically flip-flopped, to re-excavate fish ponds and "diversify."[15] The Chen Village peasants frustratedly watched the value of their workpoints decline from one year to the next.

---

[14]   During the harvest seasons, when the teams were very short of labor, the men's top rating temporarily was set at 15 workpoints and the top women's at 12, to take account of the longer and tougher workdays. But the wage spread among the men and, separately, among the women remained as narrow as during the regular seasons.

It is evident in the figures presented in the main text that the lowest rating ever given to a man was higher than the highest rating allowed for a woman. The traditional view that defined all men's work as *ipso facto* superior to women's work had persisted. But in about 1968-69, this came under challenge. Some of the young women from Canton who had settled in Chen Village began agitating for better ratings for women and were able to convince some of the strong young unmarried women to join in. Recalls a young man: "At that time other communes were talking about 'equal work, equal pay' for both men and women, so the young women settlers felt they could begin talking about it in Chen Village. A woman of 7.5 workpoints actually might work better than a man of 9; but the problem was that the women couldn't plough. This was the weak men's last resort. Ploughing had always been a man's job, and it was an important job. There were two women in my team who could plough pretty well on their private plots, but the men would never ask a woman to do any ploughing when allocating labor." As a group, the men of Chen Village were adamant: 7.5 remained the women's maximum.

[15]   See Chen, Madsen and Unger, *Chen Village*, Ch. 9.

The stronger team members, finding themselves with a shrunken portion of an annually shrinking pie, began to feel that neighbors who contributed less to team output were unjustly benefiting at their expense. Some of them began to slacken in their work and to recoup their declining earnings by putting more energy into their private plots. As increasing numbers of the best laborers stopped serving as pacesetters, the pressures upon the others to keep up were relaxed. Ultimately whole teams began to slough off. The influence of the peer group milieu had swung almost 180 degrees. Before, even lazy members had had to work well lest they be accused of taking advantage of all their neighbors' hard work. Now, conversely, people were shunning hard work for fear of being taken advantage of.

The Dazhai system was malfunctioning in villages throughout China. For once, the Party leadership in Beijing grew concerned. Hints appeared in the government press as early as 1971-72 that, if need be, teams should abandon the remnants of their Dazhai effort and revert to task rates. Many of the team cadres in Chen Village would have liked to comply. But they were reluctant to go out on a limb. Until recently, task-rate systems had been condemned in the mass media for encouraging selfishness and "petty-bourgeois thinking." More than mere hints would be required now to dispel the team cadres' fears of plunging into a dangerous political blunder.

Higher levels in Guangdong Province provided them in 1973 with an "emperor's new clothes" solution. A new slogan was announced: "Repudiate Liu Shaoqi's task rates; permit Mao Zedong's task rates." So far as the Chen Villagers could see, the two systems seemed entirely similar; but the verbal legerdemain made it safer to revert.[16]

Under the Dazhai system of face-to-face appraisals, the stronger workers had felt embarrassed to recommend sharply reduced earnings for weaker friends. Under task rates, however, everyone would simply be paid in accordance with what they produced. There would never be a need to confront neighbors directly and personally in any meetings. The weak would be able to blame not neighbors' appraisals but only their own slow labor for their low incomes. Task rates, in short, provided an effective means to rewiden the earnings gap between the stronger families and the weaker.

The team memberships accordingly were divided on the issue of Dazhai versus task rates. An interviewee recalls,

> Our labor squad's head is strong and so's his wife, so they wanted to revert to task rates. But the squad head's elder brother is lame and his wife is near blind, and they *hated* task rates. So right among those relatives, you found a

---

16   In a village in a different region of Guangdong, according to an emigrant interviewee, a different political ploy was offered: "When Lin Biao fell in 1971, this so-called Dazhai system was said to have been distorted by him, as an example of his empty-headed politics. They began talking about adopting the correct policy of 'to each according to his work'." That village returned to the task-rate structure in 1972.

"contradiction," one wanting to go back to task rates and the other strongly opposed.

A couple of the brigade-level leaders in Chen Village sided with the weaker and the poorer. But almost all of the team heads threw their weight toward task rates. It would bring an end to their unhappy need to badger team members into doing work. One after another in the summer of 1973, the team heads steered their teams back into task-rate programs.

Task Rates and Contracting Revisited

Even though task-rate payments again were structured exactly as under "Liu Shaoqi's task rates," in one respect the revived system now did operate differently. In the mid-1960s, before Dazhai, few ordinary peasants would have bawled out a teammate who did sloppy work, for traditionally to cause someone to lose face had been a breach of etiquette. But under Dazhai, a "social contract" had been erected. Under its ground rules, anyone overly careless could be loudly reprimanded. This Dazhai norm now carried over into the revived task-rate system's operations: "Nowadays [1975], if folks get caught transplanting the seedlings too carelessly, just so as to get more planted in a hurry, other folks would tell them off." The concern about "face" had been turned on its head: whereas earlier the norms involving face had protected careless workers from being criticized, the threat of public embarrassment now helped keep potential offenders in line. But even with this, the renewed system all but invited shortcuts. Interviewees report that when task rates again became the basis for rewards, the quality of work worsened.

A great many of China's villages, by the accounts of China's official news media, were, like Chen Village, caught in agricultural slumps. In fact, large numbers of these villages apparently were facing considerably greater problems than Chen Village. The Party Central Committee in Beijing reacted in the late 1970s. Mao had died; the radical Gang of Four had fallen shortly thereafter; and the new leadership, once entrenched in power, felt willing to countenance a marked further retreat from the Dazhai system. If under task rates China's peasants were not working hard enough or effectively enough, or were not caring enough about the quality of their work, then the teams ought to revert to a system that tied payments even more directly to the productivity of each person's labor. It was now felt that perhaps the very size of the teams (that large pool of some fifteen to fifty households) inhibited peasants from seeing clearly enough the connections between their own work contribution and their returns from collective productivity. The national leadership decided that the solution would be to encourage teams to decentralize and to hand over decision-making and the sharing of profits to smaller labor groupings.

The new directives came down through the Guangdong provincial Party in early 1979.[17] In compliance, the Chen Village teams organized small labor squads of several families, which negotiated quotas with the team leaders, planted and tended the fields, and divided among themselves the quota payments and the bonuses for surplus production. Within another year, again under official urgings, Chen Village shifted to individual household contracts, paralleling the contract system of the early 1960s. Indeed, production was allowed to decentralize to the point that even harvesting was entrusted to family hands. Beyond a quota of grain that had to be sold to the state, households were to be allowed to keep or sell privately all the crops they grew.

Conclusions

Chen Village, in a period of two decades, had swung from a household contract system to the Maoist experiment of Dazhai appraisals and then, like a pendulum that has mounted the crest of its arc, had fallen back by degrees to the opposite crest of the arc and a revived program of contracts and family farming. By 1981, agricultural production, though not land ownership, had been largely transferred into private hands in the village.

What should we make of this long swing into the Dazhai system and back?

It is clear, for one thing, that in Chen Village there was a pattern to these shifts. The household contracts of the early 1960s, the subsequent system of task rates, the Dazhai method, and the reverse shifts were all introduced partly as solutions to the problems that had emerged in the immediately preceding programs of remuneration.

What we witnessed, however, was not simply an evolving sequence of local problems and local responses. Intervening was a complex interplay between state and collective. Each new program was "suggested" by the state. This intervention was based partly upon the state's general awareness of the problems faced in China's collectives, but sometimes, as with the Dazhai system, it was based also upon the Party leadership's ideological commitment. Once a program was introduced, the teams did possess some leeway in modifying each remuneration system as they wanted, but they always had to keep an eye fixed on Party policies to make sure they were operating within the parameters of what was politically permissible. For instance, the Chen Village teams were quietly able to alter the shape of the Dazhai program several times as stopgap remedies to local difficulties, but they had to stick with an ostensibly Dazhai-type framework until new upper-level suggestions let them pull free in 1973.

It was observed that in Chen Village the Dazhai program operated reasonably well in the rice fields (if not in appraisal sessions) until about 1971—and within just another two years the village was allowed to abandon the Dazhai scheme. But

---

[17]   Canton Radio, January 21, 1979, in *Foreign Broadcast Information Service: China Daily Report,* January 24, 1979, p. H1.

that had not been the experience of many other communities (including several in my small sample of other Guangdong villages). Caught from the start with a Dazhai system they could not handle successfully, they still had to make the pretense of an effort, at a considerable cost to agricultural productivity.

In this respect, despite all the problems it faced, Chen Village was among the more fortunate villages. In fact, its experiences with the Dazhai system were considerably better than any of the other villages that I know about through interviews. A Four Cleanups cadre workteam had carefully laid the groundwork in Chen Village for the Dazhai experiment; the new system had been willingly accepted by many of the villagers; and their faith was rewarded for several years with rapidly rising living standards. Chen Village accorded us a glimpse of a community grappling, initially with success, to operate almost solely on the basis of collective interests.

This being the case, what do Chen Village's experiences say about a production team as a "community," or about its members' capacity to cooperate for collective goals?

It was observed, for a start, that the Chen Villagers, though always concerned for their own family interests, were not exclusively so. They understood that concerted efforts to raise agricultural productivity would raise living standards all around. And most of them even were willing to support the Dazhai method's more egalitarian apportionment of wages—just so long as the increased welfare of their less capable neighbors was not ultimately at their own family's expense.

The difficulty was to reconcile the family's and the community's interests. Here, the production teams always faced the "free-rider" problem. Not all of one's neighbors could be expected to put collective goals on a par with their own more narrow interests, and thus, not all of them necessarily would contribute their fair share of work. That being so, who but a fool would exhaust himself laboring hard in behalf of such "free-riding" neighbors?

The Dazhai experiment promised answers to this conundrum. As observed, it was introduced into Chen Village in the midst of a major Mao study campaign. With Mao's sacred thought preaching the higher morality of the collective road to prosperity, shirkers under Dazhai risked being tagged as politically and morally backward. Pressures could effectively be brought to bear on this point, for the peasants' private concerns had always been of two types. While concerned with their own economic well-being, many team members were equally concerned about their standing in the community. In the mutual-appraisal sessions, this desire for a better status could be employed to counter the tugs both of laziness and of personal short-term interests.

There were dilemmas here, however. To ensure conformity, the Dazhai system could play upon the strength of community sanctions—but only by exacerbating the small-minded anxieties to retain "face" traditionally common to an in-grown village milieu. In the end, as has been seen, the Dazhai wage program bent and broke under tensions partly of its own making. When the heightened competitive desires among neighbors to defend their status resulted, at one and the same time, in an erosion of team morale and an inordinately narrow wage gap, the strongest and most respected workers began to consider themselves the victims of free riders. As has been observed, when they opted to spend more of their time and energy on their private plots, the Dazhai system of work incentives and community sanctions collapsed from within.

Ultimately, in that long reverse swing of the pendulum away from the Dazhai system, the household contract system resolved the same problems of controlling free riders that the Dazhai method had tackled—but from the opposite extreme. Household contracts—essentially, a return to family farming—eliminated the difficulties associated with collective cooperation by, quite simply, terminating collective cooperation.

By pushing for collective goals by way of instigating a contest among team members to preserve "face," the Maoist Dazhai program had frayed the very social fabric it sought to strengthen. In Chen Village, it had left in its wake a diminished faith in collective solutions—indeed, as shall be observed in the next chapter, a willingness among the majority of the peasantry to dismantle the collective organization altogether. The failed Maoist dream has bequeathed an ironic legacy.

II

The Post-Mao Countryside

Chapter Five

DISBANDING COLLECTIVE AGRICULTURE

China's move away from collective agriculture affected the lives of three-quarters of a billion people. It constituted the single most important policy shift in China since the introduction of collectives in the mid-1950s.

In an attempt to examine decollectivization and the return to family farming while interviewees' memories were still fresh, I conducted a series of interviews in mid-1983 with twenty-eight emigrants from the Chinese countryside. They were working in Hong Kong at the time and regularly returned to their home villages to visit their parents, spouses and children. Eighteen of them were from villages in Guangdong Province, and the remaining ten came from villages spread across eight other provinces and regions.[1] All of the twenty-eight had returned home on at least one extended visit, ranging from a week to several months in duration, during the year prior to the interviews.

At the time, such an interview survey was well-nigh impossible to organize inside China. Chinese officials saw no advantage in providing foreigners with room to conduct a survey that might pose ticklish questions about politically sensitive policies. Nor, in the absence of such on-the-spot surveys, did China's news media provide any sort of reliable substitute for interviews. In fact, for reasons that will be discussed below, the Chinese press consistently distorted coverage of what was occurring in the countryside during the early 1980s. The consequence was that the picture painted in the Chinese press of how decollectivization came about and the part played in it by farmers differed markedly from the accounts of interviewees.

Who Divided the Land: the State or the Farmers?

The Chinese press at the time of decollectivization conveyed the impression that villages throughout China were permitted, at their own discretion, to determine what type of agrarian system they would adopt. The slogan blazoned by the news media was *Yin di zhi yi* (Implement in accordance with local conditions), and detailed descriptions of all sorts of locally determined solutions filled the Chinese media. A 1981 handbook portrayed fifteen quite different systems supposedly

---

[1]   These ten interviewees came from Anhui, Fujian, Hubei, Jiangsu, Jiangxi, Shandong and Zhejiang provinces, and a suburban Tianjin farming district.

being tried out simultaneously in the countryside,[2] running the gamut from specialized large-scale work groups in villages where mechanization and irrigation networks were well developed, to near-total abandonment of collectives in China's poorest districts. There, said the news media, families were dividing up all the fields and farm equipment and each household was beginning to work its own allotment separately, almost as though the fields were private holdings. Initially, the Chinese press claimed that only the 10 percent of China's villages that were the most impoverished would ever adopt this least collectivist of all options.[3] But according to the Chinese mass media of 1981-83, this system of independent family production (variously called *bao gan dao hu* [contracting management to the household] or, more commonly, *dabaogan* [big management contracting])[4] was preferred eventually by the vast majority of China's peasantry. So, claimed the Chinese press, after trying out various other methods, village after village, even in the wealthier districts, opted to break up the collective holdings. By early 1984, newspapers proclaimed that more than 90 percent of China's agricultural production teams, by popular grassroots demand, had decided to decollectivize into family-operated smallholdings.[5]

Reports from interviewees suggest a rather different scenario of decollectivization. Fully twenty-six out of the twenty-eight villages in my sample had indeed decollectivized into family smallholdings by the end of 1982. But contrary to official proclamations, twenty-four of the twenty-eight interviewees related that in their own villages the decision as to precisely what type of system would be adopted was made exclusively by officials at levels far above the village. In only two villages had the team cadres and peasants themselves taken the initiative, and in one of these cases they jumped the gun and swung over to family smallholdings in a belief that the instructions to do so would soon come down from above.[6] All of the other twenty-six villages passively waited for upper levels to tell them what to do; and when the upper levels did move, in only two of

---

[2]   Liu Hongli et al., *Nongye shengchan zerenzhi* (Agricultural Production Responsibility Systems) (Shanghai: Renmin Chubanshe, 1982 printing).

[3]   *Hong Qi* (Red Flag), No. 20, 1980, pp. 11-15.

[4]   To avoid confusion, henceforth only the term *dabaogan* will be employed, since the phrase *bao gan dao hu* closely resembles the title of a different method of decentralized production that will be discussed later in the chapter, *bao chan dao hu*.

[5]   For example, *Renmin ribao* (People's Daily), January 18, 1984, p. 1.

[6]   An account of the machinations in this community is in Jonathan Unger, "De-Collectivization in a Guangdong Village: An Interview," in John Burns and Stanley Rosen (eds.), *Policy Conflicts in Post-Mao China: A Documentary Survey with Analysis* (Armonk: M.E. Sharpe, 1986), pp. 274-79. The community, a remote hamlet, constituted a production team, and the team head's brother (my interviewee), who had emigrated to Hong Kong, had written home to relay Hong Kong newspaper reports that a return to household farming was already spreading across the Chinese countryside.

these villages were the peasantry informed that they could choose for themselves whatever system of production they preferred. Of the remaining twenty-four, fully twenty-three were shifted, without choice, into the *dabaogan* system of family smallholdings. Only one village among the twenty-eight received orders *not* to adopt family smallholdings—and this was a village of a rather uncommon type: one that specialized in sericulture. Presumably as a means of assuring state control of silk-cocoon sales, the instructions to the village stipulated that its silkworm rearing was to remain firmly in the collective sector.

Chinese newspapers and journals in the first half of the 1980s reported that many of the suburban vegetable-producing villages similarly retained a collective structure. The articles stressed that the sophistication of the irrigation networks in such villages, the high degree of mechanization there, and complex marketing schedules all would preclude the fragmentation of land into tiny family-managed plots. In late 1982, I wandered into a suburban village of this type near Beijing that had indeed adopted a system of specialized work squads rather than moving to decollectivize. But that Beijing village may not have been representative of the vegetable-producing villages of that time. My sample of twenty-eight villages includes two that specialized in vegetable production for urban markets—one near Guangzhou and the other near Tianjin—and both villages followed instructions in the early 1980s to divide all their fields into family smallholdings.

In short, my interviews suggest that most of the Chinese countryside was channeled from above into a single type of organizational structure, irrespective of the types of crops grown or the level of local economic development. Moreover, contrary to the repeated claims of the Chinese news media and top political leaders alike, very few villages were offered any choice in the matter. In the years since my 1983 interviews, I inquired in eight other villages in different parts of China as to how decollectivization had occurred, and all eight villages had similarly been shifted into family smallholdings (*dabaogan*) without any local choice in the matter.

Why do the interview findings differ so dramatically from the official press coverage of government newspapers at that time? Had China's top leadership directed the news media to engage in deliberate and sustained distortions as to the real nature of the decollectivization process? Or were the leaders in Beijing themselves not entirely cognizant of the manner in which their programs for change in the countryside were being carried out at the grassroots? The evidence from the interviews and from Chinese publications, coupled with what we know of past campaigns in the People's Republic, strongly suggest that both factors were at work simultaneously.

To understand why this confusing scenario of half-conscious distortion occurred, it is necessary to look back to 1977, after Mao's death, when China's new leadership, in an attempt to revitalize the agricultural economy, began gingerly to dismantle the various "ultra-leftist" rural policies of the previous decade. To restore incentives, in 1977 some of the leadership in Beijing had begun pressing for China's production teams to decentralize into the hands of smaller labor groupings (*bao chan dao zu*). Under the new dispensation, as was observed for Chen Village in the previous chapter, a team's lands were to be distributed among smaller labor squads, which were to hand in the yields at harvest's end in exchange for payments from the production team. In turn, the squad was supposed to apportion these payments among its members on the basis of how much work each peasant individually had accomplished.

In my sample, eleven of the twenty-eight villages had experienced this program of decentralization between 1977 and 1980; and every one of these eleven villages simply had obeyed directives coming down to them, rather than being given leeway to take any initiative themselves.[7] Just as significantly, the decision as to whether a given village should participate or not did not follow any discernible standards of economic logic.[8] Villages had been selected in a seemingly arbitrary fashion by county and commune-level officials who had concluded that it was politically expedient to demonstrate that villages under their own jurisdiction were shifting into the new program.

This decentralization into labor squads brought mixed results. In some of the villages surveyed, productivity improved; in others, peasants continued to exhibit a disinclination to labor. Some of the new leaders who were politically associated with Deng Xiaoping were convinced that these lingering problems could not entirely be blamed upon any residual peasant disaffection with the radicalism and bureaucratic interference of Mao's final years. The persisting difficulties, they apparently believed, stemmed from a more far-reaching problem of two-and-a-half decades' duration: too great a degree of socialism had originally been imposed.

Two and a half decades earlier, during the mid-1950s, a debate had occurred within the Party's top echelons. Leaders like Liu Shaoqi had felt that China was not yet ready for collectivization. As long as modern agricultural machinery was not widely available and farming remained labor-intensive, farmers should work their own plots of land. Mao, championing the other side in this debate, had argued that China should not delay until agricultural mechanization was feasible. He was convinced that production in a system of collective agriculture would climb by means of a more efficient large-scale organization of land and labor. Mao pushed his beliefs through in 1955-56 in a "high tide" of collectivization.

---

[7]   During the same years, two other villages in the survey participated in a scheme called *bao chan dao ren* (contracting to the individual). Under this, the sowing and harvesting of the fields remained a collective endeavor, but each farmer was separately assigned responsibility for all of a given field's weeding and other maintenance, in exchange for team workpoints. In both of the villages that temporarily tried this program, the decision to implement it was imposed from above. Why they were selected is unclear; the two did not differ significantly from other villages in my sample in terms of political history, income, crop types, and so forth.

[8]   For example, these eleven villages in the sample had not, as a group, been noticeably poorer or better off than the seventeen villages that did not participate, nor had their experiences with collective agriculture been discernibly less satisfactory.

Now, in the late 1970s, part of the leadership was indicating that the Party's agrarian policies since the mid-1950s may have been misguided.

A small percentage of the peasantry in some of the poorest parts of China were simultaneously beginning to test, in the late 1970s, whether they could return to family farming. As was observed in Chapter One, in such impoverished marginal agricultural districts, but not elsewhere, officials under Mao had customarily looked the other way when peasants violated state policy. The evidence strongly suggests that it was only in these desperately poor districts that villages dared in the late 1970s to take the initiative in moving beyond labor squads. One of the villages in my sample was located in precisely such a marginal district—Fengyang County in Anhui Province, which coincidentally would subsequently become famous in China as the first county to move in this direction. This was one of the only two villages in my interview survey that did not simply respond to orders from above. My informant from this village has confided:

> I was the team accountant at the time, and I said to the team head that since the labor squads weren't working out well, let's just hand out the fields to the families. On our own initiative, we secretly did so in early 1979. I kept two account books, one for the authorities above us and one for real. I was prepared to be punished, but I felt that with villagers going hungry, dividing up the land made the most sense.

This interviewee was lucky. In January 1979, in the wake of a drought, the provincial Party secretary, Wan Li, visited Fengyang County and declared, "family sideline production shouldn't be restricted, let them do it. . . . In fact, individual farming is nothing to get excited about. . . . I only fear that production will not be raised. As long as production is increased, any method is fine."[9] That same year, the illicit effort of one particular backwater hamlet in Fengyang to divide up the fields among households was endorsed by the Party committee of the prefecture that contains Fengyang County, and two forms of household farming in this prefecture's poor counties received the prefectural leadership's blessing.[10]

---

[9]   Joseph Fewsmith, *Dilemmas of Reform in China: Political Conflict and Economic Debate* (Armonk: M.E. Sharpe, 1994), p. 29. On this and the subsequent series of events, also see Dali L. Yang, *Calamity and Reform in China*, pp. 149-176.

[10]   The former Party secretary of this prefecture has written an article describing these early events, which makes clear the role played by himself and Wan Li in supporting, legitimizing and promoting household production. He also describes how, after Wan Li was promoted out of Anhui, the new provincial leadership temporarily sought to reverse Wan's policies. It is of political interest that the article's Conclusion openly contradicts the wealth of evidence presented in the main body of the article by suddenly upholding the Party's legend that decollectivization was entirely spontaneous, and a stirring title was appended in keeping with this official Party line: Wang Yushao, "Dabaogan shi yiwan nongmin de zijue xuanze"

Under *bao chan dao hu* (contracting production to the household), the first of the experiments that were sanctioned under Wan Li's aegis in 1979 (he personally endorsed it in February of that year),[11] each family, under the supervision of its team, was allocated responsibility for cultivating given plots of land. As was observed in the previous chapter, this was the same system, using the very same title, that Chen Village and many other villages had temporarily adopted nearly two decades earlier in the devastating wake of the Great Leap Forward's collapse. Once again in the late 1970s in Fengyang County, the production team provided each family with implements, seed, and fertilizer, and at harvest time the family delivered all the crops to the team, which paid the family in workpoints based on the size of the yields. The family, in short, was given the freedom to organize its own daily labor, but it could not decide for itself what to grow and it could not sell any of the crops on its own.

Under the second experiment, *dabaogan* (the so-called big management contracting), land ownership also remained with the team, but the individual households could use the land that was allotted to them to diversify into any crops they liked just so long as they used a portion of the land to help meet the team's crop-quota deliveries to the state. They could sell their remaining crops on their own, either to the state purchasing stations or on the free market. This *dabaogan* system would leave little role for the collective teams. For all intents and purposes, team members would be transformed into independent peasant smallholders (albeit without the right to sell the land or to put it to nonagricultural uses). Fengyang County, the home of my interviewee, became the officially sanctioned pioneer of this system: in early 1980 Wan Li visited the production team in Fengyang that had first received permission to practice *dabaogan*, and personally endorsed the system for this type of terribly impoverished district.

Wan Li was among the more prominent of Deng Xiaoping's backers, and his endorsement of household cultivation in impoverished districts gained political visibility when, in early 1980, he was elevated to the Party Politburo in Beijing and appointed deputy premier in charge of agriculture. Very soon after arriving in Beijing, during the Spring Festival, he received support for his Anhui policies from top leaders such as Chen Yun and Hu Yaobang,[12] and within a few more

---

(Household Farming Was Entirely the Self-Determined Choice of the Peasants), *Dangdai wenxian* (Current Documentation), No. 6, 1998, pp. 37-42. On what actually occurred in Anhui, see also Xu Yueyi, "Anhui nongcun dabaogan de qiyuan he fazhan" (The Origins and Development of Household Farming in Anhui Villages), *Dangdai Zhongguo shi yanjiu* (Historical Research on Contemporary China), No. 6, 1998, pp. 27-36. I am grateful to Warren Sun for bringing these sources to my attention.

11   Xu Yueyi, ibid., p. 27.

12   Ding Longjia, *Gaige cong zheli qibu: Zhongguo nongcun gaige* (Reform Took Off from Here: Reforms in China's Villages) (Hefei: Anhui Renmin Chubanshe, 1998), p. 145. On the support group in Beijing that lobbied for *bao chan dao hu* and *dabaogan*, which included

weeks, in May 1980, Deng Xiaoping personally weighed in on behalf of his programs. Deng declared in a speech that

> After the relaxation of agricultural policy, some places suitable to *bao chan dao hu* have adopted it, and the change for the better has been quick. In Anhui province's Feixi county, where the great majority of the production teams have adopted *bao chan dao hu*, the increases in production have been big. . . . In Fengyang county, most of the production teams have adopted *dabaogan*, and in a year's time they have *fanshen*ed [the farmers' circumstances have been completely altered in a favorable way]. . . . Currently some of our cadres don't sufficiently consider what is appropriate to local conditions, to do things that economically benefit the masses of people. They still handle things in the old ways, and their thinking isn't liberated.[13]

Deng did not specify that other regions of China should adopt *bao chan dao hu* or *dabaogan*. Nor was his speech published or quoted in the news media. But at a central forum he had committed himself to the schemes' legitimacy and viability and had challenged rural officials to show their colors.

At the time, across a number of fronts, Deng's faction was pressing the point that it was necessary to abandon rigid dogma and "seek truth from facts." Such a premise implied that the leadership's legitimacy should be judged in terms of its pragmatic accomplishments. Anything less than rapid success for the controversial shifts away from collective production would provide opponents of the Deng faction with a strong case for bringing down Wan Li; and that, in turn, might even weaken Deng Xiaoping. Very clearly, his faction had a major stake in the success of the *bao chan dao hu* and *dabaogan* experiments. Since *dabaogan*, even more than *bao chan dao hu*, represented a repudiation of collective agriculture, it became a particular point of contention between Deng's backers and a number of provincial and lower-level rural leaders across China. Some of them saw Deng's various proposals for economic reform as ideologically retrograde, and others feared to let *dabaogan* be implemented anywhere in their territory lest they ultimately be accused of anti-Maoist thinking, just as had repeatedly happened to unwary Party leaders during the past two decades.

To counter such resistance, starting in the latter half of 1980, in general terms, without naming anyone, Party bureaucrats at county and lower levels who opposed letting poor villages turn toward the program began to be attacked in the press for ultra-leftist thinking. The hint was effective. Having learned from experience always to tack with the political winds, rural officials soon were endeavoring to show that the ultra-leftist tag most certainly did not apply to

---

Deng Liqun and a group of well-connected young people, see Joseph Fewsmith, *Dilemmas of Reform in China*, Ch. 1.

[13] See Deng Xiaoping, "Guanyu nongcun zhengce wenti" (On Questions of Rural Policy), *Deng Xiaoping wenxuan* (Selected Writings of Deng Xiaoping) (Beijing: Renmin Chubanshe, 1994), pp. 315-17.

themselves. In several provinces such as Heilongjiang, Hebei and Jiangsu, where provincial Party secretaries held firm against *dabaogan*, this push was temporarily stalled, but even there, albeit more slowly, increasing numbers of villages were soon being shifted into *dabaogan*.

To be sure, the Deng faction had not called for a division of the land among households in all or even most parts of China, nor would such calls be made publicly for several years to come. The press continued throughout to stress that such divisions in team property would be of benefit largely to the poorest and most poorly organized villages. But after the middle of 1980 the shift toward *dabaogan* began to take on many of the bureaucratic features of the collectivization drive of 1956. In that earlier time, in reaction to pushes from Mao, provincial and county officials had competed to demonstrate their dedication and the progressive spirit of their districts by prodding rapidly growing numbers of villages into socialism, supposedly voluntarily. Now, in the early 1980s, a similar yet contrary campaign was rippling across China. The officials this time were competing to show that they could outdo each other in re-introducing the peasant smallholding economy.

From the latter half of 1980 onward, as this contest quietly gathered momentum, villages in many parts of the countryside were being shifted into the *dabaogan* family smallholding system irrespective of whether they were poor or well off. My survey data illustrate this clearly. Seven of the villages in my sample adopted the *dabaogan* system of household smallholdings in 1980, another fourteen in 1981, and another four in 1982; and there were no significant differences in living standards among these three sets of villages. Nor, if we concentrate on just the eighteen villages in Guangdong Province (so as to reduce the possibility of any distortions in my data caused by differing provincial policies), do we find any substantiating evidence for the claims of China's news media that *dabaogan* was being tried out first among the poorer villages. The Guangdong villages in the sample that shifted to *dabaogan* in 1980 were no poorer on average than those that shifted in 1981, and the latter were no poorer than those in 1982; nor did the villages that shifted earlier tend to be situated in poorer counties or prefectures. As a consequence of this piecemeal rush by rural officials to conform politically, by the end of 1983 97.8 percent of all of the production teams in China had parceled out their land to households in the *dabaogan* system, according to official Chinese government statistics.[14] In line with the "one cut of the knife" conformity of the Chinese political system, 99.1

---

[14]   *Jianguo yilai nongye hezuohua shiliao huibian* (A Compilation of Historial Materials on Agricultural Cooperativization Since the Establishment of the People's Republic) (Beijing: Zhonggong Dangshi Chubanshe, 1992), p. 1390. According to these official statistics, only 1.7 percent of the production teams had been shifted into *bao chan dao hu* as of the end of 1983.

percent of all of China's production teams had adopted the system by the close of 1984.[15]

It is not clear whether the leadership in Beijing was altogether aware that the claims of the news media had been false when the press trumpeted during the first one-and-a-half years of the new rural campaign that *dabaogan* was being adopted largely in poor districts or when the newspapers proclaimed the spontaneous, voluntary, grassroots nature of all of the villages' turn toward the program. After all, much as in the 1956 collectivization campaign, the various levels of the bureaucracy were apparently reporting upward precisely what the leadership was hinting it wanted to hear: in this case, that the villages in their jurisdiction were voluntarily choosing *dabaogan*.

The lie would have been given to such an Emperor's New Clothes arrangement had the peasantry in much of China resisted decollectivization. But quite to the contrary, my interview survey of 1983 suggests that the great majority in most villages welcomed the new developments (though we shall also see later that a minority were adamantly opposed). Most of the households were calculating that with *dabaogan* they would have the freedom to scramble for a living more effectively. Before, the state had been regularly imposing irrational policies from above; now decollectivization into a myriad of family smallholdings promised to loosen the bureaucracy's stranglehold on production. Before, brigade and team cadres had had the authority—and a daily need—to bring pressures to bear against ordinary peasants; now the system of near-independent family smallholdings would entirely eliminate the cadres' daily supervision and, by pulling the land and other resources out of their control, would severely curtail their powers over the peasants. Under the collectives, the peasantry had been required to devote most of their days to raising low-priced grain on the collective fields; now many peasants foresaw that, by controlling the use of their own time, they would be able to put their spare hours into endeavors that paid better. One of the interviewees observes that when *dabaogan* was initiated: "We felt like birds freed from a cage." Within Party circles, the knowledge that the program was popular among the peasants seems to have effectively obscured the issue of whether the change was being implemented voluntarily or not.

Notwithstanding this popular support for the dissolution of collective production, it is not at all certain whether, if the peasants had been given a chance to select a new system on their own, most of the villages would have adopted *dabaogan* as their first choice. To subsist as independent agricultural households entails palpable risks. In case of illness or a failed crop, families no longer would be able to count on the team's pooled collective land and resources as a safety net against personal disaster. My interviews contained a clue that, had the decision been the peasants' to make, many communities might well have stopped short of dividing the collective property to such an extent: of the only two villages in my

---

[15]   Ibid.

sample that were allowed to select a new system on their own, one did opt for *dabaogan*, but the second of these villages decided to reject *dabaogan* in favor of the more collectivist *bao chan dao hu* system.

In sum, the evidence suggests that a complex and unplanned interplay between the top and bottom levels of the bureaucratic structure, involving ambiguous directives from the top and competitive pressures among politically nervous lower-level officials, had culminated in the countryside's near-total abandonment of the collectives. There had been no master plan, no deliberate effort from above to steer all of rural China uniformly down a single path. Yet, due to the nature of Chinese political organization and the legacy of Maoist bureaucratic practices, that is precisely what occurred. By a peculiar concatenation of events, all of rural China was launched into an entirely new agrarian order.

This is not to say that the top leadership was at all displeased with the outcome. The supposedly voluntary surge toward decollectivization seemed to vindicate their view of what had gone wrong in the countryside during the previous two and a half decades.

Most Western-language specialists in the field of China studies, with a few notable exceptions,[16] have presumed that a very different scenario of decollectivization occurred in China in the late 1970s and early 1980s. Several publications have strongly influenced the field, arguing that the great bulk of China's farmers spontaneously took the initiative to decollectivize and return to family farming, in the face of government opposition or stand-offishness. For instance, Andrew Watson, based upon the articles that were appearing in the Chinese press in the early 1980s, argued that "the pressures came from below and proceeded to force the pace of change thereafter" and that "throughout the period of the growth of the production responsibility system [that is, the return to household farming] ... the central authorities and theoreticians have been in the position of reacting to and sanctioning developments that had already taken place."[17] Kate Zhou, in a book that gives all credit to the peasants, claimed that while "officials were looking the other way" the farmers across China parceled out the fields in a "spontaneous, unorganized, leaderless, non-ideological,

---

[16]   For some exceptions see, for example, Kathleen Hartford's excellent "Socialist Agriculture is Dead; Long Live Socialist Agriculture! Organizational Transformations in Rural China," in Elizabeth Perry and Christine Wong (eds.), *The Political Economy of Reform in Post-Mao China* (Cambridge: Harvard University Press, 1985); also Joseph Fewsmith, *Dilemmas of Reform in China*, Ch. 1; also David Zweig, *Freeing China's Farmers: Rural Restructuring in the Reform Era* (Armonk: M.E. Sharpe, 1997), Ch. 2, esp. pp. 61-74.

[17]   Andrew Watson, "Agriculture Looks for Shoes that Fit: The Production Responsibility System and Its Implications," *World Development*, Vol. 11, No. 8 (1983), pp. 712, 714. Also see Andrew Watson, "New Structures in the Organization of Chinese Agriculture: A Variable Model," *Pacific Affairs*, Vol. 57, No. 4 (Winter 1984-85), pp. 621-45.

apolitical movement."[18] Daniel Kelliher claims in a much-cited book that inasmuch as nationally uniform policies had been imposed upon the farmers for decades, their very sameness of circumstances drove the farmers in the late 1970s and early 1980s to undertake similar strategems from below to return to family farming: "Though peasants were atomized, the body of rural China moved because so many of its atoms lunged in the same direction at the same time."[19]

Let us pause briefly to focus on Kelliher's work, since it is the best researched of these works and has influenced the China studies field more than any other writing on this topic. I would suggest that Kelliher's own raw evidence regarding the return to household farming, on pages 55-69 of his book *Peasant Power in China*, points to a scenario of events that contradicts his conclusions. He emphasizes the quiet swing back to family farming in impoverished districts of Wan Li's province, Anhui, and observes that in Hubei, the province he directly studied, the scenario was quite different. There,

> Led by such collective officials, Hubei stayed safely to the rear of the maverick reform provinces. . . . Only in the middle of 1980, following cues from Beijing, did Hubei approve the giving of land contracts to a few households. . . . In spite of this unfavorable setting, family farming grew spontaneously in Hubei. In isolated parts of the province peasants gave up on collective farming altogether and turned to household contracting. . . . It was limited to counties like Lichuan, . . . a poor, sparsely populated area where both government vigilance and collective organization were weak.

Elsewhere in the province, according to Kelliher, some of the farmers took advantage of the orders from above in the late 1970s to institute labor squads. They pursued their own preferences by forming these with fellow lineage members and kin. In a few places that he cites—only half a dozen citations in all from the Hubei press—farmers went further and divided up the team's land, tools and animals. But Kelliher does not clearly draw distinctions as to whether or not these were reports on poor fringe districts. What he does note, though, is that in several of the handful of cases that he cites, local people were aware that the highest Party leaders approved of such moves. He cites one group that stated: "To act in this way is in conformity with the spirit of instructions from higher authority!"[20] Notably, too, other than citing these half a dozen isolated local cases, nowhere does Kelliher examine the process by which all of the rest of Hubei Province's villages shifted over to family farming, and he never broaches the question of why and how every village ended up adopting one and the same type

---

[18]   Kate Xiao Zhou, *How the Farmers Changed China: Power of the People* (Boulder: Westview Press, 1996), p. 8.

[19]   Daniel Kelliher, *Peasant Power in China: The Era of Rural Reform, 1979-1989* (New Haven: Yale University Press, 1992), p. 31.

[20]   Ibid., p. 68.

of system, *dabaogan*. He simply jumps forward from that handful of labor squads to an unsubstantiated concluding sentence regarding decollectivization: "However circumscribed peasant power may have been, it was still the peasants' creation, not the program of the strong state, that finally became policy."[21]

To sum up, none of the authors who have asserted that Chinese farmers were the prime movers of decollectivization conducted interview surveys to see whether the official documentation from China was correct or not, nor have they examined the memoirs of the officials who first initiated the shift. Instead, they and much of the rest of the China studies field have essentially adopted the Chinese government's claims that decollectivization was voluntarily initiated by farmers.

Dismantling Collective Property: Which Level Held Responsibility?

In sharp contrast to the prevailing assumptions, my interviewees from diverse parts of the Chinese countryside were in accord as to what occurred: other than in two remote hamlets, the farmers in these 28 communities did *not* take any initiatives. And the interviewees are quite specific as to where the initiative lay. In almost all cases, county officials, not those at higher or lower administrative levels, took responsibility for pushing through the shift to independent smallholdings. The evidence on this is strong. Most of the interviewees reported that all of the villages in their own county were shifted into the system of family smallholdings at about the same time, whereas the villages of adjoining counties, even of counties that were in the same prefecture, normally adopted it at a different time. Within each county, moreover, almost every village used exactly the same criteria to determine how to divide up the land, whereas the villages of different counties employed somewhat different mechanisms and standards.

To a striking degree, the county officialdom imposed inflexible procedures for decollectivization on the teams. It was partly that an imperious bureaucracy, in keeping with habit, still insisted upon dictating to China's peasantry what they must do. But in a more positive light, county officials probably also wanted to assure that the division of the collective's lands was accomplished fairly. If village-level cadres had controlled the process, they might have permitted some households, through special connections or corruption, to receive better land than others. Among the twenty-four villages in the survey that were instructed from above to adopt *dabaogan*, in only two did the village cadres have a relatively free hand in the land distributions, and blatant favoritism did occur in one of these two villages. In a third village, in a generally overcrowded delta county where most of the peasants worked outside agriculture, the problem of potential favoritism was resolved by letting fields out to the highest bidders.

As a precaution against local corruption, the other twenty-one villages were made to adhere to a set of complicated procedures that for most counties was

---

[21]   Ibid., p. 69.

broadly similar. First, each team graded all of its fields according to fertility—in most of the counties into two or three grades, but in one county into as many as nine grades. Next, for each grade of land a lottery was conducted to determine the specific plots each household was to receive. As a result, every family received several small scattered plots of different grades. A Chinese government survey in 1984 revealed that, as a result, the average household held 10.7 small plots.[22] The interviewees from all twenty-one villages in my sample agree that, to the best of their knowledge, both the lottery and the apportionment of these plots were accomplished in an entirely above-board and honest fashion.

When initiating this distribution of land, a decision had to be made as to whether it should be apportioned according to the size of households or according to the amount of labor they had available to work the fields, or by some combination of the two. In a heavily overcrowded village, fairness might best be served by granting the greatest weight to household population, so that a family with two invalid grandparents and a number of small children would have an adequate share of land to support its own grain needs after meeting its compulsory grain sales quotas. On the other hand, in villages with relatively large amounts of land, where labor shortages were normal during the harvest busy season, it made sense to allot land more in accordance with labor power, in order to avoid saddling the families that had few hands and many mouths with more land than they could manage.

This reasoning was taken into account in the apportioning of land—but bureaucratic rigidity all too often subverted the intentions. From interview reports, it seems that the officials at county level normally estimated the situation of an entire county and concluded that, say, a preponderance of villages were overcrowded or, alternatively, that most of the villages experienced labor bottlenecks at peak seasons. On the basis of such a conjecture, a blanket decree was usually issued, covering every village in the county. In most of the counties of interviewees, the county leaders decided that the villages suffered from over-crowding, and they decreed that land be distributed on a purely *per capita* basis. A nationwide survey of villages subsequently conducted for the State Council revealed that in 69.4 percent of the villages the farmland had been divided entirely based on the size of each household.[23]

The county officials were rigidly perpetuating the political campaign custom of "slicing with one stroke of the knife," imposing a single set of guidelines everywhere in the same county, oblivious to the specific circumstances and needs of each of the villages below them. As a result, decidedly inappropriate standards were imposed upon some 20 percent of the villages in my sample; and in these

---

[22]   James Kaisung Kung, "Egalitarianism, Subsistence Provision, and Work Incentives in China's Agricultural Collectives," *World Development*, Vol. 22, No. 2 (1994), p. 181.

[23]   *Cunji tudi zhidu de biange: Zhongguo nongqu 280 cun nongdi zhidu diaocha de chuji* (Changes in the Land System at the Level of the Village: A Preliminary Survey Report on 280 of China's Villages) (Beijing: State Council, 1992).

villages the households with too few hands or too many mouths to feed immediately were placed in precarious circumstances.

The financial situation of such households was doubly threatened. Before, under the collectives, production team granaries had been required by state decree to lend such families sufficient grain for their consumption needs even when they did not have the money on hand to pay for it.[24] But these families had been regarded by other peasants as free riders; as one interviewee sourly told me: "We others in the team had had to raise those families' kids for them." He and the majority of his team had wanted to divide the fields partly because they thought they could be more productive on their own but partly, too, because they saw decollectivization as a way to get out from under "raising those other families' kids" at a cost to their own incomes.[25]

With the return to household farming, the families with a large number of dependents to feed faced another worry. From 1954 onward, as was noted in Chapter One, China's agricultural production teams had been obliged to sell an annual quota of crops at a fixed low price to the state. Such crop quotas had compelled the countryside to provide the cities with stable supplies of cheap foodstuffs and industrial raw materials, enabling the government to industrialize at lower cost. With decollectivization, the government kept this quota system intact. When the land was distributed to households, the teams passed on to the individual families a fixed responsibility for the quota grain deliveries by attaching to each plot of grade-one land a quota determined by the plot's recent record of productivity.

For most families this was preferable to what had prevailed before, since any new gains in production would now be entirely theirs to keep. But giving every household full responsibility for a fixed quota also held a menacing potential in the eyes of some interviewees. Henceforth, if a family could not grow enough to fulfil its portion of the quotas, it would be obliged either to buy expensive grain on the free market to resell to the state at a loss or, in some villages, would have to make up for the deficit grain in cash. Today, this crop-quota system ostensibly has been abolished, but in many regions—especially those that depend most heavily upon grain production, it persists under other names.

---

[24] During the period of collective agriculture, such families had gone into long-term debt to their team. This accumulated debt gradually was supposed to be deducted from the family's wages when the children grew old enough to begin earning incomes in the team. But such repayments were set so far in the future that other team members tended to consider the grain more as a gift from team coffers than a loan.

[25] This interviewee noted that, as a means of clearing off the longstanding grain debts, when the fields and agricultural implements were distributed in his team, the households with debts did not receive a full share of the latter. Another interviewee remarked that under the new system of agriculture, "there's little relief grain available from the brigade or team; if someone suddenly falls sick in your family it's your own tough luck."

Faced with a need to produce a surplus to fulfill the delivery quotas, the families with a large number of dependents were not the only ones worried about the return to family farming; so also were the elderly without close relatives[26] and the families headed by women or by weak or chronically ill men. According to a sympathetic interviewee, whereas "before, if they weren't physically able-bodied they were given lighter work and still got their workpoints, now they'd have to take care of the entire agricultural process, including all the really heavy work." However, the majority of the able-bodied peasantry were little concerned with the new difficulties that would be faced by their unfortunate neighbors. Each family, said the interviewees, simply looked to its own interests. How decollectivization was viewed by these divergent interests can be seen from the following figures: overall, going by the interviewees' accounts, in the surveyed villages something like three-quarters of the households were in favor of decollectivization and something like a quarter were opposed.

Not just land was distributed, but also the essential tools of production, from shoulder poles to winnowing baskets, normally at no charge. In two-thirds of the teams in the survey, the draft animals were given or sold off to families or groups of families through lotteries or auctions. Additionally, eleven out of the eighteen teams that owned tractors sold these into private hands, sometimes on instalment plans so that the less well-endowed families could participate in the bidding. The county authorities did not play a strong role in disposing of this public property, since it was less crucial to the survival of the farm households. Thirteen of the fourteen villages with commercial fishponds auctioned off their use, usually in multiyear contracts to whichever families were willing to bid the highest annual rent. This pattern also applied to orchards. In some 60 percent of the surveyed villages, factories and workshops remained under brigade or team management, but in the other 40 percent of the villages these, too, were leased in multiyear contracts to rural entrepreneurs, who in some instances were not even village residents. By 1983, throughout rural China, the collective property holdings had largely been dismantled.

A New Political Relaxation and Economic Diversification

The commands to dissolve the system of collective agriculture and the selling off or leasing out of other productive assets trimmed the rural bureaucracy's powers. With the changeover to independent smallholdings and the strengthening of

---

[26]   Welfare cases such as the childless elderly had good reason to be worried. They used to receive not just free grain but also, under the "five guarantees" system, free home repairs and a monthly pittance in cash from their production team. Once *dabaogan* was instituted, in some teams not only were their grain guarantees cut back or withdrawn, but so too were these other welfare provisions. One of the precipitating factors was a shrinkage of team financial resources. My survey evidence suggests that, as early as 1983, the welfare system was more severely curtailed in villages where the teams' earnings from the rental of ponds, orchards or factories amounted to relatively little.

market-economy forces, the rural officials—from county headquarters down to village Party committees—oversee far less than they previously had, and thus have fewer means at their disposal to impose their will. As early as 1983, one of the interviewees observed: "If these so-called cadres tell the peasants to do something today, the peasants don't always carry it out. We farmers are practical: if we don't depend on earning collective workpoints that you control, why listen so much to you?" In short, the arbitrary power of rural officials to exact cowed compliance from the peasantry has been weakened.

Another beneficial change was the near-abandonment by the government of political campaigns as mechanisms of top-down control. Beijing under Deng Xiaoping's guidance was intent upon giving a politically exhausted populace greater regularity and security in their lives. The state would no longer be so intrusive, with the single exception of family planning. In this milieu, villagers have turned back toward traditional anchors—reconstructing lineage halls and local temples, giving ancestral altars pride of place again in their homes, and once again participating in lavish ceremonies to mark weddings, funerals and the other key events in the life cycle.

Between 1982 and 1985, the Party-state also enacted steps to reduce the Party's dominance over all aspects of rural administration. There was now to be a "separation of Party and government" (*dang zheng fenkai*), to allow local government functions to operate more routinely.[27] As a symbol of this, the politically laden titles "commune" and "brigade" were abolished, and these levels of government reverted to the pre-revolution titles of "township" (*xiang*) and "administrative village" (*xingzheng cun*). Under Mao the slogan had been "Politics in Command," and the political atmosphere aroused by the Party had bludgeoned people into conformity. Local governments would no longer explicitly be enlisted in such an effort. They were now charged more with a mandate to promote economic development than to protect Party ideology.

For several years almost all parts of rural China fared well economically under this new dispensation. Even though many of the households that had feared the shift to household farming did witness immediate declines in their livelihoods—in one of the villages in my sample, commune-level officials went so far as to impound the furnishings and household goods of families that were unable to fulfill their quota deliveries—the crisis for such families often was relatively short-lived. In half of the villages in the sample, grain yields soon shot up sufficiently, through a much more efficient application of labor and fertilizer than under the previous cumbersome management of the collective, to allow even households that were short of labor to meet all of their grain needs. For most of the other families in such villages, cash incomes from grain rose dramatically,

---

27   The consequences during the first decade of decollectivization of this and other administrative reforms are discussed in Tyrene White, "Political Reform and Rural Government," in Deborah Davis and Ezra F. Vogel (eds.), *Chinese Society on the Eve of Tiananmen* (Cambridge: Harvard University Press, 1990).

since the government guaranteed to buy almost all of the over-quota grain at a price 50 percent higher than for quota grain.[28] In the other half of the surveyed villages, as of late 1982–early 1983 (when most of my interviewees had last been home), the families with few hands and too many mouths were still suffering from the effects of decollectivization. But grain yields continued to climb throughout China in 1983-84, which apparently extricated a large number of these remaining families from their economic difficulties. In the summer of 1984, a series of interviews very similar to those analyzed here was conducted by Jean Oi, who discovered that far fewer of the households were any longer in dire trouble.[29] Instead, her interviewees reported a contrary predicament. In many districts the bulk of the farmers were now burdened by too *much* grain. Local government marketing agencies, short of storage and shipping facilities, were refusing to buy up all the surplus grain that the state technically was obliged to purchase. Since private grain wholesaling was not yet permitted, the farmers were stuck with their surpluses.

Even so, there was a rising tide of rural prosperity. For one thing, farmers had quickly begun shifting away from grain into other crops. Until the late 1970s, in addition to the grain quotas, strict designations had been imposed on land use, so that specific fields had to be put under grain or under other designated quota crops. These dogmatic specifications had all but strangled any possibilities for crop diversification. But even before the shift to family farming reached most villages, the production teams had been relieved of these acreage requirements. So long as the households managed to hand in their grain quota, they were now free to turn to whatever crop best suited the soil. "Before," an interviewee reported, "we were forced to grow rice even on swampy land, with miserable results; today we raise water chestnuts there." The benefits in improved productivity and profitability deriving from Ricardo's law of comparative advantage were demonstrated in China's villages in the early 1980s in almost textbook fashion. In addition, the government in 1979-80 began providing better farmgate prices for most types of agricultural produce, and farmers thereby doubly benefited from any increases in productivity. In point of fact, incomes had begun rising noticeably even before the return to family farming, due to the removal of land use restrictions and this improvement in farmgate prices.

A further reason for enhanced living standards was increased efficiency in the use of a family's labor power. In the latter years of the commune period, as observed in the previous chapter, the pace of work had slowed. Now, with their own families the sole beneficiaries of fast, efficient work, farmers pushed themselves. An examination of the records of a village in northern Zhejiang Province in the early 1990s discovered that rice production required only a third the time per acre, and wheat only half the time under family farming, compared to

---

[28]   This guarantee was rescinded in later years.

[29]   Personal communication from Jean Oi.

the preceding period of collectives.[30] The households with adequate labor power could now strive to quickly plant and harvest sufficient grain on part of their fields and then use the remaining land for growing labor-intensive, high-priced commercial crops. Many of these families also found the time to grow animal feed on the hillsides and began raising large numbers of hogs and poultry for the market, or rented the village ponds and raised carp for urban consumption.

Diversification was not limited to agriculture: in fact, income-generating activities outside of agriculture soon began to predominate in many villages.[31] Some families with labor to spare became heavily involved in cottage industry, even during the growing seasons. Memories of such skills had survived the quarter-century collectivist period during which government policy had all but decimated these local specializations.

Chinese statistics for China as a whole showed a rise of 67 percent in real *per capita* peasant incomes between 1978 and the end of 1982.[32] My own small survey for late 1982–early 1983 found a very similar overall gain in real incomes. In many of the villages a good part of this rise *preceded* household farming. My survey suggested that major gains came from the increases in farmgate prices that the government had begun implementing at the end of the 1970s and, at about the same time, from the release of hitherto underutilized labor that dogmatically had been tied to grain cultivation. But as just seen, the return to family farming greatly spurred labor efficiency, enabling farmers to take full advantage of these earlier policy shifts. Per capita peasant incomes leaped another 14.7 percent in real terms in 1983, a point at which all of China's households were engaged in family farming, and climbed yet again in 1984 by exactly the same percentage.[33]

Among other things, the return to household farming was accompanied by a release of spare family labor from the fields. Some of this spare labor, especially from the less prosperous districts, was beginning to spread out across China in

[30]   Zhang Letian, "Nongcun shequde shehui fenhua yu zhenghe" (Stratification and Integration in a Rural Community), *Zhanlue yu guanli* (Strategy and Management), No. 4, 1994, p. 91.

[31]   Extensive fieldwork in a well-off village in Sichuan Province by a group of Danish scholars in 1987 illustrated clearly the importance of off-the-farm income; Peter Fenger, Steen Folke, Allan Jorgensen, Peter Milthers, and Ole Odgaard, "Occupational Patterns and Income Inequality in a Sichuan Village," *Copenhagen Papers in East and Southeast Asian Studies*, No. 5, (1990), p. 78. For a rural site near Nanjing see Flemming Christiansen, "The De-rustication of the Chinese Peasant? Peasant Household Reactions to the Rural Reforms in China since 1978," Ph.D. dissertation, (University of Leiden, Netherlands), 1990, p. 121. For sites in Henan Province, see Zhu Ling, *Rural Reform and Peasant Income in China* (London: Macmillan, 1991), pp. 78, 80.

[32]   This figure was adjusted to account for inflation (*Beijing Review*, No. 20, May 16, 1983, p. 7.

[33]   The figure for 1983 appeared in *Renmin ribao* (People's Daily), May 2, 1984, p.1, and the official figure for 1984 in *Beijing Review*, No. 16, April 22, 1985, p. iv.

search of opportunities. It will be seen in the next chapter how large numbers of such labor migrants were soon working for wages in the better-off villages.

The Retreat from Cooperation

Farmers in the prosperous villages preferred to hire the extra agricultural labor they needed, whether from afar or from within their own village—even in circumstances where, alternatively, they could have become involved in cooperative labor efforts. Interviewees cited cases in their villages of small groups of relatives or friends who started to help each other temporarily during the agricultural rush seasons, but as of late 1982–early 1983 cooperation did not normally extend beyond that. Even though, as noted earlier, a fair number of the peasants would initially have preferred a system of agriculture that provided some pooling of resources against the risk of personal disasters, once a return to family farms was instituted the peasantry showed a marked disinclination to organize any pooling of land on their own. In only four of the twenty-eight surveyed communities had any families banded together to work their fields together year-round, and the reports from two of these villages highlighted the unusual nature of such a relationship. In one, the only families that chose to join their fields together as a cooperative venture were three brothers of Hakka ethnic descent; they were the only households of Hakka origin in the village and "there had always been a bit of discrimination against them."[34] In the second and somewhat similar case, five cousins of bad-class political status not only pooled their land but even determined each household's earnings through a workpoint system similar to what they had used under the collectives. The irony is that for three decades the government had repeatedly eulogized the majority population of good-class peasantry as altruistically stalwart supporters of socialism; yet two of the only four cases of full-time cooperation among a sample of twenty-eight villages involved groups of relatives who had been targets of discrimination under the collectives. As a defense they, and not the favored majority, had developed a strong sense of mutual help conducive to cooperative production. On the contrary, other peasants have declined to adapt their two decades of experience with socialism to fit present conditions, even where a pooling of resources might have proven advantageous.

This reluctance to cooperate has presented a problem for agriculture. Notwithstanding the impressive gains in agricultural production achieved since decollectivization, a number of predictable inefficiencies did result from the division of land and the dispersal of resources. The slivers of field that families received were often too small to be machine-plowed, and most tractors began to be used instead by their new owners to haul heavy supplies on the roads. Irrigation, too, became more difficult to coordinate once the large collective fields were carved up into smallholdings, especially when the cultivators of the various

---

[34] See Jonathan Unger, "Decollectivization in a Guangdong Village: An Interview," p. 277.

small plots were intent on growing different crops with different growing seasons. In three of the surveyed teams, it became necessary to re-dig irrigation channels or to re-divide the land; in two other teams, there was a need to create a new post, paying a person out of collective funds to determine and supervise a fair flow of water. Yet even such measures have not always effectively offset the new difficulties arising from land fragmentation.

Chinese newspapers in the early 1980s reported extensively that households were supposedly banding together to apply insecticides or to buy and operate farm machinery, etc. But as of late 1982–early 1983 such ventures had been inaugurated in only four of the villages surveyed. In other villages the only evident co-ownership schemes involved the sharing of draft animals among groups of two or three households; and usually it had been officials who had organized this at the time of decollectivization. My subsequent investigations in rural villages revealed that even these very modest schemes for co-ownership largely collapsed over time. When I interviewed farmers in more than a dozen villages in Yunnan Province in 1988, for instance, interviewees repeatedly told me that villagers were wary about co-owning property of any kind. They were not even ready to lend equipment or draft animals to one another, let alone co-own them. In one hamlet that I visited, a dozen draft animals had been sufficient to plow the large collective fields; in contrast, in the late 1980s the hamlet's 56 households owned 70 water buffalo and cattle since, as it was explained to me, difficulties in cooperation between families precluded much sharing of animals during the plowing season. Even today, two decades after decollectivization, there are few signs in China that economic pressures or economic opportunities have pushed farm families toward any greater coordination of resources.[35]

This is not to say that families refuse to cooperate with one another in other ways. They regularly lend a hand to relatives and neighbors in house building or in providing needed field labor during the busy seasons or when a new fishpond needs to be dug. In the largely agricultural villages that I have visited in China's interior, there is little hiring of labor for such purposes: friends and neighbors provide their labor for free, and receive in return only a meal or two as tokens of

---

[35]   A paper by Mark Selden deals with cooperation between farm households in the 1990s, and he similarly found little cooperation. He notes that "In general, it appears that the collective experience has made villagers wary of mutual aid beyond the scale of kin and close friends." See Selden's "Household, Cooperative, and State in the Remaking of China's Countryside," in Eduard Vermeer, Frank Pieke and Woei Lien Chong (eds.), *Cooperative and Collective in China's Rural Development* (Armonk: M.E. Sharpe, 1998), p. 36. A village studied by Ellen Judd contains more extensive cooperation than I have discovered in other sources; there "land groups" have been established among families with adjoining fields. Most of these groups are composed of relatives, and the most common form of cooperation among them involves the sharing of power-driven water pumps for irrigation. In a few of the groups, two or more households work their land together year-round, but these turn out to be households of brothers or of fathers and their grown sons. Ellen R. Judd, *Gender and Power in Rural North China* (Stanford: Stanford University Press, 1994), pp. 35-41.

appreciation.[36] It is an interesting phenomenon. In villages like the one in Yunnan where families were wary about lending draft animals to other households, people are more willing to give away their labor, which is "cheap," than to lend or share their property, which is in much shorter supply.

Even such statements need to be qualified. Where some particular endeavor promises high profits but a single family would not be able to handle it alone, some families are willing to bite the bullet and cooperate in co-ownership. In many of the villages I have visited, for example, some of the villagers could readily name a few other families with whom they were willing to cooperate on endeavors if development-aid credit could be made available: any sizeable loan would pose too great a risk to shoulder alone. The Chinese villager is often a pragmatic "economic man," carefully weighing risks and possible profits, and is willing to put aside worries about co-owning assets when faced with the prospect of substantial income gains.

The Push from Below to Readjust Landholdings

Also for pragmatic reasons, many farmers are reluctant to move entirely away from the collective period when it comes to the ownership of land. In most villages, every five or six years much of the land has been reallocated between households as the size of some families has increased and others decreased. In a 1992 survey, 89 percent of the sampled villages had carried out such readjustments in landholdings—in many villages, more than once.[37] Surveys have also shown that most farmers prefer this, and are opposed to establishing a system of purely private smallholdings in which their own individual property rights are secure. In the most carefully conducted of these surveys, a 1994 questionnaire survey by James Kung and Liu Shouying of 800 farm families in eight counties, only 14 percent of the respondents declared that they preferred land ownership rights to be held by each household; all the rest preferred that ownership should ultimately remain with the collective and state, and fully 65 percent favored taking land away from households that lost a member through death or through a daughter marrying out, and redistributing the plots to families that had grown in

---

[36] This has changed substantially in villages that have become highly commercialized and prosperous. On this see Scott Wilson, "The Cash Nexus and Social Networks: Mutual Aid and Gifts in Contemporary Shanghai Villages," *The China Journal*, No. 37 (January 1997), pp. 91-112. Villages that are less commercialized and continue to rely on mutual labor assistance are discussed in two excellent books: Andrew Kipnis, *Producing Guanxi: Sentiment, Self, and Subculture in a North China Village* (Durham: Duke University Press, 1997), esp. pp. 30-31; and Yunxiang Yan, *The Flow of Gifts: Reciprocity and Social Networks in a Chinese Village* (Stanford: Stanford University Press, 1996), esp. pp. 42, 89-90.

[37] James Kaisung Kung, "Equal Entitlement Versus Tenure Security Under a Regime of Collective Property Rights: Peasants' Preference for Institutions in Post-Reform Chinese Agriculture," *Journal of Comparative Economics*, Vol. 21, No. 2 (1995).

size through new births and incoming brides. Notably, only 19 percent of the respondents were opposed to such periodic land redistributions.[38]

Why should farmers favor such a system? The answer became apparent to me when I conducted research in a relatively poor village in Yunnan Province in 1988 that had never implemented such readjustments in land. There, the families that contained several teenagers at the time of decollectivization in 1982 had initially done well. They often had enough hands available not only to work their allotted fields but also to handle various economic activities outside agriculture. But in the half decade since then, shifts in the life cycle of families had altered the economic circumstances of the village's various households. One villager whom I interviewed related that in 1982 he had received five portions of land for himself, his wife, and his three teenage sons (he had no daughters), but these fields now had to support, in addition, the son's wives and children: eleven people in all. They were barely scraping by.[39] He was anxious for the village to enact a re-adjustment of fields.

Compare this case with that of a middle-aged couple from the same village with three recently grown children—one son and two daughters—who similarly received five portions of land at the time of decollectivization. As the daughters married and moved away, the son and his parents were now left with a large five-portion block of property that, if land readjustments are not carried out by the village, will be the son's alone to inherit. Yet even in this family, interestingly, the son fretted that his future prospects were shaky, since he himself now had two

---

[38]   James Kung and Shouying Liu, "Farmers' Preferences Regarding Ownership and Land Tenure in Post-Mao China: Unexpected Evidence from Eight Counties," *The China Journal*, No. 38 (July 1997), p. 48. On such reallocations of land also see Cheng Yuk-shing and Tsang Shu-ki, "Agricultural Land Reform in a Mixed System: The Chinese Experience of 1984-1994," *China Information*, Vol. 10, Nos. 3–4 (Winter 1995/Spring 1996), pp. 44-74.

[39]   Such families often had been able to accumulate some money when their children were teenagers, but the bulk of this money soon had had to be spent to acquire wives for their sons; a son's marriage is an extremely expensive proposition today, often costing more than the annual income of a household. Interestingly, families invariably divide when the eldest son marries, rather than endure the frictions of an expanding household. The newlyweds move into a new house and the eldest son takes with him his share of the family property, including a portion of the fields that had been allotted to the family. As each succeeding son marries, he too "divides the household" (*fen jia*) and takes with him his inheritance. The youngest son stays with the parents after his marriage, and it is he who inherits the ancestral house and the remaining family property when the old couple passes away. The daughters take with them a small dowry when they marry, and this is their sole share of family property. They, too, inherit nothing when their parents die. The division of family property at so early a point, decades before the older generation's death, poses serious obstacles to the diversification of peasant household endeavors and to long-term investment planning. Problems of land division that would have taken a very long time to be played out in Western societies were already plaguing rural China less than a decade after decollectivization.

sons, and the fields allotted to him some day would have to support their wives and children. Almost all families that rely strictly on farming have had to face the dilemma that, whatever their current circumstances, their prosperity would rise and fall with shifts in their family's demographic cycle.[40]

Accordingly, in surveys of farmer preferences even the wealthier households, looking forward in time, preferred a system of periodic land readjustments. In the 1994 survey by Kung and Liu, 43 percent of the high-income villagers favored readjustments of land away from households that lost family members through death or marriage, compared to only 24 percent who were opposed. Even village households with a high share of off-farm income preferred such readjustments, by a margin of 55 percent to 18 percent, perhaps in recognition of the possibility that some day they too might need to return to full-time farming.[41]

In light of this solid preference, it is ironic that a government that still touts itself as socialist instituted regulations in 1993 to put a stop to the reallocation of landholdings. Beijing decreed that land tenure should be frozen for a period of at least thirty years without any further readjustments. The government was following the strong advice of economists in the government's thinktanks, who had been strongly influenced, in turn, by Western economists. The Chinese economists and their Western mentors were enamored with the notion of "property rights" and "security of tenure" and did not deign to notice or care about what the farmers themselves wanted.

Village governments have been far more attuned to the farmers' needs. Numerous reports from China reveal that most village governments ignored the 30-year directive, and continued periodically to readjust landholdings to take account of changes in the size of households. In the late 1990s, the central government finally began to enforce its 30-year decree more rigorously, and the early results of this have borne out the worries of farmers about the consequences of being at the wrong point in the family cycle. In a hill village in Qinghai Province in 2000, I visited a young family that was barely subsisting on gruel and neighbors' charity. The husband had lived with his widowed mother and brother on three portions of land until his marriage in 1997, when he took his one portion

---

[40] This peasant family cycle of increasing and decreasing prosperity is quite similar to what Chayanov discovered in his famous study of the pre-revolution Russian peasantry. See Alexander V. Chayanov, *The Theory of Peasant Society*, republished in 1966 (Homewood, Ill.: R.D. Irwin Publishers). In large parts of Czarist Russia, families similarly were allocated larger or smaller shares in the village land as the size of their household increased and declined. This was done by villagewide custom, without government involvement.

[41] Kung and Liu, "Farmers' Preferences Regarding Ownership and Land Tenure," p. 45. This was especially the case among households with high levels of nonfarm income who resided in districts that were still largely agricultural. In districts that had largely turned to nonagricultural pursuits, a majority of the farmers felt secure enough of their future prospects to answer in the negative to the question of taking back land from families that had lost members (p. 59).

with him. That is not enough land to support himself, his wife and their two babies, and with land reallocations blocked, the family members were visibly malnourished and inadequately clothed. As time passes and as more families in villages such as this begin to suffer from inadequate landholdings, we can expect village communities once again to buck central government commands and to quietly redistribute land.

Chapter Six

LEAVING THE VILLAGES

A widening gap in income and living standards within villages had become evident as early as 1982-83. It was partly that the shift away from collective agriculture gave advantages to the more capable and more entrepreneurial farmers. But even more important was that some families quickly had begun to earn a substantial part of their livings outside of agriculture. During the previous several decades of socialism, while the rural economy had expanded, essential rural services in commerce, transport, repair work, and residential construction had been curtailed. A vacuum was created, and in the climate of economic liberalization of the early 1980s, a surge of peasants rushed to fill it.[1]

My interview survey of 1982-83 revealed that only a year or two after the villages had abandoned collectives, some families with labor to spare were already becoming heavily involved in cottage industry, even during the growing seasons. In other families, some of the men were quitting their villages for much of the year to work at urban construction sites or other pursuits, leaving the off-season agricultural chores in the hands of their wives, parents and teenage children. In fact, as of 1982-83 a majority of the men from 21 of the 28 villages that I surveyed—these were mainly the villages in relatively well developed coastal provinces or close to cities—had found ways to earn money outside their own community.

The residents of some villages did especially well at such enterprises. A large number of men from one village, for example, turned successfully to ironmongery during slack seasons, drawing upon village traditions. Most of the households of a second village drummed up orders in Guangzhou for hand-crafted quilts, a traditional specialty of that village. A considerable number of peasants from a third village began manufacturing and peddling beancurd delicacies in the nearby

---

[1]   Fei Xiaotong in 1957 wrote an essay—republished in Fei Xiaotong, *Chinese Village Close-up* (Beijing: New World Press, 1982)—in which he argued that a great many peasants depended upon income earned outside the fields to supplement what could be obtained from grain. He implied that the new collectives, in cutting off such avenues, were inflicting needless hardships on the peasantry. For putting forth this observation, Fei was criticized in both the 1957 Anti-Rightist campaign and the Cultural Revolution. Now, long after the fact, he has been proven right: the substantial gains in the incomes of most peasant families during the post-Mao era have been due largely to the types of endeavors that Fei Xiaotong had sought to protect: crop diversification, cottage industry, rural transport, animal husbandry and hired-out labor away from home.

city, much as their families had done in pre-revolution days. Several other villages parlayed urban contacts into lucrative jobs in the building trades. In one case, a village official had, over the past couple of decades, developed special connections with the cadres of a large urban factory, which led to a growing number of semi-permanent jobs for men from the village repairing factory buildings. In a second case, an entrepreneurial peasant managed to hustle a subcontract in construction work in a city close by, set himself up as a labor boss, and began hiring fellow villagers as his crew.

Through diverse means, including the establishment of manufacturing enterprises within their own villages, many of the entrepreneurial and able-bodied families that had spare labor increased their incomes many-fold. By the 1990s, when I traveled into villages to conduct interviews, such families were competing to build larger homes and were buying color TV sets and video cassette recorders.

The Safety Valve: The Flow of Migrant Labor to the Richer Rural Districts and Cities

Farmers from China's poor regions were affected by the new liberalization of the 1980s in a different way. Under Mao, from 1960 onward they, like all farmers, had been forced by a tight residence permit system to remain rooted where they were. If they had tried to find regular work at a distance from their original place of residence they were likely to be detained by police. Even if they could evade detection, they normally would find no means to purchase food, especially in the cities, as all basic foodstuffs required ration coupons. The residents of overcrowded communities in areas with depleted soils remained trapped at home, unable to search for work elsewhere to relieve their poverty. One of the consequences was that during the two decades between 1960 and 1980, the gap in living standards widened considerably between the better-off and poorer rural districts.[2]

Though the Mao-era residence permit system has remained in place up to the present day, during the early 1980s, in some cases even preceding decollectivization, farmers from the poor districts were informally able to leave their villages for many months at a time to find temporary work, as I discovered in my interview survey of 1983. Much as in pre-Liberation times, they began to work during the busy agricultural seasons as hired hands in the villages of the more prosperous districts, in some cases tending the fields full-time for households that were now earning enough from nonagricultural endeavors to enable them to quit agricultural labor altogether.

---

[2]   On this widening differential during the Maoist period, see Nicholas Lardy, *Agriculture in China's Economic Development* (Cambridge: Cambridge University Press, 1984), Ch. 4; and Peter Nolan and Gordon White, "The Distributive Implications of China's New Agricultural Policies," in Jack Gray and Gordon White (eds.), *China's New Development Strategy* (London and New York: Academic Press, 1982).

Hired laborers from the poor districts began drifting into the richer villages through other means, too. In one village in my 1983 sample, not far from Guangzhou, most of the local people found after their return to family farming that they could harvest enough rice for the entire year in their first crop, but lacked the know-how to cultivate vegetables commercially as a second crop. In the early 1980s they sought work outside of agriculture during the summer months and contracted out their land to vegetable "specialists" (*shifu*) from an impoverished district of north Guangdong's Chaozhou (Swatow) district, who brought in their own hired helpers with them. Elsewhere, in a village in central Guangdong, the head of a production team successfully bid for a small timber forest and imported rural laborers from a poor part of Hunan Province as lumberjacks.[3] In yet another Guangdong village, a brigade tile factory was leased out to an entrepreneur from the Chaozhou area, who brought with him a workforce of villagers from his own district. Overall, in the early 1980s outside laborers were being hired, sometimes from quite a distance, in almost half of the 28 surveyed communities. Not surprisingly, these tended to be the better-off villages.

In some of these cases, ongoing links were quickly erected between particular richer and poorer districts: Hakkas from Mei County, Guangdong, finding year-round work in a Hakka village in Jiangxi Province; eight peasants from a village in Guangdong's overcrowded Chaozhou region contracting to rent for five years the unwanted marginal fields of a production team two hundred miles to the south and moving there with their families for the duration; farmers from a village in Sichuan Province finding employment as farmhands in a prosperous village on the Guangdong seacoast and, within a year of their arrival, forging more complex linkages between these two far-away communities by arranging the marriages of five women from their village into households of the host village.

As of the early 1980s, the wages earned by the migrant laborers from poor districts were reasonably good by the standards of most rural Chinese. In the villages in the sample they amounted to some two to five *yuan* per day (the higher figure was reported for the peak harvest seasons), in circumstances where at home they had previously been earning well under one *yuan* a day. Over time, however, as the channels between poor and richer districts improved and the numbers of migrant laborers increased, the wages of such migrant workers have declined in real terms. In the wealthier parts of the countryside, they have generally evolved into a poorly paid underclass that does the hardest and most dirty work.[4]

---

[3]   This is discussed in Jonathan Unger, "Decollectivization in a Guangdong Village," pp. 277–78.

[4]   One example of this from the late 1980s is a rural township of non-Chinese hill peoples in Yunnan Province that had become wealthy on the proceeds of village- and township-owned mines. There—and in Chen Village, too—most of the farming and almost all of the heavy labor was being done by a large number of impoverished immigrants. (The wealthy Yunnan township is discussed in Jonathan Unger and Jean Xiong, "Life in the Chinese Hinterlands

Under present Chinese law, such immigrants are denied any rights to permanent residence. They are there only at the sufferance of the local populace and the village public-security organs, and can be ejected from the village at any moment their presence is no longer wanted. As a group, they are reluctantly tolerated by the best-off local villagers, who generally hold them in disdain and view them as economically needed intruders into a tight-knit community. And they are eyed with even greater suspicion and resentment by the poorer members of the local community, whose livelihoods they undercut. An interviewee from a village in Guangdong noted in 1990, "Some of my neighbors who rely on farming for a living have to go out to work to supplement their incomes, but they now only earn about 5 *yuan* a day from that. Even then this kind of work is not always available. Their opportunities and pay are threatened by the availability of migrant laborers who are paid 2 *yuan* a day plus a couple of meals." (This was after a period of high inflation, and 2 *yuan* was worth far less than in 1983.) It is understandable in these circumstances that an atmosphere of palpable tension and mistrust between the have-not immigrants and indigenous villagers has become evident across parts of China.

The great bulk of the available work in the richer parts of the countryside is today found in factories. Such enterprises had begun sprouting in the 1980s in very large numbers in the countryside of the coastal region, along transport routes and in the rural areas near cities. Many tens of millions of workers have found employment in such enterprises on a full-time basis. One analysis claims 100 million such workers in 1993, and another source estimates 130 million half a decade later.[5]

China's rural factory workers derive from two distinctly different types of backgrounds. Especially in the 1980s, local residents who were recruited into enterprises owned and operated by village and township governments generally earned incomes that were considered good—better certainly than was available locally from farming. There was therefore competition during the 1980s and early 1990s to obtain such jobs, and the employees who were recruited tended to come from the better-connected families in the district—for instance, relatives of village officials and of the factory's own managers. In many districts, some of the other workers bought their way in: their families could only secure a factory job for them by purchasing a fixed number of shares in the enterprises. In these

---

Under the Rural Economic Reforms," *Bulletin of Concerned Asian Scholars*, Vol. 22, No. 2 [April 1990], esp. pp. 11-12).

[5] Dorothy J. Solinger estimates that some 100 million were employed in 1993. *Contesting Citizenship in Urban China: Peasant Migrants, the State, and the Logic of the Market* (Berkeley: University of California Press, 1999), p. 155. A Chinese source has a higher estimate, claiming that 120 million people were in such employment in 1993; see *Renmin ribao* (People's Daily), May 11, 1995. As of 1998, according to Scott Rozelle, Linxiu Zhang, and Jikun Huang, "China's War on Poverty" (unpublished ms., October 1998), the number of such rural enterprise employees stood at 130 million (p. vi).

circumstances, precisely the families who were already among the more successful in agriculture tended to gain access also to the earnings in local industry.[6]

However, as time passed rural factory workers increasingly were hired from among the migrants from China's poorer districts in order to secure cheaper labor. The status and circumstances of this second type of worker, who now number in the tens of millions, are altogether unlike those enjoyed by the workers of local origin. For instance, in the rural districts of Guangdong Province near Hong Kong where I have conducted fieldwork, a very large number of foreign-funded firms have established factories, and during the 1980s the local governments arrived at a special arrangement with the foreign investors. In each of the local factories two discrete labor markets were created so as to ensure relatively high pay in a fixed number of factory positions for employees from the nearby villages. For performing similar jobs, immigrant workers from elsewhere in China earned far less.[7]

The same holds true for many of the factories throughout the countryside that are owned by local governments. But as these factories encountered increasingly stiff competition over time, they have met this by turning increasingly to cheaper migrant laborers, who are made to work harder and longer than the local workers they replace. A lot of factories have been able to cut their workforce in the process, while some others, unable to meet the competition, have been closed. The result is that rural industry has begun providing fewer jobs for local and migrant workers alike. During the heyday of the 1980s, they reportedly were expanding their employment by some 13 million people per year. In the early 1990s this slowed to gains of some 7 million employees per year, by the mid-1990s it slowed further to 3 million annually—and by the latter part of the 1990s the rural factories were reportedly shedding employees at a yearly rate of about 3 to 4 million.[8]

From early on, other migrant workers were entering the cities in very large numbers. In Beijing, for instance, they were estimated to number 1.6 million by 1994, and in Shanghai 3.3 million.[9] They have undertaken the onerous low-paid work that urban people declined to do at construction sites and sweatshops, or as maids, sanitation workers, dishwashers, and so on. State-owned factories, anxious

[6]   For an excellent case study of this, see Minchuan Yang, "Reshaping Peasant Culture and Community: Rural Industrialization in a Chinese Village," *Modern China*, Vol. 20, No. 2 (April 1994), p. 159.

[7]   On this see Chan, Madsen, and Unger, *Chen Village Under Mao and Deng*, pp. 304-7.

[8]   On this, see an interview with Wen Tiejun of the Ministry of Agriculture's Economic Research Center in *Nanfang zhoumo* (Southern Weekend), August 24, 2000, p. 2.

[9]   Cheng Li, "Surplus Rural Labourers and Internal Migration in China," in Borge Bakken (ed.), *Migration in China* (Copenhagen: Nordic Institute of Asian Studies, 1998), p. 47.

to cut costs, have also recruited them in large numbers as low-paid "temporary" workers, while laying off comparable numbers of higher-paid urban workers.

By the very nature of this surge of rural migrant labor, which the officials have dubbed the "Blind Flow" (*mang liu*), accurate national figures are not available as to how many migrants from the countryside have sought work away from home at any given time. Official Chinese claims during the mid-1990s settled broadly on 70 or more million,[10] while analyses of household surveys for 1995 show that approximately 50 million migrants that year were living away from their registered places of residence for more than half a year.[11] This flow of people is a vast number, equivalent to the entire workforces of the United Kingdom and France combined. Among the rural migrants, as of 1995 some 9.6 million had found long-term work in *urban* areas[12] and, by other calculations, some 25 million at the beginning of 1998 had found urban work of either long or short duration.[13]

Who Are the Migrants?

Over time, an ever increasing proportion of the transient rural outflow has been coming from a considerable distance, pouring out of villages in the poor inland regions.[14] As of 1995, in Shaanxi Province, which has stagnated economically in the post-Mao period and has witnessed a decline in rural incomes and increasing poverty,[15] 29 percent of the rural men reportedly had left their villages to find

---

[10]   A survey by China's Ministry of Labor, for instance, estimated 72 million as of 1995. See Azizur Rahman Khan, "Poverty in China in the Period of Globalization," *Issues in Development Discussion Paper 22* (Geneva: International Labor Office, 1998), p. 41.

[11]   Li Shi, "Labor Migration and Income Distribution in Rural China," in Carl Riskin, Zhao Renwei, and Li Shi (eds.), *China's Retreat from Equality: Income Distribution and Economic Transition* (Armonk: M.E. Sharpe, 2001), p. 306.

[12]   Ibid., p. 307.

[13]   Pun Ngai, "Chinese Labour at the End of the 20th Century," *China Review 1999* (Hong Kong: The Chinese University Press, 1999), p. 337.

[14]   For evidence on this, see Dorothy J. Solinger, *Contesting Citizenship in Urban China*, p. 163; and Scott Rozelle, Li Guo, Minggao Shen, Amelia Hughart, and John Giles, "Leaving China's Farms: Survey Results of New Paths and Remaining Hurdles to Rural Migration," *The China Quarterly*, No. 158 (July 1999), pp. 371, 375.

[15]   In a survey of 16 provinces by Stephen Morgan, Shaanxi was the only one in which the heights of 17-year-old rural girls actually declined between 1979 and 1995 (the same was true for the province's 17-year-old urban girls), indicating a persistent economic recession in that province. Stephen Morgan, "Richer and Taller: Stature and Standards of Living in China, 1979-1995," *The China Journal*, No. 44 (July 2000). During the latter half of the 1990s the decline in rural incomes in Shaanxi continued. Farmers' incomes dropped by 4 percent in 1997 and fell by a further 5.1 percent in 1998. *Zhongguo gongshang shibao* (China Business Times), May 2, 1999.

jobs.[16] Across much of inland China, this exodus in search of temporary work has continued to swell, driven by depressed agricultural commodity prices. In 1998, as one example, the numbers of migrant workers leaving inland Sichuan Province climbed to 4.5 million, up from 4 million a year earlier.[17]

The poor, but not the poorest households, are heavily represented among such migrants. Statistics suggest, for instance, that the greatest concentration of emigrants in Sichuan Province in 1994 came from counties that were about average in income for Sichuan, and the emigrants stood a bit below the national poverty line.[18] Among the households of emigrant workers from Sichuan, the wages that they remitted accounted for about 20 percent of total family income and some 50 percent of the families' cash income.[19]

As might be expected, men outnumber women among the tens of millions of migrants, but as the years have passed an increasing proportion of the flow has consisted of young women. It was obvious during my research trips in Guangdong that most of the light-industry workforce there, which assembles electronic parts and toys for export, stitches together clothing and staffs textile mills, is composed of migrant women from the countryside. A large number of these workers (and the male workers, too) arrive through a form of chain work migration. As just one example, interviews conducted outside the factory gates at a large apparel enterprise in rural Guangdong revealed that most of the women workers were from Hunan Province, introduced to the factory by cousins and friends already employed there. Similarly, at construction sites that I visited in Beijing most of the men came from rural parts of Sichuan Province and worked at the same sites as acquaintances. Surveys suggest that the great bulk of the rural migrant workers similarly have specific destinations and jobs awaiting them when they leave home.[20] What looks to the officialdom and urban populace to be a dangerously uncontrolled "Blind Flow" is not at all a blind flow.

---

[16]   Rozelle et al, "Leaving China's Farms," p. 375.

[17]   *Zhongguo jingji shibao* (China Economic Times), March 31, 1999.

[18]   World Bank, *Sharing Rising Incomes: Disparities in China* (Washington, D.C.: World Bank, 1997), p. 55.

[19]   Ibid., p. 57.

[20]   See, for example, Ying Du, "Rural Labor Migration in Contemporary China: An Analysis of Its Features and Macro Context," in Loraine A. West and Yaohui Zhao (eds.), *Rural Labor Flows in China* (Berkeley: Institute of East Asian Studies, University of California, 2000), p. 83, which finds that the "vast majority" of the 295 migrant workers from surveyed households in Sichuan and Anhui Provinces had followed the lead of relatives and fellow villagers to obtain jobs. In a different survey of 600 migrant workers in the Shanghai-Jiangsu region in 1995, it similarly was found that fully 88 percent of the workers had headed for a specific job when they left their village. Zhao Shukai, "Organizational Characteristics of Rural Labor Mobility in China," in the same volume, p. 233. Also see the survey by Xin Meng in the same volume.

A disproportionate number of the migrants are young and unmarried. Surveys in China indicate, in fact, that a substantial majority are under the age of 30.[21] During the 1990s this migrant labor appears to have come most frequently from homes that had reached the point in the family cycle where the children had reached adulthood but had not yet married—and thus had not yet received any extra allotment of land through the village's periodic land readjustments.[22]

Toughing It

In particular, young migrants make up by far the greatest part of the migrant labor force in factories. Many of the manufacturing plants hire only young people so as to be more sure of their physical endurance. As one factory owner told me, "By the age of 30, we bosses feel they can't keep up, and we prefer to take on younger women instead."

Life in these factories is truly grueling. The work often lasts ten to twelve hours a day, six or even seven days a week without respite. The factory dormitories are frequently spartan and bleak, with ten to twenty workers sharing a room crowded with double-bunk beds.[23] For many of the workers from the countryside, it is a question of lasting out very tough work for some years prior to marriage, saving as much as possible out of relatively meager earnings.

---

[21] Hein Mallee, "In Defence of Migration: Recent Chinese Studies in Rural Population Mobility," *China Information*, Vol. 10, Nos. 3-4 (Winter 1995/Spring 1996), p. 117. Also see Rozelle et al., "Leaving China's Farms," pp. 375-78. Also see Ying Du, "Rural Labor Migration," p. 77.

[22] Examining a survey of farm households in Anhui and Sichuan Provinces, Nansheng Bai found that the average number of workers in a migrant family was larger by 0.6-1.0 persons in Sichuan and by 0.3-0.8 in Anhui. Nansheng Bai, "The Effect of Labor Migration on Agriculture: An Empirical Study," in Loraine A. West and Yaohui Zhao (eds.), *Rural Labor Flows in China* (Berkeley: Institute of East Asian Studies, University of California, 2000), p. 133. This situation is also suggested by survey findings which show that the households with members working away from home had, on average, smaller portions of land per laborer than households with no members away from home. See, for example, Hein Mallee, "Agricultural Labor and Rural Population Mobility: Some Observations," in the same volume. This article notes that in a survey of 2,838 rural households, those with members working as migrants averaged 1.58 *mu* per worker, as against 1.83 *mu* for households with no migrant workers (p. 47).

[23] See, for example, an excellent article by Mobo Gao about the factory conditions faced by migrant laborers from his own native village in Jiangxi Province: "The Rural Situation in Post-Mao China and the Conditions of Migrant Workers: The Case of Gao Village," *Bulletin of Concerned Asian Scholars*, Vol. 30, No. 4 (October 1998), p. 73; also see Tan Shen, "The Relationship Between Foreign Enterprises, Local Governments, and Women Migrant Workers in the Pearl River Delta," in Loraine A. West and Yaohui Zhao (eds.), *Rural Labor Flows in China* (Berkeley: Institute of East Asian Studies, University of California, 2000), pp. 292-309.

On the positive side, the money remitted by this emigrant workforce to their families at home helps to reduce the plight of those remaining behind in impoverished districts. This transfer of funds is one of the only mechanisms helping to moderate the growing gap between the poorer regions and the prosperous, rapidly developing regions.

On the negative side, however, the government holds to a residential registration (*hukou*) policy that all but ensures that the migrant workers are at the mercy of employers and receive lower wages under worse conditions than otherwise would prevail. To work in the cities and the prosperous rural regions, each migrant today is required to obtain a temporary residence permit, and if they lose their job they also lose their right to stay on in the area. China is one of the only countries in the world with such residence restrictions, alongside North Korea and, formerly, South Africa. The practice puts the workers at a terrible disadvantage *vis-à-vis* their employer, a fact which a large number of employers exploit to the hilt. They insist upon locking up the temporary residence permits and the workers' identity papers, making it difficult for workers to leave.[24] Employers are supposed to be legally forbidden from doing so, but local officials almost invariably turn a blind eye. Because the residential registration policy prohibits the migrant workers from the countryside from ever settling locally, the officials never consider them as part of their own constituency, and accordingly are more willing to see them exploited. There is a strong added incentive where the local governments themselves own the factories or are the co-owners of joint ventures with foreign partners.

The exploitation appears worst among migrant workers with little education. The more "up market" factories, which produce brand-name merchandise and maintain stringent quality controls, normally require school graduation certificates, and often use junior high school graduation as the cut-off point. Workers with less education often end up at factories that pay illegally low wages and that take advantage of workers' vulnerability in a whole variety of other ways. Conditions there are sometimes truly abusive, with wages withheld for months on end, inadequate food, and various forms of corporal punishment.[25] Fines for infractions of work rules or for absences from work are draconian, leaving some workers with barely any pay at the end of the month. Since the

---

[24]   Anita Chan, "Globalization, China's Free (Read Bonded) Labour Market, and the Chinese Trade Unions," *Asia Pacific Business Review*, Vol. 6, Nos 3 and 4 (Spring–Summer 2000), esp. pp. 262-68; the article also appears in Chris Rowley and John Benson (eds.), *Globalization and Labour in the Asia Pacific Region* (London: Frank Cass, 2000), pp. 260-81.

[25]   Conditions in factories of this type are movingly described in Anita Chan, "The Culture of Survival—Lives of Migrant Workers Through the Prism of Private Letters," in Perry Link, Richard Madsen and Paul Pickowicz (eds.), *Popular Thought in Post-Socialist China* (Boulder: Rowman & Littlefield, 2002). Also see Anita Chan, *China's Workers Under Assault* (Armonk: M.E. Sharpe, 2001); and Mobo Gao, "The Rural Situation in Post-Mao China," esp. pp. 74-75.

migrants from the poorer areas tend, on average, to have received less education, they are most often the ones trapped in such factories. Even when the factory's treatment of them blatantly violates national laws, they have nowhere to turn when, as is so often the case, the local authorities are solidly aligned with the bosses.

Such workers are not the only victims of the central government's residential policies and local government discrimination. Migrants who arrive in a city or prosperous rural district and whose labor is not needed are soon rounded up by police, detained in special holding centers where conditions are often worse than in the normal prisons, and then deported back to the countryside. In Shanghai alone there were 40,000 such detentions and deportations in 1993, 80,000 in 1996, and 100,000 in 1997.[26]

The number of such deportations in urban areas across China mounted in the late 1990s as cities became anxious to provide jobs to the growing numbers of home-grown urban unemployed, their ranks swelled by layoffs at state enterprises. One city after another took strong measures to staunch the inflows of rural labor. In April 1998 the Beijing municipal government ordered that 120,000 migrant workers be dismissed from work so as to open up their jobs for the local unemployed. The city subsequently announced in late 2001 that only 20 percent of the employees in the service sector (not including domestic servants) henceforth were allowed to be rural migrants, and all of the migrants in Beijing would need to hold junior high school graduation certificates. Shanghai in 1998 prohibited rural migrants from working in twenty-three job sectors and placed the tightest bans on the service sector, which the city government wanted to reserve for laid-off Shanghai workers.[27] The head of the Sociology Institute of the Chinese Academy of Social Sciences has written that, all told, about 20 million people with rural registrations were obliged to leave the cities during 1998-99.[28] On the face of it, this is far too high an estimate, but it gives some indication of the very sharp decline in urban opportunities.

Even before this downturn, most of the people from the very poorest villages of China could not afford to search for a job. The unskilled laborers from the poorest villages are, for one thing, among the least likely to have developed successful chain-migration linkages—and they cannot readily afford the transport

---

[26]   Zhao Shukai, "Criminality and the Policing of Migrant Workers," *The China Journal*, No. 43 (January 2000), p. 102. Also see *Not Welcome at the Party: Behind the "Clean-Up" of China's Cities—A Report on Administrative Detention under "Custody and Repatriation"* (New York: Human Rights In China, September 1999). 57 pp.

[27]   Pun Ngai, "Chinese Labour at the End of the 20th Century," p. 337. Also see *South China Morning Post* (Hong Kong), February 10, 1998; also *Beijing qingnian bao* (Beijing Youth News), October 29, 2001, p. 3.

[28]   Lu Xueyi, "Nongmin zhen ku, nongcun zhen qiong" (The Peasants Are Suffering, Villages Are Genuinely Poor), *Dushu* (The Reader), January 2001.

costs and weeks of time required to hunt for a job on their own. Their difficulties
are greatly compounded by the deportation programs, since they face the total loss
of their expenses if they are detained and deported back to the countryside. If they
do find a job before that occurs, they are precisely the type of migrant who all too
often gets entrapped in the worst of the exploitation described above—leaving
them at year's end with little or nothing to show for their labor. In the truly
impoverished villages that I have visited in China's hinterlands on behalf of anti-
poverty projects, few villagers try to engage in long-distance job migration. The
obstacles are too high, the costs too great, and the potential rewards too
precarious.

Just one example among many was provided in December 2000 in a hill
village in the western province of Qinghai. A group of half a dozen young
women, knowing that there was little decent work available in eastern China, had
responded that year to an advertisement that jobs were available to the west in
Xinjiang, working for the government's Construction & Production Corps.
Alongside a horde of others who had responded to the notices, they had spent
months of grueling labor cultivating and picking cotton for a state farm. But the
pay was so low that they earned only enough for their daily food and their travel
fares and they returned to the village empty-handed. No-one in the village, I was
told, would be foolish enough to go out of province again in search of work.

Instead, to supplement what they can make in agriculture, large numbers of
poor hill villagers in Qinghai—mostly men—seek work within the province, in
road building, construction work and the like. Staying away from home for weeks
at a time during the agricultural slack seasons, they are able to earn only about
300 *yuan* a month (US$40). I was repeatedly told, moreover, that they regularly
risk being cheated by employers out of even that pittance. With so little to be
earned in migrant labor, and with income opportunities scant at home, residents
of impoverished villages are in a bind.

The overall effect, as the coastal regions and the more fertile districts took
advantage of the reforms and families there increasingly prospered off the farm, is
that the gap in living standards between the prosperous and the poor inland
districts of rural China has been widening over time. This widening has been
exacerbated in recent years, as has been seen, by a drop in the income earned by
unskilled migrant workers as the competition among them for jobs has
intensified.[29] This drop has occurred as the rural factory work force declined, as
financially troubled state factories cut back on hiring them, and as their numbers
swelled in the cities and in rural regions such as in Xinjiang.

To come to grips with the very different circumstances of those in the
countryside who are doing well and those who are not, the following two
chapters—Chapters Seven and Eight—will examine the households and districts

---

[29] A survey in Henan Province in 1998, for instance, found that the level of the wages and
remittances of migrant workers from that province was already in decline by 1997. *Jingji
yanjiu cankao* (Economic Research Materials), No. 1223 (November 12, 1998), pp. 39-40.

that have prospered, and then Chapter Nine will investigate the dilemmas faced today by impoverished villages and households in the hinterlands of China.

Chapter Seven

THE EMERGENCE OF PRIVATE ENTREPRENEURSHIP
AND NEW CLASSES

While farmers in the interior struggle to make ends meet when they attempt to supplement their agricultural income with migrant labor, in the better-off parts of the countryside new strata of very prosperous households are being generated through personal economic endeavors and through becoming employers of others' labor. The greatest source of personal wealth in these districts lies in the rise of private industry. While a high proportion of rural industry is owned by local rural governments, during the past decade the *private* rural industrial sector has been growing at a much quicker rate.[1] As a result, according to official statistics, by 1997 the total profits of rural private industry surpassed those of rural collective industry.[2] Some of these private factories were established by the families of officials or were "privatized" into their own hands. But a great many other factories were started by ambitious individuals with few connections to the officialdom.

---

[1] On the emergence and initial growth of the rural private sector (including private petty commerce) during the 1980s and early 1990s, and also on the difficulties across China that the small entrepreneurs faced, see Susan Young and Yang Gang, "Private Enterprises and Local Government in Rural China," in Christopher Findlay, Andrew Watson, and Harry X. Wu (eds.), *Rural Enterprises in China* (New York: St. Martin's Press, 1994). An accelerating growth of private enterprise during the 1990s was evident even in the type of rural area that has, up to now, been dominated by collective industry; on this, see Jean Oi, "The Evolution of Local State Corporatism," in Andrew Walder (ed.), *Zouping in Transition* (Cambridge, Mass.: Harvard University Press, 1998), pp. 35-61. Oi notes, for example, that "by the end of the decade it was no longer economically advantageous [for the officials in a county in Shandong that she researched] to rely exclusively on collectively owned township and village enterprise," and that "By the early 1990s, private firms became a new target of local plans, and the sector began to receive the kind of preferential treatment earlier reserved for public firms" (p. 36). Gregory Ruf, who returned to rural Sichuan to conduct research in the summer of 1998, discovered trends favorable to the private sector that were very similar to what Oi observed in Shandong (personal communication from Ruf). Also see Susan Young, "Ownership and Community Interest in China's Rural Enterprises," in Kjeld Erik Brodsgaard and David Strand (eds.), *Reconstructing Twentieth-Century China* (Oxford: Oxford University Press, 1998), esp. pp. 116-24.

[2] *Zhongguo xiangzhen qiye nianjian 1998* (1998 Chinese Rural Enterprise Yearbook) (Beijing: Zhongguo Nongye Chubanshe, 1998), p. 107.

Private Rural Factory Owners: A Case Study

It becomes important to examine the emergence of these truly private entrepreneurs, inasmuch as private industry is likely to have a rapidly growing influence in shaping China's economic and political future. I will focus on an especially prosperous township in Guangdong Province, Xiqiao, a former commune of 135,000 residents in the Pearl River delta that was almost entirely agrarian until the mid-1980s and that has experienced a surge of private entrepreneurship in the years since. Today it boasts well over 2,000 factories, including more than 1,600 textile firms. The vast majority of the factories—and every one of the textile factories—are privately owned by local people.

The next chapter—Chapter Eight—will examine in detail the relations between the local state and society in Xiqiao Township, while the first sections of this chapter will examine the personal backgrounds and attributes of the successful private businesspeople there. In investigating this, it will be asked whether there is something culturally "Chinese" about the ways in which the successful entrepreneurs have proceeded, and a comparison will be made with the rapid development of small and medium-sized private industrial enterprises in Taiwan a few decades ago.

During fieldwork in 1997, it was possible to wander Xiqiao Township unimpeded and unsupervised, going into villages and factories and homes to discuss, in private, the experiences and attitudes of local factory owners and other residents.[3] Township and village officials were also interviewed under more formal arrangements, as well as the top officials of the two local business associations. One of these, the Textile Chamber of Commerce,[4] which has a highly restrictive membership of 38 of the most successful factory owners in the township (all males),[5] mailed a questionnaire on my behalf to its members inquiring about their backgrounds and present circumstances, and the responses that were received will be used to supplement the information obtained from interviews.

---

[3]   This interview research was undertaken in collaboration with Anita Chan. We were accompanied by Eva Hung and Lam Tao-chiu, who at the time were Ph.D. students at the Australian National University. I am grateful to them for their participation in this research.

[4]   The Chambers of Commerce in China are offshoots of the even more exclusive Federation of Industry and Commerce (Gongshanglian). The Chinese government's strategy in establishing these exclusive associations for elite businesspeople is explained in Jonathan Unger, "Bridges: Private Business, the Chinese Government and the Rise of New Associations," *The China Quarterly*, No. 147 (September 1996), pp. 795-819.

[5]   Although the wives often play a very significant role in the success of the businesses, men usually occupy the top formal position in Xiqiao's firms. This is similar to what Ole Bruun found among retail shops in the city of Chengdu. *Business and Bureaucracy in a Chinese City: An Ethnography of Private Business Households in Contemporary China* (Berkeley: Institute of East Asian Studies, 1993).

The Historical Background to a Private Sector Boom

Why do some districts in China "take off" in private sector industrialization, and others do not? In the case of Xiqiao, the reasons are clear and can be traced back in time.

The district had long concentrated on rearing silkworms, and in imperial times an intensive local cottage industry of silk spinning and weaving had developed alongside this. This was mechanized in the latter part of the 19th century.[6] After the Communist Party came to power, the district's small mechanized silk-weaving enterprises were amalgamated into three commune-owned factories, and alongside this, spinning and weaving on wooden hand looms continued at home as collectively run efforts of agricultural production teams. Indeed, the state required the teams to fulfill production quotas for silk thread and also for fabric.[7]

In 1984, as China and particularly Guangdong began to "open up" under Deng, several risk-taking technicians and workers from the three collective textile factories quit their jobs and struck out on their own, starting up tiny private factories containing a few electric looms apiece. With cloth in very short supply in China in the mid-1980s, whatever the tiny new factories produced was snapped up by customers. Seeing the profits that could be made, neighbors rushed to open their own enterprises. In some of the township's villages, by the late 1980s close to half of all the families owned factories.

Xiqiao Township quickly had begun to specialize. It soon no longer manufactured any silk cloth at all: for rising labor costs and pollution curtailed the cultivation of mulberry bushes and the rearing of silkworm cocoons. Some of the first factories had started off manufacturing artificial silk fabrics, and before long they and the other factories in the township switched to using other chemical

---

[6]   A local merchant with a strong mechanical bent named Chen Qiyuan revolutionized silk spinning in the early 1860s by inventing steam-driven silk spinning machinery. He erected a factory in his home village in Xiqiao in 1872—in the process becoming the earliest native modern industrialist in China. See, for example, *Chen Qiyuan yu Nanhaixian fangzhi gongye shi* (Chen Qiyuan and the History of the Textile Industry in Nanhai County) (Nanhai: Renmin Zhengzhi Xieshang Huiyi, 1987). Also see a description of Chen and illustrations of his inventions in Sucheta Mazumdar, *Sugar and Society in China: Peasants, Technology, and the World Market* (Cambridge: Harvard University Press, 1998), pp. 362-64.

[7]   Before and just after the rise to power of the Communist government, almost all of the weaving had been done by men, but in the 1950s, after the introduction of agricultural collectives, the men were assigned to farmwork and it was the women who took up the hand-loom weaving. Due to this cottage industry, during the three and a half decades of the Maoist period most local women gained some knowledge of what textile weaving entailed. Herein lay one of Xiqiao's comparative advantages once China again opened the door to private rural factories. In a great many of today's family-owned factories, it is the wife who oversees loom production, while the husband negotiates contracts with wholesalers and other customers.

fibers along the lines of nylon. Within a few years every textile factory in the township was concentrating on making such cloth for China's domestic clothing market.

As this boom in small textile factories took off, information and ever improving technical know-how very easily circulated within the bounds of the local township, but did not so readily spread beyond the township's localized social networks. So, too, in an industry that must adjust rapidly to changes in fashion and to the shifting seasonal buying patterns of wholesalers, knowledge of the national market became centered in Xiqiao. As the first locale in south China to produce large quantities of synthetic-fiber cloth for the open market, Xiqiao had rapidly attracted purchasing agents from garment factories throughout the country. By the 1990s they were arriving each year by the thousands, and they became the eyes and ears of Xiqiao's factory owners, enabling local producers to keep abreast of market trends across China.

In an increasingly competitive business, the difference between high and low profits depends upon gauging which types of cloth, pitched at what weave and quality, will sell best during the next season. To produce outside of a major production and wholesaling center such as Xiqiao condemns a manufacturer to comparative ignorance of fluctuations in market conditions, while to produce within Xiqiao enables a reasonably capable entrepreneur to stay sensitively attuned to the national market. Once Xiqiao had carved out a sizeable manufacturing niche, thus, it could consolidate a position as one of China's most important manufacturing centers of cloth from artificial fibers.

Xiqiao exemplifies "location theory" with a vengeance. Localized technical know-how and knowledge about the wider market has kept Xiqiao's enterprises invaluable steps ahead of the competition in what Paul Krugman, in a study of similar localized geographic specializations around the world, has called "the locking in of transitory advantages."[8]

Xiqiao is not unique in the degree to which it specializes successfully. Xiqiao lies in Nanhai County, and each of the rural townships in the county has similarly developed a special niche in which it has become preeminent. One rural Nanhai township is awash with tanneries; another specializes in aluminum frames for windows, dominating the Guangdong market; another township specializes in shoes and socks. The township directly next door to Xiqiao concentrates on

---

[8]   Paul Krugman, *Geography and Trade* (Leuven: Leuven University Press; and Cambridge: MIT Press, 1991), p. 10. Also Edward H. Lorenz, "Trust, Community, and Cooperation: Toward a Theory of Industrial Districts," in Michael Storper (ed.), *Pathways to Industrial Development and Regional Development* (London and New York: Routledge, 1992). Historically, the phenomenon exists in Xiqiao's own area of specialization, textiles. In the Industrial Revolution in late 18th- and early 19th-century Britain, the cotton textile industry likewise became "closely localized" for somewhat similar reasons. Wilfred Smith, *An Economic Geography of Great Britain* (London: Methuen & Co., second edition, 1953), pp. 469, 475.

ceramic tiles and is crammed with hundreds of large and small ceramic tile factories, private and collective enterprises alike, all of them entirely locally owned, belching out fumes from kilns that operate around the clock.

Such local concentrations of mutually competitive enterprises are not unique to this corner of China. In Zhejiang Province's Wenzhou Prefecture—which not coincidentally is famous in China as a bastion of private production—by the close of the 1980s one rural township was reportedly producing 70 percent of all the buttons in China and another township was producing 40 percent of China's low-voltage electrical switches.[9]

The Attributes of Private Entrepreneurship

Not everyone in such locations is equally entrepreneurial. Within Xiqiao, there has been a winnowing out process over the years. Some of those who opened factories have developed extremely profitable businesses that continue to expand while others have found it difficult to expand in the face of increasingly stiff competition or ultimately were forced out of business. What are the reasons for these differences? What types of personal and family characteristics have contributed to success or failure? And what aspects of entrepreneurship do all of these businesspeople share in common?

To examine a *common* ingredient of entrepreneurship first, almost all of the private businesspeople in Xiqiao had initially formed a partnership with friends or relatives or neighbors in order to amass sufficient capital to establish a small manufacturing enterprise. These partnerships usually splintered into small family firms once the enterprise contained enough machines to make separate operations viable. One of my interviewees, for example, had first opened a textile factory in 1984 as one of six partners, and after frenetically buying new looms as production expanded, he and his colleagues had dissolved the partnership in 1986, divided up the machines, and amicably gone their separate ways. In running a business, one's immediate family normally took precedence: in terms of trust and in a desire to bring one's own children into the business. Partnerships among brothers are more liable to last, but in Xiqiao even most of these have dissolved over time.

Yet at the same time, some of the successful enterprises do retain the form of partnerships. These are people who are able to break the mold of a familistic approach to business. This non-family-bound approach prevails more commonly among the most successful of the entrepreneurs than among the township's business population as a whole. This can be seen in my sample of the successful businesspeople who belong to the elite Textile Chamber of Commerce, which is highly selective in its recruitment and contains only the most successful and prominent businesspeople. My survey of them reveals that about half are still members of partnership firms, which is considerably higher than the rate for

---

9   Keith Forster, "The Wenzhou Model for Economic Development: Impressions," *China Information*, Vol. 5, No. 3 (Winter 1990-91), pp. 53-64.

Xiqiao's textile firms at large. But precisely because they operate as a partnership, they find it necessary to avoid anything that smacks of a family business. As a prime example, a businessman whose family I have known since I first visited Xiqiao in 1986 remains today a member of a partnership; and rather than risk disrupting the relationship, my acquaintance prudently has made no attempt to place his sons in the firm even though the eldest is glumly unemployed.

Although the great majority of Xiqiao residents do not come from families with prior generations in the weaving industry, close to half in my survey of successful businesspeople in the Chamber of Commerce do. The grandparents of a fair number of them had been employed in the industry before the revolution, and a fair number of their parents had followed suit during the period of collectives. Many of the Chamber of Commerce members had also personally had experience in textiles through employment in the commune's collective textile factories. And several of those who did not have that background had served during the period of agrarian collectives as supply and marketing agents for the village governments and production teams, giving them an obvious leg up in commercial experience.

In Xiqiao's family firms, the wives often oversee production, while their husbands take care of sales. Among the surveyed Chamber of Commerce members who operated family firms, about half were married to women who had had prior experience as textile factory workers, far higher than was true for the women of Xiqiao as a whole.

Sorting through my interview files for villages elsewhere, it becomes clear that this type of profile is not unique to this district. Even in largely agricultural districts, success in a local specialization or in farming[10] often seems to be related

---

[10]   The salience of family history also comes through clearly in a survey by the anthropologist Yunxiang Yan that focused on which families in a middle-income north China village have become well off and which have not. Forty-one percent of the families of pre-Liberation middle-peasant stock in this village had become prosperous since decollectivization, compared to less than 10 percent of the families from pre-Liberation poor peasant origin. See Yan Yunxiang, "The Impact of Rural Reform on Economic and Social Stratification in a Chinese Village," *The Australian Journal of Chinese Affairs*, No. 27 (January 1992), pp. 9-10. One apparent reason for this difference in outcomes is that, unlike the former poor peasants, the pre-Liberation middle peasants and their children had had to learn to be particularly conscientious in their work habits under the collectives for fear of being criticized as politically retrograde. But a second and probably more important reason for the success of these middle-peasant families lies in the traditional knowledge of economically useful techniques and the cultural skills and attitudes that have been passed down within these families.

This appears to be the case not just in China. Ivan Szelenyi has discovered through surveys in rural Hungary that successful rural entrepreneurship there also adheres to the households that before the socialist era were middle peasant. (See his *Socialist Entrepreneurs: Embourgeoisement in Rural Hungary* (Madison: University of Wisconsin Press, 1988).

to family know-how that was handed down through the generations or, alternatively, to prior personal work experience: a tractor driver or auto mechanic under the collectives held definite advantages when it came to earning money privately in the post-Mao rural transport industry.

An interesting fact in Xiqiao is that few of the successful businesspeople in the Chamber of Commerce have any background at all in the political establishment or are members of the Party. In Xiqiao, with its large and essentially independent private business community, a capacity to perform well in a highly competitive market, not political access to resources or outlets, is what counts. Elsewhere in China, however, political clout and political connections appear to have considerably more bearing on private business success.[11]

A further characteristic common to the Chamber of Commerce members in Xiqiao is their relative youthfulness. As of 1997, the eldest of them for whom I had information was only 43 years of age, after having been in business for more than a decade. Most had started a factory for the first time while still in their twenties. They are risk-takers, largely having jumped into the business in the first half of the 1980s, when it was still a politically risky undertaking.

To expand their businesses, these businesspeople prefer to resort to a high level of savings and reinvestment, rather than depend on bank loans. Even though the Xiqiao township government provides members of the Chamber of Commerce with priority access to bank loans, only about half of them turn to such credit in any meaningful way. Almost all of them prefer to rely primarily on personal savings and borrowings from relatives and friends. These businesspeople have taken calculated risks at various stages of their careers, but most of them appear to prefer to do so with their own capital rather than carry high levels of debt.

In keeping with this preference, an ethic of frugality exists within Xiqiao's business community. Prosperous families build substantial houses for themselves, but not often on the grand scale seen in other wealthy parts of the Pearl River delta. Nor are there many upmarket restaurants in Xiqiao. Rather than compete among themselves to show that they can live ostentatious lifestyles, Xiqiao businesspeople instead strive competitively to position themselves better for the future through upgradings of machinery and plant. Interviews with local

---

[11]   Both urban and rural studies portray efforts by private businesspeople to ingratiate themselves with the officialdom and even to volunteer for political duties in order to secure needed political connections, and several studies have shown, too, that the families of political officials do well in business due to their connections. See, for example, David Wank, "Private Business, Bureaucracy, and Political Alliance in a Chinese City," *The Australian Journal of Chinese Affairs*, No. 33 (January 1995), pp. 55-71; Ole Bruun, *Business and Bureaucracy in a Chinese City*, Ch. 5; Ole Odgaard, "Entrepreneurs and Elite Formation in Rural China," *The Australian Journal of Chinese Affairs*, No. 28 (July, 1992), pp. 89-108; Susan Young, *Private Business and Economic Reform in China* (Armonk: M.E. Sharpe, 1995).

proprietors revealed that many pursue very high rates of reinvestment in their enterprises, often amounting to well over half of their total earnings.

Can we speak of a common "Chinese" pattern to this entrepreneurship? To a large extent, we can. Although very little research has yet been conducted on the strategies for establishing and successfully expanding private enterprises elsewhere in rural China, at least one parallel study does exist: research was carried out in a village in Fujian Province that is filled with private footwear factories, asking similar sets of questions regarding the attributes of the more successful businesspeople, and the findings are very similar to Xiqiao.[12]

In many respects China's rapid rural industrialization resembles what occurred in earlier decades in Taiwan. There, too, most of the surge in manufacturing occurred in small-scale industry, and a great deal of this small-scale private industry was dispersed in Taiwan's countryside.[13] In these parallel circumstances, were similar patterns of entrepreneurship evident?

For a start, in Taiwan, as in Xiqiao, partnerships have been a very common means to amass the capital to initiate a new small-scale enterprise—and, again similar to Xiqiao, these in turn have tended regularly to dissolve into family

---

[12]   Just as in Xiqiao, a great many of the enterprises in this Fujian village were started as partnerships between friends and relatives; and then, once successful, most of these were divided up into family firms. In these family enterprises, the wife similarly plays a significant management role in overseeing production: the Fujian study in fact notes that in many of them "the men are in charge of matters external to the firm; the wives are in charge of what goes on inside it" (*nan zhu wai, nü zhu nei*). The report also notes, though, that much as in Xiqiao, some of the "successful shoe factories have already discarded the family-firm form of management." Finally, almost all of the factory owners in the Fujian village, again akin to Xiqiao, have opted to expand their operations through high rates of personal savings and reinvestment rather than turn to bank credit. Chen Xiangshui and Ding Yuling, "Gaige kaifang houde siren qiye jingying: Fujian Jinjiang Yijiacun de xiechang qiye" (The Management of Private Enterprises in the Period of Reform and Opening: Footwear Manufacturing Enterprises in Yi Family Village, Jinjiang Township, Fujian Province), in *Huanan nongcun shehui wenhua yanjiu lunwen ji* (A Collection of Essays on Society and Culture in South China's Villages) (Taibei: Zhongguo Yanjiuyuan Minzuxuesuo [Taipei: Ethnology Institute of the Academia Sinica], 1998), pp. 287-310.

[13]   In the mid-1960s, 95 percent of the manufacturing enterprises in Taiwan employed fewer than one hundred employees (Richard Stites, "Small-Scale Industry in Yingge, Taiwan," *Modern China*, Vol. 8, No. 2 [April 1982], p. 248), and the rate of growth in industrial employment was greater outside of the urban centers than in them. Thus, according to Taiwan's 1971 industrial census, half of all industrial employment lay in rural districts. See Samuel Ho, "Decentralized Industrialization and Rural Development: Evidence from Taiwan," *Economic Development and Cultural Change*, Vol. 28, No. 1, p. 83. Also see Alice H. Amsden, "Big Business and Urban Congestion in Taiwan: The Origins of Small Enterprise and Regionally Decentralized Industry," *World Development*, Vol. 19, No. 9 (September 1991), pp. 1121-35.

firms.[14] A 1993 interview survey in Taiwan found that 70 percent of the surveyed small and medium-sized enterprises had been founded as partnerships, but at the time of the survey only 29 percent of these partnerships survived; and half of these surviving partnerships were among brothers.[15] The other enterprises were all run as family firms. Again, much as in Xiqiao, the surviving partnership firms in Taiwan had to be careful to operate on unbiased, non-familistic premises. Even when the partnership was between brothers, the inclination to favor one's own nuclear family had to be resisted, to the point that other family members were kept off the payroll: "If one had hired a family member in the partnership company [among brothers], it could be interpreted as expanding one's power in the company, and will cause suspicion among the others."[16]

Too, in many of the small and medium-sized family firms, especially in Taiwan, the wife plays a role in overseeing some of the enterprise's internal operations.[17] In all of these various respects, in Taiwan and Xiqiao the patterns of establishing small manufacturing firms display strikingly similar characteristics.

In Taiwan in the 1960s and 1970s, a great many of the small manufacturing firms were started by people who had gained a sense of their industry by working first as employees in similar factories (a survey in Taiwan showed, for instance, that 60 percent of the owners of shoe factories had originally been shoe workers).[18] Such employees had frugally saved toward the day they could

---

[14]   A study in Hong Kong likewise found a pattern of initial partnerships that dissolve into family firms, even when the initial partners are brothers. Wong Siu-lun, "The Chinese Family Firm: A Model," *The British Journal of Sociology*, Vol. 36, No. 1 (March 1985), p. 62.

[15]   Wang Hong-zen, "Mobility Patterns and Strategies Among Taiwan's Small and Medium-Scale Business People," Ph.D. dissertation, Australian National University, 1998, p. 110. In a parallel light, the data from the 1992 General Survey of Social Change in Taiwan shows that only 13 percent of the small and medium-scale companies on the island are partnerships (ibid.).

[16]   Ibid., p. 112. Similarly, a study in Lukang, a small city in Taiwan, found that "Most partners in Lukang businesses are brothers, or fathers and sons. . . . The business [with brothers as partners] is described as 'just like a corporation. . . .' Partnerships between brothers do not endure indefinitely, and there are no large, complex businesses run jointly by several brothers and their sons." Donald R. DeGlopper, "Doing Business in Lukang," in W.E. Willmott (ed.), *Economic Organization in Chinese Society* (Stanford: Stanford University Press, 1972), p. 317.

[17]   For Taiwan, see Susan Greenhalgh, "Families and Networks in Taiwan's Economic Development," in Edwin A. Winckler and Susan Greenhalgh (eds.), *Contending Approaches to the Political Economy of Taiwan* (Armonk: M.E. Sharpe, 1988), p. 23; Wang Hong-zen, "Mobility Patterns and Stretegies." Both of these sources note that the wife or another female family member often takes charge of the firm's accounts.

[18]   Gwo-shyong Shieh, *"Boss" Island* (New York: Peter Lang, 1992), p. 178.

establish a small factory of their own.[19] Again we see this pattern replicated in Xiqiao.

Once an enterprise in Taiwan was successfully established, the proprietor, just as in Xiqiao, normally engages in a high rate of reinvestment to upgrade and expand the business: most of the successful small and medium-sized businesspeople in Taiwan prefer not to borrow from banks for these purposes despite the ready availability of credit.[20]

All told, thus, the means by which would-be entrepreneurs have developed small-scale industrial enterprises in Taiwan and Xiqiao have directly parallel elements: a similar risk-taking initiative when opportunities opened for small-scale manufacturing; a similar turn to partnerships to gain an initial foothold as a small manufacturer; a similar tendency to dissolve these partnerships eventually in favor of family-based firms; a similar role for the spouse in supervising some of the firm's internal operations; and a similar propensity for the proprietor to save and reinvest out of profits in order to upgrade and expand the business rather than be reliant on bank loans. Faced with a somewhat common set of circumstances, would-be entrepreneurs in the two regions appear to have responded to opportunities in terms of a common set of "Chinese" practices.

Xiqiao provides a bird's-eye view of practices and trends that I believe will become increasingly salient throughout rural China. There remains little doubt today that private enterprise will become progressively more important in China's economic life in the decades to come,[21] and we can expect that the patterns found in Xiqiao will be reproduced a thousand times over. As just one example, we can expect attempts by would-be small entrepreneurs across China to form partnerships as a means to amass the capital needed to establish small enterprises—with many such partnerships in turn dissolving into separate family firms. It is a pattern for developing private enterprise that has strong social roots in China. But we can also expect that, as in Xiqiao, the entrepreneurs who are able to transcend the family-firm tradition will, overall, do better.

The Economic Success of Government-Favored Households

In Xiqiao, the businesspeople do not have much need for government favors in order to get ahead. Competitiveness on the market is what counts. That is less true today in most of rural China, where it is important to a family's economic success to secure access to whatever resources the government has it within its power to dispense. On the whole, the households that are already financially better off have enjoyed a distinct edge in getting such preferential treatment, not

[19]   Wang Hong-zen, "Mobility Patterns and Strategies."

[20]   Ibid., According to Wang, large numbers of such businesses do take out loans from banks, but principally as part of a complicated tax dodge that has become commonplace in Taiwan.

[21]   For evidence, see footnote 1.

only informally through their better "connections" but also through the state's explicit policy preferences.

This "bet on the strong" bias in government policy is exemplified by the government's special financial backing for so-called "specialized households" (*zhuanye hu*)—prosperous peasant families that are chosen to receive favored access to subsidized inputs *because* they are already generating a higher income than their neighbors. A pertinent example here is a village in Yunnan Province that I visited where, under a provincial government program to sow and fertilize hill pastures, thirty of the wealthiest families—less than 10 percent of the village's households—had been granted near-permanent leases in 1987 to most of that village's common pasturelands. From what could be gathered from interviews with local farmers, corruption or favoritism had not been evident here. But the criteria by which the thirty families had been selected by government officials had stressed their financial soundness: the families needed to possess sufficient incomes and assets to ensure that they would be able to repay on time the loans extended to them on special favorable terms to fence and stock the pastures. In short, provincial support and subsidies have gone to an already advantaged minority, with the consequence that a majority of the families in the village have lost access to common grazing lands. They have ended up on the outside of fences looking in.[22]

When this problem was broached with the provincial official who had jurisdiction over this pasture-development project, she quoted an official slogan that has been associated with Deng Xiaoping and that takes dead aim at Maoist egalitarianism: "Some families should be allowed to get rich sooner than others." Implicit in the slogan is the presumption that other families will later have an opportunity to 'catch up'. But this has in fact become out of the question now that most of the village's pasturelands have been closed off to them. What is occurring, in almost all aspects of the rural economy, is that some advantaged families, often with government assistance, have gained near-permanent control over local assets, be they ponds or orchards or local industry or pastures.

This "bet on the strong" bias can also be observed clearly in China's Hainan Province, where in late 1993 I supervised a random survey of 69 farming families in six relatively prosperous rural townships that specialize in growing winter vegetables. Among these 69 families, only 9 (13 percent) had succeeded in securing loans from the government Agricultural Bank or Credit Association during the previous year. The average household income of the families who obtained these loans had amounted to Y63,000 that year, and they borrowed, on

---

[22]   A disgruntled peasant from this village, interviewed while tending sheep as a hired hand on his more fortunate neighbor's fenced pastures, defiantly claimed that he would somehow build his own large flock anyway, even without access to good pasturage. From his tone of voice, it was obvious that he did not genuinely see this as a viable plan; rather, he seems to have been trying to express his own angry refusal to accept that, in one fell swoop, a new economic/social structure in the village had been erected upon unequal access to property.

average, Y26,000 apiece. This compared to an average household income of only Y8,500 among the other households. Interviews revealed that the majority of these latter families had also wanted to borrow for investment purposes, but that official banking policy had favored loans to those already rich—and to those with personal influence. In all, the survey that I supervised in 1993 of 214 households in this and other parts of rural Hainan Province revealed that only 9.8 percent of the families—the better connected and financially better-off households—had received any formal loan during the past year.

China's tax system is also regressively skewed to the advantage of the rural wealthy. One study has shown that the richest 10 percent of the rural Chinese population as of the early 1990s received 26 percent of the total rural income but paid only 13 percent of the taxes[23]—that is, they were taxed at only half the rate paid by the rest of the rural population. (One reason is that taxes are largely on land, which each family in a village, rich or poor, possesses in relatively equal measure, while non-agricultural sources of income are lightly or irregularly taxed, if at all.) In China today, those who enjoy a head start then get assisted by the government's lending and tax policies and pull yet further ahead of their neighbors. A consequence is that wealth has become increasingly concentrated in the hands of the most prosperous households, due partly to the entrepreneurial initiative of a capable minority and partly to government policies that favor the already affluent—and sometimes, too, to unofficial "connections" in the form of nepotism and corruption.

A good illustration of the latter was revealed during interviewing in 1991 in a moderately well-off village along the Guizhou-Yunnan provincial border. The economically most successful man in the village had enjoyed a single advantage: a very valuable "connection" to a minor official in the county town. The two had served together in the army, and on their return to civilian life the army buddy had used family connections to get a posting to the county's Foreign Trade Bureau. There, he had garnered for his rural friend a monopoly commission for the purchase from farmers of dried ginger and buckwheat, and had also secured for his friend a low-interest loan from the Foreign Trade Bureau for the purchase of a truck.

In one rural township of Hainan Province that I visited, according to the deputy township head, almost all of the loans from local bank branches and credit associations went to the relatives of township and village officials and to wealthy households, who reportedly often used the money to rent the land of neighbors who were short of capital and then sometimes employed those neighbors as hired hands. In yet another district, the head of a township confided that much of the credit went to households who had relatives employed at the Agricultural Bank and local credit associations. In 1990 an interviewee from a village of boat people in Guangdong Province told me that "the poor in my village are those who have

---

23   Azizur Rahman Khan, Keith Griffin, Carl Riskin and Zhao Renwei, "Sources of Income Inequality in Post-Reform China," *China Economic Review*, Vol. 4, No. 1 (1993), p. 24.

no money to buy boats. Only the people with power could get the loans to buy any boats." Throughout rural China during the past two decades, it appears that both the politically connected and the financially better-off households have enjoyed a distinct edge in gaining access to whatever bank credit or grants become available.

Not surprisingly, Chinese farmers declare themselves to be far less resentful about wealth that has been acquired through what they consider legitimate means—hard work and skill—than wealth acquired through such official connections. The extent of these latter practices, and their impact on the creation of a new monied class, should not be underestimated. It is a source of rising political tension.

Self-enrichment Among Rural Officials

Again and again in my interview research, it became clear that a disproportionate number of the newly successful households have risen from the ranks of the local cadres.[24] It is not just "connections" and corrupt practices that have given such men (very few are women) a head start over their neighbors. Unlike the ordinary peasantry, the socialist era had provided them with a good training in business: experience in handling sizable sums of money, in managing groups of workers, in dealing with the officialdom, and in taking charge of management decisions in a complex agricultural regime. It is ironic that many of the men favored with leadership positions under the collectives have, for that very reason, benefited subsequently from the demise of agrarian socialism.

But a second factor appears to be more important. Alongside the return to family farming in China in the early 1980s, the state's deliberate pullback from its domination of village life simultaneously weakened the central government's hold over the conduct of rural officials. Increasingly, they have taken advantage of this pullback to favor their own private interests and those of their favorites, unimpeded by fears of anti-corruption campaigns or purges.

Throughout the Chinese countryside, such a trend was evident from the very start of decollectivization. Even though the distribution of ordinary agricultural land was egalitarian and relatively free of corruption, the leasing or sale of production-team and village assets other than farm fields—the orchards, fishponds, village factories, and equipment—all too frequently favored the families of the Chinese officials involved in their disbursement. Sometimes they improperly sold or very cheaply leased these assets to themselves. Other times, though the bidding processes were technically open and fair, they were the only

---

[24]   This is also the clear finding of a rural household survey devised by Andrew Walder: "Rural Cadres and the Market Economy in the Deng Era: Evidence from a National Survey," in John Wong and Zheng Yongnian (eds.), *The Nanxun Legacy and China's Development in the Post-Deng Era* (Singapore: Singapore University Press and World Scientific, 2001), pp. 95-120.

villagers with sufficient know-how and market connections, and thus the only ones to make a bid.[25]

In addition, village officials have been able to use their power to secure payoffs from other rural families. They can do so because the rural population continues to be dependent upon the goodwill of village and higher-level rural cadres to get access to credit, new housing sites, and licenses to engage in business. Chinese peasants frequently need to resort to currying these cadres' favor through gifts of money and shows of deference.

Corruption most certainly is involved here. But to consider it simply as corruption may miss an important ingredient undergirding these transactions— new types of patronage networks are emerging. Even where entrepreneurial families do not already have any special *guanxi* relationships in place, by persistently giving gifts they can curry the favor of the various officials who might be helpful to the operation and expansion of family enterprises. Under the collectives, of course, patron–client relationships between cadres and peasants had also existed, but now an already prospering peasant family's wealth provides a distinct advantage in sealing such relationships.

Previously, under the communes, the range of potential patrons was greatly restricted. Because only a small group of local cadres had controlled all of a village's economic and political affairs, all patronage had flowed through them. Now a more pluralistic structure of patronage has developed. For different sorts of favors, villagers can go to different patrons, rather than to a single set of village cadres. This growth of diffuse patron–client networks provides the farmers with considerably greater freedom to maneuver, and their autonomous building of patronage links has further eroded the former rigid structuring of rural power.

Nevertheless, the cadres are being allowed to trade off some of their power for wealth, joining the new monied elite that is emerging. As an example, a survey of a north China village discovered that fully 54 percent of the village's officials who have held positions during or since decollectivization had become wealthy by local standards. This compares to only 16 percent of the villagers as a whole. Interestingly, too, only 17 percent of those who had once been village officials but no longer held office at the time of decollectivization have become wealthy since then. Regardless of the skills they had earlier acquired as local cadres, without power over village resources they have done no better economically than the ordinary farmers.[26] As of the mid-1990s in this village, the village Party secretary had advanced his own household from being one of the poorest to one of the richest in the community, and his two grown sons'

[25]   See, for example, Jonathan Unger, "Decollectivization in a Guangdong Village," p. 277.

[26]   Yan Yunxiang, "The Impact of Rural Reform," p. 10.

households were the two wealthiest in the village.[27] Similarly, computer analysis of a countywide survey in a different rural county in north China revealed "Over 100 percent of the difference [in incomes] between households with and without village-level cadres is explained by . . . the political rents associated with the position."[28] As an example, access to extra land is necessary to plant orchards or to erect substantial chicken coops and animal enclosures, and village officials in this county comprised 33 percent and 38 percent, respectively, of the top 1 percent of earners in fruit production and animal husbandry.[29] Here and elsewhere in rural China, the importance of power and office in the attainment of wealth is obvious.

If this is true of current-day Chinese village officials, their counterparts in the market towns and county capitals hold even greater opportunities to divert money into their own pockets. An example taken from Huidong County in Guangdong, one among many in my interview files, illustrates how blatantly the powers of office can be turned to the self-interest of such officials. An interviewee has explained that the sons of the leading officials of his rural township opened car repair garages, and almost simultaneously a local regulation was promulgated that all motor vehicles had to pass safety inspections every year, with these garages the only ones licensed to make the required repairs.

Such opportunities to make private money through one's control of public authority are especially available in the rich coastal and suburban districts, where local private entrepreneurs are getting into businesses that oblige them to have frequent interactions with local government offices. More significant, the leading officials in these districts supervise an array of collective factories that can be milked for their own benefit. These opportunities escalated during the 1990s when the central government encouraged the conversion of collectively owned factories into "share-holding cooperative enterprises" (*gufen hezuozhi qiye*). Many rural officials and enterprise directors enriched themselves by transferring substantial chunks of the factory shares to themselves.[30] The pickings are far more

---

[27]   Yan, Yunxiang, "Everyday Power Relations: Changes in a North China Village," in Andrew Walder (ed.), *The Waning of the Communist State* (Berkeley: University of California Press, 1995), p. 226.

[28]   Jonathan Morduch and Terry Sicular, "Politics, Growth, and Inequality in Rural China: Does it Pay to Join the Party?" *Journal of Public Economics*, No. 77 (2000), p. 349. Interestingly, the answer to the question posed in the article's title is, no, being a rural Party member confers no direct benefits through wealth enhancement; only the power of *officeholding* counts significantly.

[29]   Ibid., p. 351.

[30]   Interesting examples of these machinations are discussed in Sally Sargeson and Jian Zhang, "Reassessing the Role of the Local State: A Case Study of Local Government Interventions in Property Rights Reform in a Hangzhou District," *The China Journal*, No. 42 (July 1999), pp. 77-99.

meager in the hinterlands. In the six most impoverished counties in the interior of southwest China where I conducted research in the 1990s, not one contained even a single private factory, and publicly owned factories were very few and far between.

The richer areas have spawned a vigorous growth of both private and collective industrial and commercial activity and, at the same time, two types of elite wealthy households: first, some of the cadres and their relatives and friends, who have been converting official positions into sources of private income; and second, entrepreneurs who have risen through their own skill and resourcefulness, such as those of Xiqiao. Before, under the collectives, throughout rural China there was a single hierarchy that was grounded in differential access to power; now there are two. One is still intimately associated with political and administrative power, but with power increasingly perceived as a means to wealth; and the second originates independently in ownership of economic assets, which in turn is used, when necessary, to buy political cooperation and protection. In certain circumstances these two sets—the Mandarins and the entrepreneurs— have come into conflict, with the officialdom of some districts fitfully moving to suppress or to ruinously milk the latter. But increasingly the two elites have developed a *modus vivendi*, and indeed have begun to coalesce. In some cases this has come about through business partnerships. Even more often, the sons of officials have placed themselves among the entrepreneurs with their parents' strong assistance. In yet other cases, strategic intermarriages have emerged between the offspring of officials and those of wealthy entrepreneurs that bring such families directly into the same fold.

The development of this new hybrid class during the course of the past two decades does not bode well for the poorer sectors of the rural populace. As just one example, intervention by local officials is often the only available means to ameliorate the harsh Dickensian work regime in some of the private rural industrial enterprises. But the merging of the local power elite and the new monied elite would likely spell an end to the willingness of local officials to intervene in defense of workers.

Chapter Eight

LOCAL GOVERNMENTS AND PRIVATE ENTERPRISE:
A CASE STUDY[*]

Relations between the rural populace and the grassroots levels of government vary enormously across China. One reason is that the very nature of the power wielded by a local rural government today is strongly influenced by the extent of local industrialization and, just as importantly, by the *type* of factory ownership that prevails locally.

Thus far, most studies have concentrated on rural districts where the officials of the villages and rural townships have engineered the development of publicly owned, not privately owned, industry.[1] Under Mao, such officials had received mixed signals from above. While on the one side they had been encouraged to start local factories, on the other they had been denied access to most kinds of industrial inputs, which were largely reserved for China's state-owned enterprises. They also were usually forbidden from erecting factories that produced goods that competed with the lumbering state-owned industrial sector. Under Deng, these restrictions gradually disappeared, and the countryside was given the go-ahead to take advantage of its lower administrative and labor costs. A huge surge in rural industrialization ensued, starting in the 1980s and

---

[*]   Anita Chan co-authored parts of this chapter and I am grateful to her for this input. The research project was funded by the Asia Research Centre at Murdoch University and by the Australian National University.

[1]   This was especially the case with studies up through the mid-1990s. See, for example, Pei Xiaolin, "Township-Village Enterprises, Local Governments, and Rural Communities", in Eduard Vermeer, Frank Pieke, and Woei Lien Chong (eds.), *Cooperative and Collective in China's Rural Development* (Armonk: M.E. Sharpe, 1998), pp. 110-36; Minchuan Yang, "Reshaping Peasant Culture and Community: Rural Industrialization in a Chinese Village", *Modern China* Vol. 20, No. 2 (April 1994), pp. 157-79; Jean Oi, "The Role of the Local State in China's Transitional Economy", *The China Quarterly*, No. 144 (December, 1995), pp. 1132-49; Nan Lin, "Local Market Socialism: Local Corporatism in Action in Rural China", *Theory and Society*, Vol. 24 (1995), pp. 301-54; and John Wong, Rong Ma, and Mu Yang (eds.), *China's Rural Entrepreneurs: The Case Studies* (Singapore: Times Academic Press, 1995). An excellent detailed examination of this phenomenon, focusing on a township in Shandong Province, is Ray Yep, "Rural Entrepreneurs and the Changing State-Society Relationship in China in the Reform Era," Ph.D. dissertation, Oxford University, 1998.

accelerating in the 1990s.[2] For most of the past two decades, until the past few years, the rural industrial sector was the fastest growing portion of the most rapidly developing nation on earth, and until the past decade the ownership of these factories predominantly lay with the rural governments. Jean Oi, who has written a good deal about this phenomenon, states that such "local governments have taken on many of the characteristics of a business corporation, with officials acting as the equivalent of a board of directors."[3] Since they control the revenues from the publicly owned factories, they can shift new investments and resources from one enterprise to another, and to non-industrial parts of the public sector as well, much as a conglomerate shifts resources between its subsidiaries. The local officials also control access to coveted employment in the factories, and through this and their control of revenues they can build patronage relationships with large numbers of local constituents.

A second genre of rural industrialization is exemplified by the counties lying adjacent to Hong Kong, where an enormous amount of investment in rural factories has been undertaken by Hong Kong and Taiwanese corporations.[4] In Chen Village, for example, there is practically no indigenously owned industry today, either collective or private, since the village government and the local people alike feel incapable of competing successfully against the experienced, well-capitalized foreign investors. The Party secretary of Chen Village controls sizable funds by renting out public land and buildings to foreign companies, and through the rental fees he has been able to construct a new village school and other public facilities and to develop a substantial personal patronage system. But the village government here has become a one-man show, dominated entirely by the Party secretary, since as a simple rent-collector he has no need for any additional personnel.[5]

---

[2] The fixed assets of the rural enterprises increased at a phenomenal rate of 27 percent per annum in the five-year period between 1985 and 1990 and then at an even more sizzling rate of 37 percent per year between 1990 and 1995. Jean Oi, *Rural China Takes Off* (Berkeley: University of California Press, 1999), p. 82.

[3] Jean Oi, "Fiscal Reform and the Economic Foundations of Local State Corporatism in China", *World Politics*, Vol. 45, No. 1 (October 1992), p. 100. Also see her book *Rural China Takes Off*. Also Victor Nee and Sijin Su, "Institutions, Social Ties, and Commitment in China's Corporatist Transformation", in John McMillan and Barry Naughton (eds.), *Reforming Asian Socialism: The Growth of Market Institutions* (Ann Arbor: University of Michigan Press, 1996), p. 120. Also Gregory Ruf, *Cadres and Kin: Making a Socialist Village in West China, 1921-1991* (Stanford: Stanford University Press, 1998); also see his "Managing Interests: Collective Property Rights and Village Enterprise in Rural Sichuan", in Jean Oi and Andrew Walder (eds.), *Property Rights and Economic Reform in China* (Stanford: Stanford University Press, 1999).

[4] These districts include the former Bao'an County and Dongguan and Huizhou Counties.

[5] On this see Chan, Madsen and Unger, *Chen Village Under Mao and Deng*, pp. 316-20.

A third variant is found in rural districts in the hinterlands that have experienced almost no industrialization. After decollectivization and a return to family farming, village officials there no longer directly control any economic resources, and some of these villages find it hard to extract revenues from recalcitrant householders. In such villages public services are underfinanced and village schools are sometimes near collapse. Such villages suffer from a weakness of leadership and a loss of community cohesion.[6]

A very different scenario is evident, finally, in rural communities where private industry predominates. One such area is Wenzhou Prefecture in Zhejiang Province[7] and a second is Xiqiao Township in Guangdong, which was discussed in the previous chapter and will again be the focus of attention in this chapter. It will be seen that in a district like Xiqiao the very nature of private industrial development significantly affects the texture of the relations between the local Party-state and residents.

Few rural districts can be expected to experience Xiqiao's phenomenal industrial growth or to develop the numbers of private factories that have sprung up there, but a strong argument can be made that as time passes, more and more rural districts will similarly contain a preponderance of private enterprise. In light of this, Xiqiao township may point the way to how local government institutions will operate in the future in much of rural China. The chapter's conclusion will analyze the signal differences between the shape of local governance today in districts like Xiqiao as against rural districts where other patterns of industrialization thus far have predominated.

When examining the relationship between local governments and industry, it is also important to distinguish between the different levels of local government. We will examine, in turn, what this entails for the village governments, for the former agricultural production teams, and for the township level of government in

---

[6]   On such villages, see Kevin O'Brien's description of what the Chinese call "paralyzed villages", in his "Implementing Political Reform in China's Villages", *The Australian Journal of Chinese Affairs*, No. 32 (July 1994), pp. 51-53.

[7]   Wenzhou Prefecture, comprising a city and eight counties in Zhejiang Province, has been much studied as a whole, but less so at the grassroots level from within local townships and villages. In this respect, the writings on Wenzhou are not parallel to the chapter you are reading. Good general studies of Wenzhou from the early 1990s, when foreign observers were fascinated by the "Wenzhou model", include Keith Forster, "The Wenzhou Model for Economic Development: Impressions", *China Information*, Vol. 5, No. 3 (Winter 1990-91), pp. 53-64; Yia-Ling Liu, "Reform From Below: The Private Economy and Local Politics in the Rural Industrialization of Wenzhou", *The China Quarterly*, No. 130 (June 1992), pp. 293-316; Allen Liu, "The Wenzhou Model of Development and China's Modernization", *Asian Survey*, Vol. 32, No. 8 (August 1992), pp. 696-711; Kristen Parris, "Local Initiative and National Reform: The Wenzhou Model of Development", *The China Quarterly*, No. 134 (June 1993), pp. 242-63; and Peter Nolan and Dong Furen (eds.), *Market Forces in China: Competition and Small Business—The Wenzhou Debate* (London: Zed Books, 1990).

Xiqiao. As a general example, a large number of authors have written about the publicly owned TVEs (township and village enterprises) as if they comprise a single category of enterprise—as if the question of what level of local government owns and administers an enterprise is of no consequence. But it will be seen that such writings ignore the different financial constraints, the different types of officials overseeing the operations of local industry—private firms and TVEs alike—and the different constituencies and influences faced respectively by township and village governments.

In Xiqiao, in an environment in which there is a large amount of private business activity, what roles do the several levels of local government play? Do they help out the 2,000-plus local private manufacturing firms[8] in the capacity of a local "developmental state";[9] or are the local authorities antagonistic to private industry? Are the authorities entrepreneurial on their own account, establishing new publicly owned factories in competition with the private ones? Or are the local governments essentially parasitical and a burden upon the local populace? Are the various levels of local government strong or weak? Do the local governments, indeed, make much difference at all to local development?

The short answer to these questions is that the local administrations in Xiqiao, at both the village and township levels, do play a developmental role. But the intensity and efficacy of these efforts vary considerably between villages and between administrative levels, for reasons that will be observed. We will first examine the village governments (formerly, under Mao, production brigades), then the sub-village economic cooperatives (the former agricultural production teams), and finally the Xiqiao township government (formerly the commune administration).

Village Governments: A Tale of Two Communities

Xiqiao's twenty-six village governments have good reasons to serve as promoters of private industrialization. Not just the local populace's prosperity but also a good part of the village-level revenues depend upon this. But some of the village leaderships hustle to help develop industry far more entrepreneurially than others.

---

[8] In addition to the 1,600-plus textile weaving factories in Xiqiao, several hundred other private factories have been established in the township, in some cases related to the textile trade, as with spinning and dyeing factories, but in many cases not.

[9] This term has been common in the literature on East Asian capitalist development, referring to a government that actively seeks to create the conditions for economic development by protecting and encouraging key sectors of the economy, by facilitating investment, and by itself investing in needed infrastructure. More recently, the term has also been applied to China. For instance, Marc Blecher and Vivienne Shue posit that a Chinese county government that they have studied successfully functions as a local developmental state. See their *Tethered Deer: Government and Economy in a Chinese County* (Stanford: Stanford University Press, 1996).

It is partly a question of village histories and opportunities and partly a question of the personalities and capabilities of village leaders. This can be illustrated by focusing on two of the villages in the township, Lianxin and Jiancun.

In the first half of the 1980s Lianxin had been among the very first villages to witness an explosion of private entrepreneurship in the textile industry. The village had a significant advantage, in that one of the three commune-owned textile mills was located in the village, and thus a sizable number of the households there had gained crucial experience working with electric looms and large-scale textile production. But a second important factor was that the village government did not try to hinder private enterprise during the mid-1980s, when Beijing had not yet made it clear whether private factories would be politically tolerated over the long term. In that climate, the village officials had been risk-takers and had leased out factory sites to anyone who wanted to set up their own weaving establishment. Given a double head start—experience in the weaving industry and early access to private manufacturing—a great many villagers joined in the scramble to establish small factories. At the height of the rush in the latter years of the 1980s, as many as 450 such factories had opened in the village.

Even today, after the smallest and least capable have been weeded out, this village of 920 local families (3,550 people in all) contains more than 300 textile manufacturing firms—mostly family-owned enterprises, but including a number of partnership firms. All told, thus, close to half of all the households in the village are wholly or partly the owners of factories. These employ more than 6,000 migrant workers. In the decade between 1986 and the end of 1996, according to mimeographed village documents, the value of production in the private enterprises had leaped by more than 3,300 percent. From this industry, the village government collects very sizable revenues.

At the same time, the Lianxin village government, rather than just content itself with revenue collecting, has also sought actively to develop publicly owned industry. In 1991 a new village Party secretary decided to make his mark through this. He did not attempt to compete with the private textile factories; it was not feasible for a collective enterprise to try to match their efficiencies in production.[10] Instead, he looked across to the township next door. While Xiqiao Township was concentrating on textile production, Nanzhuan Township, just across a narrow river, had developed a very different specialization in floor and wall tiles. From very small beginnings in the early 1980s, Nanzhuan Township had come to dominate the south China market. Seeing this success, the Lianxin village Party secretary had the village government borrow close to a hundred million *yuan* in bank loans to erect a vast tile factory. He imported sets of

---

[10] This type of decision not to compete head on with the private sector is commonplace throughout Nanhai County. A book on Nanhai's rural industrialization is clear on this point. See Wang Ying, *Xin jiti zhuyi: xiangcun shehui de zai zuzhi* (The New Collectivism: Rural Society's Reorganization), (Beijing: Jingji Guanli Chubanshe, 1996), p. 33.

advanced machinery from West Germany and hired specialists in ceramic tile manufacture from other parts of China. The facility is of truly awesome size, with huge halls containing computerized conveyor-belt kilns the length of football fields. In the early 1990s a property boom was in full swing in Guangdong, and this was generating a voracious demand for construction tiles. Whatever was produced by the new factory could be sold for a good profit, and so the village government took out a series of additional huge loans to erect a further three gigantic tile factories in quick succession, within less than two years. A number of other village governments in Xiqiao scrambled to follow suit. By 1997 the township contained twenty-three behemoth tile factories.

Whereas textile manufacture in Xiqiao has become an entirely private endeavor, tile manufacture has become the local village governments' speciality and the focus for the local officials' entrepreneurship. The concentration of these tile factories in a small area, similar to the concentration of private textile enterprises, gives them an edge over the isolated factories of other regions. Taking advantage of this, as of 1997 1.8 billion *yuan* had been invested in this industry by village governments in Xiqiao Township—constituting fully six-sevenths of these governments' total industrial assets.[11] With textile and tile production both expanding dramatically in this entirely bifurcated pattern of entrepreneurship, Xiqiao development races, as it were, on two legs.

In Xiqiao, what counts the most for officials' personal prospects is doing well economically, and Lianxin Village's Party secretary was rewarded for his success. He was elevated in 1995 to serve simultaneously as the Party secretary and head of government of Xiqiao Township—the new local political kingpin. In departing Lianxin, he essentially was able to select his own successors: and for the posts of village head and village Party secretary he chose two local businessmen who had done very well in textile manufacturing.[12] The criteria for success in private enterprise and in public office are beginning to converge—a process that is deeply modifying the nature of village Party cells.

Jiancun, a village of 2,360 residents in 680 households, provides a counterpoint to Lianxin. Jiancun was the native village of the 19th-century inventor/industrialist Chen Qiyuan, who had built in the village China's first

---

[11]   While tile manufacture dominates village-level investment, some of the village governments also participate in other types of ventures. In addition to the four tile factories, the Lianxin Village administration also owns a cloth-dyeing factory (these tend to be collective enterprises in Xiqiao). A different example is the village next door to the township market town, whose village government not only owns a huge tile factory, but also a rubber factory, a watch parts factory, and a construction firm. When that village's administration is approached to sell or lease land, it negotiates to have the new building projects handled by its own construction firm.

[12]   In interviews with Lianxin's two new leaders, it transpired that they continued to own the textile enterprises, and relatives were running the businesses for them for the duration of their tenures in office.

mechanized firm, a silk-spinning factory. Silk spinning, not weaving, continued to predominate in the village through the first half of the 20th century, so when the new Communist authorities in the 1950s chose where to locate the three collective weaving factories, Jiancun lost out. Consequently, when the door was thrown open to private textile manufacture in the early 1980s, the villagers here were less well positioned to exploit the opportunity in terms of recent experience and know-how.

But it was also a question of village government attitudes. Over the past few decades the political leaders of Jiancun have been a cautious lot. It is a leadership that has been unchanged since collective days: all three of the village leadership posts have been occupied, in rotation, by the same tightknit group of three people. Over the past two decades, again and again they have waited to see how other villages fare before they themselves contemplate any new ventures.

Back in 1986, I had spent several days in Jiancun at a time when it was not yet clear in China that private factories would continue to be politically tolerated. During that 1986 visit, I spent time with a young former production-team head who had jumped into the private textile boom two years earlier—but not in his own village of Jiancun. When village leaders in 1984 denied him permission to establish a factory in the village, he had gone into partnership with his brother-in-law from Lianxin to build a textile factory there. Today, the Jiancun government is anxious to attract textile-weaving factories to the village so as to increase village revenues, but the late start has hurt. The village now contains only forty-some textile factories (one-eighth the number of Lianxin) and only sixty manufacturing enterprises of all types.

Collective-sector enterprises were politically safer in the early years of the Deng era, and the Jiancun village government set up its own textile factory in 1983. But the venture failed and the village government pulled out in 1988. It leases the plant today to a local private businessman for an annual rent. The village government in fact no longer operates any collective factories at all. As the village Party secretary confides: "We're more inclined toward renting out land and our old buildings and getting people to invest. We trust in rent." When other villages plunged into massive investments in tile factories, the Jiancun government held back: "We felt that setting up collective enterprises was difficult—too risky. It would have meant taking out enormous loans, and would have required us to construct huge buildings, and the enterprises would have been hard to operate. Others offered to assist us to set up a tile factory—specialists came—but we refused. We ourselves don't have the skills to oversee that type of operation. Collective enterprises are bound to fail."

Still, in its own modest way, the Jiancun village government tries to be entrepreneurial. Like other village governments in Xiqiao, it obtains loans for village factories that wish to upgrade their equipment. Using its influence as an official organ, it had borrowed 7 million *yuan* from banks and from the township finance bureau at rates of interest in 1997 of 15-17 percent, and the village government then re-loaned these funds at the same interest rates to local enterprises. The explicit policy is to give priority to "assisting the strong, the big and the finest" of the enterprises, partly on the grounds that these can best guarantee repayment of the loans, but even more so because they are the most likely to succeed over the long term and to provide the village government with the highest potential revenues.

The villages of Xiqiao compete with one another to rent out land for private-sector factory sites. In doing so, they no longer think in terms of favoring just local applicants. As one example, by offering slightly better terms than the other villages in Xiqiao the Jiancun village Party secretary succeeded in wooing an investor from Heilongjiang Province—a former textile wholesaler who used to frequent the Xiqiao market—to set up a new 4 million *yuan* textile factory in Jiancun and to settle there with his family. The rent he pays for his factory site and his local business taxes and fees are set at the same rate as for other manufacturers in the village, and the village government re-loans investment funds to him on the same terms as to other local borrowers. Xiqiao's eagerness to remain at the cutting edge of the domestic textile market has, in other words, begun breaking down traditional parochial attitudes toward "outsiders."

Helping Out Private Businesses

Every month each village's public-security officer goes door to door to each factory to collect a "management fee" (for the textile factories, a charge of 90-100 yuan per operating loom, depending on the village). In some of the villages that do not own tile factories, such as Jiancun, this levy is the village administration's main form of revenue. The village public-security officer also collects the bulk of the industrial taxes and fees on behalf of the township and county,[13] and most of these similarly are based on how many operating looms each textile factory possesses. From my rough calculations, the combined taxes and fees amount to some 15-20 percent of the enterprises' profits.

But in their efforts to spur industrial expansion, village officials in Xiqiao are careful to reduce even this modest impost. The method is simple. Regulations state that if a factory is going through a slow period, the idle looms are not taxed. Village cadres and local factory owners alike confided to me that every month the village officials deliberately under-report the numbers of looms in operation, and do so evenhandedly, across the board, for all of the factories. Every village for

---

[13]   In Xiqiao, the enterprises need to pay a total of thirteen taxes and fees each month. Two are dubbed taxes (*shui*)—a national tax and a regional tax that gets divided up between Guangdong Province and Nanhai County—while all of the local township levies are labeled "fees" (*fei*). In China, the revenues that are needed to support each of the local government bureaus are not bunched together into a single omnibus government fee; instead, each local organ of government imposes its own separate fee: a fee for the township education authorities, one for the fire department, one for sewage, one to support township development, one to support the township commerce bureau, and so forth (on this, see Ch. 10). To limit the inconvenience, however, almost all of these taxes and township and village fees are collected from the enterprises in one lump sum by the village public security officer.

which information was obtained carries out this under-reporting to just about the same degree.

By doing so, they are undercutting not just village revenues, but also the township government's revenues. The township's leaders are well aware of this practice, yet they approvingly turn a blind eye. One leading township official explained that taxes and fees need to be kept below the levels permitted under the national government's tax and fee regulations, so as to keep Xiqiao's textile factories competitive with other textile districts in China. Re-investment in increasingly better machinery, I was told, depends upon keeping funds in the factory owners' hands through low tax and fee levels. The officials are anxious, at all levels of local government, not to kill the geese that lay the golden eggs.

To be sure, the village officials also gain some personal monetary benefits from this method of collecting fees. Two interviewees who own factories in Xiqiao (they come from villages other than Lianxin and Jiancun) confided that every month, under the table, they pay the village official who inspects their factory a modest amount for each of the looms that escapes taxation. Every factory owner in their villages, they noted, gives the same standard rate of payoff, which apparently is then shared out among the village's other officials.

These factory owners do not see the payments as evidence of the local officials' corruption, however. Generally, as will be seen, factory owners do complain about officials' corruption, but this particular payment is regarded more as a gratuity. One reason for this perception may be that this under-reporting of looms is often financially disadvantageous to the village officers, even when the payoffs are taken into account. Under directives from the county, the Xiqiao Township government determines the village officialdom's salaries each year by six criteria, which largely weigh how much revenue they have generated through fee and tax collections.[14] Yet this strong monetary incentive to boost the collection of fees does not seem to outweigh in village officials' minds the longer-term importance of expanding the village-based industries. The pressures from within the village apparently are sufficient to keep them to this course, as is their knowledge that strong industrial expansion will raise their own income base in the *future*. They can look across to Lianxin, the village with the best record of prior industrial expansion, where the top three officials' salaries averaged Y190,000 apiece in 1997. In Jiancun, in comparison, the three top officials' salaries averaged Y43,000.

---

14   The six criteria that the township's Village Enterprises Office uses to determine the salaries of the leading officials of a village are: the village government's total revenues; the difference between this year's revenues and last year's; the amount of "management fees" collected; the ratio of depreciation to total output in any village-owned industry (low is good); the village government's fulfillment of Party and administrative directives; and its fulfillment of tax-collection duties.

Y190,000 would be considered a princely sum in most parts of China. In China as a whole, the average rural household income was only Y8,100 in 1996.[15] But Xiqiao is far richer than other parts of the country. In Lianxin Village, the average household's net income amounted to Y80,000 in 1996, according to the village government's official calculations—and successful businesspeople earn far more than that. The two businessmen who took over the Lianxin Village leadership in 1995 were able to take the pose in an interview that they were making a financial sacrifice to fulfill their civic duty.

The extent of the township's economic boom is such that even with the lowered fees from factories, village government revenues in Xiqiao are comfortably high, even in Jiancun. The fees plus the rents from fish ponds and from the ten village enterprises that the Jiancun village government leases out generate, altogether, enough revenue for it to picture itself as a benefactor in providing village services. Jiancun spent Y100,000 to equip the village primary school with a computer lab, a further Y60,000 on the school library, another Y100,000 for the school's music room, and another Y300,000 to renovate the village nursery school. It finances an old people's home and supports a small medical clinic. Lianxin Village goes further, with an even better-equipped school, four nurseries containing more than 400 toddlers, and a health clinic that boasts three doctors. Yet even taking account of these expenditures, enough revenues are available from village-level rents and endeavors that none of the local governments in Xiqiao feels a need to levy any general taxes on village households.[16] Again, the situation here is very different from China's less well-off rural districts, where, for reasons that will be discussed in Chapter Ten, high local tax impositions have put a heavy burden on villagers.

Businesspeople's Attitudes toward Village Officials

Despite the efforts of the village and township governments to serve as benefactors, to keep taxes and fees on businesses modest, and to promote local industrial development through loans and other services to local enterprises, most of the factory owners who were interviewed in Xiqiao consider the local governments to be of very limited and tangential importance to the success of

---

[15]   *Zhongguo nongcun jingji nianjian 1997* (1997 Rural Statistical Yearbook of China), pp. 51, 280. The yearbook does not directly list the average rural household income, so this figure was derived from the yearbook's separate listings of the average per capita rural income and the average rural household size.

[16]   Specific fees for services on a user-pays basis are nonetheless still imposed for families wishing to avail themselves of these. For instance, school pupils need to pay an annual tuition fee, and in one village in the township parents complained that they each were being asked to contribute Y1,500 to build a new junior high school. The township similarly imposes a variety of user fees such an annual road-use fee for motorcycles.

their businesses. They obtain their inputs entirely on the market, and themselves must scramble to sell their textiles in a highly competitive national market. They hire their own workforce off the street and, despite the local officials' programs to help secure bank loans for them, very largely raise their own capital through reinvestment of profits, borrowings from relatives and friends, and direct bank loans. Interviewees indicated that they feel little need to wine and dine officials, or to ply the local officials with gifts to secure their patronage, nor do they feel it to be of any particular advantage to subordinate themselves to the officialdom in other ways in order to survive and prosper in their businesses. In all of this, the textile-factory owners of Xiqiao appear to act quite differently from the medium-sized businesspeople who have been studied in a number of other locales in China, both urban and rural.[17] The private sector in Xiqiao has expanded to the point where it possesses its own *gravitas* and carries its own weight socially and (albeit passively) politically.

In these circumstances, despite the village governments' efforts to be of assistance to local business, the officials are viewed by villagers in essentially negative terms. Indeed, interviewees in the villages repeatedly claimed in private that the officials are almost all corrupt. They complained that the village governments' accounts are not transparent and that expenditures by the village governments to support village services are inadequate compared to the presumed revenues. The implication is that the funds are disappearing into the pockets of the officials. The villagers may well be right in their accusations, but local corruption is not as blatant as in other parts of the Chinese countryside that I have visited. Interviewees in Xiqiao find it difficult, when voicing their suspicions, to pinpoint specific instances of any corrupt diversion of village funds or any unexplained high living standard among the village officials. Whatever the extent of corruption there may be, it needs to be kept well hidden from a noncomplaisant populace.

---

[17] See David Wank, *Commodifying Communism: Business, Trust, and Politics in a Chinese City* (Cambridge: Cambridge University Press, 1999); also his "Private Business, Bureaucracy, and Political Alliance in a Chinese City", *The Australian Journal of Chinese Affairs*, No. 33 (January 1995), pp. 55-71, and his "Bureaucratic Patronage and Private Business: Changing Networks of Power in Urban China", in Andrew Walder (ed.), *The Waning of the Communist State* (Berkeley: University of California Press, 1995), pp. 153-84; also Ole Bruun, "Political Hierarchy and Private Enterprise in a Chinese Neighborhood", in Walder (ed.); Dorothy Solinger, "Urban Entrepreneurs and the State: The Merger of State and Society", in Arthur Rosenbaum (ed.), *State and Society in China: The Consequences of Reform* (Boulder: Westview Press, 1992), pp. 121-42; Jean Oi, "Rational Choices and Attainment of Wealth and Power in the Countryside", in David Goodman and Beverly Hooper (eds.), *China's Quiet Revolution: New Interactions Between State and Society* (Melbourne: Longman Cheshire, 1994), pp. 68-69, 71; Ole Odgaard, "Entrepreneurs and Elite Formation in Rural China," *The Australian Journal of Chinese Affairs*, No. 28 (July 1992), pp. 89-108; and Susan Young, *Private Business and Economic Reform* (Armonk: M.E. Sharpe, 1995), pp. 67-92.

Attitudes toward alleged corruption in Xiqiao contrast sharply, for instance, with the districts nearer to Hong Kong such as the Chen Village region. There, gifts and payoffs are regularly and often openly presented to village and township officials in pursuit of a very broad range of favors, and graft in the use of public funds also appears to be widespread. But officials there are not considered corrupt unless they grossly overstep the amounts that other local officials take for themselves.[18] There is no such view in Xiqiao. Quite the contrary. Even in the absence of concrete evidence, the officials as a group are assumed to be corrupt— intolerably so—and to be indecently squandering public money.[19] A large independent business community that sets the tone of local opinion is flexing its muscles through such talk. In the court of local public opinion in Xiqiao, the officialdom has been placed decidedly on the defensive. This in turn may well keep the village leadership's corruption in check.

In many parts of China, newly prosperous businesspeople can be seen regularly flaunting their wealth through extravagantly expensive restaurant meals and ostentatious consumerism. It is partly that they feel a need to fete officials, and partly too a *nouveau riche* mentality, augmented by a feeling, carried over from the 1980s, that it is better to spend one's gains before these get milked.[20]

Not so in Xiqiao. With continued success dependent upon repeated upgrading of machinery and reinvestment in their enterprises, an ethic of frugality prevails locally. Prosperous businesspeople build decent houses for themselves; and some successful factory owners gratify their egos by setting up young mistresses in second homes. But on the whole, Xiqiao's businesspeople do not squander money on ostentatious living.

The local community holds its officials to the same standards of frugality. In Jiancun, for example, the village leaders are careful not to dine ostentatiously or

---

[18] On this see Chan, Madsen and Unger, *Chen Village Under Mao and Deng*, p. 287.

[19] In a study of a village in Shaanxi Province, Xin Liu has observed a similar community phenomenon as in Xiqiao: "The issue is not whether the cadres are corrupt or not; rather, it is the extent to which these allegations of corruption have become part of a larger force reconstituting the public sphere by way of a moral discourse." Xin Liu, *In One's Own Shadow: An Ethnographic Account of the Condition of Post-Reform Rural China* (Berkeley: University of California Press, 2000), pp. 178-79.

[20] This consumerism was true even of the district in China best known for private enterprise, Wenzhou prefecture in Zhejiang Province. Businesspeople in Wenzhou apparently felt less secure than in Xiqiao that they could retain reinvested private assets over the long term: "Another response to potential risks posed by doing private business within a state socialist context is reflected in a decision on the part of many peasant entrepreneurs to engage in a high level of consumption rather than reinvestment in and expansion of the enterprise. Wenzhou became known in the late 1970s and 1980s as a region where people spent their money extravagantly not only on housing and clothing but also on weddings, funerals and grave sites." Kristen Parris, "Local Initiative and National Reform", a paper presented at the Association for Asian Studies convention, 1992, p. 25.

to buy fancy new official autos using public funds; and for many years they delayed building a new village headquarters and remained in an old dank run-down building inherited from the Maoist period.

Distrusted nonetheless by many of their fellow villagers, they have been reluctant to convene villagewide meetings. As a woman who owns a factory in Jiancun observed, "If they call a meeting we'll go to bawl them out; so they won't call meetings any more."

The Former Production Teams and the Institution of a New Villagewide "Shareholding System"

The rapid industrialization of Xiqiao has already affected the grass-roots administrative structure in another important respect. To accommodate to the changes in the village economy, in recent years the former agricultural production teams have been collapsed into a villagewide organization.

Under Mao, the production teams had arguably been the most important level of organization so far as farmers were concerned, inasmuch as team leaders organized their working lives and their livelihoods in turn depended upon their team's production. In the early 1980s, after the fields had all been distributed to individual households to farm independently, the teams largely lost their original purpose and functions. But they continued to exist as legal entities. Retitled here and in some other parts of China as "economic cooperatives" (*jingji hezuoshe*) in the early 1980s, they continued to own their original share of the agricultural land. During the 1980s and early 1990s, when land was rented out for fish ponds or factory sites or agri-business,[21] these so-called economic cooperatives divided the proceeds among their members each year. In short, a sharp distinction had been maintained between the assets owned by the former brigade (the village government), whose revenues go into improving village services, and the landed assets of the former production team level (the "economic cooperatives"), the rents from which have largely been distributed among its constituent households.[22]

But this latter system had begun to run into problems in Nanhai County due to industrialization. Land-use planning has been introduced, with each village allowed by the government to zone only one or two specific large blocks of agricultural land for industrial purposes. An "economic cooperative" whose land

---

[21] To ensure that the cities of Guangzhou and Foshan are well supplied with fresh vegetables, the provincial government allows the district to concentrate on these rather than grain, and specialist farmers from as far away as Hunan and Guangxi are among those who make bids to lease farmland. Some 10 percent of all the agricultural fields in Xiqiao have been leased out in this fashion to people who are not native to Xiqiao.

[22] In this particular rural township, 75 percent of the land rent gets distributed to the villagers. The village governments, which take responsibility for collecting the rents, retain the other 25 percent.

happened to lie in the village's zone for industrial use could now reap high revenues by renting out factory sites, while an "economic cooperative" whose land lay in a zone designated for agriculture lost out. Tensions between them were mounting over this. The township government, in response, finally decreed in 1994 that all of the land of each village would be combined into a single villagewide cooperative that would entirely absorb the separate remaining assets of the former production teams.[23]

The township government's decision coincided in time with, and was implemented in combination with, a set of directives from the Nanhai County government in 1993-94 ordering that a "village cooperative shareholding system" (*nongcun gufen hezuozhi*) be instituted.[24] Under this, the system of "economic cooperatives" would be reconstituted so that each resident would receive stock shares and annual dividends from the land rentals. At first blush, the new terminology suggests that the former production teams' assets were being "corporatized" and that the stock shares that have been handed out to each individual villager represent a form of privatization.

But this is not at all what has occurred. Whatever the intentions of the government, the values and cohesion of the village community as a social collectivity are being reasserted in Xiqiao in a new and more egalitarian shape than before. At the same time that the assets of all of the "economic cooperatives" were combined into a single villagewide "village cooperative shareholding system," each village in Xiqiao was given leeway to decide who is eligible to receive how many shares. The effect, interestingly, has been very similar to what membership in the village brigade and production teams used to entail in the Maoist collective era—with a twist that is in line with traditional Confucian principles of respect for age.

In Jiancun, for example, each infant whose parents are native to the village receives one share at birth (immigrants to the village and their descendants are completely excluded, not to speak of the migrant workers who hold only

---

[23]   Isabelle Thireau, a French sociologist who specializes in rural China, has conducted research at a neighboring township where many of the "economic cooperatives", and the production teams before them, are separate small natural villages or hamlets. She has told me that the villagers there successfully opposed the combining of their cooperatives' landed assets at the level of the administrative village (*guanli qu*), claiming that the money would be embezzled by the *guanli qu* cadres and that they themselves would lose property rights over their own small natural village. In Xiqiao, in comparison, the sense of village community coincides with the administrative designation of it, and so opposition to combining the assets of the "economic cooperatives" was far more muted.

[24]   The two relevant directives were republished in Nanhaishi nongcun gaige shiyanqu bangongshi (Nanhai County Office for Village Reform Experimental Districts), *Nanhaishi nongcun tudi gufen hezuozhi lunwen ji* (Collected Treatises on Nanhai's Village Land Shareholding Cooperative System) (Nanhai: no publisher listed, 1995), pp. 334-45. The national Ministry of Agriculture first started promoting this system at selected sites in 1990.

temporary resident status). The native young people hold one share up to the age of 17; those between the ages of 18 and 35 hold two shares; when they reach the ages of 36 they are given an extra share and hold three shares until the age of 55; and every native community member over 55 holds four shares.[25] A person's shares disappear when he or she dies, and a female loses her shares when she marries out of the community, though she gains an equivalent amount of shares in her husband's village as she enters it. A village family that moves away similarly loses its shares and dividends—village residence is necessary to remain part of the community—but the shares reappear if the family moves back and thereby re-enters community life.

All of this is similar to how production teams used to determine who shared in the pool of team incomes in the days of Mao. Children born to team members gained a share in the team assets and were entitled to a given portion of grain each year, with adults allotted a higher portion, while women who married out of the team lost team membership and their share of team assets, as did families who moved away. In short, with the economic reforms and industrialization in Xiqiao, the lowest-level structures of economic community and its entitlements have not been replaced by a system of permanent, saleable, and inheritable asset shares. Rather, the new system perpetuates the community values and the definitions of community membership of the collective era.

In some of the other counties in the Pearl River delta, the assets of the former production teams have similarly been transformed into village-wide "shareholdings" in the land. So, too, as other rural districts in China industrialize, they may well move in the same direction as Xiqiao, toward a villagewide "shareholding" system. But if so, we should not assume that Chinese landholdings are being privatized into property companies. Rural China marches to its own drumbeat.

With the annual dividends, it is now better in Xiqiao to be registered as a village resident than to hold an urban or market-town residence certificate, and the villages guard their official residence (*hukou*) status jealously. The investor from Heilongjiang who poured Y4 million into a textile factory in Jiancun was allowed to build a large house there and to bring his family to live in the village permanently, but the village has barred him from purchasing a village *hukou* even for a large sum of money.

The cash distributions to households in Xiqiao in 1996 from the "shareholding cooperative system" ranged from some Y1,000 to more than Y10,000. This wide variation was due partly to the large differences in the revenues obtained in each village from leasing out factory sites, fish ponds, and

---

[25]   At another village in Xiqiao, we were told that the village leadership had decided that each child between the ages of 1 and 7 holds one share; two shares between the ages of 7 and 12; 2.5 shares for ages 12–20; up to four shares for each village member over 40.

agricultural fields.[26] In Lianxin, the size of the annual dividends to households is some 3-4 times higher than in Jiancun. Villagers, it is obvious, today hold a direct vested interest in local economic development.

In each village, a management board oversees the new villagewide "shareholding cooperative system." This board is composed of an elected representative from each of the former "economic cooperatives." But the board is normally chaired by the village Party secretary or village head, and the system appears to have come under the effective control of the villagewide leadership. Some interviewees expressed a suspicion that a portion of the funds from leases are being illicitly diverted into the cadres' hands, in line with their suspicions about the overall probity of local cadres. Valid or not, such suspicions make village officials feel even more on the defensive. In Jiancun, without prompting, the Party secretary and other village leaders sought to reassure me more than once that the land-lease dividends are being appropriately distributed, and they noted, too, that the amount of money distributed would need to be raised soon in order to allay villagers' qualms about the new shareholding cooperative board.

The Township Government—Developmental or Ineffective?

Like the village governments, the Xiqiao Township government today actively promotes local private business. However, a key question to be addressed is whether the township authorities' programs and investments, overall, have been effective or not.

Pushing Private Industrialization

Certainly, on the plus side, the Xiqiao township authorities put in the effort. In fact, in order to ride herd on any village governments that might be laggard in spurring local development, the township head has established a system whereby the deputy township heads and other top leaders each get assigned to keep a close eye on the development of a few specific villages.

One consequence is that the Jiancun village government finds itself in ongoing disagreement with a deputy township head who has been assigned to oversee the village. He has pushed energetically for a rapid expansion of paved road linkages criss-crossing village territory—to be financed largely at village expense. In an interview he portrayed himself as a modernizer seeking on behalf of the Jiancun village populace to overcome the sluggish parochialism of village

---

26   Some villagers in Xiqiao no longer want to obtain an allocation of land, and they are not obliged to do so. This leaves tracts of agricultural land available for rent. People from other parts of China who want to relocate to Xiqiao in order to raise high-priced produce for the nearby urban markets are allowed to bid for large sections of this land on the same terms as native villagers. They are permitted to move into the village with their families, but again cannot obtain a local *hukou*. Given this, they pay higher fees for their children's schooling and other village services than do the local villagers.

cadres. But the village authorities in contrast portray themselves in interviews as representatives of local opinion against a profligate higher authority that seeks to saddle their village with one type of expense after another.

The township government also sees itself as responsible for improving the local textile industry's production methods. Worried that Xiqiao might lose its standing in the national textile market, township leaders keep a watchful eye on the major centers elsewhere in China that produce chemical-fiber cloth. A group of township officials led by the township head took an investigative trip to the textile centers in Zhejiang Province, Xiqiao's major competitors, and returned with warnings that these were gaining on Xiqiao. Anxious for Xiqiao to strengthen its competitive edge, the township authorities decided to subsidize purchases by Xiqiao factory owners of a new generation of looms that cost some Y120,000 apiece. In this and other programs to provide support to the private sector, the township administration (similar to the village governments) generally favors the more prosperous, larger entrepreneurs, feeling that they have the best chance of expanding local production against outside competition.[27]

The township government also sees itself as firmly behind local interests *vis-à-vis* the 70,000 temporary migrant workers from poorer parts of China who have flooded into Xiqiao. These migrants comprise about half of the township's total workforce,[28] predominantly as manual laborers. Practically every one of the women who tend the textile looms, for example, and the great bulk of the men working at local construction sites are migrants, as are 70 percent of the workforce in the collective tile factories.

---

[27]   Two of the avenues through which the township reaches out to the most successful local businesspeople are the Nanhai Textile Chamber of Commerce (*Nanhaishi fangzhi tongye shanghui*), which the county government helped to initiate in late 1995 and whose headquarters lies in Xiqiao, and the Xiqiao branch of the Non-Governmental Entrepreneurs Civic Association (*Minjian qiyejia gonghui*), which the township government helped establish in 1994. Both were provided with free offices by the township government, and both organizations are staffed by government-paid officials. These are elite associations, with membership limited to a few dozen of the most prosperous businesspeople. The status and independent wealth of the members is reflected in the fact that gradually the two associations, albeit founded and partially funded by the authorities, are becoming vehicles for the expression of this business constituency's views and interests. (On the workings of the elitist Chambers of Commerce and their parent organization, the national Federation of Industry & Commerce, and the complex relationships of these with the government, see Jonathan Unger, "Bridges: Private Business, the Chinese Government, and the Rise of New Associations", *The China Quarterly*, No. 147 [September 1996], pp. 795-819). A study containing interesting material on the Entrepreneurs Civic Association in Nanhai County is Sun Bingyao, "Xiangzhen shetuan yu Zhongguo jiceng shehui", (Rural Township Associations and Grassroots Chinese Society), *Zhongguo shehui kexue jikan* (Chinese Social Science Quarterly) (Hong Kong), No. 9 (Autumn 1994).

[28]   The total native population of Xiqiao amounts to 135,000, and about half of them are children or retired elderly or for other reasons not part of the local workforce.

The township government, in keeping with its self-image of actively supporting local industry, allows the local enterprises to violate national labor laws. This is the case, too, it appears, with almost all local governments in south China. National laws stipulate that workers must be paid overtime rates 50 percent higher than their normal wages, and 36 hours of overtime has been set as the legal maximum per month.[29] Yet a majority of the migrant female textile workers in Xiqiao labor at the looms twelve hours a day, seven days a week—far in excess of the legal maximum limit. And they receive piece-rate wages without any bonuses or premiums for overtime work, again in violation of the national statutes.

The township authorities also turn a blind eye to the fact that most of Xiqiao's factories retain the first several weeks of a worker's wages as a "deposit" (yajin). Any worker who quits within less than a year sacrifices the full amount. This so-called deposit obliges workers who are unhappy with an employer to remain there, sometimes under onerous conditions. Bonding labor in this way is against national labor laws. Yet in most of south China it is commonplace.[30] In Xiqiao, a woman worker who resigned from her job and thereby lost the "deposit" lodged a complaint with the labor bureau, but the head of the bureau explained to me that he had sided with the owner inasmuch as the owner was from Xiqiao and because the owner, not the worker, paid labor management fees to the bureau and other local taxes.[31] Whatever the national statutes, the township government looks after its own clientele.

Notwithstanding this, the migrant labor force is less poorly treated in Xiqiao than in many other districts in Guangdong. Since the local populace depends on migrant workers to do most of the production-line work in the textile and tile factories, they want to be sure of a continued steady flow into Xiqiao of capable, skilled workers. Again and again, local residents proclaimed to me that people from outside the district are welcomed, a sentiment echoed by the township government. In contrast, in many other districts in the delta, migrants are resented and harassed by both the local populace and the local governments. In the rural townships that lie between Hong Kong and Guangzhou, for example, local people complain that the migrants are responsible for rising crime rates and that they will swamp the local population if their numbers are not controlled. In those districts, the migrant workers' temporary residence cards and work permits are regularly checked by local police in the streets, and if they cannot produce a card they often

---

[29]   See the Labor Law of the People's Republic of China, adopted at the 8th National People's Congress, July 5, 1994 (Jingji ribao [Economic Daily], July 6, 1994, p. 2).

[30]   On this see Anita Chan, "Globalization, China's 'Free' (Read Bonded) Labour Market, and the Chinese Trade Unions", in Chris Rowley and John Benson (eds.), Globalization and Labour in the Asia Pacific Region (London: Frank Cass, 2000), pp. 260-81.

[31]   Employers pay an annual labor management fee of Y48 to the township's labor bureau for each migrant worker (none is required for local workers).

are beaten up and forced out of the district.[32] The reason, I believe, is that in these districts the bulk of the local industry is foreign-owned and foreign-run, mostly by Hong Kong and Taiwanese manufacturers, and thus the local populace and local governments do not have a strong vested interest in maintaining the influx of factory labor, let alone making them feel welcome.

The Township Government's Own Brand of Entrepreneurship

Akin to the village governments, the township government makes no effort to participate directly in textile production alongside the private enterprises. Township officials readily state that in the family-owned firms, without layers of staff on their payrolls and without pensions to pay, production costs are considerably lower than a township-owned collective factory would face. Thus, rather than compete head on, the three textile-weaving enterprises that the commune (township) had operated under Mao have switched to other avenues of revenue: two have been leased out to private operators; and the third factory has turned to producing spare parts for the local industry.

The township government instead has sought to develop its own specific niches for investment. It has converted the money-making enterprises that it owns into six public conglomerates, whose assets include the single largest tile factory as well as a further 34 enterprises in a range of industrial and commercial endeavors. Unlike the village officials, who feel pressures to seem publicly frugal, those in charge of these conglomerates feel more insulated, with less need to win residents' approval. As just one illustration of this, the semi-retired head of the township conglomerate that runs the township government's hotel was assigned a luxury Lexus sedan and chauffeur.

The township level principally looks to develop an entrepreneurial fiefdom in tourism. Xiqiao is dominated physically by a large craggy mountain that rises dramatically from the flat delta. It is a curiosity in a region with few similar landmarks, and for centuries had been a visiting site for the delta's wealthy. Guangdong Province's ongoing boom has generated a new large moneyed stratum, and the township and county governments decided some years ago to try to cash in on this by developing a tourist trade. In 1994 the township was declared a Tourist Holiday District, and the former township Party secretary, an old Party bureaucrat with no business experience, started spending money with a vengeance to develop the mountain into a dazzling tourist mecca.

An artificial lake was engineered halfway up the mountain, linked to the lowlands by an aerial tramway. In the center of the lake an elaborate water screen devised from a row of high-jet fountains, using special equipment imported from France, was installed to project a 3-D film documentary extolling Xiqiao. Elsewhere on the mountain, vast elaborate gardens were planted for tourists to

---

[32]   On local attitudes toward and police treatment of the migrants in those districts, see Chan, Madsen and Unger, *Chen Village Under Mao and Deng*, pp. 300-308.

wander through. At a vista near the peak, an extraordinary many-stories-high bronze statue of the goddess Guan Yin has been erected—indubitably one of the largest metal statues in the world. At the base of the mountain, an equally huge concrete statue has been constructed of the redoubtable Wang Daxian, a Taoist sage who enjoys the status of a popular god. How all of this extravagant construction work was supposed to translate into township-government earnings is not entirely clear, as even one of the officials in charge of the investment conceded. It is doubtful that the vast sums of money that have been lavished to convert the mountain into a tourist showpiece will ever be recouped. The project bears the earmarks of political leaders who are not accountable for their expenditures. The glory of a high-profile accomplishment seemed more important to the project's creators than did the project's bottom line.

Even before its completion, this grandiose tourism scheme had an adverse impact on Xiqiao residents in one important respect. Traditionally, families buried their dead in scattered tombs on the vast slopes and ridges of Xiqiao Mountain, at sites they deemed propitious in terms of geomancy. The thousands of tomb sites seemed unbecoming to an officialdom intent on tidying up the mountain for the tourist trade, and the claim was laid that the incense burned during the yearly "sweeping the tombs" festival posed a fire hazard to the mountain forests. So in the name of modernization and development, a large imposing cemetery has been constructed at the foot of the mountain, and orders were issued that all households must relocate their family tombs to the new site. Adding insult to injury, these families were required to pay for the new burial plot. Each relocation costs upward of Y20,000, more than many families could readily afford. Residents and village officials alike were vociferous in their complaints to me, united in a common anger at what they saw to be the effrontery and ruinous exactions of upper-level bureaucrats. In October 1997, Xiqiao gained international news coverage when thousands of angry protesters besieged township government offices and clashed with police after the authorities had begun forcibly removing graves from the mountain.[33] If residents hold suspicions about the usefulness and probity of village officials, they feel far more estranged from the township officialdom.

They can point in particular to another township government project that they consider wastefully expensive—and at their own expense. The township administration borrowed large sums to erect a new wholesaling district just outside town for the Xiqiao textile industry. The new district consists of many hundreds of adjoining three-story buildings, all alike, each containing a wholesale outlet downstairs and offices upstairs. Until the latter part of 1997, the private factories had rented small, run-down, relatively cheap shopfronts along the

---

[33]   *China News Digest*, October 24, 1997, citing Agence France Presse and the Hong Kong daily newspaper *Ming Bao*. In the riot's aftermath, I have learned, the officials ultimately rescinded their order that the tombs be relocated.

downtown streets, alleyways and courtyards, where factory owners spent much of their time negotiating and chatting with purchasing agents and wholesalers from throughout China. The scene seemed too backward and untidy for the taste of the township authorities—and the new wholesaling district they had constructed needed tenants—so they issued a regulation in the name of urban planning that required the factories to close down their downtown sales outlets. Factory owners furiously complained that purchasing space in the new wholesale district added to their business expenses while making no difference to their volume of sales. To them, the project looked like just another drain on local resources, from which only the township government profited.[34]

Conclusions

The different levels of local government in Xiqiao differ in their sensitivity to the pressures of popular opinion. Though the township government does feel the weight of popular pressure from below—enough so for it to strive to prove itself a facilitator for local private business—it nonetheless is far enough removed from the direct pressure of public opinion to expend money in wastefully unpopular ways and to impose unpopular decrees. In comparison, the village governments are exposed more directly to grass-roots opinion, which is dominated by a large local constituency of independent businesspeople.

Writers on the rural political and economic system in China do not usually focus on this important distinction between the different levels of rural government. To cite just one example among many, Jean Oi has written that "Somewhat akin to a large multi-level corporation, the county can be seen as being at the top of a corporate hierarchy as the corporate headquarters, the township as the regional headquarters, and the villages as companies within the larger corporation."[35] Such a perception of a unified top-to-bottom government machinery does not take account of the very different positions occupied by village, township and county governments, the different constituencies they need or do not need to pay heed to, and the divergent institutional interests, divergent strategies and frequent differences of opinion (and occasional antagonisms) between the local governments of different levels.

A second, equally important factor to take into consideration when addressing China's rural political scene is that, as earlier noted, the circumstances in different districts differ very considerably. For instance, whereas the behavior of village cadres in Xiqiao is tacitly constrained by public opinion, many other

---

[34]   For a different view of such wholesaling centers—focusing on one established by a county government in north China—see Marc Blecher and Vivienne Shue, "Into Leather: State-led Development and the Private Sector in Xinji", *The China Quarterly*, No. 166 (June 2001), pp. 368-93.

[35]   Jean Oi, "The Role of the Local State in China's Transitional Economy", p. 1138. Also see Oi's *Rural China Takes Off*, pp. 103-15.

rural districts differ in this respect. Where village officials hold the great bulk of the village-level industry in their own hands in the form of collective enterprises, as in the villages that Jean Oi and others have studied, the officials have the wherewithal to dominate village life and opinion. Similarly, village cadres in the districts where foreign-financed factories predominate are able to control the rents from the factory sites. These rents are a major source of residents' incomes, and through this the officials there also hold a strong hand in their communities. In both of these latter types of villages, an important mechanism of control centers on the patronage the officials are able to dispense, through which they are able to establish local political machines based upon concentric circles of patron–client dependency. This especially appears to be the case in the villages with a large degree of collective industry, where access to jobs as well as funds lies at the discretion of the local cadres.[36] In contrast, much of the populace in Xiqiao, including the bulk of the most influential residents, are financially and occupationally independent of the local government, so patronage mechanisms there are correspondingly weak. This comparison between different types of rural districts is summarized in Table 1, below.

In all three types of locales—those where private industry, collective industry and foreign-financed industry predominate—local officials have sought to provide improved public services such as schooling, old people's homes, and so forth. In all three types of areas, officials feel an obvious need to serve as public benefactors in order to bolster residents' support for the local administration. Here a stark contrast exists with impoverished villages (also listed in Table 1) which possess little revenue from industry or other sources. The officials there do not have the material means to serve either as patrons or as community benefactors. The Chinese government has referred to some of these as "paralyzed villages," containing "cadres with low spirit and energy who do not put their hearts into village work."[37] While village cadres retreat from their duties and village services decline, the township and county officials in such districts are apt to resort to coercive methods to extract taxes and fees from a hard-pressed peasantry. They take on the attributes of a predatory state.[38]

---

[36] On this, see the sources cited in footnotes 1 through 3 of this chapter.

[37] Quoted by Kevin O'Brien in "Implementing Political Reform in China's Villages", *The Australian Journal of Chinese Affairs*, No. 32 (July 1994), p. 51.

[38] As an example of this, a study of two poor rural counties in Guizhou Province found that the local governments, short of their own sources of income, acted in a coercive, predatory fashion toward the farmers, forcing them to grow tobacco at a loss in order to replenish local government coffers. See Yali Peng, "The Politics of Tobacco: Relations Between Farmers and Local Governments in China's Southwest", *The China Journal*, No. 36 (July 1996), pp. 67-82.

Table 1: Rural Communities by Predominance of Enterprise Ownership Types

	Private Industry	Collectives	Foreign Industry	No Industry
Societal pressure on officials	High in villages, less so at township	Low	Low	Medium in villages, higher levels sometimes predatory
Local government control of patronage	Limited	High	Medium	Low
Welfare services	Yes	Yes	Yes	Barely
"Developmental"	High (Lianxin) Medium (Jiancun)	High	Medium	Low

   In sharp contrast, the village governments in Xiqiao are "developmental," seeking actively to expand the local productive base rather than passively neglect their duties or rapaciously milk the local economy. As has been seen, they become facilitators for private business in the process, seeking to provide improved infrastructure and low tax regimes for the private sector. But our focus on two villages in Xiqiao—Lianxin and Jiancun—reveals two very different "developmental" strategies at work. In Lianxin, as has been observed, in addition to fostering private industry the village officials have greatly expanded the village-owned industrial sector by way of heavy investments in tile manufacture. The Lianxin officials are acting as risk-taking public entrepreneurs in a fashion similar to the rural areas that Jean Oi and others have studied, where collectively owned industry has flourished. Jiancun meanwhile has eschewed that route, its officials preferring instead simply to provide an infrastructure that is attractive to industry in order to gain the bulk of its revenues through rentals and fees. In this regard, the Jiancun government has fallen back on a more passive "developmental" strategy similar to what prevails in the counties adjoining Hong Kong, where village administrations actively seek to be land developers and rentiers rather than engage in industry directly.

Notably, though, the officials in both Lianxin and Jiancun, as seen above, are akin in one signally important respect: they similarly seek to nurture local private industry. This goes against the findings of most previous observers of the Chinese scene that local officials (i) give priority and advantages to publicly owned industry over private industry and (ii) insist on relationships in which private entrepreneurs are subordinate and dependent on them. In other local areas in China, researchers have perceived efforts by the local bureaucracy to corral and control private entrepreneurs, and they have observed the efforts made, in response, by private businesspeople to do favors and cement personal bonds with the local officialdom.[39] Xiqiao village governments, Lianxin and Jiancun alike, point to a very different scenario, one that very likely is already becoming increasingly widespread in China as the numerical weight of private proprietors increases. It is a scene in which, as in Xiqiao, local governments that seek faster local development actively encourage private industry[40]—and where, in turn, an independent constituency of local businesspeople begins to tilt the balance in its own favor in terms of influence at the village level. In the years to come, this is bound to have very substantial ramifications on local Chinese politics and society.

---

[39]   Several excellent urban and rural studies in the mid-1990s focused specifically on these efforts of private businesspeople to ingratiate themselves with officials, sometimes to the point of volunteering for political duties in order to secure needed political connections. On this, see footnote 17.

[40]   Jean Oi, who conducted research in the 1980s in a Shandong county where collectively owned rural industry received an overwhelming priority in what she dubbed "local state corporatism", returned to her research site during the 1990s to discover a shift in precisely the direction we describe. Jean Oi, "The Evolution of Local State Corporatism", in Andrew Walder (ed.), *Zouping in Transition: The Process of Reform in Rural North China* (Cambridge: Harvard University Press, 1998), p. 36.

Chapter Nine

POVERTY IN THE RURAL HINTERLANDS:
THE CONUNDRUMS OF UNDERDEVELOPMENT

While Xiqiao surges ahead economically, many other parts of rural China do not. Compared to the recent past, China increasingly contains "two nations," to paraphrase Disraeli, one of prosperous households and one of poor households. To varying degrees, this is occurring within villages. Even more evidently, though, it is occurring between regions, as some boom and others stagnate. An analysis of State Statistical Bureau survey data for 1988 and 1995 showed that within that period of seven years deep rural poverty in the eastern region of China had fallen from 9 percent to 5 percent and in the central region had declined from 20 percent of the population to 13 percent; but in the western region it had actually increased substantially, from 26.5 to 31 percent of the inhabitants.[1]

For rural China as a whole, growing disparities in rural incomes can be seen clearly in the Gini coefficient (the most commonly used index of inequality of income), which has progressively widened for rural China during the post-Mao period, from 0.2 in 1978 to 0.4 or above by 1995.[2] Income disparities appear to

---

[1] Bjorn Gustafsson and Wei Zhong, "How and Why has Poverty in China Changed? A Study Based on Microdata for 1988 and 1995," *The China Quarterly*, No. 146 (December 2000), pp. 989-90.

[2] One Chinese source calculated that the Gini coefficient expanded from a narrow 0.21 in 1978 to 0.33 in 1993. Tang Ping, "Wo guo nongcun jumin shouru shuiping ji chayi yanjiu" (Research into the Levels and Disparities in Income among China's Village Residents), *Jingji yanjiu cankao* (Economic Research Reference Materials), No. 158 (October 14, 1994), p. 27. Another Chinese source claims that by 1995 it further widened only marginally, to 0.34 (Zhang Ping, "Zhongguo nongcun jumin quyujian shouru bupingdeng yu feinong jiuye" (Regional Rural Chinese Income Inequality and Non-agricultural Employment) *Jingji yanjiu* (Economic Research), No. 8 [August 1998], p. 60). A third Chinese analyst, however, has calculated the coefficient as being considerably wider: reaching 0.34 by 1988 and 0.43 by 1994. *Xinhua wenzhai* (New China Digest), No. 2 (1996), pp. 16-19. Two Western academics have calculated a Gini coefficient of 0.42 for 1995, widening from 0.34 in 1988. See Azizur Rahman Khan and Carl Riskin, "Income and Inequality in China: Composition, Distribution and Growth of Household Income, 1988 to 1995," *The China Quarterly*, No. 154 (June 1998), p. 237. The World Bank's calculations, while slightly more moderate, point in the same direction, estimating that the Gini coefficient reached 0.39 in 1995. World Bank, *Sharing Rising Incomes: Disparities in China* (Washington, D.C.: World Bank, 1997), p. 1. The most recent official

have continued to widen since then. A Gini coefficient of 0.4 is considered wide for a country as a whole, which encompasses urban wealth as well as the rural poor. That the Gini coefficient has exceeded 0.4 just within the confines of China's countryside is extraordinary, especially when one takes into account the fact that two decades ago rural China exhibited an unusually narrow Gini coefficient.

The Crisis in Agricultural Livelihoods

This sharp widening reflects the fact that even though the Chinese economy has been developing rapidly for most of the past two decades and off-farm income opportunities have lifted large parts of rural China into prosperity, circumstances have been less than kind for those families in the interior of China who have remained largely in agriculture. The terms of trade for their produce, which improved sharply in the late 1970s and early 1980s, began to turn far less favorable after 1984, as government policy changed and the quota prices and farmgate prices for most of the important types of agricultural produce were pressed downward in real terms. Especially in districts too far from cities to specialize in lucrative vegetable growing, farmers' living standards began to stagnate and in a great many cases declined. Taking all rural household income into account, real income had risen dramatically by some 10 percent annually in rural China between 1978 and 1984, but during the next half-decade stagnated. The real per capita rural income in 1990 (338 *yuan*) was almost exactly the same as in 1984-85 (336 *yuan*).[3] Throughout the 1980s off-farm income in the more commercialized parts of the Chinese countryside had continued to rise, but this was offset by a marked decline in real *agricultural* income during the last half of the decade. Those families who were stuck entirely in farming were very noticeably hurt.

The 1990s witnessed much the same story. Overall, agricultural output continued to rise, but pricing policies worked against the farmers. As the Chinese journal *Agricultural Economics* explained in 1998, "During the 1990s the size of the government's grain quotas has expanded, farmers' tax burdens have grown, the cost of agricultural inputs has doubled, and the scissors differential between industrial and agricultural prices has continuously increased. All this has eaten up any profits the farmers had begun to see. Farmers toil throughout the year with little to show in the end, and even lose money in the process."[4] In the last couple

---

calculation by the Chinese government's State Statistical Bureau shows a Gini coefficient of 0.34 for 1999 (www.stats.gov.cn as of June 2001), but as will be seen in the following pages, I do not believe this to be reliable due to lower-level officials' involvement during the data gathering.

[3]   Scott Rozelle, "Stagnation Without Equity: Patterns of Growth and Inequality in China's Rural Economy," *The China Journal*, No. 35 (January 1996).

[4]   *Nongye jingji* (Agricultural Economics), No. 5, 1998, pp. 17-18; also see the Party journal *Qiushi* (Seek Facts), No. 3, 1998, pp. 46-49, for a very similar statement.

of years of the 1990s, the situation continued to worsen throughout China's huge grain belt, as prices for grains and other basic foodstuffs dropped sharply (overall, between 1997 and 2000 agricultural prices plunged by some 30 percent).[5] Large numbers of farming families who had escaped poverty found themselves falling back below the poverty line.

The Chinese government's figures for the rural poor as a whole show a rapid diminution in their numbers, from 131 million in 1986 to 75 million in 1993, down to 50 million by 1997, and to 26 million by 2000.[6] But these figures were collated from the data provided to Beijing by local governments, whose officials had good reason to hand in inflated income figures in order to show their superiors their success in developing their local bailiwicks. A blatant example of this from my own fieldwork experience is a particularly poor village in the hill country of Yunnan Province. The village's Party secretary confided that during the 1980s a visiting workteam of county officials had demanded that the village Party secretary's reports henceforth should raise every family's cash incomes by Y100 so that the officials could claim they had eliminated poverty. In reality, severe poverty remained entrenched in the village, and at the time of my visit in 1988 a third of the families could not afford to purchase matches or salt.[7] The cumulative official figures from the countryside include a large number of such grave distortions and thus are quite unreliable.[8]

The estimate of Chinese rural poverty that today is most often used in the West is that of the World Bank, which has redefined the poverty threshold in China to make it equivalent to US$1 per person per day on a purchasing power parity basis. The Bank calculates that some 106 million Chinese lived below this

---

[5]   Lu Xueyi, "Nongmin zhen ku, nongcun zhen qiong" (The Farmers Are Suffering, Villages Are Genuinely Poor), *Dushu* (Reading), January 2001.

[6]   *China Daily*, November 18, 2000.

[7]   Jonathan Unger and Jean Hung, "Zou fang Yunnan shancun ting xinsuan de gushi" (Bitter Tales Heard Through Interviews in a Yunnan Mountain Village), *Chaoliu* (Hong Kong), No. 31 (1989), p. 62. Another researcher notes, "During my visit to Yilong County of Sichuan in May 1999, the official at the township economic station complained that the income data indicative of moving out of poverty were based on instructions from the township head; the latter had just asked him to fill in income data that would be slightly higher than the poverty graduation income set by the county government, with no regard for the real income of the peasants." Luk Tak-chuen, "The Politics of Poverty Eradication in Rural China," in Lau Chung-ming and Jianfa Shen (eds.), *China Review 2000* (Hong Kong: Chinese University Press, 2000), p. 523.

[8]   *Nongmin ribao* (Farmers' Daily), March 6, 1999, contains an article explaining that this type of false reporting on villagers' incomes is quite common. An accompanying letter to the editor notes that the official statistics on incomes are collected by county statistical bureaus that often do not survey homes directly but simply rely on the unreliable claims of village officials. A trenchant English-language exposé of this and other types of blatant distortions in the creation of Chinese rural statistics is Yongshun Cai, "Between State and Peasant: Local Cadres and Statistical Reporting in Rural China," *The China Quarterly*, No. 163 (September 2000), pp. 783-805.

very stringent poverty line as of the end of 1998.[9] The vast majority of these are rural, and by the World Bank's calculation they comprised 11.5 percent of China's rural population. But these estimates, too, were largely based on the suspect figures handed in to the central government by local officials.

Two economists, Carl Riskin and Li Shi, devised their own interview surveys in 1988 and 1995 of households drawn from the State Statistical Bureau's rural household sample, and they have found—completely contrary to the Chinese government's claims—that there was "virtually no decline in the poverty rate between 1988 and 1995." They observe that over this period of time, "since the rural population grew, the absolute number of rural poor increased."[10]

Two distinctly different types of poverty among able-bodied farm households are evident today. The first pertains to farmers in areas like the grain belt whose land is capable of producing a sizable surplus beyond their own needs but who are caught in a situation of rising costs and falling farmgate prices. The second type of impoverished rural households live in agriculturally marginal districts, and must struggle on poor-quality soil simply to try to raise enough to feed their own families. As a group, they constitute the poorest of the poor.

What does this poverty entail for this latter group from the agriculturally marginal regions? The British government aid agency sponsored a large interview survey in 1999 in the poverty regions of China's southwest and Ningxia Province, and its report noted that a substantial number of the impoverished families who were interviewed "did not have enough to eat at all for some months of the year."[11] They are what specialists in development studies call the "absolute poor." Many other families in these regions enjoy sufficient food most years, even if the diet is limited largely to carbohydrates, but they still face the risk of food shortages during years of bad weather. This was the case in the villages of Qinghai Province where I conducted research in 2000. In the wake of a seasonal drought many families there did not have adequate foodstuffs to see them through the winter. Some were relying on emergency government grain deliveries to

---

[9]   The 1998 World Bank figure appears in "Zhongguo: zhansheng nongcun pinkun," a March 2000 article appearing on a Chinese-language website operated by the Beijing office of the World Bank (www.worldbank.org.cn). For earlier statistics, and an account of how these purchasing-power estimates were derived, also see World Bank, "Poverty in China: What Do the Numbers Say?," *Background Note: The World Bank*, 1996, 6 pages. The absolute poor— those without enough food to eat—stood at 70 million in 1995 by World Bank estimates. World Bank, *Sharing Rising Incomes: Disparities in China* (Washington, D.C.: World Bank, 1997), p. 4. The World Bank estimates that in 1981 28 percent of the population had been among the absolutely poor (p. 11), so a reduction to 70 million, if true, would be a major accomplishment.

[10]   Carl Riskin and Li Shi, "Chinese Rural Poverty Inside and Outside the Poor Regions," in Carl Riskin, Zhao Renwei and Li Shi (eds.), *China's Retreat from Equality: Income Distribution and Economic Transition* (Armonk: M.E. Sharpe, 2001). I am grateful to Professor Riskin for allowing me to read this paper prior to its publication.

[11]   Louise Beynon and Zheng Baohua, *Understanding Rural Poverty and Poverty Constraints in China* (London: DFID report, July 2000), p. 5.

survive. A substantial portion of China's absolute poor live in the twelve western and southwestern provinces,[12] in agriculturally marginal regions that are especially prone to natural disasters, and their location exacerbates the precariousness of their situation. Again and again in my trips into impoverished villages in these regions I encountered families who had struggled up out of poverty briefly only to be thrown back into it by the vagaries of nature.

In short, the rural poor in China tend to be highly vulnerable, in that they have little in reserve to guard against misfortunes. Not just a dry spell of weather, but also the infestation of a field, the death of a draft animal, or the illness of a working family member can be catastrophic for such a family. Any such occurrence can force the family to sell off some of the assets it needs for production, deplete the family's capacity to purchase the inputs it needs for the next year's crops, and destroy a poor family's chance of repaying an interest-bearing loan.

Although I have had an opportunity to witness poverty firsthand while conducting research for my own private purposes over the years, most of my opportunities to conduct interviews within poor villages arose while undertaking appraisals of community needs on behalf of international development agencies. These included a two-month trip to Yunnan Province in 1988, during which interviewing was conducted in thirteen villages; a second trip of two months by jeep in 1991 to conduct interviewing in nineteen hill-country villages in the three southern provinces of Guangxi, Guizhou and Yunnan; several weeks spent in impoverished townships of Hainan Province in 1993-94; and visits to poverty villages in six counties in Qinghai Province in 2000.

Entrenching Poverty: The Drawbacks of Government Policy

What I found was that some of the households even in the worst-off regions are doing relatively well, partly through off-farm endeavors. This was graphically visible in the new houses that have been built in some of the villages. However, it was equally clear that many families in these regions have become trapped in a desperate predicament.

It is a predicament caused, in part, by government policies that have exacerbated rather than reduced socio-economic differentiation over the past two decades. In Chapter Six, a significant example of this was observed in the residence-permit restrictions imposed by the central government on migrant workers from the countryside. This policy damages the livelihoods of practically all of the migrants, whose wages are depressed by the fact that they are allowed to compete only for the worst jobs and are placed at the mercy of their employers. The policy is particularly injurious to the interests of people from the poorer villages, who cannot afford to seek out jobs in circumstances where they are likely to be deported.

---

[12]   *China Overcoming Rural Poverty* (World Bank Report No. 21105-CHA, October 2000), para. 1.7.

Other policies have also had adverse effects on the poorer households. For a start, within each region, taxes discriminate against the poorest households, since the taxes are based largely on agriculture and take less account of other sources of income. A survey in the mid-1990s, based on 500 rural households that were selected randomly from poor regions spread across China, concluded that "the taxes appear to be highly regressive, with households in the lowest quintile paying a higher *absolute* amount than those in the top quintile" of the surveyed rural households.[13] Another survey found that while the average rural household in 1995 directly lost 3.4 percent of its total income to taxes and fees, impoverished households in the poor regions paid 5.6 percent.[14] In a third survey, conducted in 1994 in a poor rural township in Shanxi Province, the average rural household paid 12.3 percent of its income in taxes and fees, while the local wealthy paid only 0.13 percent.[15] The poor households in non-poor regions fare even worse. In a 1995 survey, it was found that such transfers to governments absorbed fully 15.7 percent of their total incomes, an excruciatingly high burden for a very impoverished family.[16] Analyzing the survey, Riskin and Li conclude that the "government and collective seem to be major contributors to rural poverty in non-poor regions."[17]

Notwithstanding this, the impoverished households in the better-off districts may be in a less onerous situation than their conterparts in the poor regions, given that the local governments of the better-off districts provide better public services such as schooling and offer marginally better welfare benefits—enough, usually, to ensure that the impoverished households do not literally go hungry. The local authorities in the poorer parts of the hinterlands do not have similar financial resources at their disposal, and the poorest there—unless they are disabled or

---

[13]   Wu Guobao, Sue Richardson and Peter Travers, "Rural Poverty and its Causes in China", *Working Papers of the Chinese Economy Research Unit* No. 96/2 (University of Adelaide, 1996), p. 12. Italics in the original. Azizur Khan makes a further claim that "In rural China the poor (ultra poor) pay 'net taxes' at a rate that is 27 (36) times higher than the 'net tax' rate paid by the non-poor". Azizur Rahman Khan, "Poverty in China in the Period of Globalization", *Issues in Development Discussion Paper No. 22* (Geneva: International Labor Office, 1998), p. 46.

[14]   Carl Riskin and Li Shi, "Chinese Rural Poverty Inside and Outside the Poor Regions", Table 6.

[15]   Xiong Jingming (Jean Hung) and Yang Wenliang, "Nongmin fudan" (Peasant Burdens), in Xiong Jingming (ed.), *Jinru 21 shiji de Zhongguo nongcun* (Chinese Villages Entering the 21st Century) (Beijing: Guangming Ribao Chubanshe, 2000), p. 469. See Xiaobo Lu, "The Politics of Peasant Burden in Reform China", *The Journal of Peasant Studies*, No. 25, No. 1 (October 1997), p. 119, for a 1992 survey of a Guizhou township, which found the poor paying a far higher percentage in taxes than the prosperous.

[16]   Carl Riskin and Li Shi, "Chinese Rural Poverty Inside and Outside the Poor Regions", Table 6.

[17]   Ibid.

elderly widows covered by the Civil Affairs Bureau—are sometimes left without any type of safety net at all.[18]

The poorest farmers' chances of producing and retaining enough grain to feed themselves are damaged by a third government policy—that regarding irrigation. In China's impoverished agricultural regions, a lack of irrigation is arguably the single greatest obstacle to substantially higher production and improved livelihoods. These poor regions almost all suffer from too little regular water, and the benefits of installing small-scale local irrigation can be enormous. In most of the villages that I have visited in China's southwest and Qinghai, I asked about the yields from the irrigated plots in the village compared to equivalent nearby unirrigated plots. On average, the yields on the irrigated fields are double the unirrigated fields in a non-drought year. And while the crops on the irrigated plots are largely unaffected during droughts, the yields of the non-irrigated plots sometimes drop almost to zero.

Fortunately, it is relatively inexpensive to install small-scale irrigation in most of these villages. This is almost all hill country, and a small dam of earth and stones can be constructed by farmers at the foot of a nearby hill to catch runoffs of rainwater. The dam and pond are normally sealed in cement to prevent water leakage, and a pipe or sealed irrigation ditch carries the water downhill to the fields. Why, then, do the great majority of poor villages still lack stable irrigation works? This is because, by government design, banks are not supposed to make loans for irrigation. Under policies that date back to the period of collectives, the higher levels of government are instead supposed to provide free grants for irrigation projects. The village governments and farmers therefore have to queue patiently for decades on end awaiting state grants, which today are very few and far between. This is especially the case in poor regions, where the provincial and county authorities have very constricted budgets. The ultimate effect of Chinese government policies is that irrigation projects that offer excellent returns and that would have been put in place long ago under a different system are still on hold. Poor villages and households suffer the consequences.

Poor farmers are also hurt by a fourth government practice. They cannot afford chemical fertilizers and in most parts of China have been cut off from loans from the government-controlled banks and credit associations to purchase any. Such fertilizers are particularly needed given the very infertile soils of most impoverished areas. Extensive household interviewing that I conducted during the late 1980s and early 1990s in the impoverished hill country of China's southwest revealed a doubling or in some cases even a tripling in grain output by families that could afford sufficient chemical fertilizers in comparison to neighbors who could not afford any. One vital reason is that the improved grain seeds now on the market depend upon sufficient soil nutrients. Thus, in a lot of these villages

---

[18]   This paragraph is based upon my own on-the-ground observations. It should be noted that Riskin and Li find otherwise, and conclude from their survey that "the poor in both regions received about the same amount of public transfer income" (ibid.).

chemical fertilizer use is the dividing line between households that are able to upgrade to the high-yield varieties and households that cannot. It is the difference between development and hunger.

In these circumstances, various state welfare agencies do intervene to keep the very poor from starving. The poorest of the poor obtain some free relief grain during a couple of months a year. But even these grain deliveries are usually not sufficient to stave off hunger pangs in the late winter and early spring. Officials in two of the counties that I visited in the poor hill country noted the absurdity of delivering free grain to families when these same families could, more cheaply, greatly increase their own grain yields if provided with some chemical fertilizer.

Many of us hold reservations about chemical fertilizers because their misuse sometimes produces damaging side-effects: to soil structures, rivers and ecosystems in general. But the alternative in rural China, notably, spells hunger and stark poverty, as families that cannot afford chemical fertilizers struggle to raise crops in fields that lack nutrients. To be sure, such families add to the fields whatever organic fertilizers they can find; but on the whole, the families that use chemical fertilizer simultaneously add *more* organic fertilizer to their fields than can households that lack chemical fertilizer. The reason is simple: families with bigger crops also gain more silage as a by-product, are therefore better able to raise livestock, and are able to recycle these animals' manure back into their own fields. And fortunately, this assiduous use by Chinese farmers of organic fertilizers (including, of course, household feces) to supplement applications of inorganic fertilizer helps to offset the potentially deleterious effects of chemical fertilizer misuse on soil structures.

Misuse certainly exists, however. Discussions with agricultural specialists in China reveal that a great many Chinese farmers—and even local Chinese agricultural extension officers—know little about how to apply fertilizers in ways that will retain a balanced soil. Higher yields mean more trace elements sucked out of the soil, and many of the farmers know nothing about the need to replace trace elements. They know little about optimum levels of fertilizer use, and when they can afford to buy all of the fertilizer that they feel they need, they reportedly spread on too much. China would do well to use the mass media to provide advice to farmers on the use and abuse of chemical fertilizer. But certainly, unless some miraculous genetic engineering of crops can provide a cure-all to the problem of depleted soils, chemical inputs remain all too necessary.

The Credit Trap

In Mao's day, each rural market town contained a publicly-owned credit association. When the collective fields were divided up among households in the early 1980s, these credit associations, which accept interest-bearing savings deposits in the rural areas, became the main source of loans to support the individual families' farming. They initially gave priority to providing credit of 3-12 months' duration to enable families to buy agricultural inputs at the start of the growing season or to buy animals for fattening and quick resale or to tide a family breadwinner over a sudden illness.

The credit associations, however, have come under strong pressure from the state to be business-like in their operations. They therefore normally reject the poorest households' requests for loans on the grounds that such households cannot guarantee repayment, as they do not possess collateral. The applicant's own residence and the fields the family has been allotted do not count as collateral, as evictions of families are next to impossible. This latter policy is worthy of praise, since it protects rural families in China from descending into the status of landless laborers. But it also means that they need to fall back on draft animals or pigs or other movable assets as their collateral. And these families do not have the wherewithal to raise animals precisely because they lack fertilizer and cannot grow enough to feed themselves, let alone livestock. Families can get trapped with persisting low yields in this vicious circle.

In my village interviews, these poorest households sometimes came across as the least competent: the breadwinners were ill-experienced in planning household production, or less physically able-bodied, illiterate, less mentally agile, simply feckless or given to drink. In other cases, they had simply had the ill-fortune of seeing all their animals die of illness or their crops fail in a natural disaster. In a poor community in Yunnan, for example, the hamlet head observed to me in 1991, "Last year the tobacco and corn were badly damaged by a hail storm. So a bunch of families couldn't repay the short-term loans they had taken out to buy fertilizer. But the local credit association needs money, and so couldn't take this natural disaster into account." These families consequently were not allowed to borrow as usual from the credit association, and so descended into the ranks of those who must get along each year without fertilizer. Similarly, two households from a different village who entrepreneurially borrowed some 2,000–3,000 *yuan* apiece from the local credit association in order to raise medicinal herbs saw their entire crops destroyed by a mysterious ailment. Beggared by their debts, they too became trapped in a vicious circle of no fertilizers and thus no improved seed varieties or other modern inputs, from which they could see no escape. Overall, in the three dozen impoverished villages that I have visited in Yunnan, Guangxi and Guizhou Provinces, somewhere between 10 and 15 percent of the households had fallen into this trap, unable to afford any chemical fertilizer whatsoever. In the worst off villages, a majority of the families were in these straits.

In many parts of China, the credit associations' lending policies tightened considerably during the 1990s, making it increasingly hard even for families above the poverty line to borrow the short-term credit they needed for their crop inputs. In an increasing number of provinces applicants now needed to find a guarantor who would accept part of the risk. Making the task even more difficult, in many areas it was stipulated that unless the applicant had substantial assets the guarantor must be the village head. Since serving as guarantor would involve personal risk to a village head, it is very difficult to obtain such backing. In Hainan Province, I supervised a survey in 1993-94 of 214 rural households spread across both prosperous and impoverished townships. The survey revealed that only 9.8 percent of the families had received any formal loan within the past year, and these households were largely among the wealthiest in their communities.

One reason for this deliberate tightening up of credit availability is that much of the credit associations' lending volume was being diverted away from the villages to support the development of rural industry and other non-agricultural endeavors. This is even more the case with the other normal source of rural credit, the Agricultural Bank, which, despite its title, is largely a vehicle through which money gets drawn out of the countryside for non-agricultural investments. On average, the Agricultural Bank has been lending only some 16-17 percent of its portfolio to households,[19] and almost all of this has gone to the richest.

All of these factors add up to a growing credit crisis within many rural communities. The head of a relatively well-off village told me in 1994 that "The poorer villagers here can't even *think* of getting credit." The situation is far more bleak for almost all of the farmers in the poorest rural townships, since whatever limited amount of credit is made available through the credit associations—after much of their funds have been pumped out of the villages—must depend entirely upon local deposits, and poor areas get few deposits. In an impoverished township where I lived while conducting research in 1993, in a mountainous ethnic-minority region of Hainan Province, only a single loan had been made to any of the township's farm households over the previous two years, according to the township's leadership, and that loan had gone to a village head. In a nearby, somewhat better-off township, four out of the twenty local villagers whom I interviewed had secured credit, but three of these recipients were again village officials.

If credit were available, it appears that many of the farmers would want to borrow even at high interest rates. A visit to one household in that impoverished township in Hainan turned into a round-table discussion with the host and four neighbors. All of the farmers said they would be willing to secure loans even at the maximum commercial interest rates that were being charged at the time by the Agricultural Bank—1.9 percent per month, compounded.

In most of the Chinese countryside, when formal credit is unavailable farmers turn instead at times of need to relatives and close friends for the money to buy fertilizer and other production inputs. But in the poorer villages, a farmer's relatives and friends usually are caught in similar financial straits. When desperate, farmers increasingly have had to turn to usurers at rates of 50 percent or more in the impoverished districts, sometimes reaching as high as 240 percent.[20]

---

[19] Albert Nyberg and Scott Rozelle, *Accelerating China's Rural Transformation* (Washington D.C.: World Bank, 1999), p. 27.

[20] Guo Xiaoming and Xue Xiaoming, "Xindai" (Credit), in Xiong Jingming (ed.), *Jinru 21 shiji de Zhongguo nongcun* (Chinese Villages Entering the 21st Century) (Beijing: Guangming Ribao Chubanshe, 2000), p. 412.

The Central Government's Poverty-Reduction Programs

The government is well aware of the predicament faced by the poor, and a number of special programs have been established that are targeted specifically toward helping impoverished families. In particular, the State Council established a Leading Group for Poverty Reduction in 1986, and in the fourteen years up to mid-2000 this organ had funneled a total of 138 billion *yuan* into poverty-reduction efforts.[21] In 1999 alone, 26 billion *yuan* (US$3 billion) of central government funds were budgeted to these ends.[22] Almost all of these funds have been targeted toward 592 designated "national poverty counties." A quandary, though, is that today more than half of the rural poor live in counties that have not been designated an official poverty county,[23] and most of these poor live in non-impoverished villages. By government policy, they are cut off from most forms of poverty assistance.[24]

Within the nationally designated poverty counties, lists of impoverished households are usually drawn up based on village heads' appraisals. As a means to minimize the corrupt diversion of aid funds, notice boards in each village listing these poor households are mandated in a good number of the counties. To a certain extent this safeguard works. Interviewing turned up a number of very poor households that have received interest-free or low-interest loans under this program. But the central government's efforts to constrain corrupt diversions of the funding have not always been successful. In the course of my rural household interviewing, I came upon several instances where quite prosperous households had been provided with substantial aid-the-poor credit; and in all of these cases the households were closely connected to important local officials. In one case, for instance, when I asked to interview a recipient, the man I was escorted to was the township Party secretary's elder brother, who lived in a well-furnished home.

Even officially, the central government has not always required that the aid-the-poor credit be directed toward a poor rural household. Starting in 1989 and lasting through the first half of the 1990s, priority was given to lending such funds instead to county factories, even to private firms, in the mistaken belief that this would provide considerable work for the poor and thus have a trickle-down

---

[21]   State Council Leading Group Office for Poverty Reduction, *China Poverty Paper*, Beijing, May 2000, p. 32.

[22]   World Bank, *Quarterly Update on China*, March 2000, p. 14.

[23]   On this, see Riskin and Li, "Chinese Rural Poverty Inside and Outside the Poor Regions."

[24]   In the autumn of 2001, the central government released a document announcing that the distribution of poverty would be reinvestigated and a new list of "poverty counties" would be drawn up. It indicated that up to 30 percent of the poverty funds would be set aside in future years to assist impoverished villages that were not on the new "poverty county" list, but notably, this funding would all go to poor villages, and the impoverished households in non-poor villages would still be excluded from the anti-poverty program. (*South China Morning Post* [Hong Kong], September 20, 2001).

effect. In 1992 and 1993, at the height of this program, about half of all of the subsidized poverty-reduction loans were lent to industrial enterprises in the nationally designated poverty counties.[25] But Beijing belatedly discovered that the program had "minimal or no poverty reduction impact."[26] The poverty counties are poorly located for industrial development, and many of their enterprises, public and private alike, started losing money. Rather than promoting development, the expanded publicly-owned enterprises became a drain on local government coffers. The central government eventually abandoned the trickle-down argument and by 1996-97 the Leading Group for Poverty Reduction was specifying that loans were to be aimed instead directly at impoverished village households. Nevertheless, rural governments sometimes continue to divert the poverty funds to county industry. In December 2000, the deputy head of the poorest county in eastern Qinghai advised me that the county was currently directing 30 percent of the aid-the-poor credit provided by the central government into county-based industry, much of it private.

In recent years, the Leading Group in charge of China's anti-poverty work has moved into channeling funds into micro-credit programs for the most impoverished farmers. By 1998, micro-credit schemes had been established in some two hundred impoverished counties, with central government funding of about 800 million *yuan*,[27] and the program has been expanded since then. The projects draw inspiration from the experience in Bangladesh of the Grameen Bank for the poor (whose founder was awarded a Nobel Peace Prize), and in replication of the Grameen model, the loans need to be repaid in small increments at weekly or monthly intervals. And like the Grameen model, Chinese villagers form a small group of four to seven member families, and each group is not eligible for further loans to any of its members if one of the members defaults. This mechanism takes the place of a requirement for collateral or a guarantor, in contrast to China's normal bank or credit association loans. And because no-one in a group can receive a further loan if any other member defaults, the program is supposed to provide an incentive for group members to help one another with advice about how to make good use of their micro-credit.

In the best of circumstances—in particular, in some of the micro-credit programs separately sponsored by the World Bank and the UNDP in China—this micro-credit concept works reasonably well. But in almost all cases, it has run into problems that were inherent in the very nature of the program. In Bangladesh's densely populated countryside, there are large numbers of landless poor women who engage in petty trade, and the Grameen Bank lends largely to this type of poor women. By borrowing from the Bank to increase their stock of

[25]   This is from paragraphs 8 and 10 of a second volume produced for internal distribution alongside the joint World Bank report *China Overcoming Rural Poverty* (2000).

[26]   *China Overcoming Rural Poverty*, paragraphs 3.26-27.

[27]   Ibid., para. 3.33.

goods, they are able to earn enough through daily sales to repay loans on a weekly basis. But the poor in China's programs are farmers in marginal hill country, whose earnings are largely postponed till harvest time or till after an animal has been raised, fattened and sold. China's major current poverty-reduction initiative is being stymied by the very fact that it was shaped to fit the circumstances of a very different type of poor in Bangladesh.[28] An illustration is provided by Dangchang County, the poorest county in Gansu Province, which itself is one of China's poorest provinces. Dangchang was provided with 3.6 million *yuan* to disburse as micro-credit to the poor, but the county distributed only 2 million of this, in part because its micro-credit program required repayments within a shorter period than impoverished farmers needed to recoup any agricultural investment.[29]

A number of the other programs financed by the Leading Group operate just as rigidly. But the very large sums of money that the Chinese government has pumped into poverty-reduction projects in the nationally-designated poverty counties have had an effect. A set of surveys analyzed by Azizur Rahman Khan and Carl Riskin show that the numbers of rural Chinese caught in what they call "extreme poverty" declined by about 22 percent between 1988 and 1995. This rate of decline was almost twice as high as they found to be true for the rural poor as a whole.[30] During the following half dozen years between 1996 and 2001, it appears that with aid-the-poor funding continuing to flow into impoverished counties, the numbers in absolute poverty have continued to decline at least modestly. During this same half decade of 1996-2001, the far larger numbers of rural families across China who are impoverished, but less abysmally so, remained persistently high, and probably even increased due to the falling prices for agricultural produce and the decline in opportunities for off-farm work.

Poverty and a Crisis in Access to Schooling and Medical Care

While education and medical-care delivery in prosperous rural districts such as Xiqiao have improved dramatically over the past two decades, the story is quite different in the impoverished regions. This is another respect in which rural China consists of "two nations."

It is vital that the children in impoverished regions should receive primary-school education. Illiteracy and innumeracy would condemn them to a lifetime of poverty, unable to take good advantage of new farming techniques and unable to

---

[28] These observations are based on discussions in Beijing in 2000 with Chinese academics and officials who specialize in this area, as well as my own interviews with local officials and trips into villages in Qinghai Province to study two of the more successful local micro-credit programs: one operated by the UNDP and the other by a foreign government aid agency.

[29] *Jingji xinxi bao* (Economic Information Daily), January 11, 2000.

[30] Azizur Rahman Khan and Carl Riskin, *Inequality and Poverty in China in the Age of Globalization* (New York: Oxford University Press, 2001), p. 77.

obtain a job in modern industry. As was observed in the chapter on labor migration, a lack of education already condemns their elder brothers and sisters to the most poorly paid work in the worst of the industrial sweatshops.

Yet in many of the poorer counties the education system today is in crisis. During the Maoist period, the central government largely left the local rural areas to fend for themselves, providing few resources, and little has changed. The central government continues to leave it up to county administrations, village governments and parents to foot the lion's share of the costs of schooling, and in poor districts they are very hard-pressed to do so. Under the collectives, the leaderships of impoverished villages were able to divert funding from the collective coffers into the village school before the members of the production teams received their wages. But today, with the land divided among households, there are no such collective funds in these villages to draw from.

The county governments are supposed to step in to maintain education, but when county budgets are very tight, education often gets short shrift. With insufficient county funding available to do more than pay for some of the teachers' salaries, the village schools are sustained on the principle of "user pays": rural parents have to pay tuition fees to cover a great many of the expenses. School budgets are inadequate as a consequence. In some of the poorest villages that I have visited, there are not enough desks and chairs to go round, and children are requested to bring their own. Where the county governments do not provide sufficient funding to help with teachers' salaries, it becomes hard to attract adequate staff, and the quality of teaching can be as bad as the school facilities. Many of the teachers in the poorest villages are themselves not adequately educated.

Even though the facilities and teachers tend to be far worse in the poorer districts, the school fees there tend to be as high as or even higher than in the better-off areas of rural China, since the latter schools receive more generous local government support. An example of how expensive rural education has become for households in poor areas is provided by a survey conducted in a rural county in Hubei Province. It found that 40 to 50 percent of a family's net income is absorbed by student expenses if all of the children are at school. Not surprisingly, school attendance in some parts of that county had fallen below 50 percent.[31] In Qinghai Province, I gathered information on school expenses in half a dozen villages, and as of the 2000-2001 schoolyear the charges averaged about 120-160 *yuan* per year for primary school and up to 400 *yuan* per year for ninth grade.[32] These are very poor communities where per capita annual incomes amount to less than 600 *yuan*.

---

[31]   *Nongmin ribao* (Farmers' Daily), October 13, 1999.

[32]   More than half of these charges are for textbooks. The national Ministry of Propaganda has had a monopoly on the distribution and sale of all textbooks through the New China Bookshop chain that it controls, and it has jacked up prices several times more than what the books cost to produce. A senior Chinese education specialist in Beijing related to me in 2000 that the

Impoverished parents whom I interviewed in these villages are very concerned that their children will be severely disadvantaged in life if they receive little or no education—that they will be cheated, will be less adept at farming and other occupations, and will not be able to adapt to the ongoing changes that are sweeping China. To a degree that is at once touching and inspiring, parents in these poor villages generally make major sacrifices to keep their children in school, even when it means cutting back on the quality and quantity of food consumed and on other very basic essentials.

But it is also clear, in examining my field notes on education from more than three dozen villages in the 1990s, that the poorer the household and village, the more likely that children will drop out of school early; the better off the household and village, the more likely that all of the children, including the girls, will be in school. In the poorest households of poor villages, one or more of the children is likely never even to have entered primary school, especially the daughters. Girls marry out into other families when they grow up, while boys stay in the family, and farmers know that in old age they will need to rely exclusively on their sons' earning power. Given this, the education of girls in poor families is more frequently sacrificed.

In the poorest parts of the countryside, with low funding, a complete six-year primary school education may not even be available to any of the children. In one village in Yunnan Province that I visited, no schooling was available after the fourth grade because the school's poorly paid teacher was too busy supporting his family through farmwork. In an even poorer village in Guizhou Province, the village school only went up to second grade. In a third village, where schooling during the period of collectives had been offered through fourth grade, that was no longer the case. Instead, each year only one grade of children was now taught, and the school's only teacher advanced from grade one to grade six with this one group of students. All other children have had to hike to another village for their schooling, or else wait for the local school's six-year school-grade cycle to be repeated.

In short, a crisis exists in impoverished areas, in which some poor students cannot afford to attend primary school and some schools are not fully functioning. Given that this crisis persists in elementary education, it is surprising that, in a sweeping move in the late nineties, the central government decreed that education

---

Education Ministry has battled for years to end the monopoly and reduce prices, but he noted that the Propaganda Ministry is a more powerful ministry and has continued to collect a "rent" from Chinese parents worth billions of *yuan* a year. In June 2001 the Education Ministry, responding to counter this, announced that the (relatively small) sum of 100 million *yuan* (US$12 million) would be allocated to provide free textbooks to children in poor counties beginning in the autumn 2001 semester. More importantly, it also finally succeeded in announcing that competition and bidding would be introduced into both the publication and distribution of textbooks starting that autumn. As of the time of writing this, it remains an open question whether the Propaganda Ministry will accept this; a number of reform measures of various types in the past have been announced but then blocked.

must be universalized up through ninth grade. What made the decree doubly unrealistic is that the central government has given no indication that it will supply the funding even to universalize primary education, let alone grades 7 through 9. Nonetheless, parts of the decree are being strictly enforced. In the counties in Qinghai that were visited in 2000, some of the very impoverished parents who have pulled their children out of primary school were arrested, put on trial and heavily fined— though the effect is nullified by the fact that they have no money to pay any fines and also obviously cannot afford to pay the hefty fees for their children to attend school. In the midst of this campaign, in a poor Muslim village in Qinghai the village Party Secretary admitted that some 30-40 percent of the primary-school-aged children—including the great majority of the girls—were not enrolled, and there was little the government could do to enforce attendance.

The central education authorities have also been unrealistic in a different respect. In the late 1990s Beijing decreed that schools everywhere in China must provide a "quality education"[33] and strongly indicated that this included primary-school English classes and classes on operating computers. In Qinghai, plans were obediently put in place in 2000 in very poor villages for rural primary school teachers who themselves do not know English to teach the language, and rural township education departments that cannot afford to fix broken windows at primary schools or to provide desks and chairs in classrooms were purchasing the obligatory computers. The central education authorities were demanding that all of China must be fully "modern" and were imposing that vision (without adequate funding) in ways that are incongruous with the terrible difficulties facing destitute schools and parents.

The medical-care systems in such villages are often in as bad shape as the schools. To China's credit, practically all villages have an appointed medical officer. But in the poorer regions they tend to be no better trained than the barefoot doctors of the past. The only pay these part-time personnel receive from government sources is a sum for each innoculation they provide, and the amount is so small that some of the village medical officers are negligent in carrying out this duty. "User pays" underpins all other services, and poor farmers generally try to avoid the expense of being tended to by such an ill-trained neighbor.

For more than rudimentary treatment, they can go to the township medical clinic, which is staffed by genuine salaried doctors. But in the poor areas that I have visited, county and township budgets do not stretch far enough to cover more than 65 to 70 percent of what the doctors are supposed to receive as a salary—and even this amount is often months in arrears. The clinics are supposed

---

[33]   On the "quality education" drive in a prosperous rural county, see Andrew Kipnis, "The Disturbing Educational Discipline of 'Peasants'," *The China Journal*, No. 46 (July 2001). "Quality education" also entails efforts to reduce rote learning and cramming for examinations in China's school system, and Kipnis' paper explores why this aspect of "quality education" undermines the prospects for rural students at his fieldsite to get admitted into higher education.

to make up the difference through charges to patients. Across rural China, they tend to make the bulk of their income by prescribing and selling medicines, and this very often has meant overprescribing and overcharging for medicines. Officials at the national Ministry of Health, whom I interviewed in Beijing in 2000, are well aware of this, as are county and township officials, but they generally consider it too difficult to try to root out the practice. The end result is that many ill people avoid treatment, and the rural clinics tend to be seriously underutilized, especially in the poorer regions. Preventable diseases such as turberculosis have been gaining ground in rural China.

Officials at a couple of the very poorest townships that I visited in Qinghai Province in 2000 insist that there, overprescribing and overcharging is not a problem inasmuch as most patients cannot afford the medicines they truly need even without a doctor's markup. A vicious circle ensues, in which an illness of a working family member pushes a family further into poverty, putting medical care even further out of reach. Recurring ill health makes it that much more difficult for families to lift themselves out of poverty, and is one of the most pernicious aspects of the poverty trap. A weak and underfunded Ministry of Health and local governments do little to assist.

The Special Problems of Impoverished Ethnic Minorities

Education and health care are in especially poor straits among many of the impoverished non-Han peoples of the interior, to an extent that warrants special mention. Most of them speak their own ethnic group's language at home, and so becoming literate in Chinese at school is that much more difficult for them, since they must first obtain command of what is initially a foreign language. The women in particular are at a disadvantage, as they have fewer opportunities than the men to learn to speak Chinese. This makes it that much harder for them to access health care and other services outside their village.

The great majority of the populace of non-Han descent reside in the southwestern and western regions—and often in agriculturally marginal hill country and the dry range lands that border deserts. Many are therefore destitute. In point of fact, the ethnic minority peoples comprise a disproportionately high percentage of China's absolute poor.[34]

The plight of these people can be seen clearly in China's southwestern provinces. Over the past millennium, Han Chinese immigration into the region was accompanied by the slow, forced retreat of most of the indigenous peoples southward and upward into the mountains.[35] The consequence is that in Yunnan Province, where a bit over one-third of the population is listed as belonging to the

[34]   *China, Overcoming Rural Poverty* (Beijing: Joint Report of the Leading Group for Poverty Reduction, UNDP and the World Bank, 2000), p. 9.

[35]   On the historical process of Han immigration and the consequences for the indigenous populations, see C.P. Fitzgerald, *The Southern Expansion of the Chinese People* (Canberra: Australian National University Press, 1972), Ch. 4.

ethnic minorities, 70 percent of them live in mountainous districts.[36] In Hainan Province, similarly, the progressive penetration of Han settlers pushed almost all of the indigenous Li people into the southern half of the island province. Today few Li remain in the north, whereas they comprise close to half of the population of the six southernmost counties, and within these counties, as I discovered in my travels, they live predominantly in poor hill country away from the agriculturally richer lowland coast.

Many of the ethnic people of the southwest are becoming acculturated to Han customs and gradually losing their own. As just one example among many, in Bama County, Guangxi, where the flat arable lands are occupied almost entirely by Zhuang who very largely follow local Han customs, I was told by officials that, in contrast, the remote East Mountain district was Yao territory that reputedly has not been much touched by modern Chinese ways. Yet a visit to several hamlets there, scrambling down narrow paths into hollows among the mountains, revealed quite a different picture. Chinese kitchen gods and Chinese village gods are prevalent, and in clothing, cuisine and most other respects these Yao villagers are similar to the local Han (and Zhuang). When asked how they differ from the Han, they tended to place emphasis upon the fact that the Yao hold the disadvantages associated with impoverishment. To them, that is the essential 'ethnic' distinction, other than the fact that they speak a different language at home. The differences between them and the local Han, one of them said, are that the Han know how to plan out agriculture better, and

> during the slack season some of the Han can go off to be carpenters and blacksmiths. We can't because we don't have the know-how. Our homes differ from the Han, too, in that they use tile roofing while we can only afford thatch. If we could afford to, we'd live in Han homes. No, no, there's no conflict between Yao and Han culture. None. No, we wouldn't mind, if we lived where the Han are the majority, if we were to speak Chinese at home—and wouldn't mind if our grandchildren couldn't speak Yao. [He and two neighbors chuckled at the silliness of my question, that it was naive to think that they should mind.]

During several research trips, I was able to conduct interviewing in farm households of Buyi (Bouyei), Li, Miao, Yao, Yi and Zhuang extraction in counties scattered across the back country of the southwest. A great many of the interviewees similarly regarded themselves as being a type of poor second-class Chinese and similarly wanted to escape that condition.

This perception of their ethnicity, as being a mark of low status and poverty, can be seen in marriage patterns. Although the majority of each ethnic minority intermarry among themselves, some of the young women, especially in mixed communities, marry into Han households. That is, these women, as is the case in many societies, have opportunities to practice hypergamy: upward mobility

---

[36]   *Minzuxue yu xiandaihua* (Ethnic Studies and Modernization), No. 2, 1985, p. 11.

through marriage into a higher social status grouping than they were raised within. The converse, for a young Han woman to marry a Li or Zhuang or Yao or Miao man, is rare in the countryside.

The predominant Han image of the impoverished ethnic groups of the southwest is the same image that many of these people have learned to hold of themselves: as embarrassingly poor and backward, as socially and materially so disadvantaged that they are manifestly inferior to the Han. This image is exemplified by an anti-poverty project that the Hainan provincial government has carried out among the Li. This provided grants of 1,000 *yuan* to a number of Li households to help finance the erection of Chinese-style brick homes. The Lis' thatched houses better suit the tropical climate, but Chinese-style houses are perceived to be superior precisely because they are associated with Han-ness. Notably, the program specified that these house-building grants were only to be made available to Li who live in thatched housing within sight of asphalted roads. The Hainan countryside contains few such roads: and these tend to be frequented by tourists from other parts of China and by foreigners. Thatched housing was not seen by the officials as legitimate or as picturesque because of its ethnic character, but rather as an embarrassment: as the Li personifying a primitive poverty that is unbecoming to Hainan's image. Among the Li themselves, it was noticeable in the villages that I visited that the most prosperous Li tend to build brick and tile-roofed homes similar to the Han, despite these being stifling in the sultry tropical climate.

House styles are not the only aspect of the material culture of the minority peoples that the Han officialdom hold in low regard. As an example, a Western agronomist with whom I was traveling in Guizhou Province in 1991 was perturbed that the government agricultural extension service was trying to persuade the local Buyi and Miao farmers to give up the cultivation of varieties of buckwheat and rye that were well suited to the local climate, to be displaced by varieties of dry rice that are more vulnerable to the mountain country's extreme climatic conditions. The Han officials who were locally in charge of agricultural services were puzzled by the Western agronomist's view, as a shift toward rice seemed to them an undeniable mark of the local populace's "progress."

It is not just these minorities' material culture that officials look down upon. During my travels, rural Han cadres made repeated off-the-cuff comments disparaging various impoverished ethnicities on intellectual and moral grounds. The officials perceive the behavior of these ethnic minorities largely as "slow" and "backward" and "childlike". This naively open prejudice is expressed to a foreigner even by university-educated Han, who, for instance, repeatedly described the Li as happy-go-lucky, lazy, watermelon-eating natives of dubious moral stature[37] (a description quite similar to the stereotype of southern black

---

[37]   Other examples of the stereotypical view of the Li are provided in Nancy S. Netting, "The Deer Turned Her Head: Ethnic Options for the Hainan Li," *Bulletin of Concerned Asian Scholars*, Vol. 22, No. 2 (April 1997), pp. 3-17, esp. p. 14. For a book-length discussion of Han images

people in America half a century ago). This openly bigoted image is reinforced by the titillated Han view of them as being sexually loose. Smutty locker-room jokes about the Li and other minority hill groups were bandied about on a daily basis among the Han colleagues who accompanied me on our four-wheel-drive research. The soft-core pornography industry in China is practically built around this image.[38]

At the same time, an identity as an ethnic minority can carry its own rewards. The government pursues an affirmative action program that makes it easier for students from the ethnic minorities to get through admissions exams at the higher reaches of the education system; and much more significantly, in some districts and provinces the ethnic minorities can have one more child than can Han under the government's birth-control program.[39]

Thus, notwithstanding the prejudices of many Han officials, it should not be concluded that the Chinese government is guilty of openly discriminating against these peoples. In fact, in contrast to Beijing's record in Tibet and Xinjiang, the central government deserves credit for handling relations with the ethnic groups of China's southwest more humanely than some of the nations of Southeast Asia

---

of the ethnic minorities of southwest China, see Susan D. Blum, *Portraits of "Primitives": Ordering Human Kinds in the Chinese Nation* (Latham: Rowman & Littlefield, 2001).

[38] Chinese pornography frequently uses minority peoples of the southwest as an excuse to present photographs of women with bare breasts (often using Han prostitutes against southwest China backdrops) and stories of sexual free abandon. The technique circumvents censorship by projecting the eroticism as exoticism, a trick that, at its most subtle, *National Geographic* made famous many decades ago in America. In recent times the Han have tended to be relatively puritanical when it comes to sexual matters, at least in terms of their public acknowledgement, and this stereotyping of the minority peoples at one and the same time portrays them as being not just "different," but lasciviously less moral. It became evident to me from the backseat of four-wheel drives that my Han colleagues had a doubly degrading image of the southwestern minorities: that the jokes and anecdotes about a lack of sexual control are not just the stuff of voyeuristic fantasies but simultaneously cast the minorities as truly lower class. For a discussion of the ethnic-minority soft-porn industry see Dru Gladney, "Representing Nationality in China: Refiguring Majority/Minority Identities," *The Journal of Asian Studies*, Vol. 53, No. 1 (February 1994), esp. pp. 101-6. Also see Louisa Schein, "Gender and Internal Orientalism in China," *Modern China*, Vol. 23, No. 1 (January 1997), esp. pp. 77-78.

[39] The numbers of children that the members of an ethnic minority are permitted to have seems to depend upon how anxious a provincial government is to keep population growth under control. In Yunnan Province, the ethnic-minority communities that I visited are only allowed to have two children per couple without suffering a fine, the same number of children as are allowed to rural Han families in Yunnan. In Hainan Province, in contrast, the indigenous Li are normally allowed one more child than the Han: a Li farmer is allowed three children, one more than a Han farmer; a Li state-farm worker or city dweller is allowed two children, again one more than his or her Han workmate. (In practice, the poorest Li farmers in the villages that I visited tend to have 4-5 children. Among other things, they are too impoverished to be vulnerable to fines or other sanctions.)

have treated their own minority populations. Whatever the flaws, the Chinese government has in fact generally followed a program in the southwest to respect ethnic traditions, or more specifically ethnic folkways, and provides funding to promote the retention of dance and language and other cultural markers. Simultaneously, though, through the school system and a variety of other means, efforts have been directed toward the *de facto* cultural assimilation of all of these groups, at a pace far outstripping any previous period of Chinese history. But such an effort is common to practically all governments around the world, and in many cases it enjoys the cooperation of the local minorities in southwest China.

Significantly, too, the very shape of local administration and of land ownership helps to protect the ethnic minorities from being dispossessed of their lands by commercially astute Han, as had occurred so often previously in Chinese history. As observed in earlier chapters, the administrative shell of the previous collective era has been retained—which means that while farmers cultivate their land privately, the land continues to "belong" to the hamlet or village, and cannot readily be sold away to immigrants and entrepreneurs. At a rural township in Yunnan that I visited for several days, the Tuanjie [Unity] Yi-Bai Autonomous Township, non-Han people comprise more than two-thirds of the population, and the title "Autonomous" provides an assurance that some of the leading posts are reserved for people of non-Han origin. The township Party secretary is a Bai,[40] and the township administative head is an Yi.[41] Since land ownership ultimately rests with the township and its constituent villages, it would require the collusion of such local leaders to alienate fields and pasturelands from local use and transfer them to Han outsiders. This serves as a brake on land dispossession in cases where, say, destitute households among the local Yi individually might otherwise be vulnerable.

---

[40]   The Bai have long been assimilated to Han culture, and have a higher literacy rate in Chinese than the rural Han of Yunnan. Though today called the Bai, they used to refer to themselves and their language simply as Min Chia (*minjia*), a Chinese term meaning "commoner" or "civilian" (perhaps initially used by the Bai in counter-distinction to Chinese military colonies, where Hanyu was spoken). An interesting book on them is C.P. Fitzgerald, *The Tower of Five Glories: A Study of the Min Chia of Ta Li, Yunnan* (London: The Cresset Press, 1941). Also see Colin Mackerras, "Aspects of Bai Culture: Change and Continuity in a Yunnan Nationality," *Modern China*, Vol. 14, No. 1 (January 1988), pp. 51-84; and David Y.H. Wu, "Culture Change and Ethnic Identity Among Minorities in China," in *Ethnicity and Ethnic Groups in China*, ed. Chien Chiao and Nicholas Tapp (Hong: New Asia College, 1989), esp. pp. 15-18.

[41]   The anthropologist Stevan Harrell has written several excellent papers on the Yi and the artificial common identity with which they have been labeled. See "The History of the History of the Yi," in *Cultural Encounters on China's Ethnic Frontiers*, ed. Stevan Harrell, pp. 63-91; "Ethnicity, Local Interests, and the State: Yi Communities in Southwest China," *Comparative Studies in Society and History*, Vol. 32, No. 3 (July 1990), pp. 515-48; and "Ethnicity and Kin Terms among Two Kinds of Yi," in *Ethnicity and Ethnic Change in China*, ed. Chien Chao and Nicholas Tapp, pp. 179-98.

In the present economic climate, however, even this local administrative and land ownership structure does not always suffice to protect a local ethnic population from dispossession. In late 1993 I spent a week in the countryside of Ledong County, Hainan Province, a ruggedly beautiful landscape of rolling hills that would be a perfect setting for large-scale tropical fruit production. But the local Li populace, who inhabit all of the hill acreage, are starved of capital and so are in no position to develop, fertilize and irrigate large-scale commercial fruit orchards. The Li officialdom of one entirely Li township, fearing that it will have no other use over the coming decades for its 20,000 *mu* of hill land (6,500 acres), was in the midst of negotiating a very long-term lease, for a surprisingly small annual rent, of 15,000 *mu* of land to a semi-private enterprise titled the Chinese Mango Co., Inc. In another entirely Li township that was desperate to find a way to keep paying the salaries of its local cadres and teachers, an entrepreneurial state-owned company had recently leased, again at a dirt-cheap price, a block of hill land that local Li farmers had been planting with crops. In keeping with Han prejudices, the company had brought in a group of Han farmers from Manchuria, who presumably knew nothing about tropical fruit production, to develop the orchards, leaving the local Li underemployed and without access to needed land. At yet another site in the county, a county-government enterprise had contracted out a swathe of Li hill country and had hired unemployed Han from the county capital to plant the new orchards rather than the local Li. Whatever the safeguards of central government policy and local administrative structures, the pull of historical trends and Han prejudice is once again at work, this time in the shape of agri-business, gradually dispossessing minority hill farmers in favor of Han commercial interests. At the same time that cultural assimilation advances among the hill-country ethnic groups of the southwest, some of them increasingly are becoming marginalized, poor bystanders to China's development.

Desperate Districts

In at least some cases, then, poverty is perpetuated unnecessarily through the very forces that the economic reforms have set in motion. In other cases, it persists due to flawed government programs. In yet other cases, though, the endurance of grinding poverty is rooted in causes beyond any government's power to readily redress. In at least some places the difficulties confronting efforts to assist impoverished villages seem all but insoluble: a depressing combination of remoteness, overpopulation, poor soils, inadequate availability of water, and ecological degradation. I have encountered a number of such irremediably impoverished areas both in Qinghai and in China's southwest.

In Hualong, the poorest county in the eastern half of Qinghai, where most of the hill villages are Muslim, plans were afoot during 2000 to relocate 30,000 people during the next decade to sites more suitable to human habitation. The hill villages are at elevations of some 10,000 feet, beset by cold weather and short growing seasons. Making matters worse, shortages of drinking water force residents of some of these villages to hike a mile or more every day during the summer months to haul back enough water for them and their animals to survive.[42] Stymied as to how to help such villages develop, the government decided to move one village in 2001 to the western side of Qinghai and another village to Anxi County in Gansu Province, a county inhabited by Han Chinese. Qinghai officials admitted that the Muslim immigrants would not be welcomed there. But several members of these two communities told me that they looked forward to relocating anywhere away from their hopeless current situation.

An even more hopeless setting exists in the mountains of northern Yunnan. A narrow winding road struggles north from Yunnan's provincial capital for several slow hours and then, branching off, climbs dizzyingly upward toward Huize, an isolated county in the high country that is home to some 750,000 people. It is a route that is at once beautiful and depressing: for wherever in the plunges of cliff a scrap of mountain slope contains a pocket of soil, hungry farmers have arduously planted small patches of potatoes. Many of these patches are angled at inclines greater than 45 degrees, and farmers sometimes must strap themselves to supporting ropes to avoid falling into the gorges below. In this barren mountain country, in territory that in America or Europe would be empty wilderness, extreme Malthusian pressures are forcing peasants to wage a war with nature to survive.

One of the poorest Chinese villages that I have ever visited is perched at the top of an eroded mountain gulch in this highland county, some 10,000 feet above sea level. The residents of Dacai Village, a Han community of 125 people, barely manage to struggle through from year to year on their potato yields and their proceeds from wool sales; most years, late winter is a period of gnawing hunger. Since sheep provide their only cash income, after decollectivization each household desperately began trying to increase its own flocks on the common grazing lands. The result was overgrazing on the steep mountainsides—and severe erosion. New gullies pockmark the mountainsides, and pieces of mountain have literally cleaved off and slid into the streams below. This stretch of high country has moved rapidly toward irreversible ecological disaster.

In this particular locale, the immiseration of peasant families is not a consequence of the government's present policies. Many of the mountain villages in the county have been absolved from providing quota grain or potatoes, taxes here are kept low, and central government assistance in the form of aid-the-poor credit has been made available. But such measures do not touch upon the root causes of the area's abysmal poverty: the distance of the county from any markets, the population pressures on the land, the misuse of the mountainsides, and the devastating environmental damage that is resulting.

---

[42]   This is the case, too, among a large number of hill villages in the large karst region of the southwest: the rainfalls there are adequate but karst does not retain water, which seeps away into the limestone beneath the soil. The residents of one village in Guizhou that I have visited needed to walk three miles each way from January to May to fetch water.

Fifty percent of Yunnan had been covered in forests in the early 1950s, but most of that forest was destroyed over the past half century. This destruction proceeded at a rapid pace throughout the era of collective agriculture, under directives that land should be cleared for crops and grazing. Certainly, in the immediate district surrounding Dacai Village, all forests had disappeared long before family farming was restored in the early 1980s.

To protect the environment, the government's wisest move is to restrict villagers' use of the steep slopes and to put government funds into reforesting the mountainsides. After a series of devastating floods in the late 1990s along China's major rivers, Beijing finally acted decisively. In a new national policy covering the mountainous areas of China, mountain slopes steeper than 25 degrees are being closed off to farmers and herders. The dilemma, of course, is that the peasantry of areas like Dacai would starve if denied access to their eroding potato patches and pastures. The central government accordingly is promising to deliver supplementary foodstuffs to affected villagers for a period of at least eight years, and extending beyond that wherever necessary. Whether Beijing is successful in enforcing the closure of mountain slopes or, indeed, is willing to institute a permanent system of welfare dependency remains an open question.

A "best case" scenario would be to move part of the population of the Dacai area to more fertile districts. But the lowland areas of Yunnan are also straining with people. Nor does the growth of industry in Yunnan's cities and towns offer any immediate employment possibilities for the poor of Dacai. Men from the village have tried their luck in the provincial capital Kunming and further afield, but discovered that the competition from other poor job-seekers has driven down the wages for unskilled migrant labor to such an extent that they could not easily recoup the expense of traveling there from Dacai and living in the city while working.

Given these circumstances, the most feasible response to the plight of Dacai village lies with China's birth-control campaign, which the provincial government has been trying to enforce.[43] But even this effort realistically is aimed only at curtailing the growth of the rural population, not at reducing it; the goal in the hinterlands of Yunnan is to restrict each family not to one child but to two.[44] Even if the birth-control campaign succeeds (which it has not; many rural households throughout rural China have more than two children and thus China's population continues to grow), it will only hold the district to its present degree of overpopulation. Into the foreseeable future, irrespective of government policies, villages like Dacai face continued miserable poverty.

---

[43]   At Dacai, an over-quota birth is supposed to be penalized with a heavy fine. The fine is halved if the mother accepts a tubal ligation. But truly impoverished people cannot readily be fined when they have nothing that can be confiscated.

[44]   Dacai is a Han Chinese village; in ethnic-minority villages, the regulations in China are often more lenient, stipulating a maximum of three children.

Starting in the 1980s, Dacai reverted to traditional poor-peasant mores in self-protection. This is particularly evident in the arrangement of betrothals. The peasants of such impoverished villages face difficulties in the competition to obtain brides for their sons, and so some Dacai parents, in a throwback to time-honored practices, have entered into negotiations with other local families to swap their daughters as brides for each others' sons. In doing so, most parents are seeking as far in advance as possible to line up a fiancée for their boy: childhood engagements have again become the norm. As the village's Party secretary explained:

> The result is that most of the girls here are engaged to be married at the age of two or three; the eldest would be four or five years old. Why? Because it's an old and widespread custom, so if you wait any longer you won't find anyone acceptable to marry your son or daughter to after they grow up. Besides, if you agree to a childhood engagement, the little bride-to-be will receive new clothing each year from the boy's side.

In other words, parents in this impoverished village betroth their girl toddlers in part so as to reduce the expense of raising them. In such circumstances, to provide them with schooling is out of the question: at the time of my visit, only two girls in the village were enrolled in primary school.[45] To the peasants of Dacai, the national slogans about modernizing and developing China are no more than irrelevant catchphrases. What concerns them is simply to ensure their family's survival and perpetuation.

A number of other very impoverished villages that I have visited have not established any systems to ensure the sons' marriage, and these villages face eventual extinction. In a Tibetan village in Qinghai Province, poverty-stricken parents largely send their daughters out-of-province to marry in order to secure a higher bride price. As Tibetans and Mongols both practice Lamaistic Buddhism, they are willing to let their daughters enter Mongol families in Gansu and Inner Mongolia, while poverty keeps many of the village's young men unmarried. In a mountainous Han village in a nearby county, some 40 to 50 of the men of marriageable age—the great bulk of that generation—similarly remain bachelors, as they cannot afford the expense of a wedding and bride price. The per capita annual income in this destitute village was between 300 and 400 *yuan* as of 2000, yet the total cost in the region of a bride price and marriage ceremony amounted to about 10,000 *yuan*. The young women of the village marry out to less

---

[45]   I visited the single-room four-grade school, which was located in the attic of a small storehouse. It was cramped and dark even in the daytime, and contained desks for only half of the sixteen children who were enrolled. Most of them presumably would drop out early; only nine people in the village had ever graduated from primary school. I visited this school in the company of Xiong Jingming (Jean Hung), who has written an article describing this and a few other rural schools: "Shei lian qiong xiangzi, wei jie dushu nan" (Pity the Impoverished Countryside: The Difficulties of Schooling Remain Unresolved), *Kaifang zazhi* (Open Magazine), January 1999, pp. 75-77.

impoverished villages, while these dozens of desperate young men face a bleak future. For farmers such as the Han who culturally put a premium on the perpetuation of the male line, this inability to marry can be among the most crushing blows imposed by poverty, as terrible as hunger and ill-health.

Chapter Ten

THE KALEIDOSCOPIC POLITICS OF RURAL CHINA

Evidence has mounted of increasingly open disgruntlement among villagers in many parts of the Chinese countryside, sometimes erupting in riots. Such incidents of violence have been recorded not just in parts of the country where farmers are straining to make ends meet, but even in richer districts. Why this widespread local political discontent?

It will be seen in this chapter that one major reason is the failure of the government to successfully reshape China's rural political system. When villagers returned to tilling family farms in the early 1980s, the Chinese government largely retained the same overall framework for governing rural China that had been established by the Party during the 1950s and 1960s. This had been designed under Mao as a top-down structure to enforce central control and to facilitate periodic political mobilization. But while the structure remained the same, there has been a relaxation of central powers under the post-Mao regime, and in this situation many local officials have made use of their strategic position between state and society to develop new bases of power, often to the detriment of villagers. It will be seen, too, that this has occurred in very different ways in the prosperous and non-prosperous regions of China. Finally, the chapter will examine why and how the central government is attempting to counteract the tactics of grass-roots officials by making them more accountable through a new system of village elections.

Continuities and Discontinuities in the Post-Mao Rural Administrative Scene

Even though the politically laden titles "commune" and "brigade" were abolished during the first half of the 1980s, replaced by the titles of "township" and "administrative village," to some extent this switch is a case of old wine in new bottles: new official titles and new declarations of intent are announced while the actual shape of the rural political structure has remained largely intact. At both the township level and in villages, the Party secretary often remains the single most powerful figure, more so than the local government head, and continues to play a direct role in setting policy. As just one example, the Party secretary of a well-off township in Yunnan noted in an interview that his township Party committee "decides important policies such as economic development plans— should we take steps to help develop animal husbandry, how much encouragement should be given to grain production, how much should be mined from the township's quarries, should a road be built?"

A second form of continuity in rural administration lies in the rotations of county- and township-level leaders (but notably, not village leaders) to new posts elsewhere—within the same province or prefecture for county leaders, and within the same county for township leaders. These rural government officials also had been rotated under Mao and, before that, this had been the case with the county magistrates of imperial times. The consequences are similar, too: some of the county and township leaders today do not necessarily feel any particular attachment to the populace of the districts they command. *People's Daily* has cited a saying among such officials: "Look for half a year, work for half a year, and then it's time to get out of here."[1] In the knowledge that promotions depend upon making a splash while in office, many of these higher-level rural officials today put a premium on showy projects. They pour money into launching impressive-looking new initiatives and into erecting taller public buildings and widening and beautifying streets in the county capitals and market towns. Within a few years they have departed, leaving behind debts that need to be paid out of future local revenues. Such a scenario is surprisingly common today, particularly in the richer districts, but is found also in relatively poor areas. It is the modern variant of the dam-building and backyard steel-making campaigns in Mao's day that had been vigorously pursued by county and commune officials seeking promotion.

Another type of continuity involves the shape of the county and township administrative system. The township government is divided into a number of offices that are parallel in structure to the county government: a civil affairs office, a public security office, a legal affairs office, a financial office, a Women's Association office, and so forth. In fact, almost all of the county-level bureaus have a counterpart at the township level. Practically all of these township offices come under the dual control of both the township government and the relevant county bureau: for instance, the township's legal officer comes under the joint control of both the township government and the county judicial department. This system of dual controls was inherited from the Maoist period and reflected an effort in those earlier years to combine central controls with local Party initiative.[2] Then and now, there is often a subtle tug-of-war in this system between the township and county governments to hold predominant influence over the township-level offices. To a certain extent, the respective power of these two levels of government differs according to the type of work that each office fulfills. The finance office and the tax office in the townships usually seem to be more securely in the county government's sway. The finance office, after all, is

---

[1]   The saying is quoted in a letter published in *Renmin ribao* (People's Daily), December 11, 1999.

[2]   On this system, and on the ways that power was exercised differently under these dual controls during different portions of the Maoist era, see Jonathan Unger, "The Struggle to Dictate China's Administration: The Conflict of Branches vs. Areas vs. Reform," *The Australian Journal of Chinese Affairs*, No. 18 (July 1987), pp. 15-45.

responsible for collecting the agricultural tax, and the tax office the commercial and industrial taxes, which the county and higher levels of government are intent upon controlling. The agricultural extension services, by comparison, are not of vital interest to county authorities, and the township is allowed to play a larger role in controlling these township-level offices.[3]

In the current scene, the wealth or poverty of a particular township also plays a part in determining the degree of influence of a township government. As one example, that well-to-do township in Yunnan whose Party secretary has just been quoted is located in a relatively poor county. A consequence is that this wealthy township foots most of the costs of the township-level offices out of the profits from its own mines and other enterprises. The township's Party secretary insisted to me in no uncertain terms that, as a consequence, the township authorities effectively hold the preponderance of influence over almost all of the offices and their personnel. An impoverished township that I visited in a nearby county offers a sharp contrast. In interviews, its leaders seemed competent and energetic, more than enough to control their own bailiwick. But the township government does not own any profitable resources, and the great bulk of the revenues from the township are in the shape of agricultural taxes, quota/contract grain, and commercial taxes, which are in the control of the tax and finance offices and go directly to the county. A township is allowed to collect from households an additional "township unified tax" (*xiang tongchou kuan*), but in an impoverished township like this the amount is inadequate. To keep the township government afloat, the county government provides almost all of the funding needed for essential administrative functions and for most of the township officials' salaries. The consequence is clear-cut. The township head noted in an interview that, to his chagrin, even the township's animal husbandry station has come more under the control of the county's bureau of animal husbandry than under his own. In short, he who pays the piper calls the tune.

Sufficient evidence is not available across China to generalize with any accuracy, but it appears that the county governments normally are better funded than their townships, and that the counties usually hold the preponderance of leverage over the bulk of the township-level offices. This is somewhat parallel to the balance of influence over such offices that usually prevailed under Mao.[4] A significant change, though, is that the post-Mao era has witnessed a marked proliferation in the numbers and types of such offices, as more bureaus get

---

[3]   In the best study that I know of regarding the complicated relationship between the county and township levels of rural administration, Tao-Chiu Lam finds this distinction in the influence over township-level offices to be quite clear for a county that is about average for China in terms of living standards. Tao-Chiu Lam, "The Local State Under Reform: A Study of a County in Hainan Province, China," Ph.D. dissertation, Australian National University, Canberra, 2000.

[4]   On the situation of these township offices during the first half of the 1960s, for instance, see A. Doak Barnett, *Cadres, Bureaucracy, and Political Power in Communist China* (New York: Columbia University Press, 1967), esp. pp. 352-61.

created at county level and as these establish township-level branches. Whereas the communes had contained a dozen or so departments, townships today sometimes contain more than thirty.

To what extent has the township government's influence over villages altered during the post-Mao period? As was noted in Chapter One, during the period of Mao-era collectives village officials could not ignore central-government directives and orders, but instead could attempt much more readily to sidestep or resist commands that originated at the commune level. They knew that the commune administration, when acting on its own, was the weakest link in the Party-state's chain of command. As was also observed in Chapter One, the communes' Party leaders frequently sought to strengthen their own leverage over the localities by way of the political campaigns that punctuated rural life throughout the period of Mao's rule. Today, such political campaigns have essentially disappeared from the scene. At the same time, with the *diktat* of the central Party-state less rigorously enforced than under Mao, village leaders often feel less pressure to conform to the preferences of the far-away central state.[5] In many districts, as will be seen, the higher-level rural authorities have devised new mechanisms to get village leaders to comply with directives and targets, but these do not always suffice to bring village leaderships strictly and actively into line, except on specific issues vital to the higher levels.

Inasmuch as the village leaders' power over the villagers rests on a less solid basis since decollectivization, now that they no longer control most of the villagers' livelihoods, many village cadres follow a strategy of being accommodating and avoiding giving offense both to the villagers below them and to the township leadership that can dismiss or reward them. As Yan Yunxiang notes about a village in north China that he has researched, the village leaders there have "begun to play a role of mediator or middleman" and end up in a "double-role strategy [of] 'cheating the state and coaxing the villagers.' . . . While passively carrying out unpopular policies from above, they have become much softer when they have to interfere with the private interests of peasants, in order to avoid open resistance from the latter."[6] My suspicion is that this type of behavior is the norm in a majority of China's villages.

---

[5]   In writing this, it important to note that the comparison here is with previous periods of Party-state control. When viewed in comparison to what prevails in many countries, the writ of the higher levels in China remains strong.

[6]   Yunxiang Yan, "Everyday Power Relations: Changes in a North China Village," in Andrew Walder (ed.), *The Waning of the Communist State* (Berkeley: University of California Press, 1995), pp. 228-30. In Chen Village, similarly, the village Party secretary, "fully aware that a leader's power to exact cowed compliance from the peasantry is a thing of the past, . . . generally intrudes on the affairs of his neighbors only when mediation is called for" (Chan, Madsen and Unger, *Chen Village Under Mao and Deng*, p. 320). Interesting interviews with a village head and a village Party secretary about their situation, caught between an errant township administration and angry villagers, are in Guo Zhenglin, "Dangdai Zhongguo nongcun

However, in cases where cadres are corrupt or abuse their power, the villagers can no longer turn to the Mao-era checks and balances that had existed in the division of responsibilities between brigades and production teams. This had served modestly as a brake on the behavior of brigade cadres, as they had to negotiate with production-team heads to collect revenues for the village and to get some of their other responsibilities accomplished. But this lowest level of formal rural organization, the production team, collapsed as a locus of activity in the early 1980s after the agricultural fields were distributed to the households to farm. In most parts of China, the teams continue to exist today only in the sense that they remain the *de jure* owners of the land. In some districts they can still afford to pay for the upkeep of the team's irrigation channels by renting out fishponds or from the ground-rents of industrial sites, and in the richest districts, as in Xiqiao, the income from this may even be high enough for the teams to distribute money among their member households. But the teams no longer count as part of the political equation in villages, as the team heads no longer oversee members' farming activities or represent anyone in village affairs. Although the teams had not been able to adequately protect the interests of the peasantry under the Mao-period collectives, their effective disappearance as a meaningful institution leaves the farmers more disorganized in the face of the local officialdom.

Other forms of grass-roots organization do exist in many villages, however. In some villages lineage groups have re-emerged and have rebuilt their lineage halls. The loyalties that these groups inspire sometimes now play a part in unifying villagers, especially in single-lineage villages, and through this can play a role in giving the villagers some leverage *vis-à-vis* local officials.[7] In some villages, too, religious temples have been rebuilt, and the temple committees not only raise funds to maintain the temples, but in some cases also become a focal point for non-government-organized activity on a broad range of local concerns. In some of these villages, the temple groups have even taken the place of village authorities in providing welfare services and in raising the funds to improve village roads and other infrastructure.[8] In yet other locales, especially where the

---

de jiti weiquan xingdong" (Collective Actions to Safeguard Rights in Rural China), *Xianggang shehui kexue xuebao* (Hong Kong Journal of Social Sciences), No. 19 (Spring/Summer 2001), pp. 121-26.

A very good Chinese-language source on village officials' performance, and on the other levels of rural government, is Zhang Jing, *Jiceng zhengquan: xiangcun zhidu zhu wenti* (Grassroots Governance: Various Questions Regarding the Rural System) (Hangzhou: Zhejiang Renmin Chubanshe, 2000). I am grateful to Zhang Jing for letting me read the manuscript prior to her book's publication.

[7] See, e.g., Stephan Feuchtwang, "Religion as Resistance," in Elizabeth J. Perry and Mark Selden (eds.), *Chinese Society: Change, Conflict and Resistance* (London: Routledge, 2000), p. 174.

[8] Lily Tsai, who has conducted fieldwork in several such villages for a doctoral dissertation at Harvard University, has found instances where the temple associations raised more in donations

former production teams coincide with natural hamlets, strong communal identities and bonds may continue to exist even in the absence of a team's economic functions,[9] and this sense of social cohesion can also on occasion provide villagers with some leverage in resisting impositions from above.

But in examining the available written documentation, secondary sources, and transcripts from interviews, it appears that, where they exist, these various forms of identity and social organization are not usually put to the service of organizing farmers as a constituency *vis-à-vis* the officials who govern them. They more often act to support one local cadre or another on the basis of common lineage or hamlet, and in turn to become the cornerstones of patronage systems, to the benefit of some parts of an administrative village and the detriment of other parts. Or, when they do unite whole hamlets or whole villages, this more often helps explain the re-emergence of inter-hamlet and inter-village conflicts in many parts of China. In this sense, such groupings often serve to divide the rural population, not to provide the basis for a united and organized rural populace that might be capable of checking abuses by local officials. As will be seen later in this chapter, by the late 1980s the central government was endeavoring to erect new forms of organized representation for villagers—through elections—in order to keep a check on the conduct of village cadres.

Other types of checks against cadre abuses or corruption are weaker than in earlier times. In a departure from previous practices, starting in the early 1980s the central government's more relaxed posture toward rural society was paralleled by a lax approach to rural officials. Among other things, Mao-style anti-corruption political campaigns are no longer unleashed to target local officials for public exposure and purge. Calling off such campaigns was, in one respect, all to the good in that it moved China away from a politics of unpredictability, fear and arbitrary retribution. But the national government appears tacitly to have had a separate reason in mind. By abandoning its major technique for combating corruption, it could buy the rural officials' cooperation for economic reforms—by allowing them to materially benefit from the reforms.

Large numbers of the rural cadres have taken advantage of this, both as individuals and as a group. As the central state pulled back, independent networks have arisen of local officials who scratch each other's backs and cover up for and enrich each other, sometimes blatantly but sometimes through ingenious hidden

---

to support village services than the village governments raised. See her article in the July 2002 issue of *The China Journal.* Also see Feuchtwang, ibid., for other examples of active temple associations.

[9]   The continuing role of former production teams as a basis for community and loyalty networks sometimes is evident even in large villages such as Chen Village. For a discussion of how villagers there have turned to the former teams—and also to lineage groups—to provide a supportive sense of community, see Chan, Madsen and Unger, *Chen Village Under Mao and Deng,* pp. 321-26.

machinations. Sometimes these involve personal private gains and sometimes the enrichment of the bureaucratic units to which the officials belong.

The tensions and disappointments of the last decade of Mao's rule had left, as its heritage, an atmosphere of cynicism and opportunism among many county, township and village officers. Over the years, in many parts of rural China this has translated into officials living well at public expense. This can be seen in both well-off and economically troubled districts alike. County and township officials tend to exhibit a palpable desire for perks, seen in particular in the expensive cars that are put at their disposal. They also help each other's kith and kin to win local government contracts or obtain good public-sector employment. Local government payrolls have swelled as a result. One conscience-stricken township Party secretary wrote angrily to a newspaper to complain that even he had not been able to control an expansion of township cadre ranks—apparently forced upon him by the county officials who oversaw the township-level branches of bureaus—from 120 township-level cadres in 1990 to more than 340 in 2000.[10] Such extraordinary expansions in personnel are the result partly of elaborate favors-trading (you hire my relative and I'll hire yours) among the networks of cadres, stretching across all of the levels of the rural administrative system.

This cooperation extends to policy matters. Even though the different levels of rural government squabble over money and over different priorities on local policies, they often work together informally to protect local interests and to bend central government programs more to their own liking. A saying that has become commonplace describes this: "At the top there are policies; below, there are countermeasures" (*Shang you zhengce; xia you duice*). To a slight extent this type of behavior and the local linkages among officials had existed, too, during Mao's time. But it had been constricted then by the harsh, unpredictable nature of upper-level Party rule, which had been intent upon retaining a whip hand over the

---

[10] *Nanfang zhoumo* (Southern Weekend), August 24, 2000, p. 1. "How can the peasants bear" this expense?, the letter asked. Notably, this township was an economically poorly off one in China's grain belt. In the same issue of *Nanfang zhoumo*, p. 2, a Chinese researcher noted that townships which at the beginning of the 1980s supported the salaries of 8 officials were sometimes supporting 30 staff by the mid-1980s and an average of 300 by 2000—and that in very prosperous districts the township-level staffs now sometimes numbered as many as 800-1,000. The worst case of padded payrolls that I have come across concerns Tongxin County in Ningxia, one of China's poorest provinces. The impoverished county, with a population of 330,000, employs 11,000 officials. The head of the county grain bureau placed his 9-year-old son on the bureau's payroll and subsequently managed to get the son appointed as an official of the county procuratorate, while his 11-year-old daughter was placed on the payroll of the county organization department. The youngest salary-receiving official in the county was only four years old. The county established a Revolutionary Martyrs Cemetery Administrative Office with a paid staff of 20, composed of the wives and other family members of officials, to supervise three graves. *Jingji xinxi bao* (Economic Information News), October 31, 1999, and *Fazhi ribao* (Legal Daily), October 12, 1999.

connivances of the lower-level officialdom. Today that hand has largely been stilled.

Sometimes, when high-level policies go against the interests of villagers, the "countermeasures" put in place by the networks of local officials are to the advantage of local residents. But it appears that more often the "countermeasures" serve the rural officialdom's own purposes and are related to efforts to squeeze greater benefits from office-holding, licitly or illicitly.

Differences Among Regions

Even though much of rural China experiences the problems of corruption and bloated staffs and perks, in important respects the performance of the local officialdom varies considerably across regions. These differences sometimes relate to the forms and extent of corruption and the exactions faced by villagers, but also relate to other significant aspects of rural administration. Under Mao, when central policy was enforced far more strictly, there had been a sameness to circumstances across rural China. As was noted in Chapter One, the same government programs had been pursued throughout the great bulk of the villages, everywhere using the very same mechanisms of control. Today, in contrast, different regions, counties and townships follow different drumbeats. To understand these differences, we will examine in turn the prosperous coastal regions, the impoverished regions of the western hinterlands, and the grain belts of central China.

The Prosperous Industrializing Districts

Under Deng, rural officials were granted the leeway to take greater initiatives to develop the economy of their localities. Especially in the coastal regions and in districts near the cities, as noted in earlier chapters, they have been able to take advantage of this by developing local government-owned industry. Through this industrialization some of the township-level governments have developed their own substantial sources of revenues and their own large constituencies of workers. Officials in such townships have used the budget surpluses and their control over hirings to develop a home-grown political base. To cement local support, they have spread largesse in the form of public welfare benefits, in particular through schools and health clinics. Through this, the wealthy rural township administrations not only are able to bolster their own authority locally. As just observed, they have also been able to use their budgetary independence to attain greater autonomy from the pressures of higher-level bureaucracy.

In much the same way, the village governments have been re-strengthened markedly when they own profitable factories or control other sizable sources of income and use the revenues to create mini-welfare states, as has occurred in Xiqiao. Where village governments are relatively evenhanded in their largesse and have built up a broad-based loyal constituency within the village, they may feel emboldened to resist township policies that run counter to their village's interests. But there have also been reports about villages where the largesse and patronage has been spread in a way that internally divides the village. One example among many is a Sichuan village where, starting in the 1980s, factories owned by the village government expanded very profitably. The patronage system there created a situation where clusters of families who are related to the officials through kinship or friendship have occupied the village's economic and social upper crust, and the village's other families comprised a resentful but powerless lower stratum dependent upon access to the village's blue-collar factory jobs.[11]

Generally, though, the effectiveness of the systems of patronage and dependency in industrialized villages such as this began to erode during the 1990s. For one thing, the enterprises that are owned by the rural governments can no longer provide as many jobs to local people as in the past. In the 1980s, the local factories enjoyed local protectionism against competing goods from outside their own county or prefecture, and with monopoly profits they could afford to be generous to the local factory workforce. Their wages had been higher than what villagers could earn in the fields, and gaining access to such coveted jobs cemented the fortunate workers' obedience. But the local protectionism has largely broken down over the years as the national economy continues to marketize. To remain profitable, the local factories need to be competitive in their labor costs and so increasingly they have turned to hiring people from poorer parts of China at low wages; only the supervisory jobs remain in local hands. In the case of the Sichuanese village cited above and many other villages, this shift toward lower local employment also resulted from the shrinkage or closure of factories that became unprofitable in the 1990s, and the leasing out of others. The local authorities are left with far fewer patronage jobs to dispense.

In many of these same townships, the patronage networks have been further weakened because lucrative livelihoods outside of agriculture have emerged that are beyond the control of the officials. In particular, the latter part of the 1980s witnessed the rise of private enterprises, such as those of Xiqiao, and this trend accelerated across China in the 1990s. Sometimes these private businesses are tied to the officials, but increasingly they are not. Even though the numbers of such proprietors are ordinarily far fewer than in Xiqiao, they are becoming an increasingly independent, affluent and influential constituency on the local scene, and, as in Xiqiao, may well be in a position to provide a counterweight to the unilateral power of the officialdom. These several trends provide political and social "space" for the development of a noncompliant village constituency in the most prosperous parts of the countryside.

In a substantial number of cases, village leaders who had squandered much of their base of support within their village through abuses of power or favoritism have been able to remain in office because they are protected by their immediate

[11]   Gregory Ruf, *Cadres and Kin: Making a Socialist Village in West China, 1921-1991* (Stanford: Stanford University Press, 1998); also see his "Managing Interests: Collective Property Rights and Village Enterprise in Rural Sichuan," in Jean Oi and Andrew Walder (eds.), *Property Rights and Economic Reform in China* (Stanford: Stanford University Press, 1999). Information also based on personal correspondence with Ruf.

superiors in the township and county. Reading between the lines of reports from China about rural cadre abuses, in rich and poorer areas alike, it appears that such village leaders often participate in self-serving networks of mutual back-scratching that reach down into the villages.

These cliques of village and higher-level officials have sometimes overplayed their hand, leading to violent outbursts. One scheme in the prosperous parts of the countryside that has been reported a large number of times in the Chinese press is for officials at the county and township levels, sometimes with the assistance of village officials, to connive to rob the farmers of valuable land. The officials first decree that stretches of local farmland must be sold at a low price for the inauguration of an "industrial development zone." This land is then handed over at that price to semi-private "development companies" that the officials themselves have established and largely own, and the land is immediately resold at a very high profit for use as industrial sites.[12] In 1989 I visited a village in Baoan County, Guangdong, near the city of Shenzhen, where irate residents bitterly complained to me about village (not township) leaders who had connived to do this, apparently with the approval of their township superiors. Throughout the past decade, Chinese newspapers have reported on farmer riots in several provinces in reaction to this form of corrupt land expropriation. Such outbursts, and also non-violent forms of protests (to be discussed later in this chapter), appear to be on the increase in the wealthier parts of the countryside.

Poor Marginal Agricultural Regions

The poverty-stricken districts of China's west and southwest, which include the areas where the bulk of the ethnic minorities live, are a world away from the prosperous countryside of the coastal region. There is at once far less funding available to local governments to spread as largesse in the form of public welfare benefits and, at the same time, far fewer resources in the hands of the populace for the local officials to appropriate for their own benefit. Even though there have been reports that in some parts of the poor hinterlands the farmers are at the mercy of bloated rural township and county governments that squeeze them, my general impression is that most of the very poor districts do not suffer from official depradations to the extent reported for the agricultural heartlands (to be discussed in the next section). Just as in Maoist times, there is a realization that blood cannot be squeezed from a stone—that enough needs to be left in the hands of the impoverished peasantry to ensure their survival. To be sure, corruption is evident almost everywhere in China, but in this region it is seen most frequently in quiet diversions of central government funding, sometimes including poverty aid, with fewer blatant efforts to suck money out of the villages. The central

---

[12]   Several illuminating reports of this kind are in *Guangming ribao* (Guangming Daily), April 12, 1999; *Zhongguo qingnian bao* (China Youth Daily), June 29, 1999; *Nanfang zhoumo* (September 17, 1999); *Zhongguo qingnian bao*, January 7, 2000.

government funding that pours into the 592 designated "national poverty counties" keeps government services there going at a modest level without much taxing of the populace.

This was evident in Qinghai Province in late 2000. In a Muslim village high in the hill country, villagers reported an annual land tax of only 6 *yuan* per *mu* (about 35 *yuan* [US$4.50] per acre), and the entire village and indeed the entire county was excused from delivering any crops on quotas. A fee of 3 *yuan* had previously been imposed on each head of livestock, but as the sales prices for livestock fell in recent years this fee was removed from all livestock other than sheep. The only other fee was, ironically, a 3 *yuan* fee imposed on each household for flood control even though there were never floods in this village. That was the total extent of taxation and of taxes disguised as fees, in sharp contrast to the situation that prevails in the agricultural heartlands, as will be seen in the next section.

A dearth of public funding in a poor low-tax village means meager resources to pay the salaries of village officials. In one very impoverished Qinghai village where the average per capita income amounts to only 300-400 *yuan* a year, the village head's salary was set at just 1,000 *yuan*, but due to a lack of village revenue he received only 400 *yuan* in 2000, making it scarcely worthwhile to serve. Such a village official has few resources at his disposal to get other villagers to listen to his instructions, and he in turn has little initiative to listen to higher levels. Chinese government publications refer to these as "paralyzed villages," where village administrations barely operate and where central policies penetrate only with difficulty. Another such village was visited in Yunnan in the late 1980s. It is a village without any natural water supply, and during the early 1970s under the collectives the village government had installed a system of pipes leading from a spring a mile away. By the late 1980s the pipes leaked so badly that the system was unusable, but the village could no longer raise enough money from among its sixty-five households even to repair the pipes. Instead, the villagers once again had to lug buckets of drinking water back from the spring for themselves and their animals. The households' incomes were higher than in the early 1970s, and the crisis was not so much economic as organizational: a weakness of leadership and a loss of community cohesion. In the very villages where community organization and initiatives arguably are most needed—the poorest villages—the capacity is no longer there.

The Agricultural Heartlands

The parts of the countryside where villagers have the deepest cause for political discontent are the non-industrialized districts that lie within China's agricultural heartlands. This huge region includes areas that specialize in cotton, tobacco and other commercial crops, but it largely can be considered a grain belt, stretching from Manchuria down through the provinces of Hebei, Henan, Hubei, Hunan, Anhui, Jiangxi and across into Sichuan Province. These agricultural heartlands also include non-industrialized rural districts in the eastern seaboard provinces that are too far from a city to specialize in vegetables and need instead to rely on grain production, as well as similar agriculturally productive areas of poor provinces such as Yunnan. Farmers in all of these areas have considerable reason to feel resentful toward rural officials, and the great bulk of rural protests have arisen in these regions of China.

For one thing, as was observed in Chapter Nine, villagers who depend entirely upon agriculture for a livelihood have not shared in China's boom times. But whereas farmers in the most impoverished agriculturally marginal areas consume most of what they grow, farmers in the agricultural heartlands are very much part of a commercial economy, and they have been severely hit by the cost of inputs and the falling prices for agricultural produce. Disgruntlement at the low profits from agriculture is exacerbated by comparatively high levels of taxation compared to the other two regions.

There is a dilemma here, in that in these non-industrialized rural areas, even the current level of taxes that goes to the village government is sometimes inadequate to provide for needed public services. Under the Mao-era collectives, such revenues had been quietly siphoned off from the production teams' pooled post-harvest income before the remainder of the proceeds was divided among the village households as wages. The farmers thus had not even been fully aware of the taxes. Today, in contrast, the village officials must openly collect taxes from independent farmers, going from household to household to collect them, and these are households that are already struggling economically.

In some of the poorer districts in the agricultural heartlands, village leaders do not have the willpower or capacity to coerce the farmers to pay up. In some of these villages, so few funds are collected that schooling is seriously underfinanced. It is not just the impoverished hill villages of the western poverty areas that suffer from this. Yet despite this crisis in village-level finances and services, officials higher up at the county and township levels in the grain belt still normally push to have their own share of the taxes collected in full.

In part this is because a fiscal crisis also exists at these levels. In 1994, about half of China's counties had difficulties meeting even basic expenditures,[13] and their predicament appears to have worsened in the years since, especially in the grain belt. The fiscal crisis is exacerbated in many of these counties because township and county officials there not only have legitimate government outlays to cover but also often want a share of the bureaucratic perks enjoyed by their counterparts in better-off locales. This includes the usual fleets of cars, the wining and dining, and the relatives slotted into public-sector jobs in a bloated bureaucracy. To accomplish these ends, they need to resort to coercion to extract funds from villagers.

Their performance thus differs markedly from what occurs in the poor western marginal districts and the rich industrialized coastal districts. Local officials in the latter districts, as was noted, sometimes control ample resources through local industry both to benefit themselves *and* to create mini-welfare

---

[13]   Albert Nyberg and Scott Rozelle, *Accelerating China's Rural Transformation* (Washington, D.C.: World Bank, 1999), p. 21.

states, while in the poor western region the rural officials are aware that there are no surpluses to extract from the impoverished farmers. But in the agricultural heartlands of China, agricultural surpluses do exist. They had provided the basis there for the wealth of the landlord/gentry class of earlier times. In these grain-belt regions the county and township officials today often seek to extract these surpluses, both to keep local governments afloat and to feather their own bureau's nest.

In some parts of the country the central government during the 1990s had begun increasing the amount of low-priced quota deliveries for a number of agricultural commodities, be it cotton, silk cocoons or grain. Provincial and local authorities could not resist getting into the act. While some localities added their own extra share of quotas, in some other districts the county or township government, as monopolistic middleman, has gone so far as to force farmers to hand in an entire specialty crop at prices far below the free markets. The local government then sells these extra deliveries onward at a high market price.

These special quota impositions were being implemented in particular in districts that are well suited to specialty crops. For example, in one county in Yunnan Province that I visited in the late 1980s, the peasants were required, in addition to their grain levies, to plant tobacco entirely for sale at depressed prices to the county authorities. (Tobacco is a very major source of government revenue in Yunnan; over half of the provincial-level administration's funds derive from tobacco and cigarettes.) In one of these villages, families that refused to plant a fifth of their land in tobacco were fined 10 *yuan* per *mu* and were threatened that their land might be confiscated; in a second village, peasants who refused to provide tobacco were fined at a level of 15 percent of the ungrown tobacco's value.[14]

---

[14]   For first-person descriptions of the hardship caused by enforced tobacco planting, see Jean Hung and Jonathan Unger, "Zou fang Yunnan shancun ting xinsuan de gushi" (Bitter Tales Heard Through Interviews in a Yunnan Mountain Village), *Chaoliu* (Hong Kong), No. 31 (1989), pp. 63-64. Notably, tobacco is so profitable for local governments to tap that even in poverty districts, when these are well-suited to tobacco cultivation, township and county governments are apt to impose themselves as monopolistic middlemen so as to cream off the proceeds. An extraordinary picture of how this coercive cultivation of tobacco operates to the advantage of governments in several poor counties is provided in Yali Peng, "The Politics of Tobacco: Relations Between Farmers and Local Governments in China's Southwest," *The China Journal*, No. 36 (July 1996), pp. 67-82. Also see Xiaolin Guo, "The Role of Local Government in Creating Property Rights: A Comparison of Two Townships in Northwest Yunnan," in Jean C. Oi and Andrew C. Walder (eds.), *Property Rights and Economic Reform in China* (Stanford: Stanford University Press, 1999), pp. 75-78. Also see Guo Zhenglin, "Dangdai Zhongguo nongcun de jiti weiquan xingdong" (Collective Actions to Safeguard Rights in Rural China), *Xianggang shehui kexue xuebao* (Hong Kong Journal of Social Sciences), No. 19 (Spring/Summer, 2001), on a township in Hunan where the township government's efforts in 1996 to monopolize tobacco sales provoked first violence and then mass cheating by resisting farmers (pp. 127-28).

Township and especially village cadres alienate their neighbors by collecting taxes and crop deliveries, and so they have good reason to resist doing so—unless driven by pressures and inducements from above. Since the Mao-era political levers over cadres through campaigns or control through Party committees no longer are effective, the county and in turn the rural townships elicit the cooperation of township officials today by setting job-performance quotas each year. This technique is a carryover from Maoist times, but with a twist. Officials today are rewarded monetarily, as well as through promotions, for fulfillment and overfulfillment of their assigned quotas, and they are penalized monetarily if they do not meet these quotas. One consequence of this mechanism, across China, is that "charts of targets and progress towards those targets are ubiquitous features of township meeting rooms, offices and bulletin boards."[15] In some parts of the countryside, these monetary inducements and penalties also apply to village cadres. In a north China village studied by Yan Yunxiang, the series of bonuses stipulated by the township government for fulfilling tasks amounted to four-fifths of the total salaries of village cadres.[16] The pressures placed on grass-roots cadres by the inducements and penalties are frequently discussed in the Chinese news media. As one example, "When funds are collected from the peasants, every penny must come from door-to-door collections by village and hamlet cadres. Some locales give them time limits to make their collections. If any amount is still uncollected at the end of this period, the cadres are penalized or their salaries are withheld."[17]

Even with the inducements and penalties, in some villages in the grain belt the village heads are afraid to alienate their neighbors and prefer to ignore higher levels when the orders come down for tax and quota collections. In such cases, some of the revenues do not get collected or, more often, county and township officials periodically raid the village with police officers in tow. Thus, one way or another, even in such villages the money or produce usually gets squeezed out of households.

The county and township authorities in the grain belt are well aware that the taxes and extra quotas are hard to collect—sometimes leading to violence not only against farmers but also, from below, against themselves. But there is

---

[15]   Scott Rozelle, "Decision-Making in China's Rural Economy: The Linkages Between Village Leaders and Farm Households," *The China Quarterly*, No. 137 (March 1994), p. 114. Incentives for the managers of publicly owned rural enterprises operate in a similar fashion of targets and quotas. On this, see Jean Oi, "Fiscal Reform and the Economic Foundations of Local State Corporatism in China," *World Politics*, Vol. 45, No. 1 (October 1992), p. 114.

[16]   Yunxiang Yan, "Everyday Power Relations: Changes in a North China Village," p. 227. On this system of rewards and penalties, also see Kevin J. O'Brien and Lianjiang Li, "Selective Policy Implementation in Rural China," *Comparative Politics*, Vol. 31, No. 2 (January 1999), pp. 167-86.

[17]   *Liaowang* (Outlook Weekly, Beijing), Issue 14, 1998, p. 38, translated in *Inside China Mainland*, June 1998, p. 61.

another means to collect revenue. In this region, user fees appear to have proliferated at a faster pace than taxes. One reason is that, whereas villagers may resist paying taxes, they individually need to pay the fees if they wish to gain needed licenses or to carry out desired activities. Each department and agency independently has been permitted to try to cover its own budget shortfalls, and therefore the range of such fees has become imposing. Over time, as each department and office seeks to augment its income, they have also become increasingly indiscriminate. In some districts, for example, an animal slaughter fee is applied *en masse*, levied against households that had not slaughtered any animals as well as those that had. Inasmuch as most of the township-level offices are essentially controlled by county-level bureaus, they often have been able to establish such fees regardless of the desires of the township government, which does not itself benefit. The surge in fee revenues, in short, helps specific agencies and does not help resolve a township government's fundamental budget needs. It helps explain why the numbers of excess personnel funded by the offices have expanded so rapidly, apparently far more than the core sections of township governments.

This resort to a wide range of fees is common in much of rural China, including the wealthy coastal areas, but is felt most heavily in the grain belt. Such fees began to proliferate shortly after decollectivization. A survey of 1,000 peasant households in twenty counties of the largest of the grain-belt provinces, Sichuan, undertaken by the provincial government, disclosed that the average household's burden stood at 64 separate fees and local taxes by 1985, and this increased to 107 by 1991.[18] As of that year, such charges in Sichuan cumulatively amounted to 9.9 percent of rural income (this figure excludes the government-mandated taxes), while the charges that year in the prosperous coastal province of Guangdong amounted to only 2.8 percent of rural residents' incomes.[19]

In many districts, in addition to fees, the various supervisory offices regularly levy fines as a matter of course, often as an income-raising activity rather than as a penalty for actual violations. In some cases, these fines get assessed in an arbitrary and uncoordinated fashion. In one locale, an interviewee complained that the police offices in each township separately were seeking to extract fines from local transport operators along the main through-roads, to the extent that some operators had been driven out of business by the random, repeated, escalating expense. In other cases, the fines have become a predictable expense, equivalent to a set fee. A prime example relates to the government's birth-control program. In most of rural China, unlike the cities, a couple is permitted to have two children, and if the couple succeeds in circumventing the local government's

---

[18] "Peasant Unrest in Szechwan and Mainland China's Rural Problems," *Issues & Studies*, Vol. 29, No. 6 (July 1993), p. 130.

[19] Xiaobo Lu, "The Politics of Peasant Burden in Reform China," *The Journal of Peasant Studies*, Vol. 25, No. 1 (October 1997), p. 120.

efforts to prevent this and gives birth to an additional child, the family must pay a specified fine. In much of the countryside, the couples save up for this fine in advance. The wife stays indoors or returns to her native village for the duration of her pregnancy, and the husband troops off to the township office after the birth with money in hand. The fine is a lucrative source of income that gets shared out among the county, township and village levels of government throughout much of rural China. It puts the local governments in a conflictual situation: they are under strong pressures emanating from the central government to stringently enforce the birth-limitation decrees, yet they gain monetarily to the extent that they are lax. This is the policy area where the central authorities are most determined, enough so that township officials often do make concerted efforts to prevent the local birthrate from getting out of control—including raids to apprehend hiding women. But they are up against equally determined families, and hence they do not have to worry about insufficient birth fine revenues. Despite the strict measures that the central government has sought to enforce, China's population continues to grow.

The diverse financial exactions on villagers in China's agricultural heartlands also continue to grow. Repeated complaints and warnings by academic and government specialists appeared in Chinese journals in the late 1980s and early 1990s, but to no avail. Similar complaints have continued to appear every year since then. A national Party journal in 1998 noted, for instance, that during the 1990s "these three categories of burdens [fees and taxes, quota apportionments, and fines] have increased markedly, and the amount of the increase has far outstripped the farmers' gains in cash income."[20]

The central government has been worried about the resentment aroused by the tax and fee burdens and the local bureaucracies' heavy-handed methods, especially since these sporadically spark off mass protests. Beijing's initial response was to decree an upper limit on taxes and fees: cumulatively, they cannot exceed a maximum of 5 percent of the average income in a village. This is an unrealistically low figure, since even minimal public services and local government expenses normally cost more than that amount. This is especially true in poor areas, where that "5 percent of income" benchmark represents a smaller amount of money than elsewhere. This may be a moot point, however, since the 5 percent limit does not usually seem to be adhered to. Local officials either ignore the central government's decree or rewrite local statistics to show far higher average incomes than actually exist,[21] so that they can claim that they are staying

---

[20]   *Qiushi* (Seek Facts), No. 3, 1998, pp. 46-49. Also see, for example, Mobo Gao, *Gao Village: Rural Life in Modern China* (Honolulu: University of Hawaii Press, 1999), esp. pp. 186-96.

[21]   Reports in the Chinese media of grossly inflated local rural income figures have been frequent down through the years. Despite this, many economists continue to use such figures religiously in their work. Media reports that specify outrageous falsifications in specific locations include *Zhongguo qingnian* (China Youth), No. 9, 1998, p. 4; *Nongmin ribao* (Farmers' Daily), October 2, 1999; *Nanfang zhoumo* (Southern Weekend), October 29, 1999; *Zhongguo jingji*

within the government's 5 percent limits. A government investigation in Henan Province in 1998 revealed that the taxes and fees normally amount to 10-15 percent of the villagers' net incomes, and sometimes exceed 20 percent.[22] To a poor villager in a grain-belt province like Henan, this sucks away most of the family's income above subsistence level. It often makes it difficult for such a family to meet the high costs of school tuition charges and medical care.

Peasant Protests

As the impositions upon peasants grew, they reacted violently in some places. Between January and July 1998 alone, a total of 3,200 incidents of collective protests were sufficiently serious to be recorded at a national level, and more than 420 of these involved conflicts in which rural government buildings were surrounded by angry crowds. During that half-year period, casualties were officially reported as topping 7,400, including more than 1,200 officials and police wounded.[23]

In their demonstrations against the local officialdom, farmers regularly point to the central government regulation about the 5 percent maximum. It is a handle they can turn to in order to place the local officialdom on the defensive: that they, the farmers, legally are in the right and the local cadres in the wrong. In fact, the two largest peasant protests thus far recorded, in the grain-belt provinces of Sichuan and Jiangxi, were sparked by local government efforts to suppress farmer resistance along these lines. In the first, a villager in Renshou County, Sichuan, confronted cadres in 1993 with the 5 percent rule, refused to pay anything beyond this, posted the national regulation so that others would know about it, and rallied other farmers to his cause. When he was arrested for trying to disseminate this information about central government policy, large riots ensued and the county

---

shibao (China Economic Times), December 18, 1999; *Nanfang zhoumo*, December 31, 1999; *Jingji ribao* (Economic Daily), January 17, 2000. Local officials also have a second reason to exaggerate local incomes; it makes it appear that the local economy has done well during their tenure, and helps them to win promotions. For both reasons they bring pressure upon subordinates to falsify the figures. As a village Party secretary advised a Chinese newspaper reporter, "The real income of peasants in our village isn't more than 1,500-1,600 *yuan*. But a 2,800 *yuan* figure was forced on us by the township government. If we don't use that figure there's trouble. If you ask why the figures are faked, it's because those higher up want to add to their political record. Think about it, if the statistic for peasants' incomes goes up, the supposed proportion of burdens on peasants also falls, so you score both ways." *Jingji xinxi bao* (Economic Information Daily), October 16, 1999. Economists, beware.

[22]   *Jingji yanjiu cankao* (Economic Research Materials), No. 1224 (November 12, 1998), p. 40.

[23]   *Dongxiang* (Trends Magazine, Hong Kong), October 1998, pp. 11-12. For other reports of protests, see Thomas P. Bernstein, "Instability in Rural China," in David Shambaugh (ed.), *Is China Unstable?* (Armonk: M.E. Sharpe, 2000), esp. pp. 97-99.

government headquarters was burned.[24] In Yuandu, Jiangxi, up to 20,000 farmers rioted in 2000 under almost precisely the same circumstances. Tax collectors had tried to impose a local tax of 300 *yuan* per person at a time of declining prices for agricultural produce. When a group of farmers tried to distribute copies of an official booklet titled "Farmer's Friend" that contained the central government's directives limiting taxes and fees, the local authorities put them under arrest, precipitating massive riots and the ransacking of a township government headquarters.[25]

As illustrated by both of the above cases, rural governments often try to conceal information about central policies from the villagers.[26] But it is obvious that channels of information can no longer be tightly or effectively controlled by local authorities. Literacy is too widespread today, and villagers no longer are confined to their own small localities but go out in large numbers to work in the cities, where they mingle and exchange information with migrant workers from other parts of the countryside.[27]

Armed with such information, by far the greatest number of farmers' protests today are entirely within the letter of the law. These include signature petitions, appeals to law courts, approaches to national newspapers and magazines, and delegations of peasants traveling to seek out high-level officials to lodge direct complaints.[28] Most of these peaceful protests—and also many of the violent

---

[24]   *BBC Summary of World Broadcasts: Asia Pacific*, May 3, 1993 (FE/1678-B2/1), and June 12, 1993 (FE/1713-B2/1); also see *China News*, June 16, 1993, pp. 6-7, and June 20, 1993, pp. 1-3; *The Economist*, June 19, 1993, pp. 27-28, *South China Morning Post* (Hong Kong), June 13, 1993, pp. 1 and 5.

[25]   Associated Press, August 29, 2000; Agence France Presse, August 30, 2000; *New York Times*, September 17, 2000.

[26]   "Why is it," a national newspaper asked, "that in some locales peasants who post newspapers carrying central government policies on rural bulletin boards are accused of 'disturbing public order'?" *Zhongguo qingnian bao* (China Youth Daily), December 10, 1988, p. 5, quoted in *Inside China Mainland*, March 1999, p. 61.

[27]   See, e.g., an interesting discussion in Elisabeth Croll, *From Heaven to Earth: Images and Experiences of Development in China* (London: Routledge, 1994), Ch. 5.

[28]   On this, see, for example, Kevin J. O'Brien, "Rightful Resistance," *World Politics*, Vol. 49 (October 1996), pp. 31-55; also David Zweig, "The Externalities of Development: Can New Political Institutions Manage Rural Conflict?," in Elizabeth J. Perry and Mark Selden (eds.), *Chinese Society: Change, Conflict and Resistance* (London: Routledge, 2000), esp. pp. 120-136; and Jun Jing, "Environmental Protests in Rural China," in same, pp. 143-60; also Guo Zhenglin, "Dangdai Zhongguo nongcun de jiti weiquan xingdong" (Collective Actions to Safeguard Rights in Rural China), pp. 115-33. A particularly interesting report from China discussed how 12,688 farmers from one township (two-thirds of the township population), after losing a suit in the local court against their county government for excessive fees and levies, appealed their case to the Shaanxi Province Supreme Court and won. *Nongmin ribao* (Farmers' Daily), January 16, 1999, p. 5.

ones—involve implicit or explicit appeals to the central government against local policies, even when central policies are in part the reason for disgruntlement.[29] Farmers who in Maoist times lacked protection *from* the central state feel today that they lack protection *by* the central state, and they want more of an assertion of central power in order to enforce central edicts. Many, in fact, want Beijing to re-launch Mao-era style campaigns to catch corrupt local cadres and local Party machines that violate central regime norms and regulations.[30]

In light of these popular views, the rural unrest, no matter how severe it may become, does not appear to pose any imminent danger to the central government. The disgruntlement, after all, is not aimed against the central government; and the protests are localized and isolated from each other.

Beijing, for its own part, is increasingly willing today to promote the viewpoint among disgruntled peasants that errant local cadres are to blame for their plight, painting itself as a good, caring government. National leaders see sense in posing as allies and protectors of the farmers, just as the farmers see the sense of appealing to the central authorities in hopes of playing them off against the local officialdom. In point of fact, already by the mid-1980s, after the reforms to decollectivize the countryside had been accomplished with the local officialdom's acquiescence, the central government no longer saw as much need to placate the rural cadres. As the years passed, Beijing instead expressed increasing concern that the independent back-scratching networks of local officials impeded central authority, and the national news media was regularly encouraged to publish exposés about the local officials' impositions upon the peasantry. It was within this context that the 5 percent maximum-taxation rule was decreed and that provisions were written into the 1993 Law on Agriculture that farmers could legally "refuse" (*jujue*) to pay the excessive, unauthorized fees

---

[29] Even when the main complaint of farmers involves heavy centrally imposed crop-quota burdens, local cadres more safely get blamed. A researcher in rural Xinjiang Province who found precisely that situation observes that "Many times I was told [by farmers], 'the policies issued at the top are good, but they are not implemented as they should be.'" Ildiko Beller-Hann, "The Peasant Condition in Xinjiang," *Journal of Peasant Studies*, Vol. 25, No. 1 (October 1997), p. 103. Chinese farmers throughout much of history have had a reservoir of such faith in distant rulers. In an interesting article, Lucien Bianco points to parallels in European history: "Criticizing the local authorities by appealing to the decisions of the Politburo is the reappearance, within a Communist regime, of older beliefs deeply held by the subjects of all absolutist regimes: the King of France (or the Tsar of Russia) is thought to be betrayed by his servants." Lucien Bianco, "The Weapons of the Weak: A Critical View," *China Perspectives*, No. 22 (March–April, 1999), p. 8.

[30] Kevin O'Brien and Lianjiang Li, "Campaign Nostalgia in the Chinese Countryside," *Asian Survey*, Vol. 39, No. 3 (May–June 1999), pp. 375-93; also Lianjiang Li, "Support for Anti-corruption Campaigns in Rural China", *Journal of Contemporary China*, Vol. 10, No. 29 (November 2001), pp. 573-86.

and taxes.[31] This legal right of refusal has usually been ignored and sometimes harshly overridden by rural officials, police and the local courts.

In a further effort to lessen rural discontent and win back farmer support, the central authorities have resorted to two significant policy prongs.

The Single-Tax Reform

The first prong, unsurprisingly, directly relates to the tax and fee burden. Starting in 2000, the central authorities introduced an entirely new system in Anhui Province and parts of Shandong on an experimental basis. All of the arbitrary user fees were prohibited and only a single, centrally controlled tax was allowed. Called the fees-changed-to-a-tax (*fei gai shui*) system, it stipulated a single tax on land that was supposed to bring the average tax and fee burden down below that benchmark of 5 percent of total household income.[32] Taxation in this experiment was recentralized, with each level of government entitled to receive a specified share of the revenues from this single tax: the central and provincial governments would retain specific percentages, the county government a specified percentage, and so too the township and villages governments. In 2000, village governments in one part of Anhui, for example, received 20 percent of the unified tax.[33] In Qinghai Province, officials told me late in 2000 that, starting in 2001, under this incoming tax regime village administrations there would receive 24 percent of the revenue.

Surveys in Anhui show that the new system did reduce the tax burden. On average, the tax and fee levies paid by villagers in Anhui in 2000 reportedly fell by some 30 percent.[34] But this precipitated a crisis in rural government budgets.

---

[31]   Thomas P. Bernstein, "Farmer Discontent and Regime Responses," in Merle Goldman and Roderick MacFarquhar (eds.), *The Paradox of China's Post-Mao Reforms* (Cambridge: Harvard University Press, 1999), p. 214.

[32]   The new tax was calculated as 7 percent of the value of the yields of the fields each household possesses, with villages allowed to levy an additional surcharge of 1.4 percent to help fund village services (that is, the maximum combined tax to be allowed equals 8.4 percent of the total imputed value of a household's crops). The government's quota prices were supposed to be the measure for judging the cash value of the crops. See the article by Zhu Baoping in *Zhongguo nongcun jingji* (Chinese Rural Economy), February 2001. The assumption was that most villagers have sources of income beyond just their crop yields, and that the tax was equivalent to about 5 percent of total income.

[33]   *Zhongguo jingji shibao* (China Economic Times), February 14, 2001. This and other information comes from a special series of reports on the tax's effects that this newspaper published.

[34]   *Zhongguo jingji shibao* (China Economic Times), February 7, 2001. Journalists in Anhui who went to particular rural districts to investigate reported declines by amounts ranging from 20 percent to 40 percent. *Zhongguo nongcun jingji* (Chinese Rural Economy), No. 2 (February 2001); *Zhongguo jingji shibao*, February 28, 2001.

One township in Anhui reported its revenues had dropped by as much as 53 percent.[35] Reports suggest that, as a result, officials in many rural areas across Anhui were not paid for months on end. The central government does not appear to have been overly concerned about this, since a budget crisis of this proportion forces bloated rural bureaucracies to cut back drastically on their unneeded staff.[36] The largest wage component at the township level, though, is for education, accounting for 45 percent of township government expenditures in Anhui,[37] and when faced with a need for dramatic budget cuts, it was not always unneeded officials who faced the axe. Wage arrears and personnel cuts among teaching staff in 2000 and 2001 adversely affected schooling. Complaints also mounted that villages in Anhui would no longer be able to build schools or install new irrigation works.

The tax had other problems, too. For one, inasmuch as it was entirely based on agriculture, the tax discriminated against households that rely on farming full-time[38] in comparison to those who gain much of their income off-the-farm. Since the latter families generally are better off than the full-time farmers, the new tax system was regressive. While the agricultural tax rose under the Anhui reform, the tax reform eliminated a range of user fees, and it was the better-off households who had paid a disproportionate amount of these fees: on annual motorbike charges and the like. These households, and those with rural businesses,[39] were the biggest beneficiaries of the tax reform.

It did not take long for the government to realize that its tax reform was creating problems as serious as those it was solving. In June 2001 its implementation outside of Anhui provice was indefinitely postponed—and then reactivated for a third of China's provinces in December. The government sits on the horns of a dilemma, uncertain how best to proceed.

---

[35]   *Nongmin ribao* (Farmers' Daily), March 2, 2001; also see *Zhongguo jingji shibao*, February 7, 2001.

[36]   This benefit of the reform is pointed out, for example, in *Zhongguo jingji shibao* (February 1, 2001).

[37]   Zhu Baoping in *Zhongguo nongcun jingji*, February 2001.

[38]   Jiang Guanhuo, in an article in *Zhongguo nongcun jingji* (February 2001) on the Chao Lake area of Anhui, observed that the rise in the burden of the agricultural tax, combined with lower prices for crops, had driven some farmers in 2000 to abandon their land. In some other places the county and township governments even began maneuvering illicitly to raise extra tax revenues through the new agricultural tax. One ploy was to insist that the tax be paid in cash rather than in grain, and rather than calculate the value of farmers' crops using the delivery quota price or market price, they overvalued the crop yields by concocting an artificially inflated sales price. The result at one site in Jiangxi Province was that the tax rate stood at 13.4 percent of the actual value of crops, and at a Hebei site it stood at 11.2 percent. *Zhongguo jingji shibao*, February 27, 2001.

[39]   Jiang, in *Zhongguo nongcun jingji* (February 2001).

The Inauguration of Grass-roots Elections

As the second prong of the central government's effort to reduce farmers' discontent, reformers in Beijing urged the creation, at the village level, of an institutionalized check on cadres' power. Beginning in the mid-1980s and extending throughout the 1990s, they have argued that villagers would be more willing to abide by national-level taxes and crop quotas and birth-control policies if they were given an organized voice to overturn the diverse grass-roots abuses.[40] In 1987 the reformers in Beijing were able to push through a regulation calling for the establishment of "village representative assemblies" (*cunmin daibiao huiyi*): grass-roots legislatures that are supposed to monitor the village cadres. The government subsequently directed, more importantly, that not just these representative bodies but also the village officials—who collectively comprise a so-called villager committee (*cunmin weiyuanhui*)—should be elected to three-year terms of office through multi-candidate elections.[41]

To issue directives in Beijing is one thing, but to actually carry them through in the provinces and localities is another, and it is not known how many of China's 930,000 villages have experienced genuine elections in which residents get to nominate the candidates. For one thing, many of the incumbent officeholders in villages understandably did not see the electoral reforms to be in their own best interests, nor did many of the provincial, county and township bureaucrats. In most parts of the countryside all of these levels of officials were slow to implement village elections.

This was the case, for example, in Xiqiao Township. In this instance, it was the Guangdong provincial government that was slow to act. Rather than put village officials to the test of public opinion, the province allowed county and township governments to turn instead to direct supervision of village

---

[40]   On this see, for example, Daniel Kelliher, "The Chinese Debate over Village Self-Government," *The China Journal*, No. 37 (January 1997), pp. 63-86. The director of the State Council's Village Economy Research Section has written an excellent report analyzing the various types of corruption and abuses of power that local cadres perpetrate in villages, and he concluded by pressing exactly these arguments in behalf of village democracy. Zhao Shukai, "Shequ chongtu he xinxing quanli guanxi" (Community Conflict and New Forms of Power Relations), *Nongcun diaoyan* (Village Investigations and Research), No. 146 (November 21, 1998) [a publication of the Development Research Center of the PRC State Council], 22 pp.

[41]   On the origins and operations of these two types of village elections, see Kevin O'Brien, "Implementing Political Reform in China's Villages," *The Australian Journal of Chinese Affairs*, No. 32 (July 1994); Susan V. Lawrence, "Democracy, Chinese Style," in the same journal issue. Also see Lianjiang Li and Kevin O'Brien, "The Struggle over Village Elections," in Merle Goldman and Roderick MacFarquhar (eds.), *The Paradox of China's Post-Mao Reforms* (Cambridge: Harvard University Press, 1999), pp. 129-44; Jorgen Elklit, "The Chinese Village Committee Electoral System," *China Information*, Vol. 11, No. 4 (Spring 1997), pp. 1-13; and a special issue of *The China Quarterly* on elections: No. 162 (June 2000), pp. 465-559.

administrations by higher-level officials. In 1995, for instance, using a Mao-era technique, the county government dispatched cadre workteams to investigate each of the village administrations and to remove errant village officials by way of "guided elections" that were elections only in name.[42] It was not until 1999 that Guangdong began implementing village committee elections throughout the province, one of the last provinces in China to commit itself to doing so.

Even when they get held, in a great many villages across China the new direct elections for village officials are dominated by the township administrators or by the village incumbents, and potential rivals for office are not allowed to run on one pretext or another. And even where elections are fairly held, in some villages the selections are dominated by the most numerous lineage group, which only reinforces longstanding patterns of favoritism and intra-village antagonism. In many places, moreover, rather than allowing genuine direct multi-candidate elections to select the village leaders, the residents are provided with a list of six or seven candidates from among whom five are to be selected to serve as the village's officials. The officials who are chosen then decide how to divide up the leadership posts, under the guidance of the village Party committee. Thus the residents' influence over the composition of the village leadership is effectively minimized, as their choice is confined to the essentially negative role of vetoing one or two disliked candidates.

Yet, year by year, more and more villages do participate in elections that, to one degree or another, provide choices. In Qinghai most of the villages that I visited in 2000 had held such elections. In one, the village Party committee had nominated the two candidates for village head, but every adult resident then had an opportunity to participate in a secret ballot, and the victor won with a margin of only two votes. In a second village, the village elders selected the nominees; in a third village, each of the village's two hamlets nominated a candidate; in a fourth, each of the three hamlets nominated a candidate and the village Party branch nominated yet another. In a fifth village, the township head readily confesses he had lobbied hard to retain the incumbent village head and had even attended the election in person in order to put pressure on the residents. But in this village, a "sea selection" (*hai xuan*) method of election was held, in which each resident obtained a ballot on which he or she could list a nominee. All such names were posted publicly and voted upon, and the top five vote-getters—in this case, the three hamlet heads, the incumbent village head and the village accountant—became the official nominees. A second vote determined the two final candidates, and in the third and final round of voting the accountant was

---

42   The county workteams' operations in Xiqiao are described in *Foshan ribao* (Foshan Daily), August 17, 1995, p. 1. The workteams of officials removed one or more cadres from office in 70 percent of Xiqiao's villages. In line with national policy, they placed a stress on removing cadres who were old or had inadequate educations. Throughout the county, the cadres who were eased from office received retirement "subsidies" as compensation.

elected as village head. In seven of this township's twenty-four villages, the incumbent village heads were ousted through such elections.

The village representative assemblies, which are supposed to provide a check on the cadres, have faced their own share of problems. In many parts of China, even when elections for the village representative assembly actually get held, the local officials often make sure that the new bodies are toothless. In some villages the deputy village head, for instance, serves as the head of the village representative assembly even though the assembly is supposed to oversee him and his superior. In many villages, too, the village representative assembly is rarely called into session. In a great many places, thus, they remain ineffective, inactive, or a tool of the village leadership. But that is reported to be changing in a small minority of villages, where legislative checks and balances have begun to operate, and in some of these villages the assemblies have gained a say in supervising the village budget.[43]

The elections for village officials and for the assemblies constitute significant political reforms, especially since the Communist Party tradition is, by its very essence, anti-democratic. The Marxist-Leninist belief system had always stressed that the Party leadership holds a special mission to push history forward through its superior knowledge of Marxism and its commitment to the revolution, and that the Party stood far in advance of the at-times "feudal" ideas held by ordinary people. To select a local government by majority vote, as in "bourgeois democracy," would only reflect the average, unprogressive, unenlightened views of the people. Today, the national Party leadership does not hold to that Marxist ideology any longer in reality, but it still firmly believes in its unilateral right to power—now as the helmsmen of a developmental state. The very notion of multi-candidate elections goes against the grain of the Party's long-entrenched aversion to democratic processes.

The Party is not alone in this distrust. The bulk of China's university students and intellectuals, who normally are portrayed in the West as pro-democracy, hold suspicions about a one-person-one-vote universal franchise. They share in an urban antipathy and disdain for the countryside and a fear that the farmers are ill-equipped to vote and would be prone to support demagogues.[44]

It is ironic, then, that the farmers are the only group in China allowed to select local leaders in multi-candidate secret ballots. But perhaps it is even more ironic that urban people should have disdain for the farmers' capacity to participate in such elections. The farmers, after all, are the only portion of China's

---

[43]   Anne F. Thurston, *Muddling toward Democracy: Political Change in Grassroots China* (Washington, D.C.: United States Institute of Peace, 1998), 55 pp.

[44]   At Tiananmen in 1989, when students and intellectuals called for democracy what they meant by the word was "freedom": freedom of the press, of assembly and of association, and an impartial independent court system. They wanted the government to take into account a wider range of voices, with a widening of the decision-making elite to include themselves as an educated constituency.

population who have had prior experience in local democracy, since they had been allowed under Mao to elect their own production-team leadership. Now, in the 1990s, with the production teams hollowed out and rendered irrelevant by decollectivization, they were again to choose their grass-roots leaders, raised one degree to the village level.

In all of the elections—whether for village representative assemblies or for village leadership posts—no political parties are allowed, nor slates of candidates with common platforms, nor any overarching electoral organizations transcending the village. Elections are permitted in villages, rather than in cities, precisely because the villages are atomized. China's top Party leadership appears to believe that if elections can be restricted to a very local rural level and also isolated from the all-important structure of Party rule, they cannot provide the seeds for any organized challenge to higher-level Party rule.

The problem the Party faces, however, is that the example set by the village-level elections is contagious. Already, some reformist provincial, prefectural and county leaders have been willing to go beyond Beijing. They can observe that in many villages the present sets of elections are not sufficient to restore legitimacy to village governments. The most important village figure under the Chinese political system even today, after all, is often not the village head but the village Party secretary, still insulated from popular opinion. The village elections may be of little importance when the Party secretary retains control over village enterprises and the village's purse strings and his power trumps that of the village head and village committee.[45]

Thus, despite Leninist antipathy to allowing non-Party members to elect Party leaders, the logic of the village-level electoral reforms has led to a further step, starting in rural Shanxi Province, with elections for village Party secretary. To retain the fig leaf of Party autonomy, a two-stage election is employed in the new experiment. The first is a secret ballot of all villagers in which they can vote for as many Party members from the village as they please, and then a second ballot, confined to Party members, formally selects the secretary from among the candidates who had been approved by more than 50 percent of the voters in the first round.[46] Despite the discomfiture of the Party organization in Beijing, democracy is creeping into previously taboo areas.

The electoral process is also creeping upward out of the villages. The level of rural administration that most alienates many farmers is the township level: it

---

[45] On this see, e.g., Jean Oi, "Economic Development, Stability and Democratic Village Self-governance," in Maurice Brosseau, Suzanne Pepper, and Tsang Shu-ki (eds.), *China Review 1996* (Hong Kong: Chinese University Press, 1996), p. 136.

[46] Lianjiang Li, "The Two-Ballot System in Shanxi Province: Subjecting Village Party Secretaries to a Popular Vote," *The China Journal*, No. 42 (July 1999), pp. 103-18. By late 1999, direct elections for village Party secretaries and village Party committees had been conducted in a section of Shandong Province containing 6,500 villages. *Nongmin ribao* (Farmers' Daily), December 11, 1999.

appears to them to be the source for most of the local fees, taxes and fines. Village-level elections cannot assuage peasant discontent against township leaders; so if the process of electing officials at the lower level proves successful in restoring farmers' goodwill, why not attempt elections for rural township leaders? Even some of the top leaders in Beijing are enticed by such a notion. Jiang Zemin, China's Communist Party Secretary and President, himself tentatively endorsed the idea in 1997,[47] though the measure has not yet been officially approved.[48] However, with support from reformist officials and mass-media outlets in Beijing, in league with reformist regional officials, efforts have begun at selected spots to set the stage gradually for this next shift. Thus, bucking the official policy in Beijing, prefectural officials in Sichuan Province successfully conducted elections for a rural township chief in late 1998, and garnered widespread favorable publicity among reformers elsewhere. Within months, a township in Guangdong had followed suit,[49] and others have since then.

These should *not* be interpreted as bottom-up initiatives by the villagers themselves; they are not in a position to play any precedent-setting part in the initiation of new electoral reforms. There is a mistaken belief among some people outside China regarding this, just as there exists a similar mistaken belief that the farmers were able to take the initiative into their own hands to decollectivize in the early 1980s. But still, elections are quietly being instituted at levels above the village, engineered first in selected districts at a distance from Beijing, through the connivance of political reformers in the upper echelons of government, officials in the Ministry of Civil Affairs (the government organization that is supposed to organize and oversee elections)[50] and middle-ranking officials out in the regions. The structure of rural governance, which had largely stood unchanged since the end of Mao's era, is perhaps beginning to bend in important ways.

---

[47]   Tyrene White, "Village Elections: Democracy from the Bottom Up?" *Current History*, Vol. 97, No. 620 (September 1998), pp. 263-67.

[48]   A government circular in 1998 announced Beijing's intentions to introduce township elections so as to "introduce the practice of open administration to government bodies at the township level" (*China News Digest*, June 10, 1998), but since then the national government has not taken any further steps to legalize and enact such elections.

[49]   On the Sichuan election see, for example, "China Praises Sichuan Election: Television Report Calls Vote Key Step Toward Rural Reform," *Washington Post*, February 27, 1999, p. A12. A report on the Guangdong election is contained in *Zhongguo shehui kexue jikan* (Chinese Social Science Quarterly), No. 26 (Summer 1999), pp. 27-30. An article describing both is Joseph Y.S. Cheng, "Direct Elections of Town and Township Heads in China: The Dapeng and Buyun Experiments," *China Information*, Vol. 15, No. 1 (2001), pp. 104-37.

[50]   For an interesting study of the successful gradualist strategy by reformers in the Ministry of Civil Affairs to overcome resistance to the earlier spread of village-level elections, see Tianjian Shi, "Village Committee Elections in China," *World Politics*, Vol. 51, No. 3 (April 1999), esp. pp. 396-410.

Chapter Eleven

ASSESSING THE POST-MAO PERIOD

Though the introduction of elections may, we hope, have an impact on how the rural officialdom operates, this is only part of a much larger picture. As seen in these pages, two decades after China decollectivized agriculture and its farmers returned to household farming, the countryside is still struggling with a very wide range of problems, some of them old and some new. Much has been achieved these past two decades in higher agricultural productivity and rural industrialization. But rural living standards in a great many agricultural households away from the coast have stagnated since the mid-1980s, income disparities within the countryside have grown to an alarming extent and continue to widen, taxation under both Anhui's new single-tax regime and its predecessors has been regressive, rural education is underfunded in large parts of the countryside, much of the rural medical-care system is overpriced and beyond the means of farmers, large pockets of severe poverty persist, and as observed in the previous chapter, corruption today is rife in much of rural China.

How then should the post-collective period in rural China be assessed? Looking at the broad sweep of what occurred, an even more fundamental question can also be asked: to what extent was decollectivization beneficial, and in what ways possibly detrimental, to villagers' interests? Did China need to dismantle the collectives? Does it need to go yet further? There is a push among some Chinese economists and their Western mentors to erase the last vestiges of the collective era. They are calling for the privatization of rural industry, for an end to land reallocations and indeed for the total privatization of agricultural land. Are they right? Or are their proposals likely to aggravate the problems?

It should be obvious from the first chapters of this book that the collective era under Mao witnessed a whole range of ill-advised and at times even disastrous policies. The state had enforced mechanisms to drain off much of the agricultural surplus from the countryside on terms deleterious to the interests of farmers; the Party-state perpetuated a system of "class" labeling and persecution long after that system had lost any genuine purpose other than to manipulate the emotions of a majority of the peasantry; it promoted a wave of "struggle" campaigns that ruptured rural communities and that sapped the farmers' will to resist unfeasible top-down economic directives. These political mechanisms, while bending the countryside to the central leadership's will in the short term, over the longer term exhausted and soured much of the rural populace.

It should be noted, though, that team-based collective agriculture ultimately failed largely due to political pressures and irrational agricultural policies imposed from above, and might otherwise have survived. In the mid-1970s, people from the countryside who were interviewed in Hong Kong, including interviewees of "bad-class" backgrounds, were almost all of the opinion that the system of teams had its good points. They concurred that the teams provided members with economic security, noted that members felt a loyalty to their teams, and believed that if left to their own devices the teams were capable of spurring agricultural development.

But the state did not leave the teams alone. While Mao was alive, it was incapable of doing so. The repeated effort to bend the grassroots to the Party's will was inherent to Mao's revolutionary vision and program. The system of collectives was, as a result, repressive to an extent that too often undermined its economy. With agricultural production and living standards stagnating during much of the 1970s, many farmers had lost their patience.

Even so, when after Mao's death China's leadership, starting in the late 1970s, offered higher prices for the teams' produce and gave teams more leeway to grow the crops that best suited their soil and climate, agricultural production rose very substantially. Most observers today forget that the bulk of the remarkable upsurge in agricultural production, in off-farm income generation and in rural living standards between 1978 and 1982 occurred *before* agriculture in most villages was decollectivized. (The per capita income of rural households grew by 67 percent in real terms between 1978 and 1982, according to official figures,[1] and the Gini coefficient had not yet begun to widen: between 1980 and 1982, it in fact appears to have narrowed marginally, from 0.24 to 0.23.)[2]

Despite these gains, at the time that Chinese farmers were introduced to household farming (*dabaogan*) in the early 1980s, many were relieved to escape the heavy hand of controls over their everyday livelihoods. They were exhausted by their experience of the 1970s, when bewildering and at times tense political campaigns had been funneled through the collectives, and they were irritated by the commandist style of so many team and village leaders, which was in keeping with, and a reflection of, the broader political atmosphere of Party rule. My interview survey of 1983 revealed that farmers hoped for less interference of that type.

Yet in pitching all of China into the *dabaogan* system of family farming in the early 1980s, the government exchanged one set of difficulties for another. The land has been divided into a patchwork of plots that are often too small to be machine-plowed, and irrigation is now difficult to coordinate among so many disparate households and scattered plots of land. In some communities the door was also opened to social and political fragmentation—as in the village mentioned in Chapter Ten, where the community could no longer maintain the water pipes that it had installed under the collectives. And the new system also imposes a special problem on the poor. As seen in Chapter Nine, substantial

---

[1]   *Beijing Review*, No. 20, May 16, 1983, p. 7.

[2]   Zhang Ping, "Rural Interregional Inequality and Off-Farm Employment in China," in Carl Riskin, Zhao Renwei, and Li Shi (eds.), *China's Retreat from Equality: Income Distribution and Economic Transition* (Armonk: M.E. Sharpe, 2001), p. 215.

numbers of these families in the hinterlands are caught in poverty traps because as individual households they do not have sufficient collateral to be eligible for loans to secure fertilizer and other essential inputs. Income inequalities have risen rapidly as some households pull ahead and others remain stranded.

What should be done? One set of voices has spoken out loudly. The new agricultural system is not yet to the taste of most Western economists and their acolytes in China's think-tanks, who chorus the need for greater "free enterprise" and securely permanent "property rights." Though the system today is entirely one of family farming, the ownership of agricultural land, as we have observed, remains with the grass-roots collectives at the level of the hamlet or village neighborhood. In the belief that Chinese agriculture ultimately ought to have a system of "private property," most economists urge that the shift to a full-fledged private property regime in agricultural land should be hurried up.

Doing so would not resolve the problems listed above. And what the economists ignore is that the present system safeguards farmers against being dispossessed because of poverty and indebtedness. While we have noted the persistence of rural poverty, there are no landless in China, unlike so many other poor countries. This has been of great importance to struggling villagers throughout China. And it is particularly important for ethnic-minority peoples. As observed in Chapter Nine, hamlet-level ownership of the land protects such communities from gradual dispossession by Han farmers. Historically, one of the ways in which such people were pushed into the mountains was precisely in this fashion, as poor ethnic households went under and sold off land to Han settlers.[3]

What those who advocate "secure property rights" (i.e., private property) also ignore is that most Chinese farmers, and not just the poor among them, are worried about the prospect of private landholdings. They *prefer* to retain the current system of use rights rather than be granted outright ownership of the fields they work. A survey of 800 farmers in eight counties across China found that only 14 percent of the respondents wanted farm households to own their own land and, by a margin of 64 percent, the farmers preferred a system that periodically reassigns fields in line with changes in the size and composition of families.[4] In a separate survey conducted in Sichuan and Hunan, two grain-belt provinces, 81.5 percent of the villagers preferred such periodic reallocations of land.[5] They are concerned that during some periods of the family cycle, they will

---

[3]   This "commercial" conquest of the land of ethnic-minority households is evident, for example, in the life stories related in Hsiao-t'ung Fei and Chih-I Chang, *Earthbound China: A Study of Rural Economy in Yunnan* (London: Routledge & Kegan Paul, 1948).

[4]   James Kung and Shouying Liu, "Farmers' Preferences Regarding Ownership and Land Tenure in Post-Mao China: Unexpected Evidence from Eight Counties," *The China Journal*, No. 38 (July 1997), pp. 39, 48.

[5]   James Kung, "Equal Entitlement Versus Tenure Security under a Regime of Collective Property Rights: Peasants' Preference for Institutions in Post-Reform Chinese Agriculture," *Journal of Comparative Economics*, Vol. 21, No. 2 (1995), pp. 82-111.

not have enough land to support their families, and they empathize with other families already caught at the wrong time of a family cycle. A very recent study of a village in Hebei Province by a sociologist at Beijing University examines the delicate balance achieved in the method by which the land reallocation was carried out in this village, so as to take into account the opinions of those who would lose land as well as those who would gain. The result was a land readjustment in 1996 that received the support of almost all of the villagers.[6] In this, farmers are more practical and more fair-minded than the central government, which has been swayed by the lobbying of economists and has passed decrees that fields cannot be reallocated for a thirty-year period. This is but the latest in a series of such decrees, and it can be expected that, as in the past, many villages will disregard these government regulations and quietly continue to redistribute fields, practically daring higher authorities to stop them.

This is not to claim that Chinese farmers are idealistically egalitarian. Rather, they understand the complexity of their own circumstances better than do the armchair economists, and see a system of periodic land rotations as best meeting their present and future contingencies. Complicated attitudes seem to prevail among many farmers, in which they balk at directly helping impoverished neighbors who are not their relatives, balk at cooperating voluntarily in the ownership of draft animals, balk at paying taxes for better public services, and yet pragmatically are willing to put aside worries about co-owning assets when faced with the prospect of substantial income gains. This willingness was observed in Chapter Five in relation to agricultural endeavors that a single family would not be able to afford to handle alone. A similar willingness was observed in Xiqiao Township, where villagers are willing to enter into partnerships in establishing new industrial or commercial enterprises when that is the most feasible means of putting together enough money to start a promising business. Notably, too, in Xiqiao they seek to reinvigorate community values when given a choice. When government organs above the villages ordered the conversion of the collective land into a "village cooperative shareholding system" and left it up to the villages in Xiqiao to decide how to implement this, the villages did not give the term "shareholding" any connotation of privatization. They instead reaffirmed community ownership. By distributing annual dividends on the basis of age, instead of allowing the installation of any system of permanent, saleable, inheritable asset shares, these villages are at one and the same time perpetuating the definitions of community membership of the collective era alongside the

---

[6]   Liu Shiding, "De la préférence individuelle au choix collectif: Un cas de redistribution des terres en Chine rurale" (Individual Preferences in a Collective Choice: A Case Study of the Redistribution of Land in Rural China), in Isabelle Thireau and Wang Hansheng (eds.), *Disputes au village chinois: Formes du juste et recompositions locales des espaces normatifs* (Disputes in Chinese Villages: Forms of Justice and the Local Recomposition of Normative Space) (Paris: Éditions de la Maison des sciences de l'homme, 2001), pp. 167-203.

Confucian value system that honors age. China's villagers have their own priorities.

It is notable that the former production teams in Xiqiao were *required* to amalgamate and to establish a "shareholding" system. Even though the administrative system is looser than before, China retains a top-down framework inherited from Mao's day. But it is notable that it was the *county* government that decided to push this through in the Xiqiao area. In Mao's day, in comparison, policies generally were initiated in Beijing and rolled across China. As observed in earlier chapters, in a *de facto* devolution under Deng starting in the early 1980s, greater leeway was given to the rural officialdom to take initiatives. In some respects this was all to the good. It gave rise to an extraordinary surge of local cadre entrepreneurship in the 1980s and the first half of the 1990s, in which large numbers of villages and townships accelerated their industrial development in parts of the countryside to an astonishing extent. The vast majority of these new and expanding factories during that decade and a half were publicly owned, a demonstration that, with adequate incentives, rural collectives could successfully and profitably industrialize.

But in several important respects, as seen in this book, this loosening up by Beijing has not released villagers from being boxed in administratively. As a very significant example, it did not erase the barriers between urban and rural or even between different rural areas. In a "pass" system somewhat analogous to apartheid minus a racial ingredient, the *hukou* residence certificate policy continues to consign rural people working away from their villages to temporary jobs at worse earnings and conditions than they would otherwise obtain. It is one of the factors that holds back the living standards of families in the interior.

Nor, as a second significant example, has the relaxation of central government *diktat* over the rural governments necessarily provided villagers with an improved position *vis-à-vis* the rural officialdom. Certainly, the initial decollectivization of farming removed the daily supervision over them of cadres, which greatly weakened the cadres' hold over farmers. But the relaxation of higher-level controls over local governments was a different matter. On the one side this looser grip of the central state did provide greater room for the reassertion of local social mores, as seen in the reconstruction of lineage halls and temples. But on the other side, rural officials gained greater discretion to pursue their own individual and combined interests, often at the expense of the local populace. Examples of this were clearly observed in Chapters Seven and Ten, where it was seen how officials have been able to use their power to financially benefit their families and friends, and how they have imposed a multitude of fees to provide for the well-being of the rural bureaucracy as a whole.

As was also observed in Chapter Ten, elections at the village level have been introduced by the government as a means to check cadre abuses and relegitimize grass-roots structures of authority. It was also seen how, in seeming contravention of national regulations, elections have been quietly introduced at the rural township level at selected sites. Will the electoral reforms eventually influence the performance even of officials who sit higher up than the levels at which elections get held?

Any optimism must be tempered by a realization that a whole range of problems faced by rural families must rely upon other forms of remedy. Whatever their potential importance, village elections will not alter national policies that discriminate against rural workers. They will not improve the low prices that farmers receive for their grain, prices that will be kept low by China's accession to the World Trade Organization. They will not solve the financial difficulties experienced by families in the interior as regards medical care and schooling. They will not help develop the household economies of the several tens of millions of absolute poor. Rural China faces problems for which no quick solutions are evident on the horizon.

A Selected Bibliography

Alpermann, Bjorn. "The Post-Election Administration of Chinese Villages." *The China Journal*, No. 46 (July 2001), pp. 45-67.

Bachman, David. *Bureaucracy, Economy, and Leadership in China: The Institutional Origins of the Great Leap Forward.* Cambridge: Cambridge University Press, 1991.

Bai Nansheng. "The Effect of Labor Migration on Agriculture: An Empirical Study." In Loraine A. West and Yaohui Zhao, eds., *Rural Labor Flows in China.* Berkeley: Institute of East Asian Studies, University of California, 2000, pp. 129-48.

Bakken, Borge, ed., *Migration in China.* Copenhagen: Nordic Institute of Asian Studies Report Series, No. 31, 1998.

Barnett, A. Doak. *Cadres, Bureaucracy, and Political Power in Communist China.* New York: Columbia University Press, 1967, esp. Part III, written by Ezra Vogel (pp. 313-424).

Baum, Richard. "The Cultural Revolution in the Countryside: Anatomy of a Limited Rebellion." In Thomas W. Robinson, ed., *The Cultural Revolution in China.* Berkeley: University of California Press, 1971, pp. 367-476.

——*Prelude to Revolution: Mao, the Party, and the Peasant Question, 1962-1966.* New York: Columbia University Press, 1975.

Beller-Hann, Ildiko. "The Peasant Condition in Xinjiang." *Journal of Peasant Studies*, Vol. 25, No. 1 (October 1997), pp. 87-112.

Bernstein, Thomas P. *Up to the Mountains and Down to the Villages: The Transfer of Youth from Urban to Rural China.* New Haven: Yale University Press, 1977.

——"Farmer Discontent and Regime Responses." In Merle Goldman and Roderick MacFarquhar, eds., *The Paradox of China's Post-Mao Reforms.* Cambridge: Harvard University Press, 1999, pp. 197-219.

——"Instability in Rural China." In David Shambaugh, ed., *Is China Unstable?* Armonk: M.E. Sharpe, 2000, pp. 95-111.

Bernstein, Thomas P., and Xiaobo Lu. "Taxation without Representation: Peasants, the Central and the Local States in Reform China." *The China Quarterly*, No. 163 (September 2000), pp. 742-63.

Bianco, Lucien. "Rural Areas: Vendettas Are Back." *China Perspectives*, No. 1 (September 1995), pp. 25-29.

————"The Weapons of the Weak: A Critical View." *China Perspectives*, No. 22 (March–April, 1999), pp. 4-16.

————*Peasants Without the Party: Grass-roots Movements in Twentieth-Century China*. Armonk: M.E. Sharpe, 2001.

Blecher, Marc, and Vivienne Shue. *Tethered Deer: Government and Economy in a Chinese County*. Stanford: Stanford University Press, 1996.

————"Into Leather: State-led Development and the Private Sector in Xinji." *The China Quarterly*, No. 166 (June 2001), pp. 368-93.

Blum, Susan D. *Portraits of "Primitives": Ordering Human Kinds in the Chinese Nation*. Lanham: Rowman & Littlefield, 2001.

Bramall, Chris. "Origins of the Agricultural 'Miracle': Some Evidence from Sichuan." *The China Quarterly*, No. 143 (September 1995), pp. 731-55.

Bramall, Chris, and Marion E. Jones. "Rural Income Inequality in China Since 1978." *The Journal of Peasant Studies*, Vol. 21, No. 1 (October 1993), pp. 41-70.

Brandt, Loren, Jikun Huang, Guo Li and Scott Rozelle. "Land Rights in Rural China: Facts, Fictions and Issues." *The China Journal*, No. 47 (January 2002).

Brown, Melissa J., ed. *Negotiating Ethnicities in China and Taiwan*. Berkeley: China Research Monograph No. 46, Institute of East Asian Studies, 1996.

Bruun, Ole. "The Fengshui Resurgence in China: Conflicting Cosmologies Between State and Peasantry." *The China Journal*, No. 36 (July 1996), pp. 47-65.

Burki, S.J. *A Study of Chinese Communes, 1965*. Cambridge: Harvard University East Asian Research Center, 1969.

Burns, John. "The Radicals and the Campaign to Limit Bourgeois Rights in the Countryside." *Contemporary China*, Vol. 1, No. 4 (January 1977).

————*Political Participation in Rural China.* Berkeley: University of California Press, 1988.

Cai, Yongshun. "Between State and Peasant: Local Cadres and Statistical Reporting in Rural China." *The China Quarterly*, No. 163 (September 2000), pp. 783-805.

Chan, Alfred. *Mao's Crusade: Politics and Policy Implementation in China's Great Leap Forward.* Oxford: Oxford University Press, 2001.

Chan, Anita. *China's Workers under Assault: The Exploitation of Labor in a Globalizing Economy.* Armonk: M.E. Sharpe, 2001.

————"The Culture of Survival—Lives of Migrant Workers Through the Prism of Private Letters." In Perry Link, Richard Madsen and Paul Pickowicz, eds., *Popular Thought in Post-Socialist China.* Boulder: Rowman & Littlefield (2002).

Chan, Anita, and Jonathan Unger. "Grey and Black: The Hidden Economy of Rural China." *Pacific Affairs*, Vol. 55, No. 3 (Fall 1982), pp. 452-71.

Chan, Anita, Richard Madsen, and Jonathan Unger. *Chen Village Under Mao and Deng.* Berkeley: University of California Press, 1992.

Chan, Sylvia. "Village Self-Government and Civil Society." In Joseph Y.S. Cheng, ed., *China Review 1998.* Hong Kong: Chinese University Press, 1998, pp. 235-58.

Chao, Emily. "Hegemony, Agency, and Re-presenting the Past" In Melissa J. Brown, ed., *Negotiating Ethnicities in China and Taiwan.* Berkeley: China Research Monograph No. 46, Institute of East Asian Studies, 1996, pp. 208-239.

Chen Xiangshui and Ding Yuling. "Gaige kaifang houde siren qiye jingying: Fujian Jinjiang Yijiacun de xiechang qiye" (The Management of Private Enterprises in the Period of Reform and Opening: Footwear Manufacturing Enterprises in Yi Family Village, Jinjiang Township, Fujian Province). In *Huanan nongcun shehui wenhua yanjiu lunwen ji* (A Collection of Essays on Society and Culture in South China's Villages). Taibei: Zhongguo Yanjiuyuan Minzuxuesuo (Taipei: Ethnology Institute of the Academia Sinica), 1998, pp. 287-310.

Cheng, Joseph Y.S. "Direct Elections of Town and Township Heads in China: The Dapeng and Buyun Experiments." *China Information,* Vol. 15, No. 1 (2001), pp. 104-37.

Cheng Yuk-shing and Tsang Shu-ki. "Agricultural Land Reform in a Mixed System: The Chinese Experience of 1984-1994." *China Information*, Vol. 10, Nos. 3-4 (Winter 1995/Spring 1996), pp. 44-74.

China, Overcoming Rural Poverty. Beijing: Joint Report of the Leading Group for Poverty Reduction, UNDP and the World Bank, 2000. 121 pp.

Christiansen, Flemming. "The De-rustication of the Chinese Peasant? Peasant Household Reactions to the Rural Reforms in China Since 1978." Ph.D. dissertation, University of Leiden, Netherlands, 1990.

Christiansen, Flemming, and Zhang Junzuo, eds. *Village Inc.: Chinese Rural Society in the 1990s*. Richmond: Curzon Press, 1998.

Cook, Sarah, and Gordon White. "The Changing Pattern of Poverty in China," *Poverty Research Program Working Paper 67*. Brighton: Institute of Development Studies, 1998. 44 pp.

Croll, Elisabeth. "Development Project Objectives and the Local Environment: A Case Study of a Chinese Village." *The China Journal*, No. 18 (July 1987), pp. 127-46.

————"Short-term Field Investigations in China: A Personal View." *China Information*, Vol. 2, No. 1 (Summer 1987), pp. 17-26.

————*From Heaven to Earth: Images and Experiences of Development in China*. London: Routledge, 1994.

Davis-Friedman, Deborah. "Strategies for Aging: Interdependence Between Generations in the Transition to Socialism." *Contemporary China*, Vol. 1, No. 6 (March 1977).

Diamond, Larry, and Ramon H. Myers, eds. *Elections and Democracy in Greater China*. Oxford: Oxford University Press, 2001.

Diamond, Norma. "Defining the Miao: Ming, Qing, and Contemporary Views." In Stevan Harrell, ed., *Cultural Encounters on China's Ethnic Frontiers*. Seattle: University of Washington Press, 1995.

Du Ying. "Rural Labor Migration in Contemporary China: An Analysis of Its Features and Macro Context." In Loraine A. West and Yaohui Zhao, eds., *Rural Labor Flows in China*. Berkeley: Institute of East Asian Studies, University of California, 2000, pp. 67-101.

Elklit, Jorgen. "The Chinese Village Committee Electoral System." *China Information*, Vol. 11, No. 4 (Spring 1997), pp. 1-13.

Endicott, Stephen. *Red Earth: Revolution in a Sichuan Village.* Toronto: NC Press, 1989.

Fan, Cindy C. "Migration and Gender in China." In Lau Chung-ming and Jianfa Shen, eds. *China Review 2000.* Hong Kong: Chinese University Press, 2000, pp. 423-55.

Fei Hsiao-t'ung (Fei Xiaotong) and Chih-I Chang (Zhang Zhiyi). *Earthbound China: A Study of Rural Economy in Yunnan.* London: Routledge & Kegan Paul, 1948.

Fei Xiaotong. *Chinese Village Close-up.* Beijing: New World Press, 1982.

Feng Chongyi. *Nongmin yishi yu Zhongguo* (Peasant Consciousness and China). Hong Kong: Zhonghua Shuju, 1989, section 4, pp. 142-225.

Feng Jici. "The Cultural Revolution has been Under Way for Two Thousand Years." In *Yi baige ren de shinian*, translated in *Chinese Sociology and Anthropology*, Vol. 26, No. 1 (Fall 1993).

Fenger, Peter, Steen Folke, Allan Jorgensen, Peter Milthers, and Ole Odgaard. "Occupational Patterns and Income Inequality in a Sichuan Village." *Copenhagen Papers in East and Southeast Asian Studies*, No. 5 (1990), pp. 73-90.

Feuchtwang, Stephan. "Religion as Resistance." In Elizabeth J. Perry and Mark Selden, eds., *Chinese Society: Change, Conflict and Resistance.* London: Routledge, 2000, pp. 161-77.

Fewsmith, Joseph. *Dilemmas of Reform in China: Political Conflict and Economic Debate.* Armonk: M.E. Sharpe, 1994, Ch. 1.

Fitzgerald, C.P. *The Southern Expansion of the Chinese People.* Canberra: Australian National University Press, 1972.

Fitzgerald, John. "Autonomy and Growth in China: County Experience in Guangdong Province." *Journal of Contemporary China*, Vol. 5, No. 11 (March 1996).

Forster, Keith. "The Wenzhou Model for Economic Development: Impressions." *China Information*, Vol. 5, No. 3 (Winter 1990-91), pp. 53-64.

Friedman, Edward, Paul G. Pickowicz, and Mark Selden. *Chinese Village, Socialist State*. New Haven: Yale University Press, 1991.

———*Revolution, Resistance and Reform in Village China*. New Haven: Yale University Press, forthcoming.

Gao Gao and Yan Jiaqi. *Zhongguo wenge shinian shi* (History of the Ten Years of the Chinese Cultural Revolution), Vol. 1. Hong Kong: Dagongbao She, 1986.

Gao, Mobo. "The Rural Situation in Post-Mao China and the Conditions of Migrant Workers: The Case of Gao Village." *Bulletin of Concerned Asian Scholars*, Vol. 30, No. 4 (October 1998), pp. 70-77.

———*Gao Village: Rural Life in China Since the Revolution*. London: Hurst; Honolulu: University of Hawaii Press, 1999.

Garnaut, Ross, Guo Shutian, and Ma Guonan, eds. *The Third Revolution in the Chinese Countryside*. Cambridge: Cambridge University Press, 1996.

Gladney, Dru. "Representing Nationality in China: Refiguring Majority/Minority Identities." *The Journal of Asian Studies*, Vol. 53, No. 1 (February 1994), pp. 92-123.

———"Salman Rushdie in China: Religion, Ethnicity, and State Definition in the People's Republic." In Charles F. Keyes, Laurel Kendall, and Helen Hardacre, eds., *Asian Visions of Authority*. Honolulu: University of Hawaii Press, 1994, pp. 255-78.

Gong Xiaoxia. "Perpetual Victims: Persecution of the 'Bad Classes' during the Cultural Revolution." *China Information*, Vol. 11, Nos. 2-3 (Autumn 1996), pp. 35-53.

Griffin, Keith, and Zhao Renwei. *The Distribution of Income in China*. New York: St. Martin's Press, 1993.

Grunfeld, A. Tom. "In Search of Equality: Relations between China's Ethnic Minorities and the Majority Han." *Bulletin of Concerned Asian Scholars*, Vol. 17, No. 1 (January–March 1985).

Guo Xiaolin. "The Role of Local Government in Creating Property Rights: A Comparison of Two Townships in Northwest Yunnan." In Jean C. Oi and Andrew C. Walder, eds., *Property Rights and Economic Reform in China*. Stanford: Stanford University Press, 1999, pp. 71-94.

Guo Xiaolin. "Land Expropriation and Rural Conflicts in China." *The China Quarterly*, No. 166 (June 2001), pp. 422-39.

Guo Xiaoming and Xue Xiaoming, "Xindai" (Credit). In Xiong Jingming, ed., *Jinru 21 shiji de Zhongguo nongcun* (Chinese Villages Entering the 21st Century). Beijing: Guangming Ribao Chubanshe, 2000, pp. 389-413.

Guo Zhenglin. "Dangdai Zhongguo nongcun de jiti weiquan xingdong" (Collective Actions to Safeguard Rights in Rural China). *Xianggang shehui kexue xuebao.* Hong Kong Journal of Social Sciences, No. 19 (Spring/summer 2001), pp. 115-33.

————"Zhongguo nongcun quanli jiegou de zhiduhua tiaozheng" (The Restructuring of Power in China's Villages). *Kaifang shidai* (Open Times, Guangzhou), August 2001, pp. 34-40.

Gustafsson, Bjorn, and Wei Zhong. "How and Why has Poverty in China Changed? A Study Based on Microdata for 1988 and 1995." *The China Quarterly*, No. 146 (December 2000), pp. 983-1006.

Harrell, Stevan. "Ethnicity, Local Interests, and the State: Yi Communities in Southwest China." *Comparative Studies in Society and History*, Vol. 32, No. 3 (July 1990), pp. 515-48.

Hartford, Kathleen. "Socialist Agriculture is Dead; Long Live Socialist Agriculture! Organizational Transformations in Rural China." In Elizabeth Perry and Christine Wong, eds., *The Political Economy of Reform in Post-Mao China.* Cambridge: Harvard University Press, 1985.

He Baogang and Lang Youxing. "Cunmin xuanju dui xiangcun quanli de yinxiang" (The Impact of Village Elections on Rural Power). *Xianggang shehui kexue xuebao* (Hong Kong Journal of Social Sciences), No. 16 (Spring 2000), pp. 99-124.

Hinton, William. *Fanshen: A Documentary of Revolution in a Chinese Village* (1966). Republished Berkeley: University of California Press, 1997.

————*Shenfan: The Continuing Revolution in a Chinese Village.* New York: Random House, 1983.

Howell, Jude. "Prospects of Village Self-Governance in China." *Journal of Peasant Studies*, Vol. 25, No. 3 (April 1998), pp. 86-111.

Hsu, Robert. "Grain Procurement and Distribution in China's Rural Areas: Post-Mao Policies and Problems." *Asian Survey*, Vol. 24, No. 12 (December 1984).

Hua, Linshan. *Les Années Rouges*. Paris: Editions du Seuil, 1987.

Huang, Philip. *The Peasant Family and Rural Development in the Yangzi Delta*. Stanford: Stanford University Press, 1990.

————"Rural Class Struggle in the Chinese Revolution." *Modern China*, Vol. 21, No. 1 (January 1995).

Huang, Shu-min. *The Spiral Road: Change in a Chinese Village Through the Eyes of a Communist Party Leader*. Boulder: Westview Press, 1989.

Huang, Shu-min and Sewart Odend'hal. "Fengjia: A Village in Transition." In Andrew Walder, ed., *Zouping in Transition: The Process of Reform in Rural North China*. Cambridge: Harvard University Press, 1998.

Hung, Jean, and Jonathan Unger. "Zou fang Yunnan shancun ting xinsuan de gushi" (Bitter Tales Heard through Interviews in a Yunnan Mountain Village). *Chaoliu* (Hong Kong), No. 31 (1989), pp. 61-64.

Jacobs, J. Bruce. "Political and Economic Institutional Changes and Continuities in Six Chinese Rural Localities." *The Australian Journal of Chinese Affairs*, No. 14 (July 1985), pp. 105-27.

Jankowiak, William R. "The Last Hurrah? Political Protest in Inner Mongolia." *The Australian Journal of Chinese Affairs*, No. 19-20 (January-July 1988), pp. 273-88.

Jennings, M. Kent. "Political Participation in the Chinese Countryside." *American Political Science Review*, Vol. 91, No. 2 (June 1997), pp. 361-72.

Jing, Jun. *The Temple of Memories: History, Power, and Morality in a Chinese Village*. Stanford: Stanford University Press, 1996.

————"Environmental Protests in Rural China." In Elizabeth J. Perry and Mark Selden, eds., *Chinese Society: Change, Conflict and Resistance*. London: Routledge, 2000, pp. 143-60.

Judd, Ellen R. *Gender & Power in Rural North China*. Stanford: Stanford University Press, 1994.

Ke Bingsheng. "Regional Inequality in Rural Development." In Ross Garnaut, Guo Shutian, and Ma Guonan, eds., *The Third Revolution in the Chinese Countryside*. Cambridge: Cambridge University Press, 1996, pp. 245-55.

Kelkar, Govind, and Wang Yunxian. "Farmers, Women, and Economic Reform in China." *Bulletin of Concerned Asian Scholars*, Vol. 29, No. 4 (October 1997), pp. 69-77.

Kelliher, Daniel. *Peasant Power in China: The Era of Rural Reform, 1979-1989.* New Haven: Yale University Press, 1992.

————"The Chinese Debate over Village Self-Government." *The China Journal*, No. 37 (January 1997), pp. 63-86.

Kerkvliet, Benedict, and Mark Selden. "Agrarian Transformations in China and Vietnam." In Anita Chan, Benedict Kerkvliet, and Jonathan Unger, eds., *Transforming Asian Socialism.* Lanham: Rowman & Littlefield; Sydney: Allen & Unwin, 1999, pp. 98-119.

Khan, Azizur Rahman. "Poverty in China in the Period of Globalization." *Issues in Development Discussion Paper 22.* Geneva: International Labor Office, 1998, 54 pp.

Khan, Azizur Rahman, and Carl Riskin. "Income and Inequality in China: Composition, Distribution and Growth of Household Income, 1988 to 1995." *The China Quarterly*, No. 154 (June 1998), pp. 221-53.

————*Inequality and Poverty in China in the Age of Globalization.* New York: Oxford University Press, 2001.

Kipnis, Andrew. *Producing Guanxi: Sentiment, Self, and Subculture in a North China Village.* Durham: Duke University Press, 1997.

————"The Disturbing Educational Discipline of 'Peasants.'" *The China Journal*, No. 46 (July 2001), pp. 1-24.

Ku, Hok-bun. "Chinese Peasants' Discontent and Forms of Resistance in the Post-Reform Era." *China Review 1999.* Hong Kong: The Chinese University Press, 1999, pp. 285-308.

Kung, James Kaisung. "Egalitarianism, Subsistence Provision, and Work Incentives in China's Agricultural Collectives." *World Development*, Vol. 22, No. 2 (1994), pp. 175-87.

————"Equal Entitlement Versus Tenure Security under a Regime of Collective Property Rights: Peasants' Preference for Institutions in Post-Reform Chinese Agriculture." *Journal of Comparative Economics*, Vol. 21, No. 2 (1995), pp. 82-111.

Kung, James, and Shouying Liu. "Farmers' Preferences Regarding Ownership and Land Tenure in Post-Mao China: Unexpected Evidence from Eight Counties." *The China Journal*, No. 38 (July 1997), pp. 33-63.

Lam, Tao-Chiu. *The Local State Under Reform: A Study of a County in Hainan Province, China.* Canberra: Doctoral Dissertation, Australian National University, 2000.

Lardy, Nicholas. *Agriculture in China's Economic Development.* Cambridge: Cambridge University Press, 1984.

Lawrence, Susan V. "Democracy, Chinese Style." *The Australian Journal of Chinese Affairs*, No. 32 (July 1994).

Lee, Pak K., and Charles C.L. Kwong. "China's Rural Industrialization at the Turn of the Century." In Lau Chung-ming and Jianfa Shen, eds., *China Review 2000.* Hong Kong: Chinese University Press, 2000, pp. 359-80.

Li, Cheng. "Surplus Rural Labourers and Internal Migration in China." In Borge Bakken, ed., *Migration in China.* Copenhagen: Nordic Institute of Asian Studies, 1998.

Li, Lianjiang. "The Two-Ballot System in Shanxi Province: Subjecting Village Party Secretaries to a Popular Vote." *The China Journal*, No. 42 (July 1999), pp. 103-118.

———"Support for Anti-corruption Campaigns in Rural China." *Journal of Contemporary China*, Vol. 10, No. 29 (November 2001), pp. 573-86.

Li, Lianjiang, and Kevin J. O'Brien. "The Struggle over Village Elections." In Merle Goldman and Roderick MacFarquhar, eds., *The Paradox of China's Post-Mao Reforms.* Cambridge: Harvard University Press, 1999, pp. 129-44.

Li Shi. "Labor Migration and Income Distribution in Rural China." In Carl Riskin, Zhao Renwei, and Li Shi, eds., *China's Retreat from Equality: Income Distribution and Economic Transition.* Armonk: M.E. Sharpe, 2001, pp. 229-244.

Liu, Allen. "The Wenzhou Model of Development and China's Modernization." *Asian Survey*, Vol. 32, No. 8 (August 1992), pp. 696-711.

Liu Guokai. "A Brief Analysis of the Cultural Revolution." *Chinese Sociology and Anthropology*, Vol. 11, No. 2 (Winter 1986-87).

Liu Hongli, et al. *Nongye shengchan zerenzhi* (Agricultural Production Responsibility Systems). Shanghai: Renmin Chubanshe, 1982.

Liu Shiding. "De la préférence individuelle au choix collectif: Un cas de redistribution des terres en Chine rurale" (Individual Preferences in a Collective Choice: A Case Study of the Redistribution of Land in Rural China). In Isabelle Thireau and Wang Hansheng, eds., *Disputes au village chinois: Formes du juste et recompositions locales des espaces normatifs* (Disputes in Chinese Villages: Forms of Justice and the Local Recomposition of Normative Space). Paris: Éditions de la Maison des sciences de l'homme, 2001, pp. 167-203.

Liu, Yia-Ling. "Reform From Below: The Private Economy and Local Politics in the Rural Industrialization of Wenzhou." *The China Quarterly*, No. 130 (June 1992), pp. 293-316.

Lu, Xiaobo. "The Politics of Peasant Burden in Reform China." *The Journal of Peasant Studies*, Vol. 25, No. 1 (October 1997), pp. 113-38.

————*Cadres and Corruption: The Organizational Involution of the Chinese Communist Party*. Stanford: Stanford University Press, 2000.

Lu Xueyi, ed. *Gaige zhongde nongcun yu nongmin* (Villages and Peasants During the Reforms). Beijing: Zhonggong Zhongyang Dangxiao Chubanshe, 1992.

————"Nongmin zhen ku, nongcun zhen qiong" (The Farmers are Suffering, Villages are Genuinely Poor). *Dushu* (Reading), January 2001.

Luk Tak-chuen. "The Politics of Poverty Eradication in Rural China." In Lau Chung-ming and Jianfa Shen, eds., *China Review 2000*. Hong Kong: Chinese University Press, 2000, pp. 509-27.

Luong, Hy Van, and Jonathan Unger. "Wealth, Power, and Poverty in the Transition to Market Economies: The Process of Socio-Economic Differentiation in Rural China and Northern Vietnam." *The China Journal*, No. 40 (July 1998). Also in Anita Chan, Benedict Kerkvliet, and Jonathan Unger, eds., *Transforming Asian Socialism—China and Vietnam Compared*. Lantham: Rowman & Littlefield, and Sydney: Allen & Unwin, 1999, pp. 120-152.

Ma Xiaodong. "'Insider' and 'Outsider' Community Strategies toward Migrant Workers." In Loraine A. West and Yaohui Zhao, eds., *Rural Labor Flows in China*. Berkeley: Institute of East Asian Studies, University of California, 2000, pp. 310-32.

McKinley, Terry. *The Distribution of Wealth in Rural China.* Armonk: M.E. Sharpe, 1996.

Madsen, Richard. *Morality and Power in a Chinese Village.* Berkeley: University of California Press, 1984.

————"The Politics of Revenge in Rural China During the Cultural Revolution." In Jonathan N. Lipman and Stevan Harrell, eds., *Violence in China.* Albany: State University of New York Press, 1990.

Mallee, Hein. "In Defence of Migration: Recent Chinese Studies in Rural Population Mobility." *China Information*, Vol. 10, Nos. 3-4 (Winter 1995/Spring 1996), pp. 108-140.

————"Reform of the *Hukou* System." *Chinese Sociology & Anthropology*, Vol. 29, No. 1 (Fall 1996).

————"Migration, Hukou and Resistance in Reform China." In Elizabeth J. Perry and Mark Selden, eds., *Chinese Society: Change, Conflict and Resistance.* London: Routledge, 2000, pp. 83-101.

————"Agricultural Labor and Rural Population Mobility: Some Observations." In Loraine A. West and Yaohui Zhao, eds., *Rural Labor Flows in China.* Berkeley: Institute of East Asian Studies, University of California, 2000, pp. 34-66.

Manion, Melanie. "The Electoral Connection in the Countryside." *American Political Science Review*, Vol. 90, No. 4 (December 1996), pp. 736-48.

Morgan, Stephen. "Richer and Taller: Stature and Standards of Living in China, 1979-1995." *The China Journal*, No. 44 (July 2000), pp. 1-39.

Murdoch, Jonathan, and Terry Sicular. "Politics, Growth, and Inequality in Rural China: Does It Pay to Join the Party?" *Journal of Public Economics*, No. 77 (2000), pp. 331-56.

Nan Lin. "Local Market Socialism: Local Corporatism in Action in Rural China." *Theory and Society*, Vol. 24 (1995), pp. 301-54.

Nee, Victor, and Sijin Su. "Institutions, Social Ties, and Commitment in China's Corporatist Transformation." In John McMillan and Barry Naughton, eds., *Reforming Asian Socialism: The Growth of Market Institutions.* Ann Arbor: University of Michigan Press, 1996.

Netting, Nancy S. "The Deer Turned Her Head: Ethnic Options for the Hainan Li." *Bulletin of Concerned Asian Scholars*, Vol. 22, No. 2 (April 1997), pp. 3-17.

Nolan, Peter, and Gordon White. "The Distributive Implications of China's New Agricultural Policies." In Jack Gray and Gordon White, eds., *China's New Development Strategy*. London and New York: Academic Press, 1982.

Nolan, Peter, and Dong Furen, eds. *Market Forces in China: Competition and Small Business—The Wenzhou Debate*. London: Zed Books, 1990.

Nongmin liudong yu xingbie (Peasant Flows and Gender Distinctions). Zhengzhou: Zhongyuan Nongmin Chubanshe, 2000.

Nyberg, Albert, and Scott Rozelle. *Accelerating China's Rural Transformation*. Washington D.C.: World Bank, 1999.

O'Brien, Kevin J. "Rightful Resistance," *World Politics*, Vol. 49 (October 1996), pp. 31-55.

———"Implementing Political Reform in China's Villages." *The Australian Journal of Chinese Affairs*, No. 32 (July 1994), pp. 33-59.

O'Brien, Kevin J., and Lianjiang Li. "Campaign Nostalgia in the Chinese Countryside." *Asian Survey*, Vol. 39, No. 3 (May–June 1999), pp. 375-93.

Odgaard, Ole. "Entrepreneurs and Elite Formation in Rural China." *The Australian Journal of Chinese Affairs*, No. 28 (July 1992), pp. 89-108.

———*Private Enterprises in Rural China*. Aldershot: Avebury, 1992.

Oi, Jean. "Communism and Clientalism: Rural Politics in China." *World Politics*, Vol. 37, No. 2 (January 1985), pp. 238-266.

———"Commercializing China's Rural Cadres." *Problems of Communism*, Vol. 35, No. 5 (September 1986), pp. 1-15.

———"Peasant Households Between Plan and Market." *Modern China*, Vol. 12, No. 2 (1986), pp. 230-51.

———*State and Peasant in Contemporary China*. Berkeley: University of California Press, 1989.

———"Fiscal Reform and the Economic Foundations of Local State Corporatism in China." *World Politics*, Vol. 45, No. 1 (October 1992).

————"The Role of the Local State in China's Transitional Economy." *The China Quarterly*, No. 144 (December 1995), pp. 1132-49.

————"Economic Development, Stability and Democratic Village Self-governance." In Maurice Brosseau, Suzanne Pepper, and Tsang Shu-ki, eds., *China Review 1996.* Hong Kong: Chinese University Press, 1996.

————"The Evolution of Local State Corporatism." In Andrew Walder, ed., *Zouping in Transition: The Process of Reform in Rural North China.* Cambridge: Harvard University Press, 1998.

————*Rural China Takes Off.* Berkeley: University of California Press, 1999.

Pan Zhongqi and Tan Xiaomei. "Ethnic Conflict in China: Characteristics, Causes, and Countermeasures." *Issues and Studies*, Vol. 35, No. 5 (September 1999), pp. 137-68.

Parish, William, ed. *Chinese Rural Development: The Great Transformation.* Armonk: M.E. Sharpe, 1985.

Parish, William, and Martin Whyte. *Village and Family in Contemporary China.* Chicago: University of Chicago Press, 1978.

Parris, Kristen. "Local Initiative and National Reform: The Wenzhou Model of Development." *The China Quarterly*, No. 134 (June 1993), pp. 242-263.

"Peasant Unrest in Szechwan and Mainland China's Rural Problems." *Issues & Studies*, Vol. 29, No. 6 (July 1993).

Pei Xiaolin. "Township-Village Enterprises, Local Governments, and Rural Communities." In Eduard Vermeer, Frank Pieke, and Woei Lien Chong, eds., *Cooperative and Collective in China's Rural Development.* Armonk: M.E. Sharpe, 1998, pp. 110-36.

Peng, Yali. "The Politics of Tobacco: Relations Between Farmers and Local Governments in China's Southwest." *The China Journal*, No. 36 (July 1996), pp. 67-82.

Perry, Elizabeth J., and Christine Wong, eds. *The Political Economy of Reform in Post-Mao China.* Cambridge: Harvard University Press, 1985.

Potter, Sulamith H., and Jack M. Potter. *China's Peasants: The Anthropology of a Revolution.* Cambridge: Cambridge University Press, 1990.

Putterman, Louis. *Peasants, Collectives and Choice.* Greenwich: JAI Press, 1986.

————"The Incentive Problem and the Demise of Team Farming in China." *Journal of Development Economics*, Vol. 26, No. 1 (1987), pp. 103-27.

————"Ration Subsidies and Incentives in the Pre-reform Chinese Commune." *Economica*, Vol. 55, No. 218 (May 1988), pp. 235-47.

Qian Keping. "Zhongguo nongcun de minjian zuzhi yu zhili: yi Fujian sheng Dongsheng cun wei li" (Grassroots Organization and Administration in Chinese Villages: A Case Study of Fujian Province's Dongsheng Village). *Zhongguo shehui kexue jikan* (China Social Science Quarterly), No. 30 (Summer 2000), pp. 85-96.

Qu Tao. "Grassroots Democracy—Not All It Seems." *China Perspectives*, No. 13 (September 1997), pp. 6-10.

Riskin, Carl. "Rural Poverty in Post-reform China." In Ross Garnaut, Guo Shutian, and Ma Guonan, eds., *The Third Revolution in the Chinese Countryside.* Cambridge: Cambridge University Press, 1996, pp. 63-79.

Riskin, Carl, and Li Shi. "Chinese Rural Poverty Inside and Outside the Poor Regions." In Carl Riskin, Zhao Renwei and Li Shi, eds., *China's Retreat from Equality: Income Distribution and Economic Transition.* Armonk: M.E. Sharpe, 2001.

Rosen, Stanley. *The Role of Sent-down Youth in the Chinese Cultural Revolution.* Berkeley: Institute of East Asian Studies, University of California, 1981.

Rozelle, Scott. "Decision-Making in China's Rural Economy: The Linkages Between Village Leaders and Farm Households." *The China Quarterly*, No. 137 (March 1994), pp. 99-114.

————"Stagnation Without Equity: Patterns of Growth and Inequality in China's Rural Economy." *The China Journal*, No. 35 (January 1996), pp. 63-92.

Rozelle, Scott, and Jiang Leying. "Survival Strategies during Agricultural Recession in China's Reforming Economy." *Chinese Environment and Development* (Spring–Summer 1995), pp. 43-84.

Rozelle, Scott, Li Guo, Minggao Shen, Amelia Hughart, and John Giles, "Leaving China's Farms: Survey Results of New Paths and Remaining Hurdles to Rural Migration." *The China Quarterly*, No. 158 (July 1999), pp. 367-93.

Rozelle, Scott, Linxiu Zhang, and Jikun Huang. "China's War on Poverty." Working Paper, Department of Agricultural and Resource Economics, University of California at Davis, December 2000.

Ruf, Gregory A. *Cadres and Kin: Power, Authority, and Corporatism in a West China Village, 1937-1991.* Stanford: Stanford University Press, 1998.

————"Managing Interests: Collective Property Rights and Village Enterprise in Rural Sichuan." In Jean Oi and Andrew Walder, eds., *Property Rights and Economic Reform in China.* Stanford: Stanford University Press, 1999.

Sargeson, Sally, and Jian Zhang. "Reassessing the Role of the Local State: A Case Study of Local Government Interventions in Property Rights Reform in a Hangzhou District." *The China Journal*, No. 42 (July 1999), pp. 77-99.

Schein, Louisa. "Gender and Internal Orientalism in China." *Modern China*, Vol. 23, No. 1 (January 1997).

Schurmann, Franz. *Ideology and Organization in Communist China.* Berkeley: University of California Press, 1966.

Selden, Mark. "Post-Collective Agrarian Alternatives in Russia and China." In Barrett L. McCormick and Jonathan Unger, eds., *China After Socialism: In the Footsteps of Eastern Europe or East Asia?* Armonk: M.E. Sharpe, 1986, pp. 7-28.

————ed. *The Political Economy of Chinese Development.* Armonk: M.E. Sharpe, 1993.

————"Household, Cooperative, and State in the Remaking of China's Countryside." In Eduard Vermeer, Frank Pieke, and Woei Lien Chong, eds., *Cooperative and Collective in China's Rural Development.* Armonk: M.E. Sharpe, 1998, pp. 17-45.

————"After Collectivization: Continuity and Change in Rural China." In Ivan Szelenyi, ed., *Privatizing the Land.* London: Rutledge, 1998, pp. 125-48.

Seybolt, Peter J. *Throwing the Emperor from His Horse: Portrait of a Village Leader in China, 1923-1995.* Boulder: Westview Press, 1996.

Shen Yansheng. "Cunzheng de xing—yu chongjian" (The Village Administration's Rise and Decline—and Reconstruction). *Zhanlue yu guanli* (Strategy and Management), No. 6, 1998, pp. 1-34.

Shi Tianjian. "Village Committee Elections in China." *World Politics*, Vol. 51, No. 3 (April 1999).

Shih Chih-yu. "Public Citizens, Private Voters: The Meaning of Elections for Chinese Peasants." In Chong-pin Lin, ed., *PRC Tomorrow*. Kaohsiung: National Sun Yat-Sen University, 1996, pp. 145-168.

Shue, Vivienne. *Peasant China in Transition: The Dynamics of Development Toward Socialism, 1949-1956*. Berkeley: University of California Press, 1980.

————"The Fate of the Commune." *Modern China*, Vol. 10, No. 3 (July 1984), pp. 259-83.

Siu, Helen F. *Agents and Victims in South China*. New Haven: Yale University Press, 1989.

Skinner, G. William. "Marketing and Social Structure in Rural China." *Journal of Asian Studies*, Part I: Vol. 24, No. 1 (September 1964); Part III: Vol. 24, No. 3 (May 1965).

Solinger, Dorothy J. "The Floating Population in the Cities: Chances for Assimilation?" In Deborah Davis, Richard Kraus, Barry Naughton, and Elizabeth Perry, eds., *Urban Spaces in Contemporary China*. New York: Cambridge University Press, 1995, pp. 113-39.

————*Contesting Citizenship in Urban China: Peasant Migrants, the State, and the Logic of the Market*. Berkeley: University of California Press, 1999.

Sun Qitai and Xiong Zhiyong. *Dazhai hongqi de shengqi yu zhuiluo* (The Rise and Fall of the Red Flag of Dazhai). Henan Renmin Chubanshe, 1990.

Sutton, Donald C. "Consuming Counter-revolution: The Ritual and Culture of Cannibalism in Wuxuan, Guangxi, China, May to July 1968." *Comparative Studies in Society and History*, Vol. 37, No. 1 (July 1995), pp. 136-172.

Tan Shen. "The Relationship between Foreign Enterprises, Local Governments, and Women Migrant Workers in the Pearl River Delta." In Loraine A. West and Yaohui Zhao, eds., *Rural Labor Flows in China*. Berkeley: Institute of East Asian Studies, University of California, 2000, pp. 292-309.

Teiwes, Frederick C., and Warren Sun. *China's Road to Disaster: Mao, Central Politicians, and Provincial Leaders in the Unfolding of the Great Leap Forward, 1955-1959*. Armonk: M.E. Sharpe, 1999.

Thireau, Isabelle. "Recent Change in a Guangdong Village." *The Australian Journal of Chinese Affairs*, No. 19/20 (January 1988), pp. 289-310.

————"From Equality to Equity: An Exploration of Changing Norms of Distribution in Rural China." *China Information*, Vol. 5, No. 4 (Spring 1991), pp. 42-57.

Thireau, Isabelle, and Wang Hansheng, eds. *Disputes au village chinois: Formes du juste et recompositions locales des espaces normatifs* (Disputes in Chinese Villages: Forms of Justice and the Local Recomposition of Normative Space). Paris: Éditions de la Maison des sciences de l'homme, 2001.

Thireau, Isabelle, and Hua Linshan. *Enquête Sociologique sur la Chine 1911-1949*. Paris: Presses Universitaires de France, 1996.

Thogersen, Stig. "Cultural Life and Cultural Control in Rural China: Where is the Party?" *The China Journal*, No. 44 (July 2000), pp. 129-41.

Thurston, Anne F. *Muddling toward Democracy: Political Change in Grassroots China*. Washington, DC: United States Institute of Peace, 1998, 55 pp.

Thurston, Anne, and Burton Pasternak, eds. *The Social Sciences and Fieldwork in China: Views from the Field*. Boulder: Westview Press, 1986.

Unger, Jonathan. "'Learn from Tachai': China's Agricultural Model." *Current Scene*, Vol. 9, No. 9 (September 1971).

————"Decollectivization in a Guangdong Village: An Interview." In John P. Burns and Stanley Rosen, eds., *Policy Conflicts in Post-Mao China: A Documentary Survey, with Analysis*. Armonk: M.E. Sharpe, 1986), pp. 274-79.

————"The Hong Kong Connection: The Advantages of China Research from the Room Next Door." *China Information*, Vol. 2, No. 2 (Spring, 1987), pp. 27-36.

————"The Struggle to Dictate China's Administration: The Conflict of Branches vs. Areas vs. Reform." *The Australian Journal of Chinese Affairs*, No. 18 (July 1987), pp. 15-45.

————"Not Quite Han: The Ethnic Minorities of China's Southwest." *Bulletin of Concerned Asian Scholars*, Vol. 29, No. 3 (July–September, 1997), pp. 67-78.

Vermeer, Eduard, Frank Pieke, and Woei Lien Chong, eds. *Cooperative and Collective in China's Rural Development*. Armonk: M.E. Sharpe, 1998.

Walder, Andrew. "Rural Cadres and the Market Economy in the Deng Era: Evidence from a National Survey." In John Wong and Zheng Yongnian, eds., *The Nanxun Legacy and China's Development in the Post-Deng Era*. Singapore: Singapore University Press and World Scientific Press, 2001, pp. 95-120.

Walker, Kenneth. *Planning in Chinese Agriculture: Socialization and the Private Sector, 1956-1962*. London: Frank Cass, 1965.

Wang Jinhong. "Gaige yilai woguo nongye zhengce biandong yu nongmin liyi de xiangguan fenxi" (Analysis of Changes in Rural Chinese Policies and Fluctuations in Peasant Interests). *Kaifang shidai* (Open Times, Guangzhou), August 2001, pp. 41-9.

Wang Xiaoqiang and Bai Nanfeng. *Furao de pinkun: Zhonggu luohou diqu de jingji kaocha* (Richly Endowed Poverty: Investigations into the Economies of Backward Chinese Districts). Chengdu: Sichuan Renmin Chubanshe, 1986.

Wang Xiaotao. "The Politics of Village Elections: The Case of North Village." *Issues and Studies*, Vol. 35, No. 6 (November–December 1999), pp. 167-85.

Wang Ying. *Xin jiti zhuyi: xiangcun shehui de zai zuzhi* (The New Collectivism: Rural Society's Re-organization). Beijing: Jingji Guanli Chubanshe, 1996.

Wang Zhenyao. "Zhongguode cunmin zizhi yu minzhuhua fazhan daolu" (The Autonomy of Chinese Villages and the Road to Democratization). *Zhanlue yu guanli* (Strategy and Management), No. 2 (2000), pp. 99-105.

Watson, Andrew. "Agriculture Looks for Shoes that Fit: The Production Responsibility System and Its Implications." *World Development*, Vol. 11, No. 8 (1983).

————"New Structures in the Organization of Chinese Agriculture: A Variable Model." *Pacific Affairs*, Vol. 57, No. 4 (Winter 1984-85), pp. 621-45.

————"The Family Farm, Land Use and Accumulation in Agriculture." *The Australian Journal of Chinese Affairs*, No. 17 (January 1987), pp. 1-27.

————"Investment Issues in the Chinese Countryside." *The Australian Journal of Chinese Affairs*, No. 22 (July 1989), pp. 85-126.

————ed., *Economic Reform and Social Change in China*. London: Routledge, 1992.

Wen Tiejun. *Zhongguo nongcun jiben jingji zhidu yanjiu* (Studies on the Basic Economic System of Rural China). Beijing: Zhongguo Jingji Chubanshe, 2000.

White, Gordon. "The Impact of Economic Reforms in the Chinese Countryside: Towards the Politics of Social Capitalism?" *Modern China*, Vol. 13, No. 4 (October 1987), pp. 411-40.

White, Lynn T. III. *Unstately Power, Vol. I: Local Causes of China's Economic Reforms.* Armonk: M.E. Sharpe, 1998.

White, Tyrene. "Political Reform and Rural Government." In Deborah Davis and Ezra F. Vogel, eds., *Chinese Society on the Eve of Tiananmen.* Cambridge: Harvard University Press, 1990.

————"Village Elections: Democracy from the Bottom Up?" *Current History*, Vol. 97, No. 620 (September 1998), pp. 263-7.

Wilson, Scott. "The Cash Nexus and Social Networks: Mutual Aid and Gifts in Contemporary Shanghai Villages." *The China Journal*, No. 37 (January 1997), pp. 91-112.

Wobowo, Ignatius. "The Chinese Communist Party in the Countryside." In Wang Gungwu and Zheng Yongnian, eds., *Reform, Legitimacy and Dilemmas: China's Politics and Society.* Singapore: Singapore University Press, 2000, pp. 51-70.

Wong, John, Rong Ma, and Mu Yang, eds. *China's Rural Entrepreneurs: Ten Case Studies.* Singapore: Times Academic Press, 1995.

Woody, W. *The Cultural Revolution in Inner Mongolia.* Stockholm: Center for Pacific Asia Studies at Stockholm University Occasional Paper 20, 1993, 41 pp.

Woon, Yuen-Fong. "From Mao to Deng: Life Satisfaction Among Rural Women in an Emigrant Community in South China." *TheAustralian Journal of Chinese Affairs*, No. 25 (January 1991), pp. 139-69.

World Bank. *Sharing Rising Incomes: Disparities in China.* Washington, D.C.: World Bank, 1997.

Wu, David Y.H. "Culture Change and Ethnic Identity Among Minorities in China." In Chien Chiao and Nicholas Tapp, eds., *Ethnicity & Ethnic Groups in China.* Hong Kong: New Asia College, 1989.

Wu Guobao, Sue Richardson, and Peter Travers. "Rural Poverty and its Causes in China." *Working Papers of the Chinese Economy Research Unit* No. 96/2 (University of Adelaide, 1996).

Xiong Jingming (Jean Hung). "Shei lian qiong xiangzi, wei jie dushu nan" (Pity the Impoverished Countryside: The Difficulties of Schooling Remain Unresolved). *Kaifang zazhi* (Open Magazine), January 1999, pp. 75-77.

Xiong Jingming and Yang Wenliang. "Nongmin fudan" (Peasant Burdens). In Xiong Jingming, ed., *Jinru 21 shiji de Zhongguo nongcun* (Chinese Villages Entering the 21st Century). Beijing: Guangming Ribao Chubanshe, 2000, pp. 467-77.

Yan, Yunxiang. "The Impact of Rural Reform on Economic and Social Stratification in a Chinese Village." *The Australian Journal of Chinese Affairs*, No. 27 (January 1992), pp. 1-23.

————"Everyday Power Relations: Changes in a North China Village." In Andrew Walder, ed., *The Waning of the Communist State*. Berkeley: University of California Press, 1995, pp. 215-41.

————"The Culture of *Guanxi* in a North China Village." *The China Journal*, No. 35 (January 1996), pp. 1-25.

————*The Flow of Gifts: Reciprocity and Social Networks in a Chinese Village*. Stanford: Stanford University Press, 1996.

————*Private Life under Socialism: Love Intimacy, and Family Change in a Chinese Village, 1949-1999*. Stanford: Stanford University Press, 2002.

Yang, Dali L. *Calamity and Reform in China*. Stanford: Stanford University Press, 1996.

Yang, Minchuan. "Reshaping Peasant Culture and Community: Rural Industrialization in a Chinese Village." *Modern China*, Vol. 20, No. 2 (April 1994), pp. 157-79.

Yep, Ray. "Rural Entrepreneurs and the Changing State-Society Relationship in China in the Reform Era." Ph.D. dissertation, Oxford University, 1998.

Young, Susan. *Private Business and Economic Reform*. Armonk: M.E. Sharpe, 1995, pp. 67-92.

——— "Ownership and Community Interest in China's Rural Enterprises." In Kjeld Erik Brodsgaard and David Strand, eds., *Reconstructing Twentieth-Century China*. Oxford: Oxford University Press, 1998.

Young, Susan, and Yang Gang. "Private Enterprises and Local Government in Rural China." In Christopher Findlay, Andrew Watson, and Harry X. Wu, eds., *Rural Enterprises in China*. New York: St. Martin's Press, 1994.

Zhang Jing. *Jiceng zhengquan: xiangcun zhidu zhu wenti* (Grassroots Governance: Various Questions Regarding the Rural System). Hangzhou: Zhejiang Renmin Chubanshe, 2000.

Zhang Letian. "Nongcun shequde shehui fenhua yu zhenghe" (Stratification and Integration in a Rural Community). *Zhanlue yu guanli* (Strategy & Management), No. 4, 1994.

———*Gaobie lixiang: Renmin gongshe zhidu yanjiu* (Departing from Ideals: Research into the System of the People's Commune). Shanghai: Dongfang Chubanshe, 1998.

Zhang Ping. "Rural Interregional Inequality and Off-Farm Employment in China." In Carl Riskin, Zhao Renwei, and Li Shi, eds., *China's Retreat from Equality: Income Distribution and Economic Transition*. Armonk: M.E. Sharpe, 2001, pp. 213-22.

Zhao Shukai. "Shequ chongtu he xinxing quanli guanxi" (Community Conflict and New Forms of Power Relations). *Nongcun diaoyan* (Village Investigations and Research), No. 146 (November 21, 1998), 22 pp.

———"Criminality and the Policing of Migrant Workers." *The China Journal*, No. 43 (January 2000), pp. 101-10.

———"Organizational Characteristics of Rural Labor Mobility in China." In Loraine A. West and Yaohui Zhao, eds., *Rural Labor Flows in China*. Berkeley: Institute of East Asian Studies, University of California, 2000, pp. 231-50.

Zheng Yi. *Hongse jinian bei* (The Red Memorial Plinth). Taipei: Huashi Wenhua Gongsi, 1993, 686 pp. A greatly abridged version of the book has been published in English as *Scarlet Memorial: Tales of Cannibalism in Modern China*. Boulder: Westview Press, 1996, 199 pp.

Zhong, Yang. "Withering Governmental Power in China? A View from Below." *Communist and Post-Communist Studies*, Vol. 29, No. 4 (December 1996), pp. 363-75.

Zhou Daming, Cao Mengjun, and Lin Yuping. *Gongyouzhi yu xiandaihua: gaige kaifang houde yige Zhongguo cunluo* (Ownership in Common and Modernization: A Chinese Village after the Reforms and Opening Up). Guangzhou: Zhongshan Daxue Chubanshe, 1998.

Zhu Ling. *Rural Reform and Peasant Income in China.* London: The MacMillan Press, 1991.

———"Food Security of Low-Income Groups in Rural China." In Carl Riskin, Zhao Renwei, and Li Shi, eds., *China's Retreat from Equality: Income Distribution and Economic Transition.* Armonk: M.E. Sharpe, 2001, pp. 229-45.

Zhu Ling and Jiang Zhongyi. *Public Works and Poverty Alleviation in Rural China.* Commack: Nova Science Publishers, 1996.

Zhu Xiaoyang. *Punishment in a Chinese Village in Yunnan.* Ph.D. dissertation, Macquarie University, Sydney, 2000.

Zhu Xigang and Tian Weiming. "The System of Decision Making for Agriculture in China." *The Australian Journal of Chinese Affairs*, No. 21 (January 1989), pp. 161-70.

Zweig, David. *Agrarian Radicalism in China, 1968-1978.* Cambridge: Harvard University Press, 1989.

———"Peasants and Politics." *World Policy Journal*, Vol. 6, No. 4 (1989), pp. 633-45.

———*Freeing China's Farmers: Rural Restructuring in the Reform Era.* Armonk: M.E. Sharpe, 1997.

———"The Externalities of Development: Can New Political Institutions Manage Rural Conflict?" In Elizabeth J. Perry and Mark Selden, eds., *Chinese Society: Change, Conflict and Resistance.* London: Routledge, 2000, pp. 120-42.

Index

ethnic minorities, 50n, 187-92, 206
exploitation, 127

factories, 122-3, 125, 126-8, 145-6,
    151-70
    private, 132-40
family farming
    see dabaogan; decollectivization
favoritism, 44, 106, 139, 140-2, 143-
    6, 148, 205
    see also nepotism
fees, 154-5
    see also taxes
fertilizers, 178, 179, 180
"four bad elements", 32-4, 35, 38,
    43, 64, 69
Four Cleanups campaign, 23, 37-8,
    39, 44, 55-6, 57n, 61-2, 71, 78,
    70, 91
Four Modernizations, 47
Fujian Province, 138

Gang of Four, 16, 89
Gansu Province, 183, 193
geomancy (fengshui), 27, 59, 166
government favors, 140-2
government policy, drawbacks, 175-
    8
Great Leap Forward
    collapse, 2, 26, 74, 100
    commencement, 8
    communes, 19
    economic effect, 37, 74, 76
    radicalism, 25
Green Revolution, 82-3, 87
Guangdong Province, 11, 20, 26, 57,
    59, 60, 61, 62, 68-9, 70, 88, 90,
    102, 121, 122, 123, 132, 133-40,
    142, 145, 152, 218, 222
Guangxi Province, 52, 68, 70, 159n,
    175-96
Guizhou Province, 142, 168n, 175-
    96

Hainan Province, 141, 142, 179,
    188, 192

Hebei Province, 58, 59
Heilongjiang Province, 154, 161
Henan Province, 213
household contract system, 75-6, see
    also bao chan dao hu, dabaogan
housing, 189
Hubei Province, 105, 185
Hunan Province, 63, 125, 159n
hukou
    see residential permits

ideology, 59, 73-92
income, 111, 112, 172, 195, 207,
    212-13
    see also remuneration; wages
industry, 109, 121, 122-23, 133-35,
    147-49, 151-54, 165, 204-6, see
    also private industry; factories;
    textile industry
irrigation, 177, 224

Jiangsu Province, 56-8
Jiangxi Province, 56-7

labor hire, 113, 120-4, 164-6
land ownership, 115-18, 191-2
    see also, generally,
    collectivization;
    decollectivization
land reform, 7-9, 62, 95-118
land tenure
    see land ownership
land-use planning, 159-60
    see also readjusting landholdings
Law on Agriculture, 215
Leading Group for Poverty
    Reduction, 181, 182, 183
Line Education Campaign, 16
loans, 140, 141-2, 151, 152, 153-4,
    157, 178-80
local governments, 147-50
Loyalty campaigns, 20, 45

Mao, 1, 11, 16, 22, 24, 25, 26, 27,
    37, 44, 45, 61, 71, 72, 98, 102,
    110, 120, 148, 161, 197, 199, 203